Early Church Records
of
Burlington County
New Jersey

Volume 3

Charlotte D. Meldrum

HERITAGE BOOKS
2007

HERITAGE BOOKS
AN IMPRINT OF HERITAGE BOOKS, INC.

Books, CDs, and more—Worldwide

For our listing of thousands of titles see our website
at
www.HeritageBooks.com

Published 2007 by
HERITAGE BOOKS, INC.
Publishing Division
65 East Main Street
Westminster, Maryland 21157-5026

Copyright © 1995, 1999 Charlotte D. Meldrum

All rights reserved. No part of this book may be reproduced or transmitted in any form or by any means, electronic or mechanical, including photocopying, recording or by any information storage and retrieval system without written permission from the author, except for the inclusion of brief quotations in a review.

International Standard Book Number: 978-1-58549-054-7

TABLE OF CONTENTS

Upper Springfield Preparative Monthly Meeting Members...........1

Births and Deaths of Upper Springfield Monthly Meeting..........6

Certificates from Upper Springfield Monthly Meeting........... 33

Marriages from Upper Springfield Monthly Meeting.............. 42

Minutes from Upper Springfield Monthly Meeting.................48

Upper Evesham Monthly Meeting
Births/Deaths/Marriages/Certificates..........................69

Upper Evesham Monthly Meeting Minutes......................... 90

Birth Records of a Quaker Physician...........................100

Burlington County Marriages (Justice of Peace)................102

Burlington County, New Jersey Marriage Licenses...............103

St. Andrews PE Church - Trinity PE Church.....................115

Baptisms at St. Andrews PE Church, Mt. Holly..................117

New Jersey Catholic Baptism records from 1759-1781............118

The Register of the Church of St. Ann's (St. Mary's)..........119

Index...161

INTRODUCTION

THE SOCIETY OF FRIENDS (QUAKERS)

The major religious denomination of Burlington County in its early years was the Society of Friends. According to Woodward and Hageman the 230 Quakers, half from Yorkshire and half from London, landed in the ship, Kent, in 1677. Burlington Monthly Meeting was established in 1678.[1] The importance of Burlington in Quakerism becomes obvious when noting that The Yearly Meeting, between 1690 and 1760, met alternately at Burlington and Philadelphia until it was permanently established at Philadelphia. The first annual meeting was held at the house of Thomas Gardiner on the 28th of the 6th month, 1681.

A meeting for worship at Crosswicks was established some time after 1681; the meeting was transferred to Chesterfield Monthly Meeting in 1684 with the formation of the monthly meeting by Burlington Quarterly Meeting.[2]

The Evesham Preparative Meeting was established at Mount Laurel by the Newton (Haddonfield) Monthly Meeting. In 1717 the meeting for worship alternated between Evesham and Chester. A preparative meeting for Evesham and Chester was established in 1717/1718. A meeting for worship held entirely at Evesham was established in 1736. In 1760 the meeting for worship and preparative meeting became part of Evesham Monthly Meeting.[3] Evesham Monthly Meeting was established in 1760 by Salem Quarterly Meeting out of Haddonfield Monthly Meeting.[4]

Mount Holly Preparative Meeting was established before 1762; the name was changed from Northampton to Mount Holly ca. 1772. It was a part of Burlington Monthly Meeting until Mount Holly Monthly Meeting was established in 1776.

Upper Springfield Monthly Meeting was established in 1781 by Burlington Quarterly Meeting out of the monthly meetings of Burlington, Chesterfield and Mount Holly.

Upper Evesham Monthly Meeting was established in 1793 out of Evesham Monthly Meeting. Its first business sessions opened in 1794.

In our series of church records we have abstracted selected items from the minutes. Certain subjects (e.g., the selection of the burying ground, building the meeting house, etc.) were not included in this effort. The wording has been changed for brevity and clarity.

Quaker Marriages
The couple announced their intentions of marriage at the monthly meeting. At a subsequent meeting, usually the next meeting, the couple announced their continued intention and at a subsequent meeting the committee appointed to oversee the marriage reported

the marriage had been orderly accomplished. If the bride had children by a previous marriage a committee was assigned to ensure that the children's rights were protected. The marriage usually took place within the jurisdiction of the bride's monthly meeting. If the groom were a member of another monthly meeting he was required to produce a certificate recommending him as a worthy member and verifying that he was clear of any marriage engagements. After the marriage the bride might request a certificate (of removal) to be sent to the groom's monthly meeting indicating that the couple was planning to live "within the compass" of his monthly meeting.

In the case of marriages, the minutes sometimes contained no additional genealogical information. Other times the fact that the bride was a widow or the membership of the groom in another meeting was evident only in the minutes. And still other times information on the marriage was entirely missing from the register and from the record of the marriage certificates. That the clerk failed to record marriages was a concern to the monthly meeting and specific instructions were given to appointed members to oversee that "the marriage was orderly accomplished," AND that it was recorded in the records.

Disorderly marriages
The Friends used several different phrases to indicate that a member had married contrary to their Rules of Discipline. The terms, "disorderly marriages," "out going in marriage," "married out of the unity of Friends," or "marrying out" and "married by a hireling minister" - are virtually synonymous.[2]

Comparison to Hinshaw
William Wade Hinshaw is well-know for his monumental efforts in compiling many of the Quaker records. Volume 2 of his series, *Encyclopedia of American Quaker Genealogy* included two New Jersey monthly meetings, Burlington and Salem.[3] In the preparation of this volume he was aided by Thomas W. Marshall and Walter C. Woodward. In his introduction Marshall states that only those subjects having genealogical interest were incorporated. Omitted from the Hinshaw work were references to military service, fornication (usually alluding to pre-marital sex), marrying cousins, indebtedness, disagreements between two parties, and other situations. We have included the latter types of information.

ANGLICAN CHURCH

According to Schermerhorn in his *History of Burlington, New Jersey*, the corner stone of St. Mary's Protestant Episcopal Church was laid in 1703. He states that it was the first seat of Episcopal authority in America.[5]

METHODISTS

Francis Asbury acted as pastor of the Burlington and Trenton societies, preaching there as early as 1773. A meeting house was built in Burlington in 1789.

BAPTISTS

Baptists were settling in Burlington County as early as 1688. The Burlington Baptists as recorded in the records of the church at Lower Dublin were Thomas Bibbs; Thomas Potts and Ann his wife; Nathaniel Douglass and Emblem his wife; Edmund Wells; Joseph Wood; Ann Gill; John Joiner; Nathaniel West and Elizabeth his wife; Rev. Elias Keech. Rev. Elias Keech, the first pastor at Lower Dublin, also preached at Burlington and Philadelphia.

ROMAN CATHOLICS

The early Catholics of Burlington were ministered to by Augustinian Fathers of St. Augustine Church of Philadelphia. St. Paul's Roman Catholic Church was established ca. 1798.

SELECTED BIBILOGRAPHY

1. *Genealogical Society of Pennsylvania*, Volume II, 1903, No. 3. Register of St. Mary's Church, Burlington, New Jersey. pp. 241-302.

2. Schermerhorn, William E. *History of Burlington, New Jersey*. Burlington, New Jersey: Press of Enterprise Publishing Co., 1927.

3. Hills, Rev. George Morgan. *History of the Church in Burlington, New Jersey*. Trenton, New Jersey: The W. S. Sharp Printing Company, 1885.

4. Woodward, Major E. M. and John F. Hageman. *History of Burlington and Mercers Counties, New Jersey*. Philadelphia: Everts and Peck, 1883.

5. Eckert, Jack. *Guide to the Records of Philadelphia Yearly Meeting*. Haverford College, Records Committee of Phildelphia Yearly Meeting, Swarthmore College, 1989.

1. Jack Eckert, *Guide to the Records of the Philadelphia Yearly Meeting*, p. 23.

2. *Ibid.*, pp. 45-47.

3. *Ibid.*, p. 66.

4. *Ibid.*, p. 65.

5. William E. Schermerhorn, *History of Burlington, New Jersey*.

Burlington County

UPPER SPRINGFIELD PREPARATIVE MONTHLY MEETING MEMBERS
1782

Anthony Sykes and his wife, Mary, and their children: Samuel, Anthony, Mary, Thomas, Benjamin, Katherine and John.
Mary Brown.
Jonathan Branson and his wife, Alice, and their children: Asa and Sarah.
Caleb Newbold and his wife, Sarah, and their children: Henry, Daniel, Lydia, Caleb, Edith, Sarah, Samuel, Thomas, Hannah and Mary.
Clayton Newbold and his wife, Mary, and their children: William, Elizabeth, Susan, Mary, Rebecca, John, George and Cleayton.
Joseph Pancost and his wife, Sarah, and their children: Hannah, John and Abigail.
Sarah Newbold, widow, and children, Hannah and Rachel.
Deborah, dau. of Hannah Newbold.
Ann Newbold, wife of Thomas Newbold, and their children: Margaret, Barzillai, Joseph, Michael, Sarah and Beulah.
Robert Emely and his wife, Elizabeth and their children: John, Susannah and Mary.
Mary Wright, widow of Samuel Wright, and dau. of John Scholey.
Francis Leonard.
Caleb Shreve, and his wife, Grace, and their children: Rebecca, Reuben, Thomas and Grace.
John Wood.
Benjamin Sykes and his wife, Hannah, and children: Rebecca, their dau. and Thomas, Edith, Charles, William, John and Susannah Newbold, children of William Newbold.
John Warren and his wife, Rachel, and their children: Thomas, Susannah, John and Sarah.
Anne Steward, wife of Joseph Steward, and children: Elizabeth and Bridget.
Achsah Warren.
Asa Bak.
Richard Stockton and his wife, Sarah, and their children: Joseph, Mary, Ann, Elizabeth, Israel and George.
The children of William Wood: Thomas, Mary, Ann, Susan, Elizabeth and Margaret.
Samuel Gauntt and his wife, Hannah, and their children: Uz, Sarspeta, Asher, Reubine, Elihu and Peter.
Thomas Gaskill and his wife, Edith, and their children: Thomas, Clayton, Sarah, Caleb and Charles.
Joseph Lamb and Rebecca, his wife.
Tanton Earl and Mary, his wife, and their children: John, Joseph, Elizabeth, Mercy, Mary, Tanton and Daniel.
Thomas Earle and his children: Michael, Susannah, John, Clayton, Martha, Rebecca, Thomas, and Tucker.
Charity Garwood.
Sarah Bibble, wife of Joseph Bibble.
George Croshaw and his wife, Hannah, and their children: Sarah, Samuel, John, Elizabeth.
Joseph Wright and Rebecca, his wife, and their children: Sarah, Mary, Schooley, Joseph, Frances, and Elizabeth.
Catherine Wright, wife of Caleb Wright, and their son, Samuel.

Rebecca Shreeve, wife of Joshua Shreve, and their children:
  Gresham, Theodocia, Alexander, Leah, Isaiah, James and Charles.
Anthony Morris and Sarah, his wife, and their children: Esther,
  Alice, Joseph, Anthony, Elizabeth.
Joseph Lamb and Mary, his wife, and their dau., Mercy.
Henry Ridgway and Mary, his wife, and their children: Ann,
  Samuel, Solomon, Elizabeth, Mary and Sarah.
Mary Ridgway, widow of Job Ridgway, and their children: Rebecca,
  Job, Jonathan.
John Wright and his children, Elizabeth and Samuel.
William Fox, Jr. and Sarah, his sister.
Job Stockton.
John Croshaw.
Benjamin Antrum.
Sarah Antrum.
Thomas Earl, Jr. and his wife, Edith, and son, Anthony.
Mary Gibbs, wife of Samuel Gibbs, and her son, William Earl.
Lottice Lamb, widow of Nehemiah Lamb, and their children: Esaias,
  Samuel, Rebecca, Mary and Charttee.
David Stockton and Elizabeth, his wife, and their children: Job,
  Mary, Obediah, Mercy, Samuel and Elizabeth.

MANSFIELD PARTICULAR MEETING MEMBERS

Martin Gibbs and Rebecca, his wife, and their children: Joel,
  John, Asa, Amos and Phebe.
Mary Smith.
John Atkinson and Sarah, his wife, and their children: Hope,
  Isaac, Jane, Joseph, John and William.
Benjamin Atkinson and Ann, his wife, and their son: Job.
Hope Black, wife of William Black, and their children, Ann and
  Charles.
Mathias Herlin and Elizabeth, his wife, and their son, Mathias.
Grace Kerlin, wife of Thomas Kerlin.
Nathaniel Pope and his wife, Sarah, and their children: John,
  Nathaniel, Thomas and William.
Richard Buffin and Hannah, his wife, and their children:
  Penelope, Abigail, Sarah and Michael.
Thomas Smith and Meribah, his wife, and their children: Rebecca,
  Job, Mary and Sarah.
Rachel Talbert, wife of William Talbert.
Elizabeth Bate.
Samuel Rockhill and Hannah, his wife, and their children: Joshua,
  John and Aaron.
Joseph Antrum and Ann, his wife, and their children: Martha,
  Susannah, Sarah, John and Hannah.
Job Harvey and Mary, his wife, and his children, Peter and John.
Elizabeth Pope, widow of Joseph Pope, and their children: Joseph,
  Rebecca, Ann, Elizabeth, Clayton and John.
Thomas Scattergood.
Jersha Rockhill, wife of Amos Rockhill.
Mercy Rockhill, wife of Thomas Rockhill.
Jacob Garwood.
Michael Buffin and Elizabeth, his wife.

Sarah Linton.
Samuel Satterthwaite and Mary, his wife, and their children:
John, Reubine, Joseph, Benjamin and Elizabeth.
Edward Rockhill and Elizabeth, his wife, and their children: Amy,
Mary, Nathan.
Mary Newbold, widow of John Newbold, and their children: Martha,
Ann and Samuel.
Elizabeth Stratten.
Nathan Bokins and Joice, his wife, and their son, Edward and Mary
Bunet [Bennet], her dau.
Jonathan Barton and Sarah, his wife, and their children:
Barzillai, John and David.
Samuel Bunting.

MANSFIELD PARTICULAR MEETING MEMBERS

Isaac Decow and Mary, his wife, and their children: Samuel,
Edward, Stacy, Isaac and Joel.
Sarah Lucas, wife of John Lucas, and their children: Eben,
Thomas, John, Sarah, William and Elizabeth.
William Satterthwaite and Jane, his wife, and their children:
Ann, Samuel, Jane, Mary, Martha, Hannah and Abigail.
William White and his children: Peter, Elizabeth and Mary.
Martha Linton.
Asa Mase.
Joseph English and Sarah, his wife.
Amy Black, wife of Ezra Black, and their children: William,
Achsah, Sarah, Amy, Ezra.
Barzillai Furman and Elizabeth, his wife, and their children:
Hannah and Matilda.
Joseph Field and Rebecca, his wife, and their children: Benjamin,
Caleb, Thomas.
Martha Rockhill, wife of George Rockhill, and their children:
John, Caleb, Sarah, Mary and Martha.
Mercy English, wife of Joseph English, and their children:
Joseph, John, Amy and Sarah.
Joseph Shreeve and Sarah, his wife, and their children: Rebecca
and Abigail.
Triphena Wilson.
Joseph Talman and Sarah, his wife, and their children: Deborah,
Joseph, Mary and Martha.
Unity Pancoast, wife of Joseph Pancoast, and their children:
Benjamin, Solomon, Samuel, Joseph, Mary, Sarah, Elizabeth, Asa
and Thomasin.
Peter Ellis and Mariam, his wife, and their children: Amos,
Elizabeth, Leah, Sarah, Mary and Phebe.
Alice Curtis, wife of Thomas Curtis.
Rhode Middleton.
Mary Talman, wife of Joseph Talman.
Talman Brock.
John Black.
Abel Gibbs.
John Harvey and Ann, his wife.
Ann Ridgway, dau. of Job Ridgway.

Mary Harvey.
Phebe Cooke.
Phebe Cooke.
Hannah Cooke.
Samuel Ellis, son of John Ellis.
Isaac Bunting and Elizabeth, his wife, and sons, Ebeneazer and
 Isaac.
Thomas Wright.
William Wright and Catherine, his wife.
Isabell Ridgway, wife of Jacob Ridgway, and their children:
 Jacob, Mary, Elizabeth.
Caleb Sattergood and Mary, his wife, and their children: Caleb,
 Sarah, Joshua, Mary, Benjamin and Martha.

UPPER FREEHOLD PARTICULAR MEETING MEMBERS

William Stevenson and Mary, his wife, and their children: John,
 Alice, Samuel, Margaret, William, James and Susannah.
Isaac Ivins and Ann, his wife.
Barzillai Levins and Margaret, his wife, and dau., Hannah.
Benjamin Kirby and Rachel, his wife, and dau., Elizabeth.
Diadamia Harrison.
John Bullock and Sarah, his wife.
Mary Lippincott.
John Rogers and his children, Theodosia and Ruth.
Samuel Wright and Jane, his wife, and children: Mary, Samuel,
 Joseph and Ann.
Joseph Ogborn.
Isaac Harrison.
Mahlon Wright and Mary, his wife.
John Ellis and Elizabeth, his wife, and his children: Joseph,
 Phebe, William; their children: John, Meribah, Barzillai and
 David.
Robert Kirby and his wife, Ann, and their children: Israel,
 Phebe, Job, Abraham, Robert and Achsah.
Mary Woodard, wife of Jesse Woodward, and their children: Isaac
 and Susan.
Nathan Wright and Rebecca, his wife.
Sarah Earl.
Joshua Gibbs, Jr.
Richard Waln and Elizabeth, his wife, and their children: Joseph,
 Nicholas, Mary, Elizabeth, Richard, Rebecca, Hannah and Jacob.
Alexander Howard and Elizabeth, his wife and their children:
 Martha, Thomas, Elizabeth and Rebecca.
Abner Steward and Mary, his wife.
Joshua Gibbs and Hannah, his wife, and their children: Reuben,
 Sarah, Rebecca and Isaac.
Joseph Fowler and Meribah, his wife, and their dau. Mary.
Bridget Steward, widow of Joseph Steward, and their children:
 Thomas and Susannah.
David Wright and Sarah, his wife, and their children: Joshua and
 Moses.
Joseph Bullock and Elizabeth, his wife, and their children:
 Elizabeth, Jemina, Rebecca and Anthony.

George Bullock and Edith, his wife, and their children: William,
    Joseph, Margaret and Hannah.
Isaac Bullock and Elizabeth, his wife, and their children: Edward
    and Amy.
Ebenezer Wright and Elizabeth, his wife, and their son, Joseph.
John Lawrie and Achsah, his wife, and their children: William,
    Elizabeth, Thomas and Ann.
Isaac Wright
Elizabeth Furman, wife of Thomas Furman, and their children:
    Thomas, Rebecca, Elizabeth, Isaac, Sarah, and William.
Mercy Davenport, wife of Emanuel Davenport.
Empson Kirby and Ann, his wife, and his children: Benjamin and
    Elizabeth; her children: Meriam, Joseph and Ralf Allen
Israel Woodward and Mary, his wife, and their children: Forman,
    Susannah, John, Elizabeth, Robert and Samuel.
George Holloway and Elizabeth, his wife, and their children:
    William, Mary, Sarah and George.
Josiah Williams and his children: Sarah, Joel, Ester, Joseph,
    John and Elizabeth.
Mary Rogers.
Sarah Wardel and her children: Samuel and Mary Wardel, and Sarah
    Ivins.
Deborah Woodward, wife of Anthony Woodward, and their children:
    Anthony, Nimrod, Benjamin, Constant, Velariah and George.
Theodosia Furman, widow of James Furman, and their children: John
    and Isaac.
Thomas Wright and Mary, his wife, and their children: Achsah,
    Ann, Thomas, David and John.
Joseph Wiles.
Richard Potts
Susannah Branson.
Abner Wright and Sarah, his wife, and their children: Sarah and
    Ann.
Lemuel Fox.
Benjamin Cathrall and Sarah, his wife, and son, Benjamin.
Samuel Lippincott and Elizabeth, his wife, and their children:
    Rebecca, Joseph.
Susannah Woodward, widow of Thomas Woodward, and their children:
    Keturah, Abner, Rebecca, Mary and Elizabeth.
James Shinn and Levina, his wife, and their children: Meuin,
    Margaret and Abigail.
Heziah Levin, wife of Moses Levins.
Ann Hutchin, wife of Hugh Hutchin.
Joseph Willis.
James Robinson.
Thomas Shinn and Sarah, his wife, and their children: Rachel,
    Vincent, Unity, Solomon, Elizabeth, Thomas, Sarah and Mary.
Jonathan Steward.
Stacy Wright.
Elizabeth Parker.
Edward Parker.
Hannah Andrews, wife of John Andrews, and her son, Jacob.
Thomas Coppwerthwaite.
Sarah Levis.
Rebecca Harrison.

Samuel Emley.
Catharine Emley.
Elizabeth Wiggus, wife of John Wiggus.
Elizabeth Wright, wife of David Wright, Jr.
Mary Rogers, wife of Samuel Rogers.
John Copwerthaite.
Michael Rogers, Jr. and Ann, his wife, and dau., Ann.
Samuel Gaskill and Sybilla, his wife, and children: Nathaniel, Elizabeth, John, Mary, Samuel, Sarah, Rachell and Aaron.
Joseph Parker.
Lucretia Stevens, wife of John Stevens, and the children of John Brown, dec'd: Asher, Elizabeth, Joseph, Margaret, Ann and Rebecca Brown.
Mary Wright, dau. of Isaac Wright.
William French and Rachael, his wife, and their son, John.
Joseph Vanlaw.
Benjamin Cathrall and Sarah, his wife, and their son Benjamin.

BIRTHS AND DEATHS OF UPPER SPRINGFIELD MONTHLY MEETING

Children of Anthony Sykes, b. 5th mo, 20th da, 1717, d. 8th mo, 24th da, 1783 and his wife, Mary, dau. of Thomas Newbold, b. 4th mo, 11th da, 1729, d. 5th mo, 22nd da, 1818: Samuel Sykes, b. 3rd mo, 31st da, 1752, d. 3rd mo, 1829; John Sykes, b. 5th mo, 3rd da, 1754, d. 1st mo, 29th da, 1761; Edith Sykes, b. 7th mo, 26th da, 1756, d. 9th mo, 12th da, 1817; Anthony Sykes, b. 10th mo, 3rd da, 1759; Mary Sykes, b. 8th mo, 30th da, 1762, d. 7th mo, 28th da, 1834; Thomas Sykes, b. 7th mo, 30th da, 1764; Benjamin Sykes, b. 2nd mo, 2nd da, 1766, d. 5th mo, 18th da, 1801; Katherine Sykes, b. 9th mo, 15th da, 1768, d. 4th mo, 3rd da, 1806 [never married]; John Sykes, b. 1st mo, 19th da, 1773.

Mary Brown, sister of Anthony Sykes, b. 1707, d. 1st mo, 8th da, 1783.
Mary Wright, widow of Samuel Wright, d. 1791.

Children of Tantom Earl, b. 3rd mo, 9th da, 1731, d. 10th mo, 24th da, 1807 and wife Mary, dau. of C. Haines, b. 9th mo, 12th da, 1732, d. 6th mo, 3rd da, 1833: Thomas Earl, b. 12th mo, 13th da, 1754, d. 8th mo, 4th da, 1806; Caleb Earl, b. 12th mo, 21st da, 1756; John Earl, b. 10th mo, 25th da, 1758; Joseph Earl, b. 1st mo, 12th da, 1761; Elizabeth Earl, b. 3rd mo, 7th da, 1763, d. 4th mo, 7th da, 1791; Mercy Earl, b. 3rd mo, 19th da, 1765, d. 9th mo, 20th da, 1804; Mary Earl, b. 5th mo, 25th da, 1767; Leticia Earl, b. 5th mo, 31st da, 1769, d. 3rd mo, 15th da, 1774; Tanton Earl, b. 10th mo, 23rd da, 1772, d. 1st mo, 29th da, 1796; Daniel Earl, b. 1st mo, 21st da, 1774.

Samuel Gaunt, b. 3rd mo, 11th da, 1718 and 1st wife, Sarah, dau. of John Black.

Children of Samuel Gaunt, and Hannah, his wife, dau. of Samuel Woodman, b. 4th mo, 9th da, 1726, d. 6th mo, 13th da, 1795: Judah Gaunt, b. 9th mo, 18th da, 1750; Uz Gaunt, b. 2nd mo, 21st

da, 1753; Larsta Gaunt, b. 9th mo, 5th da, 1755; Asher Gaunt, b. 4th mo, 7th da, 1758; Reuben Gaunt, b. 11th mo, 2nd da, 1760; Elizabeth Gaunt, b. 9th mo, 11th da, 1763; Elihu Gaunt, b. 7th mo, 27th da, 1766; Peter Gaunt, b. 8th mo, 19th da, 1771.
Children of Anthony Morris, b. 5th mo, 20th da, 1722 and Sarah, his wife, dau. of Stephen Cramer, b. 9th mo, 20th da, 1726: Stephen Morris, b. 2nd da, 20th mo, 1747; Mary Morris, b. 10th mo, 24th da, 1748; Hannah Morris, b. 3rd mo, 3rd da, 1750, d. 1782; Sarah Morris, b. 3rd mo, 21st da, 1751; John Morris, b. 2nd mo, 6th da, 1753, d. 1782; Hannah Morris, b. 2nd mo, 9th da, 1755; Esther Morris, b. 1st mo, 29th da, 1757; Alice Morris, b. 7th mo, 4th da, 1758; George Morris, b. 6th mo, 2nd da, 1760; Alice Morris, b. 4th mo, 14th da, 1762, d. 7th mo, 18th da, 1758; Anthony Morris, b. 4th mo, 15th da, 1764, d. 12th mo, 1769; Joseph Morris, b. 2nd mo, 3rd da, 1767; Elizabeth Morris, b. 11th mo, 23rd da, 1770; Anthony Morris, b. 4th mo, 18th da, 1773.
Children of Benjamin Sykes, b. 6th mo, 3rd da, 1729 and wife, Hannah, dau. of Japhet Leeds, b. 11th mo, 3rd da, 1747: Rebecca Sykes, b. 12th mo, 14th da, 1781; Hannah Sykes, b. 4th mo, 22nd da, 1783; Ann Sykes, b. 12th mo, 13th da, 1787; Elizabeth Sykes, b. 3rd mo, 12th da, 1790.

Sarah Newbold, widow of Barzillai Newbold, d. 10th mo, 17th da, 1784.
Joseph Lamb, b. 6th mo, 1715, d. 7th mo, 15th da, 1794 and Rebecca, his wife, dau. of William Budd, b. 7th mo, 13th da, 1714, d. 10th mo, 1783.

Children of Thomas Earl, d. 5th mo, 17th da, 1808 and his 1st wife, Rebecca, dau. of Michael Newbold, b. 8th mo, 13th da, 1739, d. 11th mo, 16th da, 1774: Michael Earl, b. 9th mo, 25th da, 1765 and Susannah Earl, b. 9th mo, 25th da, 1765, d. 6th mo, 9th da, 1833; John Earl, b. 12th mo, 30th da, 1766; Clayton Earl, b. 1st mo, 14th da, 1768; Martha Earl, b. 1st mo, 2nd da, 1770, d. 11th mo, 26th da, 1836; Rebecca Earl, b. 2nd mo, 11th da, 1772; Thomas Earl, b. 5th mo, 20th da, 1774; Mercy Earl, b. 5th mo, 3rd da, 1774, d. 9th mo, 4th da, 1775.
Children of Thomas Earl and his 2nd wife, Leah, dau. of John Tucker, b. 1744, d. 3rd mo, 16th da, 1780: Tucker William Earl, b. 3rd mo, 15th da, 1780, d. 3rd mo, 23rd da, 1803.
Children of Job Ridgway, d. 7th mo, 18th da, 1782 and Mary, his wife, dau. of John Wright, and widow of J. Schooley, b. 5th mo, 10th mo, 1730, d. 5th mo, 11th da, 1795: Rebecca Ridgway, b. 11th mo, 3rd da, 1762; Job Ridgway, b. 7th mo, 23rd da, 1764, d. 7th mo, 16th da, 1795; Jonathan Ridgway, b. 11th mo, 23rd da, 1769.
Children of Thomas Gaskill, b. 12th mo, 28th da, 1741, d. 11th mo, 17th da, 1828 and Edith, dau. of James Bowne, b. 8th mo, 10th da, 1742, d. 5th mo, 31st da, 1804: William Gaskill, b. 9th mo, 12th da, 1765, d. 3rd mo, 30th da, 1815; Thomas Gaskill, b. 10th mo, 29th da, 1769; Clayton Gaskill, b. 2nd mo, 28th da, 1772; Sarah Gaskill, b. 6th mo, 10th da, 1774, d. 11th mo, 29th da, 1792; Caleb Gaskill, b. 6th mo, 1st da, 1777, d. 12th mo, 26th da, 1860; Charles Gaskill, b. 10th mo, 14th da, 1781, d.

12th mo, 13th da, 1817.
Children of Clayton Newbold, b. 6th mo, 7th da, 1737, d. 7th mo, 7th da, 1812 and Mary, dau. of William Foster, b. 12th mo, 12th da, 1740, d. 3rd mo, 31st da, 1809: Michael Newbold, b. 7th mo, 31st da, 1760, d. 7th mo, 1761; Charlotte Newbold, b. 1st mo, 29th da, 1762, d. 10th mo, 26th da, 1819; Hannah Newbold, b. 12th mo, 3rd da, 1763, d. 2nd mo, 1765; William Newbold, b. 3rd mo, 1st da, 1767, d. 8th mo, 17th da, 1828; Elizabeth Newbold, b. 4th mo, 23rd da, 1769, d. 12th mo, 12th da, 1841; Susannah Newbold, b. 11th mo, 25th da, 1770, d. 7th mo, 27th da, 1847; Mary Newbold, b. 4th mo, 27th da, 1773, d. 4th mo, 9th da, 1796; Joseph Newbold, b. 9th mo, 15th da, 1774, d. 2nd mo, 1775; Rebecca Newbold, b. 1st mo, 25th da, 1776, d. 1839; John Newbold, b. 11th mo, 23rd da, 1777, d. 4th mo, 20th da, 1802; George Newbold, b. 5th mo, 29th da, 1780, d. 9th mo, 8th da, 1858; Clayton Newbold, b. 9th mo, 28th da, 1782, d. 9th mo, 9th da, 1863.
Children of Richard Stockton, b. 9th mo, 24th da, 1739, d. 12th mo, 20th da, 1814 and Sarah, dau. of Joseph Stockton, b. 5th mo, 25th da, 1745, d. 8th mo, 1st da, 1813: Joseph Stockton, b. 6th mo, 15th da, 1769; Mary Stockton, b. 11th mo, 30th da, 1772; Anna Stockton, b. 11th mo, 10th da, 1773; Elizabeth Stockton, b. 1st mo, 10th da, 1776; Israel F. Stockton, b. 10th mo, 1st da, 1778; George W. Stockton, b. 3rd mo, 10th da, 1781; Job Stockton, b. 5th mo, 2nd da, 1783; Doughty Stockton, b. 9th mo, 8th da, 1785.

Aaron Morton, b. 12th mo, 16th da, 1727, d. 12th mo, 2nd da, 1802; Sarah Morton, his 2nd wife, dau. of Samuel Tilton, b. 1753.

Children of Joseph Pancoast, b. 6th mo, 6th da, 1741, d. 6th mo, 14th da, 1808 and Sarah, dau. of Joseph Ridgway, b. 1st mo, 15th da, 1748, d. 11th mo, 29th da, 1817: Elizabeth Pancoast, b. 4th mo, 8th da, 1769, d. 7th mo, 15th da, 1779; Hannah Pancoast, b. 3rd mo, 22nd da, 1770; John Pancoast, b. 7th mo, 22nd da, 1771, d. 2nd mo, 17th da, 1841; Abigail Pancoast, b. 7th mo, 21st da, 1778, d. 10th mo, 25th da, 1815; Sarah Pancoast, b. 2nd mo, 20th da, 1785.
Child of Joseph Lamb, b. 6th mo, 28th da, 1754 and wife Mary, dau. of William Earl, b. 4th mo, 17th da, 1753, d. 8th mo, 6th da, 1798: Mercy Lamb, b. 6th mo, 1st da, 1782.
Children of Rebecca Shreve, wife of Joshua Shreve and dau. of Joseph Lamb, b. 3rd mo, 26th da, 1742, d. 12th mo, 9th da, 1800: Gersham Shreve, b. 10th mo, 6th da, 1762; Theodosia Shreve, b. 4th mo, 28th da, 1766; Alexander Shreve, b. 3rd mo, 3rd da, 1769; Leah Shreve, b. 4th mo, 8th da, 1771; Sarah Shreve, b. 12th mo, 25th da, 1775; James Shreve, b. 3rd mo, 1st da, 1778, d. 9th mo, 1852; Charles Shreve, b. 4th mo, 7th da, 1781; Rebecca Shreve, b. 12th mo, 3rd da, 1785.
Children of David Stockton, b. 1st mo, 29th da, 1740, d. 4th mo, 25th da, 1787 and Elizabeth, dau. of O. Tinton, b. 9th mo, 30th da, 1735: David Stockton, b. 3rd mo, 3rd da, 1762, d. 9th mo, 28th da, 1777; Ruth Stockton, b. 1st mo, 14th da, 1764, d. 9th mo, 29th da, 1777; Job Stockton, b. 1st mo, 3rd da, 1766; Mary

Stockton, b. 3rd mo, 12th da, 1768; Obediah Stockton, b. 2nd mo, 25th da, 1770; Mercy and Hannah Stockton, b. 1st mo, 26th da, 1772, Hannah Stockton, d. 3rd mo, 24th da 1772; Samuel Stockton, b. 6th mo, 14th da, 1774; Joseph Stockton, b. 1st mo, 2nd da, 1776, d. 10th mo, 6th da, 1777; Elizabeth Stockton, b. 12th mo, 5th da, 1778.
Children of George Croshaw, d. 9th mo, 12th da, 1785 and Hannah, dau. of Samuel Gauntt, b. 8th mo, 15th da, 1746, d. 3rd mo, 24th da, 1807: Sarah Croshaw, b. 4th mo, 6th da, 1774, d. 9th mo, 23rd da, 1791; Samuel Croshaw, b. 6th mo, 9th da, 1776; John Croshaw, b. 10th mo, 17th da, 1778; Elizabeth Croshaw, b. 3rd mo, 19th da, 1781; Hannah Croshaw, b. 9th mo, 9th da, 1735.
Children of William Harris, b. 1st mo, 25th da, 1729 and Alice, his wife, dau. of James Sharkey: James Harris, b. 12th mo, 16th da, 1753; Phebe Harris, b. 9th mo, 5th da, 1755; Edith Harris, b. 3rd mo, 25th da, 1767; Sarah Harris, b. 12th mo, 24th da, 1758; Alice Harris, b. 9th mo, 24th da, 1760; Samuel Harris, b. 7th mo, 28th da, 1762; William Harris, b. 6th mo, 14th da, 1765; Ruth Harris, b. 8th mo, 21st da, 1767; Frances Harris, b. no. date.
Children of William Harris and his 2nd wife, Jane, dau. of John Richardson: Joseph Harris, b. 6th mo, 7th da, 1773; Thomas Harris, b. no. date. [Records say all children are non members.
Children of Nehemiah Lamb, b. 12th mo, 11th da, 1749 and Lettice, his wife, dau. of Amariah Foster, b. 2nd mo, 22nd da, 1755: Ejaias, b. 3rd mo, 4th da, 1773; Mary b. 3rd mo, 10th da, 1774; Samuel b. 5th mo, 14th da, 1777; Rebecca b. 7th mo, 30th da, 1780; Charlotte b. 8th mo, 9th da, 1782.
Children of Samuel Gibbs and Mercy his wife, widow of William Earl: Tantom Gibbs, b. 7th mo, 6th da, 1765; Caleb Gibbs, b. 2nd mo, 12th da, 1767; John Gibbs, b. 2nd mo, 7th da, 1769; Elizabeth Gibbs, b. 9th mo, 25th da, 1773.

Sarah Clevenger, b. 8th mo, 15th da, 1747.
George O'Neil, b. 1738 and Sarah, his wife, dau. of Ralph Smith, b. 3rd mo, 6th da, 1751.

Children of Robert Emley and Mary, his wife, dau. of Michael Newbold, b. 2nd mo, 2nd da, 1742: Elizabeth Emley, b. 10th mo, 17th da, 1767; John Emley, b. 4th mo, 25th da, 1769; Susanna Emley, b. 4th mo, 30th da, 1771; Mary Emley, b. 10th mo, 9th da, 1780.
Children of John Warren, b. 11th mo, 21st da, 1742, d. 4th mo, 27th da, 1797 and Rachel, dau. of Thomas Morrison, b. 8th mo, 29th da, 1752, d. 4th mo, 17th da, 1797: Thomas Warren, b. 12th mo, 19th da, 1775, d. 5th mo, 9th da, 1806; Susannah Warren, b. 10th mo, 18th da, 1777; John Warren, b. 9th mo, 22nd da, 1779; Sarah Warren, b. 10th mo, 1st da, 1781; Beulah Warren, b. 10th mo, 12th da, 1783; Benjamin Warren, b. 11th mo, 11th da, 1785; Rachel Warren, b. 3rd mo, 11th da, 1788; Caleb Warren, b. 5th mo, 31st da, 1790; Stephen Warren, b. 1st mo, 30th da, 1795.
Children of Job Gaskill, b. 3rd mo, 27th da, 1747 and Louis, dau. of Isaac Prickett, b. 7th mo, 30th da, 1742: Isaac Gaskill, b. 6th mo, 17th da, 1769; William Gaskill, b. 4th mo, 8th da, 1772; Hudson Gaskill, b. 11th mo, 12th da, 1774; Esther Gaskill, b.

10th mo, 10th da, 1777, d. 2nd mo, 1st da, 1780; Mary Gaskill, b. 10th mo, 10th da, 1782; Levi Gaskill, b. 9th mo, 19th da, 1785; Job Gaskill, b. 8th mo, 19th da, 1788, d. 9th mo, 13th da, 1792.

Job Gaskill removed to the State of Ohio.

Children of John Wright, b. 12th mo, 12th da, 1749 and Priscilla, dau. of Charity Garwood, b. 2nd mo, 8th da, 1751: Elizabeth Wright, b. 8th mo, 15th da, 1772; Samuel Wright, b. 3rd mo, 8th da, 1775.
Children of John Wright and Achsah, 2nd wife, dau. of John Horner, b. 3rd mo, 8th da, 1759: John Wright, b. 6th mo, 20th da, 1785; Mary Wright, b. 12th mo, 20th da, 1786, d. 1st mo, 5th da, 1809; Elisha Wright, b. 12th mo, 5th da, 1788;, d. 11th mo, 27th da, 1796; Deborah Wright, b. 6th mo, 1st da, 1792, d. 10th mo, 4th da, 1793; Rebecca Wright, b. 9th mo, 17th da, 1794; Richard Wright, b. 6th mo, 16th da, 1796, d. 12th mo, 26th da, 1796; William Wright, b. 3rd mo, 17th da, 1798.
Children of Catherine Wright, wife of Caleb Wright, and dau. of John Gardiner, b. 10th mo, 15th da, 1755: John Wright, b. 8th mo, 6th da, 1780, d. 8th mo, 26th da, 1780; Samuel G. Wright, b. 11th mo, 18th da, 1781; Henry Wright, b. 11th mo, 2nd da, 1783; Joseph Wright, b. 5th mo, 2nd da, 1785; Caleb Wright, b. 6th mo, 29th da, 1787; Benjamin Wright, b. 10th mo, 13th da, 1729; Amy Wright, b. 7th mo, 29th da, 1791; John Wright, b. 8th mo, 21st da, 1795, d. 8th mo, 28th da, 1795; Esther Wright, b. 7th mo, 22nd da, 1797.
Children of Grace Shreve, widow of Caleb Shreve, and dau. of Thomas Pancoast, b. 3rd mo, 7th da, 1734, d. 5th mo, 23rd da, 1806: Phebe Shreve, b. 5th mo, 12th da 1757; Benjamin Shreve, b. 1st mo, 7th da, 1759; Ann Shreve, b. 10th mo, 10th da, 1761; Rebecah Shreve, b. 9th mo, 30th da, 1764; Caleb Shreve, b. 10th mo, 30th da, 1766; Ruben Shreve, b. 8th mo, 16th da, 1768; Thomas Shreve, b. 9th mo, 9th da, 1770; Grace Shreve, b. 10th mo, 15th da, 1772; Mary Shreve, b. 4th mo, 10th da, 1775, d. 11th mo, 30th da, 1777.
Children of Thomas Earl, son of Tantum and Mary Earl, b. 12th mo, 13th da, 1754, d. 8th mo, 4th da, 1806 and Edith, dau. of Anthony and Mary Sykes, b. 7th mo, 26th da, 1756, d. 9th mo, 12th da, 1817: Anthony Earl, b. 4th mo, 21st da, 1780; Mary Earl, b. 6th mo, 4th da, 1783, d. 5th mo, 30th da, 1854; Leticia Earl, b. 6th mo, 16th da, 1785; Leah Earl, b. 10th mo, 24th da, 1789, d. 1st mo, 24th da, 1864; Caleb and Thomas Earl, b. 3rd mo, 7th da, 1794; Tanton Earl, b. 5th mo, 30th da, 1800.
Children of Abigail Smith, wife of Samuel Smith, and dau. of John Schooley, b. 3rd mo, 21st da, 1755: John Smith, b. 7th mo, 23rd da, 1775, d. 7th mo, 7th da, 1777; William Smith, b. 8th mo, 16th da, 1773; Charles Smith, b. 3rd mo, 25th da, 1781; Samuel S. Smith, b. 8th mo, 24th da, 1788.
Children of Henry Ridgeway, b. 12th mo, 26th da, 1749, d. 2nd mo, 1805 and Mary, dau. of Samuel Wright, b. 2nd mo, 7th da, 1752, d. 12th mo, 28th da, 1812: Ann Ridgeway, b. 12th mo, 10th da, 1771; Samuel W. Ridgeway, b. 8th mo, 12th da, 1773; Solomon Ridgeway, b. 5th mo, 9th da, 1775; Elizabeth Ridgeway, b. 10th

mo, 25th da, 1777; Mary Ridgeway, b. 2nd mo, 7th da, 1780; Sarah
Ridgeway, b. 5th mo, 12th da, 1782; Rebecca Ridgeway, b. 12th
mo, 11th da, 1785; Hannah Ridgeway, b. 5th mo, 14th da, 1787, d.
1st mo, 18th da, 1788; Henry Ridgeway, b. 7th mo, 5th da, 1791,
d. 8th mo, 23rd da, 1792; William Ridgeway, b. 11th mo, 30th da,
1793.
Children of Caleb Newbold, b. 3rd mo, 16th da, 1731, d. 3rd mo,
1781 and Sarah, dau. of Samuel Haines, b. 7th mo, 15th da, 1737,
d. 3rd mo, 10th da, 1820: Achsah Newbold, b. 1st mo, 15th da,
1757, d. 8th mo, 11th da, 1770; Daniel Newbold, b. 8th mo, 4th
da, 1758, d. 1815; Lydia Newbold, b. 12th mo, 10th mo, 1760;
Caleb Newbold, b. 11th mo, 2nd da, 1763, b. 11th mo, 17th da,
1853; Edith Newbold, b. 2nd mo, 31st da, 1766; Sarah Newbold, b.
22nd da, 3rd da, 1769, d. 3rd mo, 2nd da, 1860; Samuel Newbold,
b. 10th da, 12th da, 1771, d. 7th mo, 13th da, 1849; Thomas
Newbold, b. 9th mo, 22nd da, 1773, d. 12th mo, 1815; Hannah
Newbold, b. 4th mo, 2nd da, 1775, d. 2nd mo, 3rd da, 1821; Molly
or Mary Newbold, b. 9th mo, 29th da, 1779; d. 9th mo, 23rd da,
1862; Hannah Newbold, b. 6th mo, 23rd da, 1782, d. 1832.

Daniel Newbold m. Rachel Newbold; Lydia Newbold m. John Black;
Caleb Newbold m. Sarah Lawrence; Edith Newbold m. Thomas Howard;
Sarah Newbold m. William Bowne; Samuel Newbold m. Mary Hough;
Thomas Newbold m. Catharine LeRoy, from New York; Hannah Newbold
m. John Henry Taylor, PA; Molly Newbold m. John B. Lawrence, New
York.

Children of Joseph Southwick, b. 4th mo, 11th da, 1760, d. 1828
and Phebe, dau. of Peter Baker, b. 6th mo, 1st da, 1763, d. 10th
mo, 3rd da, 1826: Mary Southwick, b. 10th mo, 3rd da, 1786;
Samuel Southwick, b. 6th mo, 16th da, 1789; Peter Southwick, b.
11th mo, 7th da, 1791; Rebecca Southwick, b. 4th mo, 28th da,
1794; Joseph Southwick, b. 11th mo, 23rd da, 1796; Hannah
Southwick, b. no date.
Children of Jonathan Branson, b. 9th mo, 20th da, 1726, d. 3rd
mo, 16th da, 1799; Alice, his wife, dau. of Francis Atkinson, b.
8th mo, 24th da, 1726, d. 2nd mo, 2nd da, 1791: Elizabeth
Branson, b. 6th mo, 1748; Samuel Branson, b. 11th mo, 9th da,
1749; Lydia Branson, b. 8th mo, 1751; Mary Branson, b. 4th mo,
1753; Mercy Branson, b. 3rd mo, 1755; Asa Branson, b. 2nd mo,
4th da, 1757; Sarah Branson, b. 5th mo, 1759; Jonathan Branson,
b. 7th mo, 1761; Achsah Branson, b. 7th mo, 1764.
Children of Ann Newbold, wife of Thomas, dau. of Joseph Lamb:
Margaret Newbold, Barzillia Newbold, Joseph Newbold, Enoch
Newbold, Michael Newbold, Sarah Newbold, b. 2nd mo, 29th da,
1776, Beulah Newbold. [no dates for any of the children except
Sarah.]

Ann Newbold, widow of Thomas Newbold, and dau. of Joseph Lamb, d.
3rd mo, 24th da, 1787.
Mercy Rockhill, wife of Thomas Rockhill, d. 9th mo, 5th da, 1800.

Children of Uz Gauntt, b. 2nd mo, 21st da, 1753, d. 2nd mo, 9th
da, 1839, son of Samuel Gauntt and wife, Sarah, dau. of Benjamin
Jones, d. 5th mo, 16th da, 1817: Samuel Gauntt, b. 10th mo, 27th

da, 1791; Benjamin Gauntt, b. 6th mo, 18th da, 1793; Israel
Gauntt, b. 8th mo, 16th da, 1794; Lewis Gauntt, b. 7th mo, 29th
da, 1797, d. 8th mo, 15th da, 1807; Hannah Gauntt, b. 5th mo,
9th mo, 1799; Elisha Gauntt, b. 7th mo, 6th da, 1800; Jefferson
Gauntt, b. 12th mo, 3rd da, 1805.
Children of Thomas Newbold, son of William Newbold, b. 8th mo,
2nd da, 1760, d. 12th mo, 18th da, 1823 and Mary, dau. of
Anthony Taylor, b. 9th mo, 8th da, 1768, 7th mo, 21st da, 1811:
Edith Newbold, b. 10th mo, 30th da, 1790, d. 6th mo, 10th da,
1809; Anthony Newbold, b. 4th mo, 2nd da, 1791, d. 4th mo, 12th
da, 1795; William Newbold, b. 11th mo, 22nd da, 1792, d. 12th
mo, 2nd da, 1800; Michael Newbold, b. 8th mo, 4th da, 1794;
Samuel Newbold, b. 2nd mo, 2nd da, 1796, d. 8th mo, 2nd da,
1800; Thomas Newbold, b. 10th mo, 16th da, 1797, d. 11th mo,
12th da, 1800; Ann Newbold, b. 11th mo, 17th da, 1799, d. 11th
mo, 22nd da, 1858; Sarah Newbold, b. 1st mo, 27th da, 1802, d.
5th mo, 15th da, 1850; Thomas J. Newbold, b. 11th mo, 27th da,
1803; Susan C. Newbold, b. 3rd mo, 25th da, 1806, d. 1824; Mary
Newbold b. 6th mo, 25th da, 1811.

Michael Newbold m. Esther Lounes, Philadelaphia; Ann Newbold m.
William Black, Sarah Newbold m. John Rowland; Thomas J. Newbold
m. Rebecca Shreve; Mary Newbold m. 1st Anthony Taylor, 2nd
Samuel Hyett?, 3rd John Adams; 4th ? Black.

Children of Joseph Steward, b. 4th mo, 13th da, 1746 and wife,
Ann, dau. of Nathaniel Robins, b. 1st mo, 29th da, 1747: Nathan
Steward, b. 3rd mo, 19th da, 1768; Elizabeth Steward, b. 4th mo,
7th da, 1777; Bridget Steward, b. 1st mo, 26th da, 1780, d. 23rd
da, 7th da, 1783; John Steward, b. 3rd mo, 4th da, 1790.
Children of Isaac Barton, b. 1st mo, 8th da, 1754, d. 1st mo, 5th
da, 1809 son of Aaron Barton and Sempta, dau. of Samuel Gauntt,
b. 9th mo, 5th da, 1755, d. 7th mo, 18th da, 1801: Hannah
Barton, b. 10th mo, 8th da, 1792, d. 7th mo, 1st da, 1793; Isaac
Barton, b. 10th mo, 3rd da, 1795; Bathsheba Barton, b. 3rd mo,
8th da, 1798.
Children of William Newbold, son of Clayton and Mary Newbold, b.
3rd mo, 1st da, 1767, d. 8th mo, 17th da, 1828 and Hannah, dau.
of John Watson, b. 9th mo, 24th da, 1765, d. 12th mo, 5th da,
1831: Joseph W. Newbold, b. 3rd mo, 30th da, 1792, d. 8th mo,
23rd da, 1822; Watson Newbold, b. 1st mo, 6th da, 1794, d. 7th
mo, 24th da, 1800; Clayton Newbold , b. 1st mo, 22nd da, 1797;
George Newbold, b. 1st mo, 24th da, 1799; William F. Newbold, b.
9th mo, 15th da, 1800; Watson Newbold, b. 4th mo, 2nd da, 1802;
Rachel Newbold, b. 12th mo, 4th da, 1803; Hannah Newbold, b. 2nd
mo, 4th da, 1810.

Joseph W. Newbold m. Hannah Coleman; Clayton Newbold m. Susan H.
Trotten?; William F. Newbold m. Elizabeth Pancoast; Watson
Newbold m. Hannah Pancoast; Rachel Newbold m. Daniel A.
Pancoast.

Children of Samuel Haines and Anne, formerly Bickey, b. 11th mo,
5th da, 1762: Elizabeth Haines, b. 8th mo, 29th da, 1790, d.
12th mo, 10th da, 1802; Ann Haines, b. 5th mo, 19th da, 1791;

Mahlon Haines, b. 3rd mo, 22nd da, 1793; Isaac Haines, b. 2nd mo, 5th da, 1796.
Children of Isaac Horner, b. 11th mo, 25th da, 1763 and Mary, dau. of John Pitman, b. 9th mo, 12th da, 1766, d. 3rd mo, 16th da, 1810: Thomas Horner, b. 3rd mo, 1st da, 1787, d. 9th mo, 6th da, 1791; Achsah Horner, b. 2nd mo, 26th da, 1789; Sarah Horner, b. 4th mo, 6th da, 1791; Deborah Horner, b. 5th mo, 23rd da, 1793; Anna Horner, b. 7th mo, 3rd da, 1795; Hannah Horner, b. 5th mo, 22nd da, 1797; Susannah Horner, b. 4th mo, 18th da, 1799; Jonathan Horner, b. 2nd mo, 27th da, 1801; Rebecca Horner, b. 6th mo, 10th da, 1804; Chalkley Horner, b. 8th mo, 1st da, 1806, d. 12th mo, 26th da, 1807; Mary Horner, b. 9th mo, 18th da, 1808, d. 11th mo, 3rd da, 1808.
Children of Thomas Wilson, b. 8th mo, 11th da, 1744 and Ann, dau. of Thomas Price, b. 8th mo, 3rd da, 1748: Rachel b. 11th mo, 2nd mo, 1770, d. 9th mo, 18th da, 1794; Ann b. 12th mo, 9th da, 1772; Thomas Wilson, b. 2nd mo, 15th da, 1775; Sarah Wilson, b. 3rd mo, 15th da, 1777; Mary Wilson, b. 7th mo, 30th da, 1779; Hannah Wilson, b. 7th mo, 13th da, 1781; William Wilson, b. 10th mo, 26th da, 1783; Elizabeth Wilson, b. 1st mo, 11th da, 1786; Lydia Wilson, b. 1st mo, 11th da, 1786; John Wilson, b. 8th mo, 3rd da, 1788; Joseph Wilson, b. 5th mo, 24th da, 1790.

Caleb Shreve (York Road) b. 8th mo, 13th da, 1721, d. 9th mo, 27th da, 1786 and wife, Abigail, dau. of Joseph Antrum, d. 4th mo, 8th da, 1800.

Children of Alexander Shreve, son of Joshua and Rebecca Shreeve, b. 3rd mo, 3rd da, 1769 and Mary, dau. of Tantom Earl, b. 5th mo, 25th da, 1767: Joshua Shreve, b. 3rd mo, 25th da, 1793; Mary Shreve, b. 4th mo, 19th da, 1795, d. 8th mo, 11th da, 1796; Sarah Shreve, b. 7th mo, 20th da, 1797; Mary Ann Shreve, b. 9th mo, 6th da, 1799; Tanton E. Shreve, b. 2nd mo, 23rd da, 1802; Rebecca Shreve, b. 5th mo, 9th da, 1805; Alexander Shreve, b. 10th mo, 2nd da, 1812.
Children of Samuel Satterthwaite, b. 8th mo, 5th da, 1773, d. 9th mo, 20th da, 1789 and Mary, d. 5th mo, 19th da, 1782, dau. of John Crisps: John Satterthwaite, b. 10th mo, 4th da, 1758; Reuben Satterthwaite, b. 3rd mo, 5th da, 1760, d. 10th mo, 9th da, 1787; Reuben Satterthwaite, b. 3rd mo, 5th da, 1760, d. 4th mo, 24th da, 1802; Joseph Satterthwaite, b. 3rd mo, 10th da, 1762; Benjamin Satterthwaite, b. 10th mo, 5th da, 1764; Elizabeth Satterthwaite, b. 10th mo, 6th da, 1767; Mary Satterthwaite, b. no date.
Children of William Satterthwaite, b. 1st mo, 29th da, 1738, d. 5th mo, 31st da, 1817 and Jane, dau. of Benjamin Linton, b. 1st mo, 10th da, 1743, dau. of Benjamin Linton: Ann Satterthwaite, b. 1st mo, 29th da, 1769; Samuel Satterthwaite, b. 12th mo, 23rd da, 1770, d. 3rd mo, 12th da, 1851; Jane Satterthwaite, b. 9th mo, 16th da, 1772; Mary Satterthwaite, b. 3rd mo, 29th da, 1775, d. 3rd mo, 6th da, 1846; Martha Satterthwaite, b. 8th mo, 30th da, 1777; Hannah Satterthwaite, b. 7th mo, 17th da, 1779, d. 3rd mo, 6th da, 1858; Abigail Satterthwaite, b. 7th mo, 14th da, 1781, d. 12th mo, 18th da, 1793; Benjamin Satterthwaite, b. 6th mo, 11th da, 1783, d. 1st mo, 9th da, 1871; William

Satterthwaite, b. 9th mo, 26th da, 1790, d. 11th da, 10th da, 1822.
Children of Mary Newbold, widow of John Newbold, dau. of Samuel Cole, b. 6th mo, 10th da, 1731, d. 10th mo, 20th da, 1789: Rachel Newbold, b. 2nd mo, 20th da, 1759; Martha Newbold, b. 5th mo, 5th da, 1761; Ann b. 3rd mo, 5th da, 1763; Samuel Newbold, b. 3rd mo, 9th da, 1763.

Joseph English, d. 11th mo, 1785 and his wife Sarah, d. 11th mo, 1785.
Ann Gauntt, widow of Hannaniah Gauntt, and dau. of Jacob Ridgway b. 10th mo, 8th da, 1710, d. 2nd mo, 6th da, 1794.

Children of Isaac Decow, b. 2nd mo, 1st da, 1748, d. 12th mo, 22nd da, 1790 and Mary, dau. of John Taylor, b. 9th mo, 21st da, 1748: Daniel Decow, b. 10th mo, 2nd da, 1771; Samuel Decow, b. 8th mo, 17th da, 1774; Stacy Decow, b. 11th mo, 26th da, 1776; Isaac Decow, b. 7th mo, 27th da, 1778; Joel Decow, b. 4th mo, 15th da, 1780, d. 1st mo, 23rd da, 1784; Mary Decow, b. 3rd mo, 2nd da, 1782, b. 4th mo, 8th da, 1782; Achsah Decow, b. 3rd mo, 13rd da, 1783; Sarah Decow, b. 5th mo, 1785; Nathan Decow, b. 5th mo, 21st da, 1787.
Children of Peter Ellis, b. 6th mo, 17th da, 1743, d. 1st mo, 11th da, 1830 and Miriam, dau. of Amos Middleton, b. 3rd mo, 6th da, 1748, d. 9th mo, 14th da, 1823: Amos Ellis, b. 1st mo, 13th da, 1772. d. 9th mo, 18th da, 1813; William Ellis, b. 1st mo, 18th da, 1773, d. 8th mo, 27th da, 1781; Elizabeth Ellis, b. 2nd mo, 27th da, 1774; Leah Ellis, b. 10th mo, 8th da, 1775; Sarah Ellis, b. 11th mo, 2nd da, 1777; Mary Ellis, b. 3rd mo, 19th da, 1780; Phebe Ellis, b. 10th mo, 23rd da, 1782; Peter H. Ellis, b. 9th mo, 8th da, 1785, d. 6th mo, 5th da, 1811; Hannah Ellis, b. 1st mo, 15th da, 1789; Samuel Ellis, b. 7th mo, 17th da, 1791.
Children of Martin Gibbs, b. 1st mo, 4th da, 1732, d. 1st mo, 1st da, 1820 and Rebecca, his second wife, b. 8th mo, 5th da, 1782, d. 2nd mo, 27th da, 1805: Phebe Gibbs, b. 8th mo, 5th da, 1782; Martin Gibbs, b. 1st mo, 2nd da, 1791.

Edward Rockhill, d. 5th mo, 30th da, 1789; his wife, Elizabeth, dau. of Samuel Taylor, d. 5th mo, 28th da, 1798.
Mary Harvey, widow of Peter Harvey, and dau. of Godfrey Hancock, b. 12th mo, 25th da, 1723, d. 2nd mo, 26th da, 1791.
John Harvey, b. 2nd mo, 28th da, 1724, d. 3rd mo, 30th da, 1792 and Ann his wife, dau. of Daniel Tilton, b. 11th mo, 11th da, 1729, d. 8th mo, 2nd da, 1806.
Job Harvey d. 1st mo, 23rd da, 1791; his 2nd wife Mary, dau. of Samuel Satterthwaite, b. 3rd mo, 16th da, 1731, d. 11th mo, 12th da, 1790.

Children of John Atkinson, b. 10th mo, 15th da, 1727, d. 1st mo, 15th da, 1805 and Sarah, his wife, b. 7th mo, 20th da, 1738, d. 7th mo, 23rd da, 1807: Benjamin Atkinson, b. 10th mo, 17th da, 1754; Jane Atkinson, b. 10th mo, 27th da, 1756; Joseph Atkinson, b. 1st mo, 27th da, 1759; Elizabeth Atkinson, b. 12th mo, 20th da, 1760; Ann Atkinson, b. 4th mo, 10th da, 1763; Joseph Atkinson, b. 5th mo, 8th da, 1765; Hope Atkinson, b. 9th mo, 8th

da, 1767; Jane Atkinson, b. 12th mo, 3rd da, 1769; Sarah Atkinson, b. 2nd mo, 8th da, 1772; John Atkinson, b. 8th mo, 4th da, 1775; William Atkinson, b. 1st mo, 10th da, 1778.
Children of Richard Buffin, b. 8th mo, 26th da, 1745, d. 3rd mo, 24th da, 1825; and Hannah, his wife, b. 5th mo, 15th da, 1746, d. 12th mo, 22nd da, 1831: Penelope Buffin, b. 3rd mo, 16th da, 1774, d. 6th mo, 15th da, 1847; Abigail Buffin, b. 8th mo, 9th da, 1778; Sarah Buffin, b. 7th mo, 6th da, 1780; Michael Buffin, b. 10th mo, 22nd da, 1782; Levina Buffin, b. 3rd mo, 16th da, 1784; Ann Buffin, b. 7th mo, 9th da, 1787; Clayton Buffin, b. 5th mo, 21st da, 1790.
Children of Nathaniel Pope, b. 12th mo, 12th da, 1745 and Sarah, his wife, dau. of Solomon Shinn, b. 6th mo, 10th da, 1748, d. 8th mo, 10th da, 1825: Mary Pope, b. 2nd mo, 3rd da, 1771, d. 7th mo, 8th da, 1777; Samuel Pope, b. 12th mo, 21st da, 1772, d. 9th mo, 2nd da, 1773; John Pope, b. 2nd mo, 15th da, 1774; Unity Pope, b. 7th mo, 18th da, 1776, d. 7th mo, 15th da, 1777; Nathaniel Pope, b. 7th mo, 6th da, 1778; Thomas Pope, b. 6th mo, 19th da, 1780; William Pope, b. 3rd mo, 31st da, 1782; Richard Pope, b. 8th mo, 3rd da, 1784; Sarah Pope, b.7th mo, 31st da, 1786.
Children of Thomas Smith, b. 12th mo, 25th da, 1745, d. 5th mo, 22nd da, 1810 and Meribah, his wife, dau. of Amos Rockhill, b. 1st mo, 2nd da, 1756: Rebecca Smith, b. 1st mo, 13th da, 1777; Job Smith, b. 12th mo, 14th da, 1778; Mary Smith, b. 11th mo, 2nd da, 1780; Sarah Smith, b. 1st mo, 24th da, 1782; Thomas Smith, b. 3rd mo, 6th da, 1784; Margaret Smith, b. 5th mo, 5th da, 1786, d. 10th mo, 19th da, 1796; Samuel Smith, b. 5th mo, 8th da, 1788; Meribah Smith, b. 1st mo, 27th da, 1790; Amos Smith, b. 10th mo, 15th da, 1792; Joshua Smith, b. 1st mo, 11th da, 1796, d. 6th mo, 5th da, 1796.
Children of Samuel Rockhill, b. 1st mo, 15th da, 1752 and Susannah, his wife, dau. of A. Morris, b. 9th mo, 2nd da, 1755, d. 3rd mo, 21st da, 1817: Samuel Rockhill, b. 4th mo, 19th da, 1775, d. 12th mo, 22nd da, 1780; Jerusha Rockhill, b. 9th mo, 4th da, 1776; John Rockhill, b. 8th mo, 6th da, 1778; Aaron Rockhill, b. 1st mo, 11th da, 1780; Sarah Rockhill, b. 4th mo, 6th da, 1785; Samuel Rockhill, b. 6th mo, 22nd da, 1787, d. 5th mo, 29th da, 1787; Hannah Rockhill, b. 7th mo, 27th da, 1789; William Rockhill, b. 7th mo, 13th da, 1791; Samuel Rockhill, b. 7th mo, 15th da, 1793; Edward Rockhill, b. 10th mo, 31st da, 1795; Amos Rockhill, b. 12th mo, 21st da, 1797.
Children of Joseph Shreve, son of Caleb Shreve, York Road, b. 12th mo, 28th da, 1748, d. 12th mo, 22nd da, 1829 and Sarah, his wife, dau. of Samuel Taylor: Rebecca Shreve, b. 9th mo, 25th da, 1778; Abigail Shreve, b. 9th mo, 28th da, 1780; Amey Shreve, b. 9th mo, 29th da, 1782; Ann Shreve, b. 12th mo, 30th da, 1784, d. 8th mo, 8th da, 1785; Sarah Shreve, b. 6th mo, 12th da, 1786; Elizabeth Shreve, b. 8th mo, 1st da, 1788, d. 11th mo, 1840; Joseph Shreve, b. 3rd mo, 22nd da, 1791, d. 11th mo, 1872; Samuel Shreve, b. 10th mo, 19th da, 1792; Cabel Shreve, b. 9th mo, 27th da, 1796, d. 8th mo, 1832; Thomas Shreve, b. 5th mo, 20th da, 1799, d. 10th mo, 23rd da, 1825; Charlotte Shreve, b. 3rd mo, 25th da, 1802.

Barzillai Furman, b. 11th mo, 15th da, 1753, d. 3rd mo, 10th da, 1835 and Elizabeth, his wife, dau. of George Middleton, b. 10th mo, 8th da, 1747, d. 2nd mo, 3rd da, 1829: Hannah Furman, b. 12th mo, 6th da, 1779, Mahlon Furman, b. 1st mo, 14th da, 1783.
Catherine Wright, wife of William Wright, b. 2nd mo, 27th da, 1741 and dau. of Joseph Ridgway, b. 11th mo, 24th da, 1749, d. 2nd mo, 2nd da, 1792.
Amy Black, wife of Ezra Black, and dau. of Samuel Taylor d. 2nd mo, 17th da, 1796.

Children of Joseph Field, b. 4th mo, 1st da, 1754 and Rebecca, his wife, dau. of Caleb Shreve, b. 5th mo, 1st da, 1757, d. 9th mo, 7th da, 1825: Benjamin Field, b. 1st mo, 25th da, 1777; Caleb Field, b. 11th mo, 16th da, 1778; Thomas Field, b. 9th mo, 17th da, 1780; Job Field b. 4th mo, 2nd da, 1783; Abigail Field, b. 9th mo, 8th da, 1724; Joseph Field, b. 9th mo, 22nd da, 1787; Isaac Field, b. 4th mo, 29th da, 1790; William Field, b. 10th mo, 24th da, 1792.
Child of Samuel Newbold, son of Mary Newbold, b. 5th mo, 9th da, 1766, d. 11th mo, 5th da, 1795 and Mary, his wife, dau. of John Hoskins, b. 1st mo, 30th da, 1765: Martha Newbold, b. 8th mo, 14th da, 1792, d. 11th mo, 20th da, 1816.
Children of John Curtis, b. 10th mo, 10th da, 1758, d. 8th mo, 29th da, 1792 and Sarah, his wife, dau. of John Taylor, b. 12th mo, 13th da, 1764: Tilton Curtis, b. 12th mo, 9th da, 1785; John Curtis b. 2nd mo, 9th da 1787, d. 12th mo, 8th da, 1788; Achsah Curtis, b. 11th mo, 1st da, 1791.

Amy Quicksall, widow of Samuel Quicksall, and dau. of Samuel Taylor, d. 2nd mo, 10th da, 1780.
Jershua Rockhill, wife of Amos Rockhill, d. 9th mo, 11th mo, 1795.
Job Stockton, d. 1st mo, 11th da, 1789.

Children of George Craft and Elizabeth, his wife, dau. of Jacob Ridgway: Ann Craft, b. 11th mo, 30th da, 1793; Deborah Craft, no date.
Children of Edward Rockhill, son of Edward Rockhill, b. 4th mo, 11th da, 1749, d. 1st mo, 1st da, 1820 and his wife, Elisabeth, dau. of Samuel Taylor: Edward Rockhill, b. 4th mo, 4th da, 1749; Tabitha Rockhill, b. 8th mo, 3rd da, 1752; Elizabeth Rockhill, b. 6th mo, 26th da, 1754; Amy Rockhill, b. 7th mo, 20th da, 1756; Mary Rockhill, b. 7th mo, 3rd da, 1758; Nathan Rockhill, b. 7th mo, 6th da, 1764.
Children of William Carslake, b. 9th mo, 27th da, 1756, d. 3rd mo, 25th da, 1826 and Abigail, his wife, b. 6th mo, 15th da, 1765, d. 9th mo, 12th da, 1823: Edward Carslake, b. 5th mo, 25th da, 1783, d. 10th mo, 9th da, 1784; Mary Carslake, b. 10th mo, 17th da, 1785, d. 10th mo, 2nd da, 1825; Sarah Carslake, b. 7th mo, 3rd da, 1788; Ann Carslake, b. 11th mo, 13th da, 1790, d. 2nd mo, 13th da, 1861, widow of Israel Kerlin; Joel Carslake, b. 6th mo, 28th da, 1793, d. 9th mo, 10th da, 1849; William Carslake, b. 11th mo, 20th da, 1795, d. 1877; Clayton Carslake, b. 4th mo, 8th da, 1798, d. 6th mo, 10th da, 1798; Joseph Carslake, b. 7th mo, 31st da, 1799; Abigail Carslake, b. 8th mo,

12th da, 1803, d. 7th mo, 31st da, 1824.
Children of Peter Harvey, son of Job Harvey, b. 6th mo, 2nd da, 1759, d. 1st mo, 1st da, 1842 and Sarah, his wife, dau. of Lawrence Minor, b. 12th mo, 8th da, 1762: Lawrence Harvey, (a son) b. 7th mo, 30th da, 1785, d. 8th mo, 15th da, 1785; Mary Harvey, b. 11th mo, 15th da, 1787; Elizabeth Harvey, b. 12th mo, 6th da, 1790, d. 9th mo, 20th da, 1791; Charlotte Harvey, b. 6th mo, 24th da, 1792; Lydia Harvey, b. 11th mo, 19th da, 1794; Ann Harvey, b. 2nd mo, 10th da, 1797; Peter Harvey, b. 9th mo, 2nd da, 1799; Rebecca Harvey, b. 12th mo, 15th da, 1802; Minor Harvey, (a son) b. 3rd mo, 11th da, 1805.
Children of Amos Ellis, son of Peter and Miriam Ellis, b. 1st mo, 13th da, 1772, d. 9th mo, 18th da, 1813 and Mary his wife, dau. of Josiah Haines, b. 3rd mo, 14th da, 1772: Charles Ellis, b. 10th mo, 7th da, 1796; Abigail Ellis, b. 2nd mo, 9th da, 1797; Elizabeth Ellis, b. 2nd mo, 25th da, 1799; Benjamin C. Ellis, b. 10th mo, 1800, d. 8th mo, 9th da, 1802; Sarah Ellis, b. 6th mo, 4th da, 1802; Ann Ellis, b. 2nd mo, 27th da, 1804; William M. Ellis, b. 2nd mo, 9th da, 1806, d. 4th mo, 1st da, 1816; Amos and Mary Ellis, (twins) b. 8th mo, 4th da, 1808; Thomas Biddle Ellis, b. 9th mo, 18th da, 1810; Josiah Ellis, b. 12th mo, 11th da, 1812.
Children of John Emley, b. 4th mo, 25th da, 1769, and Hannah, his wife, dau. of Joseph Stokes, b. 9th mo, 9th da, 1772: Abigail Emley, b. 1st mo, 18th da, 1797; Robert Emley, b. 1st mo, 12th da, 1799; Joseph Emley, b. 3rd mo, 23rd da, 1800, d. 1842; William Emley, b. 11th mo, 14th da, 1801; Mary Emley, b. 10th mo, 8th da, 1803; John Emley, b. 3rd mo, 3rd da, 1807, d. 8th mo, 10th da, 1811; Hannah Emley, b. 12th mo, 24th da, 1809; Elizabeth Emley, b. 3rd mo, 4th da, 1814; John Emley, b. 10th mo, 19th da, 1813, d. 10th mo, 6th da, 1814.
Children of Daniel Decow, son of Isaac and Mary Decow, b. 10th mo, 2nd da, 1771, d. 11th mo, 18th da, 1844 and Margaret his wife, dau. of Samuel Taylor: Mary Decow, b. 2nd mo, 28th da, 1804; James Decow, b. 2nd mo, 1st da, 1806; Isaac Decow, b. 2nd mo, 15th da, 1808; Abigail Decow, b. 1st mo, 2nd da, 1810; Margaret Decow, b. 3rd mo, 13th da, 1812; Sarah Decow, b. 4th mo, 11th da, 1814; Anna T. Decow, b. 9th mo, 3rd da, 1817.
Children of Sarah Decow, wife of John Decow and dau. of Thomas Antrum, b. 5th mo, 16th da, 1749, d. 11th mo, 30th da, 1804: Joseph Decow, b. 10th mo, 8th da, 1768, d. 1st mo, 22nd da, 1773; Eber Decow, b. 4th mo, 26th da, 1770; Thomas Decow, b. 2nd mo, 4th da, 1772; John Decow, b. 12th mo, 25th da, 1773; Sarah Decow, b. 1st mo, 25th da, 1776; William Decow, b. 4th mo, 24th da, 1778; Elizabeth Decow, b. 9th mo, 18th da, 1780; Ann Decow, b. 7th mo, 12th da, 1782; Prudence Decow, b. 11th mo, 9th da, 1785; Robert Decow, b. 2nd mo, 15th da, 1788, d. 3rd mo, 3rd da, 1813; George Decow, b. 7th mo, 3rd da, 1790; Lydia Decow, b. 6th mo, 15th da, 1797.
Children of Benjamin Atkinson, son of John and Sarah Atkinson, b. 10th mo, 17th da, 1754, d. 1st mo, 29th da, 1810 and Ann, his wife, dau. of Martin and Rebecca Gibbs, b. 5th mo, 21st da, 1756: Joel Atkinson, b. 3rd mo, 6th da, 1782; Nathan Atkinson, b. 11th mo, 13th da, 1785; Amos Atkinson, b. 4th mo, 3rd da, 1788; Clayton G. Atkinson, b. 10th mo, 15th da, 1790; Lydia Ann

Atkinson, b. 5th mo, 31st da, 1794; Chalkley Atkinson, b. 3rd mo, 23rd da, 1797; Ann Atkinson, b. 1st mo, 14th da, 1800.

Edward Rockhill, son of Edward Rockhill, b. 11th mo, 4th da, 1749, d. 1st mo, 1st da, 1820 and Grace his wife, dau of Joshua Foster, d. 11th mo, 25th da, 1807.

Children of William Black of Mansfield, b. 2nd mo, 12th da, 1759, d. 10th mo, 7th da, 1839 and Hope, his wife, dau. of Charles French, b. 11th mo, 5th da, 1762, d. 8th mo, 19th da, 1834: Ann Black, b. 8th mo, 12th da, 1780, d. 8th mo, 24th da, 1863; Charles Black, b. 1st mo, 20th da, 1783, d. 4th mo, 9th da, 1787; Samuel Black, b. 10th mo, 22nd da, 1786, d. 9th da, 1865; Nathan W. Black, b. 10th mo, 21st da, 1789; Rebecca Black, b. 8th mo, 23rd da, 1792; William Black, b. 4th mo, 12th da, 1795; Charles Black, b. 3rd mo, 8th da, 1799; George Black, b. 1st mo, 15th da, 1802; Mary Black, b. 1st mo, 18th da, 1805.

Children of Mathias Kerlin, b. 1st mo, 12th da, 1744, d. 5th mo, 4th da, 1820 and Elizabeth, his wife, dau. of Timothy Thomas, b. 11th mo, 13th da, 1747, d. 11th mo, 15th da, 1818: Grace Kerlin, b. 2nd mo, 12th da, 1774, d. 4th mo, 29th da, 1774; Mathias Kerlin, b. 3rd mo, 14th da, 1776, d. 1st mo, 23rd da, 1823; Sarah Kerlin, b. 9th mo, 30th da, 1780, d. 10th mo, 26th da, 1782; Elizabeth Kerlin, b. 6th mo, 25th da, 1782, d. 4th mo, 6th da, 1783; Margaret Kerlin, b. 2nd mo, 23rd da, 1784.

Children of Joseph English, b. 3rd mo, 14th da, 1771 and Elizabeth, his wife, dau. of Joseph Pope, b. 7th mo, 22nd da, 1775, d. 10th mo, 26th da, 1805: Israel English, b. 11th mo, 8th da, 1798; Elizabeth English, b. 6th mo, 22nd da, 1800, d. 8th mo, 13th da, 1800; Sarah Ann English, b. 7th mo, 4th da, 1801; Rebecca English, b. 10th mo, 19th da, 1803; Mary E. English, b. 5th mo, 12th da, 1805.

Children of Benjamin Satterthwaite, son of Samuel and Mary Satterthwaite, b. 10th mo, 5th da, 1764, and Sarah, his wife, dau. of Josiah Haines: Joel Satterthwaite, b. 4th mo, 4th da, 1795; Caleb Satterthwaite, b. 12th mo, 10th da, 1796; Benjamin Satterthwaite, b. 7th mo, 29th da, 1800; Mary Satterthwaite, b. 1st mo, 21st da, 1803; Abigail Satterthwaite, b. 10th mo, 4th da, 1805.

Charlotte Shreve, wife of Caleb Shreve, d. 12th mo, 6th da, 1792.
Joseph Talman, b. 6th mo, 10th da, 1738 and wife, Sarah, dau. of J. English, b. 1st mo, 24th da, 1746, d. 1st mo, 19th da, 1799.
Abner Steward d. 6th mo, 20th da, 1801.
Sarah Biddle b. 10th mo, 16th da, 1743, d. 9th mo, 23rd da, 1807.
Children of Edward Robbins, b. 11th mo, 4th da, 1767 and Amy, his wife, dau. of Ezra Black, b. 9th mo, 10th da, 1771, d. 12th mo, 24th da, 1856: Anna Robbins, b. 9th mo, 30th da, 1790; Elizabeth Robbins, b. 8th mo, 5th da, 1792; Amy Robbins, b. 7th mo, 22nd da, 1794; Sarah Robbins, b. 10th mo, 15th da, 1796; Mariah Robbins, b. 2nd mo, 25th da, 1802; Nathan Robbins, b. 5th mo, 23rd da, 1805; Edward Robbins, b. 2nd mo, 6th da, 1807; Rebecca Robbins, b. 3rd mo, 27th da, 1809, d. 2nd mo, 12th da, 1852; William Robbins, b. 11th mo, 30th da, 1812.
Children of Joseph Talman, Jr., son of Joseph Talman, b. 4th mo,

20th da, 1769, d. 12th mo, 13th da, 1814 and Valeriah, his wife, dau. of Anthony Woodward, b. 9th mo, 11th da, 1771, d. 10th mo, 14th da, 1803: Sarah Talman, b. 1st mo, 12th da, 1795; Deborah Ann Talman, b. 12th mo, 1st da, 1797; Augustin Talman, b. 2nd mo, 27th da, 1800; Valeriah Talman, b. 6th mo, 3rd da, 1803, d. 1803.

Hope Aaronson, widow of Benjamin Aaronson, b. 2nd mo, 16th da, 1747, d. 10th mo, 22nd da, 1813.
Martha Rockhill, d. 12th mo, 19th da, 1812.
George Zillai (Zelley), d. 5th mo, 29th da, 1816.

Children of Joseph Satterthwaite, b. 3rd mo, 10th da, 1762, d. 2nd mo, 20th da, 1837, son of Samuel Satterthwaite and Elizabeth,, his wife, dau. of Cornell Stevanson, b. 12th mo, 26th da, 1761, d. 5th mo, 2nd da, 1831: Samuel Satterthwaite, b. 7th mo, 2nd da, 1790; Joseph Satterthwaite, b. 3rd mo, 27th da, 1792; Daniel Satterthwaite, b. 7th mo, 9th da, 1794, d. 3rd mo, 13th da, 1880; Mary Satterthwaite, b. 5th da, 10th da, 1796, d. 5th da, 7th mo, 1858; Reuben Satterthwaite, b. 3rd mo, 17th da, 1801; Deborah Satterthwaite, b. 12th mo, 7th da, 1803.
Children of Joseph Decow, b. 6th mo, 7th da, 1756, d. 12th mo, 22nd da, 1786 and Achsah, his wife, dau. of John Taylor, b. 10th mo, 6th da, 1760: Mary Decow, b. 3rd mo, 14th da, 1779; Joseph Decow, b. 8th mo, 14th da, 1781; Clayton Decow, b. 6th mo, 4th da, 1783, d. 2nd mo, 26th da, 1785; Clayton Decow, b. 1st mo, 7th da, 1786.
Child of Nathan Rockhill, son of Edward Rockhill, b. 7th mo, 6th da, 1764 and Hannah, his wife, dau. of William Cook, b. 11th mo, 11th da, 1763, d. 1st mo, 5th da, 1792: Hannah Rockhill, b. 12th mo, 22nd da, 1791.
Children of Samuel Gauntt, son of John Gauntt, b. 7th mo, 22nd da, 1765 and Achsah, his wife, widow of Joseph Decow, dau. of John Taylor: John Gauntt, b. 12th mo, 19th da, 1794; Samuel Gauntt, b. 1st mo, 12th da, 1797.
Children of Job Shreve, son of Caleb Shreve, York Road, b. 5th mo, 24th da, 1755, d. 8th mo, 21st da, 1826 and Elizabeth, his wife, dau. of Samuel Gauntt, b. 9th mo, 11th da, 1763, d. 9th mo, 5th da, 1827: Hannah Shreve, b. 11th mo, 18th da, 1781, d. 5th mo, 4th da, 1783; Abigail Shreve, b. 10th mo, 6th da, 1785; Hannah Shreve, b. 1st mo, 28th da, 1788, d. 7th mo, 9th da, 1788; Elizabeth Shreve, b. 10th mo, 27th da, 1789; Job Shreve, b. 10th mo, 27th da, 1789; Cabel Shreve, b. 1st mo, 31st da, 1792, d. 4th mo, 2nd da, 1792; Thomas Shreve, b. 4th mo, 21st da, 1793, d. 6th mo, 5th da, 1795; Rebecca Shreve, b. 7th mo, 1st da, 1797; Samuel Shreve, b. 7th mo, 1st da, 1797, d. 11th mo, 8th da, 1797; Cabel Shreve, b. 12th mo, 11th da, 1800; Mercy Shreve, b. 10th mo, 19th da, 1802, d. 10th mo, 9th da, 1812.
Children of Thomas Shinn, b. 9th mo, 17th da, 1749, d. 10th mo, 13th da, 1820 and Sarah, his wife, b. 3rd mo, 5th da, 1743, d. 6th mo, 25th da, 1809: Rachel Shinn, b. 2nd mo, 12th da, 1765; Vinecomb Shinn, (a son) b. 8th mo, 21st da, 1766; Unity Shinn, b. 1st mo, 21st da, 1768, d. 2nd mo, 6th da, 1803; Solomon Shinn, b. 7th mo, 15th da, 1771; Anna Shinn, b. 4th mo, 2nd da, 1773; Elizabeth Shinn, b. 2nd mo, 2nd da, 1776; Thomas Shinn, b.

9th mo, 23rd da, 1777; Sarah Shinn, b. 11th mo, 27th da, 1779, d. 5th mo, 27th da, 1802; Mary Shinn, b. 9th mo, 30th da, 1781; Zilpah Shinn, b. 7th mo, 19th da, 1783.

Meribah Shinn, 2nd wife of Thomas Shinn, d. 10th mo, 29th da, 1836.
Esther Branson, d. 4th mo, 1848.

Children of Israel Woodward, b. 10th mo, 12th da, 1735, b. 1st mo, 19th da, 1821 and Mary, his wife, dau. of John Evilman, b. 7th mo, 18th da, 1750, d. 2nd mo, 6th da, 1829: Forman Woodward, b. 5th mo, 8th da, 1768; Susannah Woodward, b. 9th mo, 23rd da, 1770; John E. Woodward, b. 9th mo, 30th da, 1772; Elizabeth Woodward, b. 7th mo, 10th da, 1774; Robert Woodward, b. 6th mo, 13th da, 1776; Samuel Woodward, b. 7th mo, 5th da, 1779; Achsah Woodward, b. 7th mo, 8th da, 1784; Alice Woodward, b. 7th mo, 8th da, 1784.
Children of Eliakim Willets, b. 11th mo, 3rd da, 1745 and Phebe, his wife, dau. of Jacob Ridgway, b. 5th mo, 21st da, 1753: Jacob Willets, b. 10th mo, 1st da, 1776, d. 7th mo, 4th da, 1778; Samuel Willets, b. 8th mo, 1st da, 1778, d. 5th mo, 3rd da, 1782; David Willets, b. 5th mo, 31st da, 1783; Elizabeth Willets, b. 5th mo, 15th da, 1785; Mary Willets, b. 8th mo, 31st da, 1787; Sarah Willets, b. 12th mo, 4th da, 1790; Ann Willets, b. 5th mo, 14th da, 1792; Phebe Willets, b. 9th mo, 10th da, 1797; Rebecca Willets, b. 2nd mo, 17th da, 1799.
Child of Michael Rogers and Ann,, his wife, dau. of Caleb Shreve: Ann b. 3rd mo, 4th da, 1783.

John Bullock, b. 7th mo, 8th da, 1712, d. 2nd mo, 5th da, 1804 and Sarah his 2nd wife, d. 6th mo, 19th da, 1785.
Bridget Steward d. 23rd da, 7th da, 1783.
Elizabeth Waln, wife of Richard Waln, d. 2nd mo, 17th da, 1790.
William Stevanson, b. 12th mo, 1st da, 1730, d. 8th mo, 30th da, 1807 and Mary, his wife, formerly Bunting, b. 2nd mo, 13th da, 1730, d. 4th mo, 4th da, 1788.

Children of Abner Woodward, son of Thomas Woodward and Clemence, his wife, dau. of Anthony Woodward, b. 12th mo, 24th da, 1766: Sarah Woodward, b. 3rd da, 2nd da, 1789; Charlotte Woodward, b. 7th mo, 14th da, 1790, d. 8th mo, 13th da, 1791; Thomas Woodward, b. 3rd da, 12th da, 1792; Apollo Woodard, b. 10th mo, 8th da, 1795; Horace Woodward, b. 11th mo, 2nd da, 1797; Eliza Woodward, b. 9th mo, 15th da, 1799; James Woodward, b. 7th mo, 1st da, 1801; Abner Woodward, b. 3rd mo, 20th da, 1803; Ann Woodward, b. 2nd mo, 1st da, 1805; Clemence Woodward, b. 4th mo, 11th da, 1806; Joseph Woodward, b. 11th mo, 28th da, 1807, d. 8th mo, 2nd da, 1808.
Children of Isaac Bullock, son of John Bullock, b. 5th mo, 27th da, 1749, d. 5th mo, 30th da, 1820 and Elizabeth, his wife, dau. of E. Rockhill, b. 6th mo, 26th da, 1754: Edward Bullock, b. 7th mo, 1st da, 1776; Margaret Bullock, b. 8th mo, 20th da, 1779, d. 1st mo, 26th da, 1780; Amy Bullock, b. 12th mo, 17th da, 1780, d. 7th mo, 1st da, 1782; Elizabeth Bullock, b. 12th mo, 21st da, 1782; John Bullock, b. 1st mo, 14th da, 1785; Isaac Bullock, b.

9th mo, 19th da, 1787; Joshua Bullock, b. 5th mo, 23rd da, 1789;
Amos Bullock, b. 10th mo, 4th da, 1791; Nathan Bullock, b. 5th
mo, 2nd da, 179?; Mary Bullock, b. 3rd mo, 14th da, 1797.
Children of Amos Bullock, b. 9th mo, 2nd da, 1752, d. 4th mo,
22nd da, 1824 and Margaret, his wife, dau. of Thomas Butcher, b.
5th mo, 11th da, 1758, d. 6th mo, 25th da, 1798: Thomas Bullock,
b. 7th mo, 31st da, 781; Sarah Bullock, b. 7th mo, 2nd da, 1783;
David Barton Bullock, b. 2nd mo, 14th da, 1785; Margaret
Bullock, b. 9th mo, 13th da, 1786; Elizabeth Bullock, b. 5th mo,
22nd da, 1789; Mary Bullock, b. 11th mo, 29th da, 1790, d. 12th
mo, 4th da, 1791; Caleb Bullock, b. 4th mo, 6th da, 1794, d. 6th
mo, 12th da, 1794; Amy Bullock, b. 10th mo, 13th da, 1795; Amos
Bullock, b. 3rd mo, 14th da, 1797, d. 3rd mo, 29th da, 1797;
Mary Bullock, b. 6th mo, 23rd da, 1798.
Children of Anthony Woodward and Increase, his wife, d. 7th mo,
7th da, 1795: Jonathan b. 9th mo, 21st da, 1761, d. 5th mo,
1765; Josiah Woodard, b. 9th mo, 18th da, 1763; Jethro Woodard,
b. 6th mo, 17th da, 1765; Clemence Woodard, b. 12th mo, 24th da,
1766; Elizabeth Woodard, b. 9th mo, 19th da, 1768; William
Woodard, b. 8th mo, 11th da, 1770, d. 9th mo, 11th da, 1770;
Phebe Woodard, b. 11th mo, 6th da, 1771; William Woodard, b. 9th
mo, 5th da, 1773; Hannah Woodard, b. 8th mo, 19th da, 1775; Mary
Woodard, b. 8th mo, 22nd da, 178; Sarah Woodard, b. 8th mo, 7th
da, 1780; Ann Woodard, b. 9th mo, 9th da, 1783.
Children of John Lawrie, b. 8th mo, 1736 and Achsah, his wife,
dau. of William Black, b. 8th mo, 4th da, 1742, d. 10th mo, 3rd
da, 1806: William Lawrie, b. 10th mo, 11th da, 1766; Elizabeth
Lawrie, b. 1st mo, 2nd da, 1775; Thomas Lawrie, b. 3rd mo, 25th
da, 1777, d. 6th mo, 3rd da, 1816; Ann Lawrie, b. 10th mo, 21st
da, 780.
Children of Jonathan Wright, d. 5th mo, 1st da, 1798 and
Elizabeth, his wife, dau. of John Williams, b. 6th mo, 10th da,
1751: Jonathan Wright, b. 12th mo, 28th da, 1774, d. 9th mo,
16th da, 1775; Mary Wright, b. 6th mo, 20th da, 1776; Hannah
Wright, b. 2nd mo, 9th da, 1778; Elizabeth Wright, b. 2nd mo,
17th da, 1780; John Wright, b. 5th mo, 9th da, 1782; Sarah
Wright, b. 10th mo, 11th da, 1784; Isaac Wright, b. 2nd mo, 23rd
da, 1787; Elihu Wright, b. 7th mo, 3rd da, 1789; Rebecca Wright,
b. 12th mo, 19th da, 1791; Nathan Wright, b. 5th mo, 4th da,
1795.

John Cowperthwait, d. 5th mo, 16th da, 1795.
Robert Kirby, b. 3rd mo, 28th da, 1736, d. 7th mo, 27th da, 1794
and Amy, his wife, b. 8th mo, 23rd da, 1736, d. 7th mo, 15th da,
1794.
Joseph Bullock, d. 8th mo, 26th da, 1792 and Elizabeth, his wife,
d. 10th mo, 6th da, 1805.
Elizabeth Barber, d. 4th mo, 6th da, 1806.

Children of John Ridgway, b. 8th mo, 14th da, 1755, d. 4th mo,
1845 and Elizabeth, his wife, dau. of David Wright, b. 3rd mo,
17th da, 1756, d. 3rd mo, 1843: David Ridgway, b. 12th mo, 5th
da, 1777, d. 6th mo, 20th da, 1778; Sarah Ridgway, b. 11th mo,
8th da, 1779; Caleb Ridgway, b. 12th mo, 4th da, 1781; John
Ridgway, b. 8th mo, 23rd da, 1784; Jacob Ridgway, b. 9th mo, 3rd

da, 1787; David W. Ridgway, b. 5th mo, 12th da, 1791; Andrew C. Ridgway, b. 2nd mo, 9th da, 1793; Thomas Ridgway, b. 5th mo, 5th da, 1797.
Children of Thomas Wright b. 12th mo, 11th da, 1744, d. 4th mo, 14th da, 1825 and Mary, his wife, dau. of D. Branson, b. 6th mo, 26th da, 1751, d. 2nd mo, 16th da, 1824: Achsah Wright, b. 12th mo, 1st da, 1773; Ann Wright, b. 1st mo, 26th da, 1776; Thomas Wright, b. 1st mo, 17th da, 1778; David Wright, b. 3rd mo, 3rd da, 1779; John Wright, b. 3rd mo, 4th da, 1781; Amos Wright, b. 6th mo, 8th da, 1783; Mary Wright, b. 9th mo, 2nd da, 1785; Elizabeth Wright, b. 11th mo, 13th da, 1787; Samuel Wright, b. 12th mo, 4th da, 1789, b. 12th mo, 26th da, 1789; Abner Wright, b. 8th mo, 26th da, 1791, d. 1st mo, 2nd da, 1792; Rebecca Wright, b. 1st mo, 3rd da, 1794, d. 1st mo, 19th da, 1795.

Nathan Wright, b. 2nd mo, 23rd da, 1737, b. 10th mo, 1st da, 1813 and Rebecca, his wife, dau. of Isaac Gibbs, b. 8th mo, 4th da, 1737, d. 4th mo, 28th da, 1811.
Elizabeth Jones, widow of Benjamin Jones, d. 5th mo, 8th da, 1814.

Children of Abner Wright, b. 11th mo, 27th da, 1746, d. 5th mo, 7th da, 1799 and Sarah, his wife, dau. of Thomas Morrison?, b. 7th mo, 8th da, 1754: Sarah Wright, b. 8th mo, 7th da, 1779; Ann Wright, b. 12th mo, 22nd da, 1780.
Children of Charles Jones, b. 12th mo, 16th da, 1762 and Mary, his wife, dau. of Samuel Ivins, b. 1st mo, 25th da, 1770: Sarah Jones, b. 3rd mo, 25th da, 1789; Elizabeth Sophia Jones, b. 2nd mo, 21st da, 1791; Charity C. Jones, b. 12th mo, 22nd da, 1793; Samuel Jones, b. 2nd mo, 6th da, 1796.
Children of John Taylor, b. 2nd mo, 18th da, 1761 and Elizabeth, his wife, dau. of J. Lippincott, b. 9th mo, 9th da, 1766, d. 12th mo, 31st da, 1810: Daniel Taylor, b. 9th mo, 11th da, 1786; Robert Taylor, b. 2nd mo, 3rd da, 1788, d. 4th mo, 10th da, 1798; Charles Taylor, b. 5th mo, 31st da, 1790; Mary Taylor, b. 10th mo, 23rd da, 1792; Amos Taylor, b. 10th mo, 9th da, 1794; Abner Taylor, b. 10th mo, 29th da, 1798; Caleb Taylor, b. 9th mo, 7th da, 1801; Elizabeth Taylor, b. 7th mo, 17th da, 1804; Hannah Taylor, b. 7th mo, 12th da, 1808.
Children of John Platt, b. 8th mo, 1749 and Alice, his wife, dau. of William Stevanson, b. 5th mo, 11th da, 1758: Elizabeth Platt, b. 7th mo, 9th da, 1785; Martha Platt, b. 12th mo, 27th da, 1787, d. 7th mo, 1790; William Platt, b. 3rd mo, 13th da, 1790; Mary Platt, b. 1st mo, 20th da, 1793; George Platt, b. 7th mo, 19th da, 1795.

Ann Gibbs, wife of Tanton Gibbs, d. 2nd mo, 8th da, 1826.

Children of John Antrim and Jane, his wife, dau. of C. Shreve, York Road, d. 5th mo, 30th da, 1786: Charity Antrim, b. 12th mo, 18th da, 1776; Isaac Antrim, b. 7th mo, 3rd da, 1779; Caleb Antrim, b. 1st mo, 23rd da, 1781; Ann Antrim, b. 2nd mo, 12th da, 1783; Abigail Antrim, b. 9th mo, 6th da, 1785.
Children of Isaac Hutchin, b. 5th mo, 27th da, 1765, d. 5th mo, 9th da, 1804 and Jane, his wife, dau. of William and Jane

Satterthwaite, b. 9th mo, 16th da, 1773: Mary Hutchin, b. 9th
mo, 20th da, 1794, d. 5th mo, 29th da, 1801; Sarah Hutchin, b.
8th mo, 8th da, 1797; Rebecca Hutchin, b. 2nd mo, 20th da, 1799;
William Hutchin, b. 9th mo, 2nd da, 1801.
Children of William French, b. 5th mo, 10th da, 1751 and Rachel,
his wife, formerly Bickney, b. 7th mo, 28th da, 1753: Lydia
French, b. 8th mo, 25th da, 1778, d. 3rd mo, 18th da, 1781;
Hannah French, b. 12th mo, 5th da, 1779, d. 5th mo, 22nd da,
1782; John French, b. 1st mo, 27th da, 1783; William French, b.
11th mo, 23rd da, 1785; Mahlon French, b. 6th mo, 12th da, 1788;
Ames French, b. 1st mo, 23rd da, 1791; Rachel French, b. 2nd mo,
22nd da, 1794.

Martha Linton, b. 11th mo, 21st da, 1724, d. 1st mo, 5th da,
1818.
Mary Rogers d. 11th mo, 8th da, 1803.

Children of Israel Kirby, b. 3rd mo, 22nd da, 1759 and Rachel,
his wife, dau. of Thomas and Sarah Shinn, b. 2nd mo, 12th da,
1765, d. 11th mo, 5th da, 1805: Achsah Kirby, b. 3rd mo, 28th
da, 1788, Sarah Kirby, b. 5th mo, 12th da, 1789, d. 8th mo, 8th
da, 1791; Aaron Kirby, b. 1st mo, 22nd da, 1791; Charlotte
Kirby, b. 9th mo, 20th da, 1792; Amy Kirby, b. 8th mo, 4th da,
1796; Sarah Kirby, b. 2nd mo, 9th da, 1798, d. 7th mo, 26th da,
1800; Israel Kirby, b. 1st mo, 1800.

Samuel Stockton son of Samuel Stockton d. 10th mo, 1837.

Children of James Shinn, b. 1st mo, 23rd da, 1745, d. 2nd mo, 2nd
da, 1809 and wife, Levina, b. 11th mo, 15th da, 1750, d. 6th mo,
15th da, 1785: Mariam Shinn, b. 11th mo, 9th da, 1774; Margaret
Shinn, b. 7th mo, 11th da, 1777; Abigail Shinn, b. 12th mo, 8th
da, 1779; James Shinn, b. 11th mo, 7th da, 1782; George Shinn,
b. 6th mo, 6th da, 1785, d. 4th mo, 1st da, 1803.
Children of John E. Woodward, b. 9th mo, 30th da, 1772 and
Rebecca, his wife, dau. of Samuel Lipincott, b. 1st mo, 19th da,
1777: Job Woodward, b. 10th mo, 24th da, 1796, d. 11th mo, 7th
da, 1796; Israel Woodward, b. 10th mo, 30th da, 1797, d. 1st mo,
25th da, 1799; Samuel L. Woodward, b. 8th mo, 26th da, 1799;
Caleb A. Woodward, b. 11th mo, 14th da, 1801; Beulah Woodward,
b. 7th mo, 6th da, 1803, b. 5th mo, 20th da, 1806; Mary Annah
Woodward, b. 8th mo, 23rd da, 1805.

John E. Woodward, his wife, Rebecca and children: Job, Israel,
Samuel L., Caleb A., Beulah and Mary Annah moved to Mt. Holly
Monthly Meeting.
Joseph Horner, d. 9th mo, 9th da, 1812.
Mary Beck, widow of John Beck, d. 1st mo, 29th da, 1816.

Children of John Ellis and Lucy, his wife, dau. of Richard
Ridgway, d. 11th mo, 15th da, 1774: Joseph Ellis, b. 1st mo,
26th da, 1763; Phebe Ellis, b. 2nd mo, 8th da, 1765, d. 10th mo,
7th da, 1802; Samuel Ellis, b. 6th mo, 20th da, 1767, d. 27th
da, 10th da, 1838; John Ellis, b. 12th mo, 17th da, 1769, d. 6th
mo, 7th da, 1773; William Hunt Ellis, b. 3rd mo, 9th da, 1772,

d. 12th mo, 1802; Peter Ellis, b. 5th mo, 1774, d. 5th mo, 1775.
Children of John Ellis and Elizabeth, his 2nd wife, dau. of
Joseph Fowler: John Ellis, b. 7th mo, 28th da, 1777; Meribah
Ellis, b. 1st mo, 3rd da, 1779; Barzillai Ellis, b. 6th mo, 23rd
da, 1781; David Ellis, b. 4th mo, 3rd da, 1783; Elizabeth Ellis,
b. 10th mo, 5th da, 1785; Peter Ellis, b. 2nd mo, 11th da, 1788;
Rebecca N. Ellis, b. 2nd mo, 1789, d. 9th mo, 1790.
Children of Alexander Howard and Elizabeth, his wife: Martha
Howard, b. 8th mo, 7th da, 1769, d. 8th mo, 21st da, 1824;
Thomas M. Howard, b. 1st mo, 14th da, 1771; Elizabeth Howard, b.
7th mo, 12th da, 1773; Rebecca Howard, b. 6th mo, 5th da, 1775,
d. 8th mo, 9th da, 1819; Mary Howard, b. 5th mo, 6th da, 1777,
d. 1st mo, 6th da, 1778.

Alexander Howard, d. 1st mo, 4th da, 1817 age 76
Benjamin Linton, b. 2nd mo, 21st da, 1736, d. 6th mo, 2nd da,
1809 age 73 and Hannah, his wife, dau. of Samuel Satterthwaite,
b. 3rd mo, 25th da, 1742, d. 6th mo, 11th da, 1825.

Children of Anthony Bullock, son of Joseph Bullock, b. 3rd mo,
31st da, 1766, d. 6th mo, 1837 and Hannah, his wife, dau. of
William Wood, b. 5th mo, 22nd da, 1769: Edith Bullock, b. 2nd
mo, 28th da, 1799; Margaret Bullock, b. 4th mo, 15th da, 1801;
George Bullock, b. 7th mo, 10th da, 1803; William W. Bullock, b.
9th mo, 25th da, 1807.
Children of John Kirby, b. 3rd mo, 17th da, 1762 and Mary, his
wife, dau. of Edmond Beaks, b. 4th mo, 6th da, 1769, d. 9th mo,
27th da, 1825: Elizabeth Kirby, b. 10th mo, 29th da, 1790; Amy
Kirby, b. 9th mo, 4th da, 1792, d. 5th mo, 3rd da, 1810; Robert
Kirby, b. 10th mo, 1st da, 1794, d. 9th mo, 20th da, 1874;
Edmond B. Kirby, b. 3rd mo, 11th da, 1797; James I. Kirby, b.
3rd mo, 27th da, 1800, d. 1874; William N. Kirby, b. 8th mo,
17th da, 1802; Mary Kirby, b. 5th mo, 18th da, 1805; Martha
Kirby, b. 3rd mo, 14th da, 1810, d. 3rd mo, 29th da, 1810.
Children of Samuel Ellis, son of John and Lucy Ellis, b. 6th mo,
30th da, 1767, d. 10th mo, 27th da, 1838 and Elizabeth, his
wife, dau. of John Henry, b. 12th mo, 30th da, 1768, d. 3rd mo,
3rd da, 1858: Susannah Ellis, b. 6th mo, 25th da, 1794, d. 2nd
mo, 27th da, 1850; Joshua Ellis, b. 2nd mo, 23rd da, 1796, d.
6th mo, 10th da, 1858; William N. Ellis, b. 1st mo, 2nd da,
1798, d. 12th mo, 31st da, 1862; Phebe Ellis, b. 12th mo, 11th
da, 1799, b. 5th mo, 24th da, 1866; Rebecca Ellis, b. 10th mo,
5th da, 1801, d. 1st mo, 9th da, 1823 age 21; Lucy Ellis, b. 8th
mo, 15th da, 1803; Nathan W. Ellis, b. 5th mo, 1st da, 1805;
Martha R. Ellis, b. 4th mo, 4th da, 1810; Elizabeth Howard
Ellis, b. 5th mo, 6th da, 1815.

Mary G. Martin, dau. of Simon Gibson, d. 6th mo, 6th da, 1829.
Mary Scattergood, widow of Caleb Scattergood, d. 1st mo, 13th da,
1836.

Children of Caleb Scattergood, b. 4th mo, 10th da, 1768 and
Sarah, his wife, b. 2nd mo, 8th da, 1772: Ann Scattergood, b.
12th mo, 12th da, 1791; Joseph Scattergood, b. 8th mo, 27th da,
1793; Jonathan Scattergood, b. 10th mo, 28th da, 1795; Mary

Scattergood, b. 2nd mo, 12th da, 1797, d. 2nd mo, 11th da, 1800;
Sarah Scattergood, b. 5th mo, 21st da, 1800; Caleb Scattergood,
b. 3rd mo, 28th da, 1802; Nathan Scattergood, b. 12th mo, 7th
da, 1803; William Scattergood, b. 2nd mo, 17th da, 1806; Martha
Scattergood, b. 6th mo, 30th mo, 1808; John A. Scattergood, b.
?; Hannah Scattergood, b. 3rd mo, 23rd da, 1811.
Children of Amos Gibbs, son of Martin Gibbs b. 4th mo, 12th da,
1767, d. 5th mo, 7th da, 1833, and Mary, his wife, b. 3rd mo,
29th da, 1775, d. 3rd mo, 6th da, 1846: John Gibbs, b. 2nd mo,
28th da, 1802; Jane Gibbs, b. 11th mo, 15th da, 1803; Anna
Gibbs, b. 8th mo, 2nd da, 1806, d. 4th mo, 20th da, 1869;
Benjamin Gibbs, b. 11th mo, 26th da, 1810; Hannah Gibbs, b. 4th
mo, 24th da, 1814, d. 7th mo, 1837

Mary Decow, widow of Thomas Decow, d. 2nd mo, 25th da, 1846.
Rachel Haines, sister of Mary Decow, d. 5th mo, 28th da, 1851.

Children of Michael Earl, son of Thomas and Rebecca Earl, b. 9th
mo, 25th da, 1765, d. 1st mo, 23rd da, 1850 and Rebecca, his
wife, dau. of Job and Mary Ridgway, b. 11th mo, 3rd da, 1762, d.
5th mo, 4th da, 1838: Mary Earl, b. 6th mo, 29th da, 1797; Lydia
Earl, b. 11th mo, 13th da, 1798, d. 10th mo, 16th da, 1829;
Martha Earl, b. 5th mo, 15th da, 1800; Michael Earl, b. 11th mo,
13th da, 1802, d. 3rd mo, 10th da, 1804; Sarah Earl, b. 4th mo,
21st da, 1805; Elizabeth S. Earl, b. 6th mo, 11th da, 1807.
Children of William Gaskill, son of Thomas and Edith Gaskill, b.
9th mo, 12th da, 1765, d. 3rd mo, 30th da, 1815 and Sarah, his
wife, dau. of James Cooper, b. 2nd mo, 5th da, 1770: Hannah
Gaskill, b. 4th mo, 6th da, 1788; Charles E. Gaskill, b. 1st mo,
7th da, 1790; Sarah Gaskill, b. 8th mo, 15th da, 1793; Robert
Gaskill, b. 11th mo, 13th da, 1797; Cornelia C. Gaskill, b. 10th
mo, 21st da, 17th da, 1804.
Children of Achsah Black, widow of William Black and dau. of
Thomas Wright no. 75, b. 12th mo, 1st da, 1773: Mary Black, b.
6th mo, 19th da, 1797, d. 6th mo, 23rd da, 1797; Elizabeth b.
7th mo, 16th da, 1799; Samuel b. 12th mo, 6th da, 1800.
Children of John Pancoast, son of Joseph and Sarah Pancoast, b.
7th mo, 22nd da, 1771, and Ann, his wife, dau. of Samuel Abbott,
b. 6th mo, 3rd da, 1780: Lucy A. Pancoast, b. 9th mo, 16th da,
1799, d. 11th mo, 17th da, 1806; Sarah Pancoast, b. 1st mo, 19th
da, 1802; Hannah Pancoast, b. 11th mo, 20th da, 1803; Joseph
Pancoast, b. 11th mo, 23rd da, 1805; Samuel A. Pancoast, b. 8th
mo, 13th da, 1807; Elizabeth Pancoast, b. 4th mo, 28th da, 1809;
George L. Pancoast, b. 6th mo, 19th da, 1811; Abbe Ann b. 7th
mo, 15th da, 1813; William Abbott, b. 10th mo, 26th da, 1817;
Lucy A. b. 9th mo, 4th da, 1825.
Children of David Branson and Sarah, his wife, dau. of Ebenezer
Antrum: Stacy, b. 1st mo, 30th da, 1792; Samuel b. 1st mo, 4th
da, 1794, d. 12th mo, 15th da, 1795; Moses b. 5th mo, 19th da,
1796.

George Oneal, b. 1738, d. 8th mo, 30th da, 1818. Sarah Oneal, b.
3rd mo, 6th da, 1755, b. 12th mo, 21st mo, 1818.

Children of Joseph Morris and Rachel, his wife, dau. of John

Zilly: Abraham Z. Morris, b. 12th mo, 21st da, 1793; Sarah Morris, b. 11th da, 7th da, 1795; John Morris, b. 5th mo, 8th da, 1798; Rebecca Morris, b. 4th mo, 12th da, 1800; Thomason Morris, b. 5th mo, 21st da, 1802; Joseph Morris, b. 6th mo, 23rd da, 1804; Rachel Morris, b. 9th mo, 6th da, 1806; Esther Morris, b. 3rd mo, 10th da, 1809; Anthony Morris, b. 8th mo, 22nd da, 1811, d. 10th mo, 6th da, 1815; Caleb Morris, b. 12th mo, 27th da, 1813.

William Douglass, b. 1st mo, 13th da, 1779, d. 1st mo, 25th da, 1810.

Child of Joseph Tantum, b. 8th mo, 26th da, 1772 and Sarah, his wife, dau. of David Kelly: David K. b. 9th mo, 2nd da, 1796.
Children of William Wilson, b. 2nd mo, 1729, d. 4th mo, 8th da, 1815 and Abigail, his wife, dau. of John Rockhill, d. 3rd mo, 1st da, 1813: Sarah Wilson, b. 2nd mo, 2nd da, 1755; John Wilson, b. 11th mo, 24th da, 1758; Tryphena Wilson, b. 4th mo, 2nd da, 1760; Tryphosia Wilson, b. 5th mo, 14th da, 1762; Mary Wilson, b. 2nd mo, 23rd da, 1764; Abraham Wilson, b. 6th mo, 6th da, 1766; Christianna Wilson, b. 5th mo, 19th da, 1768; William Wilson, b. 9th mo, 17th da, 1772, d. 2nd mo, 15th da, 1796; Benjamin L. Wilson, b. 9th mo, 2nd da, 1778.
Children of Jediah Hance, b. 7th mo, 20th da, 1767 and Sarepty, his wife, dau. of Samuel Burns?, b. 2nd mo, 27th da, 1770, d. 9th mo, 15th da, 1811: Edward Hance, b. 7th mo, 7th da, 1792; Ann Hance, b. 11th mo, 8th da, 1794; Isaac Hance, b. 8th mo, 23rd da, 1796; Eliza Hance, b. 1st mo, 16th da, 1798; David Hance, b. 8th mo, 22nd da, 1803; Hannah Hance, b. 4th mo, 23rd da, 1805.
Children of Joseph Wright and Rebecca, his wife, dau. of John Schooley: Abigail Wright, b. 7th mo, 31st da, 1748; William Wright, b. 10th mo, 2nd da, 17th da, 1750; Sarah Wright, b. 1st mo, 21st da, 1753; Mary Wright, b. 7th mo, 15th da, 1756; Schooley Wright, (a son) b. 7th mo, 15th da, 1760; Joseph Wright, b. 12th mo, 4th da, 1763; Frances Wright, b. 3rd mo, 18th da, 1765; Elizabeth Wright, b. 5th mo, 18th da, 1767; Rebecca Wright, b. 2nd mo, 23rd da, 1770.
Children of Henry Ridgway, b. 12th mo, 26th da, 1749, d. 2nd mo, 1st da, 1805 and, his wife, Mary, dau. of Samuel Wright, b. 2nd mo, 7th da, 1752: Ann Ridgway, b. 12th mo, 10th da, 1771; Samuel W. Ridgway, b. 8th mo, 12th da, 1773; Solomon Ridgway, b. 9th mo, 5th da, 1775; Elizabeth Ridgway, b. 10th mo, 25th da, 1777; Mary Ridgway, b. 2nd mo, 7th da, 1780; Sarah Ridgway, b. 5th mo, 12th da, 1782; Rebecca Ridgway, b. 12th mo, 11th da, 1785; Hannah Ridgway, b. 5th mo, 15th da, 1787, d. 1st mo, 18th da, 1788; Henry Ridgway, b. 7th mo, 5th da, 1791, d. 8th mo, 23rd da, 1792; William Ridgway, b. 11th mo, 30th da, 1793.

Ruth Stockton, b. 6th mo, 13th da, 1744, d. 2nd mo, 1791.

Children of Aaron Borton, b. 12th mo, 16th da, 1727 and, his wife, Bathsheba, dau. of Isaac Antrim, b. 9th mo, 9th da, 1730, d. 12th mo, 12th da, 1778: Mary Borton, b. 1st mo, 10th da, 1751, d. 3rd mo, 19th da, 1761; Edward Borton, b. 6th mo, 22nd da, 1752; d. 3rd mo, 18th da, 1761; Isaac Borton, b. 1st mo, 8th da, 1754; Aaron Borton, b. 2nd mo, 15th da, 1756, d. 2nd mo, 29th da, 1760; Bathsheba Borton, b. 10th mo, 4th da, 1758, d. 7th mo, 14th da, 1762; Jane Borton, b. 12th mo, 25th da, 1764.

Sarah Borton, 2nd wife of Aaron Borton, dau. of Daniel Tilton, b. 1733.

Children of Barzillia Newbold, and Sarah, his wife, dau. of Enoch Core: Thomas Newbold, b. 1st mo, 7th da, 1735; Margaret Newbold, b. 2nd mo, 21st da, 1737, d. 2nd mo, 19th da, 1739; Sarah Newbold, b. 1st mo, 21st da, 1740; Enoch Newbold, b. 7th mo, 1st mo, 1742, d. 8th mo, 15th da, 1749; Hannah Newbold, b. 3rd mo, 28th da, 1745; Rachel Newbold, b. 4th mo, 26th da, 1751; Joshua Newbold, b. 11th mo, 14th da, 1753.
Children of Isaac Borton, son of Aaron Borton, b. 1st mo, 8th da,m 1754 and Serepta, his wife, dau. of Samuel Gauntt, b. 9th mo, 5th da, 1755: Hannah Borton, b. 10th mo, 8th da, 1792; Isaac Borton, b. 10th mo, 3rd da, 1795; Bathsheba Borton b, no date.
Children of William Wood, d. 5th mo, 1778 and Hannah, his wife, dau. of Thomas Newbold, b. 5th mo, 27th da, 1734, d. 9th mo, 26th da, 1779: Edith Wood, b. 10th mo, 17th da, 1754; Mary Wood, b. 8th mo, 24th da, 1756; William Wood, b. 1st mo, 22nd da, 1759; Thomas Wood, b. 10th mo, 1761; Anna Wood, b. 12th mo, 29th da, 1764; Susan Wood, b. 8th mo, 17th da, 1767; Hannah Wood, b. 5th mo, 22nd da, 1769; Elizabeth Wood, b. 1771; Samuel Wood, b. 2nd mo, 1773; Margaret Wood, b. 9th mo, 3rd da, 1775.

Charity Garwood, d. 3rd mo, 6th da, 1795.

Children of Benjamin Jones and, his wife, Elizabeth, dau. of William Rogers, b. 1st mo, 7th da, 1733: Benjamin Jones, b. 9th mo, 3rd da, 1759; Sarah Jones, b. 9th mo, 7th da, 1761; Elizabeth Jones, b. 3rd mo, 17th da, 1763; Esther Jones, b. 9th mo, 24th da, 1765; Mary Jones, b. 3rd mo, 21st da, 1768; Joseph Jones, b. 2nd mo, 19th da, 1771; Israel Jones, b. 10th mo, 5th da, 1774, d. 1st mo, 2nd da, 1796.
Children of Samuel Ivins and Ann, his wife, b. 11th mo, 5th da, 1762: Elizabeth Ivins, b. 8th mo, 29th da, 1790; Ann Ivins, b. 5th mo, 19th da, 1791; Mahlon Ivins, b. 3rd mo, 22nd da, 1793; Isaac Ivins, b. 7th mo, 5th da, 1796.
Children of William Newbold, b. 9th mo, 10th da, 1736, d. 8th mo, 7th da, 1793 and wife, Susannah, b. 6th mo, 1735, d. 11th mo, 15th da, 1773: Barzillai Newbold, b. 4th mo, 28th da, 1758; Thomas Newbold, b. 8th mo, 2nd da, 1760; Michael Newbold, b. 8th mo, 29th da, 1762, d. 7th mo, 2nd da, 1764; Charles Newbold, b. 5th mo, 23rd da, 1764; Edith Newbold, b. 6th mo, 30th da, 1766; Mary Newbold, b. 1st mo, 1769, d. 4th mo, 1769; William Newbold, b. 4th mo, 3rd da, 1770; John Newbold, b. 3rd mo, 1772; Susannah Newbold, b. 10th mo, 31st da, 1773.
Children of Ebenezer Gaskill, b. 1744 and wife, Esther, b. 4th mo, 12th da, 1747: Lydia Gaskill, b. 7th mo, 31st da, 1779; Elizabeth Gaskill, b. 2nd mo, 14th da, 1782.
Children of Cabel Shinn, b. 5th mo, 3rd da, 1752 and wife, Mary, dau. of Benjamin Lucas, b. 6th mo, 24th da, 1751, d. 1788:

Thomas Shinn, b. 2nd mo, 14th da, 1772; Kedar Shinn, b. 2nd mo, 10th da, 1773; Sarah Shinn, b. 6th mo, 25th da, 1774.
Children of William Davis, b. 12th mo, 25th da, 1746, d. 12th mo, 9th da, 1782 and his wife, Mary, dau. of Isaac Ivins, b. 9th mo, 24th da, 1747: Isaac Davis, b. 2nd mo, 15th da, 1767; Ann Davis, b. 8th mo, 21st da, 1768; Mary Davis, b. 1st mo, 9th da, 1770; Meribah Davis, b. 8th mo, 17th da, 1771; Jonathan Davis, b. 3rd mo, 19th da, 1773; Hannah Davis, b. 2nd mo, 1st da, 1775; Job Davis, b. 8th mo, 4th da, 1777; William Davis, b. 5th mo, 19th da, 1779; Abigail Davis, b. 1st mo, 5th da, 1780; Ivins Davis, b. 12th mo, 14th da, 1780.

Asa Pointseh, son of Peter Pointseh, b. 4th mo, 5th da, 1757.

Children of Thomas Curtis, son of John Curtis, b. 1st mo, 25th da, 1737 and Alice, dau. John Beck, b. 4th mo, 15th da, 1744: John Curtis, b. 1st mo, 10th da, 1763; Thomas Curtis, b. 7th mo, 17th da, 1765; Elizabeth Curtis, b. 11th mo, 8th da, 1767; Asa Curtis, b. 3rd mo, 10th da, 1770; Susannah Curtis, b. 11th mo, 9th da, 1772, d. 5th mo, 24th da, 1773; Ann Curtis, b. 6th mo, 21st da, 2774; Benjamin Curtis, b. 4th mo, 20th da, 1776, 5th mo, 3rd da, 1776; Sarah Curtis, b. 5th mo, 15th da, 1778; Mary Curtis, b. 5th mo, 8th da, 1780, d. 9th mo, 29th da, 1793; Mary Curtis, b. 5th mo, 27th da, 1784.
Children of Barzillai Forman, b. 11th mo, 15th da, 1753 and Elizabeth, his wife, dau. of George Middleton, b. 10th mo, 3rd da, 1747: Hannah Forman, b. 12th mo, 6th da, 1779; Matilda Forman, b. 1st mo, 14th da, 1783.
Children of Joseph English, Jr., b. 10th mo, 1743, d. 1st mo, 23rd da, 1788 and Mary, his wife, dau. of Israel Butler, b. 10th mo, 1752: Joseph English, b. 3rd mo, 14th da, 1771; Arthur English, b. 3rd mo, 11th da, 1773; John English, b. 9th mo, 25th da, 1774; Amy English, b. 1st mo, 20th da, 1777; Sarah English, b. 10th mo, 2nd da, 1779; Israel English, b. 11th mo, 20th da, 1782, d. 2nd mo, 24th da, 1797; Elisha English, b. 12th mo, 9th da, 1705.
Children of Caleb Shreve, York Road, b. 8th mo, 13th da, 1721, d. 9th mo, 27th da, 1786 and Abigail, his wife, dau. of Isaac Antrim: Joseph Shreve, b. 12th mo, 28th da, 1748; Isaac Shreve, b. 6th mo, 19th da, 1750; Thomas Shreve, b. 11th mo, 2nd da, 1752; Jane Shreve, b. 5th mo, 2nd da, 1753; Job Shreve, b. 5th mo, 24th da, 1755; Rebecah Shreve, b. 1st mo, 5th da, 1757; Penelope Shreve, b. 11th mo, 10th da, 1757; Caleb Shreve, b. 7th mo, 6th da, 1761; Mary Shreve, b. 12th mo, 15th da, 1763; Sarah Shreve, b. 5th mo, 5th da, 1765.
Child of Ann Forsyth, widow of Joseph Forsyth, dau. of John Gaunt, b. 1st mo, 9th da, 1758: Ann Forsyth, b. 9th mo, 13th da, 1795.
Children of Lawrence Minor, b. 12th mo, 11th da, 1737 and Elizabeth, his wife, b. 1st mo, 25th da, 1744: Cathrine Minor, b. 3rd mo, 1st da, 1761; Sarah Minor, b. 12th mo, 8th da, 1762; Charlotte Minor, b. 8th mo, 30th da, 1766; Rebecca Minor, b. 12th mo, 29th da, 1768; Thomas Minor, b. 12th mo, 29th da, 1768.
Children of Thomas Tallman, b. 6th mo, 10th da, 1738 and Sarah, his wife, dau. of Joseph English, b. 1st mo, 24th da, 1746:

Deborah Tallman, b. 1st mo, 31st da, 1766; Joseph Tallman, b.
4th mo, 20th da, 1769; Mary Tallman, b. 1st mo, 10th da, 1772;
Martha Tallman, b. ? mo, 14th da, 1777.

Joseph Green, b. 3rd mo, 27th da, 1759.
Nathan Robbins and Anna, his wife, dau. of Godfrey Beck: no
issue.

Children of Joice Robbins, the 2nd wife of Nathan Robbins:
Elizabeth Burnet; Deborah Burnet; Mary Burnet; no dates given.
Children of Jonathan Barton, b. 7th mo, 27th da, 1741 and Sarah,
his wife, dau. of B. Newbold, b. 1st mo, 21st da, 1740:
Barzillai Barton, b. 4th mo, 13th da, 1767; John Barton, b. 11th
mo, 17th da, 1769; David Barton, b. 2nd mo, 7th da, 1774.
Children of Amy Black, wife of Ezra Black, and dau. of Samuel
Taylor, d. 2nd mo, 17th da, 1796: William Black, b. 7th mo, 19th
da, 1761; Achsah Black, b. 3rd mo, 21st da, 1764; Sarah Black,
b. 3rd mo, 28th da, 1767; Amy Black, b. 9th mo, 20th da, 1771;
Ezra Black, b. 2nd mo, 6th da, 1775.

John Harvey, b. 2nd mo, 28th da, 1724, d. 3rd mo, 30th da, 1792.
Ann, wife of John Harvey, b. 11th mo, 11th da, 1729, d. 8th mo,
2nd da, 1806.
Mary Harvey, widow of Peter Harvey, dau. of Godfrey Hanock, b.
12th mo, 25th da, 1723, d. 2nd mo, 26th da, 1791.
Children of Caleb Scattergood, b. 1713 and Mary, his wife, dau.
of Stephen Crammer, b. 10th mo, 23rd da, 1738: Caleb
Scattergood, b. 4th mo, 10th da, 1768; Sarah Scattergood, b.
11th mo, 12th da, 1769; Joshua Scattergood, b. 9th mo, 23rd da,
1771; Mary Scattergood, b. 8th mo, 31st da, 1773; Benjamin
Scattergood, b. 1st mo, 8th da, 1775; Elizabeth Scattergood, b.
1st mo, 16th da, 1776, d. 5th mo, 1777; Martha Scattergood, b.
8th mo, 2nd da, 1779.
Children of Joseph Pope, b. 11th mo, 17th da, 1743 and Elizabeth,
his wife, dau. of Joseph Lamb, d. 3rd mo, 13th da, 1781: Joseph
Pope, b. 7th mo, 17th da, 1769; Rebekah Pope, b. 4th mo, 18th
da, 1771; Ann Pope, b. 3rd mo, 8th da, 1773; Elizabeth Pope, b.
7th mo, 22nd da, 1775; Clayton Pope, b. 2nd mo, 24th da, 1779;
John Pope, b. 7th mo, 13th da, 1781.
Child of Andrew Ware, b. 7th mo, 1729 and wife, Edith, b. 5th mo,
14th da, 1732: Miriam b. 4th mo, 10th da, 1753.
Children of John Gaunt, b. 5th mo, 21st da, 1735 and Jane, his
wife, dau. of Samuel Satterthwaite, b. 1st mo, 20th da, 1735, d.
8th mo, 28th da, 1798: Ann Gaunt, b. 1st mo, 9th da, 1758; Jane
Gaunt, b. 9th mo, 2nd da, 1760; Hannah Gaunt, b. 2nd mo, 25th
da, 1763; Samuel Gaunt, b. 7th mo, 22nd da, 1765; Elizabeth
Gaunt, b. 1st mo, 31st da, 1767; Mary Gaunt, b. 5th mo, 2nd da,
1769; Phebe Gaunt, b. 9th mo, 8th da, 1771; Daniel Gaunt, b. 9th
mo, 6th da, 1776; John Gaunt, b. 8th mo, 11th da, 1780, d. 4th
mo, 6th da, 1785.

Joseph Pope, son of Joseph Pope, b. 9th mo, 17th da, 1743;
Nathaniel Pope, b. 12th mo, 12th da, 1745; John Pope, b. 8th mo,
26th da, 1747.

Children of Isaac Bunting, son of Samuel Bunting, b. 11th mo, 22nd da, 1721 and Elizabeth, his wife, dau. of Benjamin Scattergood: Ebenezer Bunting, b. 10th mo, 5th da, 1760; Benjamin Bunting, b. 4th mo, 15th da, 1762; Isaac Bunting, b. 7th mo, 18th da, 1763.

Children of Ephraim Pittman and Sarah, his wife, formerly Lippincott, b. 1st mo, 20th da, 1746: Abel Pittman, b. 9th mo, 6th da, 1768; Frances Pittman, b. 11th mo, 10th da, 1769; Elizabeth Pittman, b. 9th mo, 13th da, 1771; Ephraim Pittman, b. 2nd mo, 27th da, 1773; Robert Pittman, b. 1st mo, 13th da, 1775, d. 12th mo, 15th da, 1774; Mary Pittman, b. 8th mo, 27th da, 1776.

Children of William White and Esther, his wife, dau. of Jacob Decow: Elizabeth White, b. 12th mo, 5th da, 1745; Peter White, b. 4th mo, 7th da, 1747; Mary White, b. 9th mo, 1st da, 1749.

Keziah Pettit, dau. of Adam Pettit, b. 9th mo, 22nd da, 1758.

Children of Gamaliel Warren, b. 8th mo, 23rd da, 1749, d. 1st mo, 13th da, 1811 and, his wife, Meribah, b. 12th mo, 8th da, 1750, d. 10th mo, 29th da, 1836: Achsah Warren, b. 2nd mo, 10th da, 1776; Susannah Warren, b. 2nd mo, 15th da, 1780; Thomas Warren, b. 6th mo, 26th da, 1782; Robert Warren, b. 2nd mo, 27th da, 1785; Anna Warren, b. 5th mo, 11th da, 1788; Nathan Warren, b. 2nd mo, 19th da, 1791; John Warren, b. 6th mo, 14th da, 1793.

Ann Stockton, wife of Samuel Stockton, and dau. of William Wood, b. 12th mo, 29th da, 1760, d. 9th mo, 11th da, 1817.

Deborah Lawrie, dau. of Thomas Lawrie, d. 12th mo, 4th da, 1732.

Children of Abraham Brown, son of Joseph and Hannah Brown, b. 4th mo, 13th da, 1751, d. 5th mo, 29th da, 1830 and Jane, his wife, b. 4th mo, 29th da, 1757, d. 3rd mo, 5th da, 1825: Samuel Brown, b. 2nd mo, 25th da, 1775, d. 10th mo, 1st da, 1776; Joseph Brown, b. 5th mo, 5th da, 1776; Asher Brown, b. 9th mo, 24th da, 1777; Abigail Brown, b. 2nd mo, 13th da, 1779; Ruben Brown, b. 4th mo, 14th da, 1780; Israel Brown, b. 1st mo, 14th da, 1785, d. 1793; Allen Brown, b. 8th mo, 28th da, 1794, d. 10th mo, 22nd da, 1794; Ira Brown, b. 9th mo, 15th da, 1795, d. 9th mo, 15th da, 1795; Ezra Brown, b. 9th mo, 15th da, 1795.

Children of Simon Gilliam, b. 1st mo, 24th da, 1759, d. 8th mo, 31st da, 1839 and Anna, his wife, dau. of William Paxson, b. 7th mo, 4th da, 1762, d. 1st mo, 21st da, 1831: Mary Gilliam, b. 10th mo, 22nd da, 1784, d. 6th mo, 6th da, 1829; William Gilliam, b. 10th mo, 1st da, 1786; Isaac Gilliam, b. 4th mo, 13th da, 1788; Anna Gilliam, b. 10th mo, 30th da, 1794, d. 8th mo, 2nd da, 1798.

Children of Samuel Aaronson, b. 9th mo, 30th da, 1768, d. 9th mo, 6th da, 1835 and Elizabeth, his wife, b. 9th mo, 13th da, 1771, d. 6th mo, 10th da, 1857: John Aaronson, b. 12th mo, 30th da, 1793; Sarah C. Aaronson, b. 10th mo, 16th da, 1794; Ephraim C. Aaronson, b. 9th mo, 3rd da, 1796; Elizabeth Aaronson, b. 7th mo, 24th da, 1798; Samuel Aaronson, b. 9th mo, 6th da, 1800; Mary Ann Aaronson, b. 8th mo, 8th da, 1802; Rebecca Aaronson, b. 9th mo, 1st da, 1804; Ann b. 6th mo, 23rd da, 1807; Abigail F.

Aaronson, b. 2nd mo, 27th da, 1810; Nathan R. Aaronson, b. 3rd
mo, 5th da, 1812, d. 10th mo, 8th da, 1885; Frances R. Aaronson,
b. 7th mo, 29th da, 1814.

Nicholas Waln, son of Richard Waln, b. 10th mo, 28th da, 1763
married to Sarah, his wife, b. 11th mo, 8th da, 1779.
John Earl, son of Thomas and Edith Earl, b. 12th mo, 30th da,
1766 married to Anna C., his wife, dau. of W. Wills.
William Wright, b. 10th mo, 10th da, 1771, d. 1st mo, 11th da,
1837 married to Rebecca, his wife, dau. of S. Silver, b. 2nd mo,
11th da, 1776.
Benjamin Field, son of Joseph and Rebecca Field, b. 1st mo, 25th
da, 1777 married to Martha, his wife, dau. of J. Talman, b. 1st
mo, 14th da, 1777, d. 7th mo, 6th da, 1806.
Caleb Field, b. 11th mo, 16th da, 1778 married to Catherine, his
wife, dau. of S. Thomas, b. 9th mo, 23rd da, 1782.
Joseph Decow, b. 8th mo, 14th da, 1781 married to Sarah, his
wife, b. 11th mo, 2nd da, 1777.
Thomas Sykes, son of Anthony and Mary Sykes, b. 7th mo, 30th da,
1764 married to Mary, his wife, dau. of James Laurie, b. 1st mo,
6th da, 1771.
John Pope, son of Nathaniel and Sarah Pope, b. 2nd mo, 1774
married to Amy, dau. of Jacob French, b. 12th mo, 3rd da, 1774.
David Taylor, b. 8th mo, 23rd da, 1774, d. 1864 married to
Elizabeth, his wife, b. 3rd mo, 21st da, 1782.
Charles Gaskill, son of Thomas and Edith Gaskill, b. 10th mo,
14th da, 1781 married to Abigail, his wife, b. 10th mo, 6th da,
1785.
Thomas Letchworth married to Sarah, his wife, dau. of Samuel
Newton, b. 3rd mo, 31st da, 1796, d. 12th mo, 16th da, 1825.
Barzillai Ellis of John and Elizabeth Ellis, b. 6th mo, 23rd da,
1781 married to Mary, his wife, dau. of Ebenezer Wright, b. 5th
mo, 22nd da, 1787.
Jonathan Curtis married to Mary, his wife, dau. of Anthony and
Mary Sykes, b. 8th mo, 30th da, 1762, d. 7th mo, 28th da, 1834.
David Tantum married to Susannah, his 2nd wife, dau. of Gamabiel
Warren.
Aaron Pitman, b. 10th mo, 5th da, 1780 married to Matida, his
wife, b. 1st mo, 14th da, 1783.
Samuel Croshaw, son of George and Hannah Croshaw, b. 6th mo, 9th
da, 1776 married to Mary, his wife, dau. of Thomas and Sarah
Shinn, b. 9th mo, 30th da, 1781.
Joseph Brown, son of Abraham Brown, b. 5th mo, 5th da, 1776
married to Hannah Croshaw b. 9th mo, 9th da, 1785.
James Shreve, son of Joshua and Rebecca Shreve, b. 1st mo, 3rd
da, 1778, d. 9th mo, 1st da, 1852 married to Elizabeth, his
wife, dau. of Daniel Smith, b. 12th mo, 21st da, 1779.
David Ellis, b. 4th mo, 3rd da, 1783 married to Ann, his wife,
dau. of Jacob Middleton, b. 11th mo, 3rd da, 1786.
Thomas Shinn, Jr., b. 9th mo, 23rd da, 1777 married to Abigail,
his wife, dau. of Caleb Haines.
John Ellis, Jr., b. 7th mo, 28th da, 1777, d. 5th mo, 18th da,
1823 married to Elizabeth, his wife, dau. of Abraham Tilton, b.
6th mo, 11th da, 1786.
Richard Cook, son of Thomas Cook, b. 2nd mo, 27th da, 1784, d.

12th da, 1825 married to Elizabeth,, his wife, b. 10th mo, 27th da, 1789.
William C. Wright, son of David Wright, b. 8th mo, 18th da, 1781 married to Ann, his wife, b. 12th mo, 12th da, 1791.
John Wright, b. 3rd mo, 4th da, 1781 married to Elizabeth, his wife, b. 5th mo, 22nd da, 1789.
Joseph Gibbs, son of Benjamin Gibbs married to Elizabeth, his wife, dau. of John Ellis, b. 10th mo, 5th da, 1785.
Clayton Newbold, son of Clayton and Mary Newbold, b. 9th mo, 28th da, 1782 married to Beulah, his wife, dau. of Joseph H. Lawrie, b. 8th mo, 22nd da, 1792.
John Bishop, b. 6th mo, 17th da, 1778, d. 12th mo, 2nd da, 1863 married to Mary, his wife, dau. of Joseph Ridgway, b. 12th mo, 21st da, 1776, d. 4th mo, 6th da, 1815.
John Bishop married to Ann, his 2nd wife, dau. of William Black, b. 8th mo, 12th da, 1780.
Joseph Satterthwaite, Jr., son of Joseph and Elizabeth Satterthwaite, b. 3rd mo, 27th da, 1792 married to Elizabeth Fisher, dau. of Thomas Fisher, b. 3rd mo, 7th da, 1792.
Thomas Earl, son of Thomas and Rebecca Earl, b. 5th mo, 20th da, 1774 married to Mercy, dau. of Benjamin Burling.
Samuel Satterthwaite, son of Joseph and Elizabeth Satterthwaite, b. 7th mo, 2nd da, 1790 married to Hannah Atkinson, dau. of Caleb Atkinson, b. 2nd mo, 12th da, 1797.
Clayton G. Atkinson, son of Benjamin married to Ann Atkinson, b. 10th mo, 15th da, 1790.
Joel Carslake, son of William and Abigail Carslake, b. 6th mo, 28th da, 1793, d. 9th mo, 10th da, 1849 married to Anna Wright, dau. of William and Rebecca Wright, b. 11th mo, 20th da, 1801, d. 8th mo, 14th da, 1843.
Chalkey Atkinson, son of Benjamin and Ann Atkinson, b. 3rd mo, 23rd da, 1797 married to Mary S. Burr, dau. of Joseph Burr, b. 4th mo, 12th da, 1801.
Thomas Scott, b. 4th mo, 3rd da, 1780 married to Mary Smith, dau. of Thomas and Meribah Smith, b. 11th mo, 2nd da, 1780.
Joshua Bullock son of Isaac and Elizabeth Bullock, b. 5th mo, 23rd da, 1789 married to Deborah Corless, dau. of Joseph Corless, b. mo, 8th da, 1790.
Robert Kirby of John and Mary Kirby, b. 10th mo, 1st da, 1794, d. 1874 married to Maria Middleton, dau. of Josiah Middleton, b. 6th da, 1804.
John Brown, son of John and Susanna Brown, b. 12th mo, 1798 married to Phebe Ellis, dau. of Samuel and Elizabeth Ellis, b. 12th mo, 11th da, 1799.
Thomas Furman, son of Richard Furman, b. 9th mo, 20th da, 1787 married to Susannah, his wife, b. 6th mo, 25th da, 1794.
Samuel Woodward, son of Israel and Mary Woodward, b. 7th mo, 5th da, 1779 married to Henrietta Ridgway, dau. of H. Ridgway, b. 4th mo, 26th da, 1788.
Joseph Cox, b. 5th mo, 17th da, 1789 married to Hannah Letchworth, dau. of William Letchworth, b. 3rd mo, 8th da, 1790.
Peter Harvey, Jr. son of Peter and Sarah Harvey, b. 9th mo, 2nd da, 1799 married to Elizabeth Ellis, dau. of Amos and Mary Ellis, b. 2nd mo, 25th da, 1799.
Andrew C. Ridgway, son of John and Elizabeth Ridgway, b. 2nd mo,

9th da, 1793, d. 8th mo, 23rd da, 1844 married to Eliza Bishop, dau. of John and Mary Bishop, b. 12th mo, 17th da, 1806, d. 5th mo, 11th da, 1855.
Joseph Carslake son of William married to Abigail Carslake, b. 7th mo, 31st da, 1799, d. 5th mo, 12th da, 1861.
Thomas Martin, b. 9th mo, 8th da, 1786, d. 10th mo, 9th da, 1825 married to Mary Gillam, dau. of Simon and Anna Gillam, b. 10th mo, 22nd da, 1784, d. 6th mo, 6th da, 1829.
Isaac Gillam son of Simon and Anna Gillam, b. 4th mo, 13th da, 1788 married to Margaret Mitchel, dau. of Samuel Mitchel, b. 10th mo, 6th da, 1785, d. 3rd mo, 24th da, 1819.
Clayton Newbold, Jr., son of William and Hannah Newbold, b. 1st mo, 22nd da, 1797, d. 7th mo, 25th da, 1870 married to Susannah Trotter, dau. of Joseph Trotter, d. 7th mo, 12th da, 1835.
Caleb Newbold, son of Caleb and Sarah Newbold, b. 11th mo, 2nd da, 1763, d. 11th mo, 17th da, 1853 married to Sarah, his wife, b. 1st mo, 29th da, 1760, d. 3rd mo, 13th da, 1841.
Nathan Atkinson, son of Benjamin and Ann Atkinson, b. 11th mo, 13th da, 1785, d. 5th mo, 18th da, 1878 married to Lydia, his wife, b. 7th mo, 5th da, 1792, d. 11th mo, 24th da, 1844.
Caleb Aaronson, son of John Aaronson, b. 11th mo, 26th da, 1796, d. 1st mo, 27th da, 1853 married to Lydia, b. 11th mo, 19th da, 1794, d. 4th mo, 14th da, 1877.

CERTIFICATES FROM UPPER SPRINGFIELD MONTHLY MEETING.

3/3/1783 to Philadelphia Northern District Monthly Meeting for Benjamin Catherall, Sarah, his wife, and Benjamin his son.
6/4/1783 to Philadelphia Northern District Monthly Meeting Monthly Meeting, George Bullock, wife Edith and children: William, Joseph, Margaret and Hannah.
6/4/1783 to Philadelphia Northern District Monthly Meeting for Ann Wood.
6/4/1783 to Philadelphia Northern District Monthly Meeting for Susanna, Hannah, and Elisabeth Wood in their minority to live with George Bullock.
7/9/1783 to Burlington Monthly Meeting for Tryphena English, wife of Joseph English.
7/9/1783 Anthony Sykes requests a certificate for his son, Thomas Sykes who is placed as an apprentice to William Lavory.
7/9/1783 to Burlington Monthly Meeting for Ann Smith.
9/3/1783 to Burlington Monthly Meeting for Sarah Pittman.
9/3/1783 to Shrewsbury Monthly Meeting for Rebecca Haines.
10/8/1783 to Haddonfield Monthly Meeting for Susannah Branson.
10/8/1783 to Burlington Monthly Meeting for Able Gibbs.
11/5/1783 to Haddonfield Monthly Meeting for Benjamin Antrum.
11/5/1783 to Crooked Run Monthly Meeting, New Virginia for Scholey Wright.
11/5/1783 to Wilmington Monthly Meeting for James Robertson.
11/5/1783 to Haddonfield Monthly Meeting for Sarah Antrum.
12/3/1783 to Haddonfield Monthly Meeting for Sarah Branson.
1/7/1784 to Chesterfield Monthly Meeting for Sarah Linton, a minor.
4/7/1784 to Burlington Monthly Meeting for Mary Smith, wife of

Thomas Smith.
4/7/1784 to Haddonfield Monthly Meeting for Elizabeth Middleton, wife of David Middleton.
4/7/1784 to Philadelphia for Phebe Poultney, wife of Benjamin Poultney.
5/5/1784 to Burlington Monthly Meeting for Joseph Vanlaw.
6/9/1784 to Burlington Monthly Meeting for Solomon Pancoast, a minor, placed as an apprentice.
6/9/1784 to Evesham Monthly Meeting for Jacob Ridgway, Jr., his wife, Susannah, and children, Ellis and Eli.,
7/7/1784 to Kingwood or Hardwick Monthly Meeting for Robert Emley, and three children: Elizabeth, John and Mary.
9/8/1784 to Philadelphia Monthly Meeting for Isaac Forman, who is placed as an apprentice to Joseph Budd.
9/8/1784 to Philadelphia Northern District Monthly Meeting for Thomas Forman, Jr.
10/6/1784 to Philadelphia Northern District Monthly Meeting for William Stevenson, Jr., who is placed as an apprentice to Thomas Sattergood.
11/3/1784 to Chesterfield Monthly Meeting for Hannah Lloyd, wife of Levi Lloyd.
11/3/1784 to Chesterfield Monthly Meeting for William Cook, Jr., his wife, Diadamia, and Rebekah Harrison, a minor, who lives with them.
11/3/1784 to New York Monthly Meeting for Sarah Fox.
11/3/1784 to Chesterfield Monthly Meeting for Thomas Lawrance who is an apprentice to William Cook, Jr.
2/8/1785 to Mt. Holly Monthly Meeting for Unity Pancoast.
2/9/1785 to Burlington Monthly Meeting for Mary Lippincott.
2/9/1785 to Mt. Holly Monthly Meeting for Susannah Emley, dau. of Robert Emley in her minority to live with Samuel Hough.
4/5/1785 to Burlington Monthly Meeting for Anthony Morris, wife, Sarah and two children, Elizabeth and Anthony.
4/5/1785 to Haddonfield Monthly Meeting for Miles Gibbs, who is an apprentice.
4/6/1785 to Chesterfield Monthly Meeting for Mary Davenport.
6/9/1785 to Evesham Monthly Meeting for Jacob Ridgway.
6/9/1785 to Mt. Holly Monthly Meeting for Benjamin Pancoast, who is placed as an apprentice with Daniel Doughty.
9/7/1785 to Evesham Monthly Meeting for Elisabeth Stratton.
9/7/1785 to Woodbury Monthly Meeting for Ann Steward, wife of Joseph Steward, and her two children, Elizabeth and Bridget.
9/7/1785 to Chesterfield Monthly Meeting for Ebenezer Wright and Elizabeth, his wife, and their three children: Joseph, Ann and Mary, in their minority.
10/5/1785 to Philadelphia Northern District Monthly Meeting for Mary Wood.
2/8/1786 to Philadelphia Northern District Monthly Meeting for Thomas Gaskill, Jr., who is placed as an apprentice.
4/5/1786 to Salem Monthly Meeting for Stephen Wright and Priscilla, his wife, with their dau., Rebecca.
6/7/1786 to Fairfax, Va. Monthly Meeting for Susannah Shreve, wife of Benjamin Shreve.
6/7/1786 to Chesterfield Monthly Meeting for Elizabeth Wright.
6/9/1786 to Burlington Monthly Meeting for William White, Jr.

UPPER SPRINGFIELD MONTHLY MEETING CERTIFICATES   35

7/5/1786 to Greenwich Monthly Meeting for Hannah Newbold.
7/5/1786 to Chesterfield Monthly Meeting for Tacy Harrison.
8/9/1786 to Chesterfield Monthly Meeting for Mary Smith.
9/6/1786 to Mt. Holly Monthly Meeting for John Earl.
10/4/1786 to Chesterfield Monthly Meeting for Rachel Dawson.
10/4/1786 to Philadelphia Monthly Meeting for Mary Wistar to live with her husband, Thomas Wistar.
11/8/1786 to Philadelphia Northern District Monthly Meeting for Timothy Abbott, who is placed as an apprentice to William Savory (or Lavory).
12/6/1786 to Burlington Monthly Meeting for Charles Jones.
1/3/1787 to Chesterfield Monthly meeting for Sarah Williams.
12/6/1786 to Philadelphia Northern District Monthly Meeting for Elizabeth Beaty.
2/7/1787 to Burlington Monthly Meeting for Mary Ridgway, wife of William Ridgway.
3/1/1787 to Chesterfield Monthly Meeting for Elizabeth Wilkams.
3/7/1787 to Burlington Monthly Meeting for Penelope Zilla, wife of Daniel Zilla, to live with her husband.
5/9/1787 to Crooked Run Monthly Meeting, VA for Thomas Smith and wife, Deborah, and children: William, David, Ann, Lydia, and Copperthwaite Copeland.
6/6/1787 to Chesterfield Monthly Meeting for Susannah Forman.
6/6/1787 to Evesham Monthly Meeting for Mary Pittman, a minor, living with Amos Bullock.
8/8/1787 to Mt. Holly Monthly Meeting for Samuel Lipincott and Elizabeth his wife and their two children, Rebekah and Joseph, minors.
8/8/1787 to Mt. Holly Monthly Meeting for Achsah Warren.
8/8/1787 to Greenwich Monthly Meeting for Deborah Newbold.
9/5/1787 to Bush Creek Monthly Meeting, MD for Benjamin Harrison, wife, Meriam, and their two children, Latham and William.
12/5/1787 to Chesterfield Monthly Meeting for John Stevenson.
12/5/1787 to Burlington Monthly Meeting for Benjamin Gibbs and Rebecah, his wife.
1/8/1788 to Chesterfield Monthly Meeting for Ann, George and Josiah Forman, children of Richard Way Forman, being in their minority.
1/9/1788 to Burlington Monthly Meeting for Sarah Gibbs.
1/9/1788 to Burlington Monthly Meeting for Rebekah Gibbs, Jr.
2/6/1788 to Philadelphia Monthly Meeting for John Sykes, a minor, who is placed as an apprentice.
2/6/1788 to Evesham Monthly Meeting for Charles Jones and Mary, his wife.
3/5/1788 to Philadelphia Northern District Monthly Meeting for Elizabeth Ashton.
3/5/1788 to Mt. Holly Monthly Meeting for Martha Reeve to live with her husband, Josiah Reeve.
4/9/1788 to Philadelphia Southern District for Edith Howard to live with her husband.
5/7/1788 to Salem Monthly Meeting for Job and Elizabeth Shreve and their two daus., Abigail and Hannah.
5/7/1788 to Rahway Monthly Meeting for Mary Wright.
5/7/1788 to Chesterfield Monthly Meeting for Sarah Steward.
5/7/1788 to Evesham Monthly Meeting for Benjamin Kirby, Rachel,

his wife and Elizabeth, their dau., a minor.
6/4/1788 to Burlington Monthly Meeting for Cadawalder Foulke, Phebe, his wife and their child.
6/4/1788 to Evesham Monthly Meeting for Joseph Wright.
6/4/1788 to Philadelphia Northern District Monthly Meeting for Clayton Gaskill, who is placed as an apprentice to William Savory (or Lavory).
7/5/1788 to Philadelphia Northern District Monthly Meeting for Peter Gaunt to be placed as an apprentice with Thomas Scattergood.
7/5/1788 to Evesham Monthly Meeting for Rebecca Wright.
7/5/1788 to Evesham Monthly Meeting for Frances Wright.
7/9/1788 to Chesterfield Monthly Meeting for Ann Ivins, Sr.
7/9/1788 to Westland Monthly Meeting, PA for Sarah Smith, wife of Timothy Smith.
7/9/1788 to Crooked Run Monthly Meeting, VA for Elizabeth Holloway, wife of George Holloway and their children: William, Mary, Sarah, George and Thomas, all in their minority.
9/3/1788 to Westland Monthly Meeting, PA for Abigail Shreve, wife of John Shreve and her son, Joseph, an infant.
11/5/1788 to Chesterfield Monthly Meeting for Achsah Decow and her three children: Mary, Joseph and Clayton, all in their minority.
1/7/1789 to Middletown Monthly Meeting, PA for Samuel Wright, his wife Jane and their five children: Mary, Samuel, Joseph, Ann and Nathan.
1/7/1789 to Haddonfield Monthly Meeting for Sarah Gibbs.
1/7/1789 to Burlington Monthly Meeting for Amey Rogers to live with her husband, Samuel Rogers.
2/4/1789 to Middletown, Pa for John Forman, who is placed as an apprentice to Samuel Wright.
3/4/1789 to Burlington Monthly Meeting for Mary Pancoast, a minor, who is placed with a Friend.
3/4/1789 to Mt. Holly Monthly Meeting for Elizabeth Curtis.
5/6/1789 to Mt. Holly Monthly Meeting for Susanna Reeves.
6/3/1789 to Chesterfield Monthly Meeting for Ann Ely.
6/3/1789 to Burlington Monthly Meeting for Frances Leonard.
7/8/1789 to Philadelphia Monthly Meeting for Joseph Waln.
7/8/1789 to Burlington Monthly Meeting for Esther Morris.
7/8/1789 to Philadelphia Monthly Meeting for Richard Waln, a minor who is placed with a Friend.
7/8/1789 to Chesterfield Monthly Meeting for Susanna Antrim, a minor, dau. of Joseph Antrim, dec'd who is placed with a Friend.
8/5/1789 to Philadelphia Southern District Monthly Meeting for Ann Offley, to live with her husband, Daniel Offley.
9/9/1789 to Mt. Holly Monthly Meeting for Joseph Earl, Theodosia, his wife and their two children, Esther and Caleb, both minors.
11/4/1789 to Chesterfield Monthly Meeting for Joseph Bullock, Jr. and wife, Lydia and their three children: Mary, Susanna, and Lydia, minors.
11/4/1789 to Burlington Monthly Meeting for Joseph Morris.
1/6/1790 to Chesterfield Monthly Meeting for Thomas Antrim.
2/3/1790 to Chesterfield Monthly Meeting for Edith Lawrie.
3/3/1790 to Burlington Monthly Meeting for Joseph Green.

UPPER SPRINGFIELD MONTHLY MEETING CERTIFICATES 37

3/3/1790 to Burlington Monthly Meeting for Ephriam Pitmann, a minor, to live with Thomas Smith.
5/5/1790 to Mt. Holly Monthly Meeting for Hannah Nutt, a minor,. to live with a Friend.
5/5/1790 to Evesham Monthly Meeting for Ebenezer Gaskill and his wife, Esther, and their two daus., Lydia and Elizabeth, both being in their minority.
6/9/1790 to Philadelphia Southern District Monthly Meeting for Margaret Donaldson to live with her parents, Arthur and Elizabeth Donaldson.
6/9/1790 to Chesterfield Monthly Meeting for Susanna Wood.
6/9/1790 to Philadelphia Southern District Monthly Meeting for Elizabeth Donaldson to live with her husband, Arthur Donaldson.
6/9/1790 to Burlington Monthly Meeting for Henry Ridgway and wife, Mary, and their six children: Samuel, Solomon, Elizabeth, Mary, Sarah and Rebecca, all in their minority.
7/4/1790 to Chesterfield Monthly Meeting for Samuel Stevenson and Catharine, his wife.
8/4/1790 to Burlington Monthly Meeting for Ann Ridgway to live with her parents.
9/8/1790 to Falls Monthly Meeting, Bucks County, PA for Thomas Scattergood.
9/8/1790 to Salem Monthly Meeting for Naomi Hall.
12/8/1790 to Philadelphia Monthly Meeting for Thomas Newbold, son of Sarah Newbold, who is placed as an apprentice to James Smith.
12/8/1790 to Salem Monthly Meeting for Michael Newbold, who is an apprentice to Jonas Friedland.
1/5/1791 to Philadelphia Monthly Meeting for John Newbold.
2/9/1791 to Chesterfield Monthly Meeting for Grace Shuff after producing a certificate from Mt. Holly Monthly Meeting.
3/9/1791 to Chesterfield Monthly Meeting for Mary Stevenson to live with her sister.
3/9/1791 to Mt. Holly Monthly Meeting for Leah Burr to live with her husband.
3/9/1791 to Chesterfield Monthly Meeting for Sarah Chapman to live with her husband.
5/4/1791 to Burlington Monthly Meeting for Eliakim Willets and Phebe, his wife and their four children: David, Mary, Elizabeth and Sarah.
5/4/1791 to Chesterfield Monthly Meeting for Thomas Lawrie and Ann, his wife.
6/8/1791 to Little Eggharbor Monthly Meeting for Elizabeth Burdsall to live with her husband, Richard Burdsall.
6/8/1791 to Little Eggharbor Monthly Meeting for Caleb Ogborn, his wife, Ann and four children: Daniel, Joseph, Samuel and William, all in their minority.
7/8/1791 to Little Eggharbor Monthly Meeting for Samuel Warren.
8/6/1791 to Burlington Monthly Meeting Elizabeth Brown to live with her husband, Clayton Brown.
10/5/1791 to Mt. Holly Monthly Meeting for Abigail, Charlotte and Moses Nutt, minors to live with their parents, Moses and Elizabeth Nutt.
10/5/1791 to Mt. Holly Monthly Meeting for Ann Pope to live with her parents.
10/5/1791 to Mt. Holly Monthly Meeting for Rebecak Pope to live

with her parents.
10/5/1791 to Mt. Holly Monthly Meeting for Elizabeth Cope, in her minority, to live with her parents, Moses and Elizabeth Nutt.
10/5/1791 to Mt. Holly Monthly Meeting for Clayton and John Pope, minors to live with their father-in-law, Moses Nutt.
11/9/1791 to Pipe Creek, MD for Joseph Ogburn to live with his family.
1/4/1792 to Chesterfield Monthly Meeting for Deborah Woodward, a minor, dau. of Elizabeth Woodward.
4/1/1792 to Chesterfield Monthly Meeting for Increase Woodward, Jr.
4/7/1792 to Falls Monthly Meeting, PA for Aaron Ivins and Ann, his wife and their four minor children: Samuel, Ann, Mary and Barclay.
6/6/1792 to Burlington Monthly Meeting for Joshua Gibbs and his wife, Mary and their infant, Hannah.
6/6/1792 to Chesterfield Monthly Meeting for Lydia Williams.
7/4/1792 to Falls Monthly Meeting, PA for William Henry.
7/4/1792 to Richland Monthly Meeting for Jane Folke to live with her husband, Eneker Folke.
9/4/1792 to Burlington Monthly Meeting for John Decow, Jr. who is placed as an apprentice.
9/5/1792 to Philadelphia Monthly Meeting for Mary, Elizabeth and Rebecah Woodward to live with her mother.
10/8/1792 to Falls Monthly Meeting, PA for Isaac Ivins, Jr.
1/9/1793 to New York Monthly Meeting for Miles H. Gibbs.
3/5/1793 to Philadelphia Northern District Monthly Meeting for Beulah Sansom to live with her husband, Joseph Sansom.
3/6/1793 to Falls Monthly Meeting, PA for Edward Bullock, a minor who is placed as an apprentice to William Field.
5/8/1793 to Falls Monthly Meeting, PA for Lydia White and her husband, Joseph White and their three children: Mary, Joseph and Hannah.
5/8/1793 to Falls Monthly Meeting, PA for Lydia Bunting.
6/5/1793 to Burlington Monthly Meeting for Mary Ridgway.
6/5/1793 to Burlington Monthly Meeting for Sarah Pancost, a minor to live with her parents.
7/3/1793 to Horsham Monthly Meeting, PA for Sarah Shreve to live with her brother.
8/7/1793 to Evesham Monthly Meeting for Tacy Borden and her three children: Sarah, Thomas and Charles, minors to live with her husband, William Borden.
9/4/1793 to Chesterfield Monthly Meeting for John Thorn, [Thorne] Jr. and Tacy [Tacey], his wife, and their four children: Abraham, Diadamia, Mary and Elizabeth, in their minority.
9/4/1793 to Chesterfield Monthly Meeting for Ann Forsythe to live with her husband, Joseph Forsythe.
9/4/1793 to Burlington Monthly Meeting for Rachel Wilson, dau. of Thomas and Ann Wilson.
2/5/1794 to Redston, PA Monthly Meeting for Margaret Shreve, wife of Richard Shreeve.
3/9/1794 to Burlington Monthly Meeting for Mercy English and her four children: Amy, Sarah, Israel and Elisha all in their minority.
4/9/1794 to Burlington Monthly Meeting for Martha Antrim.

5/6/1794 to Philadelphia Northern District Monthly Meeting for
Jacob Shoebaker Waln, a minor, who is placed as an apprentice.
5/7/1794 to Chesterfield Monthly Meeting for Sarah Earl.
5/7/1794 to Mt. Holly Monthly Meeting for Peter Shinn, and Grace
his wife and five children: David, Hannah, Rachel, John and
Mahlon all in their minority.
5/7/1794 to Burlington Monthly Meeting for John English, who is
placed as an apprentice to Daniel Smith, Jr.
5/7/1794 to Philadelphia for Nathaniel Pope, a minor, who is
placed as an apprentice.
6/4/1794 to Uwchland Monthly Meeting in Chester County for Thomas
Parker.
2/4/1795 to New York Monthly Meeting for Joseph Pancoast, Jr.
5/6/1795 to Burlington Monthly Meeting for Nicolaus Busby.
5/6/1795 to Philadelphia Monthly Meeting for Ebenezer Gaskill,
his wife, Esther and their two daus., Lydia and Elizabeth.
6/3/1795 to Chesterfield Monthly Meeting for Isaac Wright.
7/8/1795 to Philadelphia Monthly Meeting for William French, his
wife, Rachel, and their five children: John, William, Mahlon,
Amos and Rachel.
7/8/1795 to Burlington Monthly Meeting for Edward Rockhill, and
his wife, Grace.
7/8/1795 to Evesham Monthly Meeting for Stacy Lippincott.
8/5/1795 to Philadelphia Monthly Meeting for Israel Stockton, who
is placed as an apprentice to John Sykes.
9/9/1795 to Falls Monthly Meeting, PA for Aaron Ivins, his wife,
Meriam and son, George.
11/4/1795 to Cecil Monthly Meeting, MD for Achsah Black, wife of
William Black, to live with her husband.
11/4/1795 to New York Monthly Meeting for Isaac Gibbs.
11/4/1795 for Susanna Clayton who has moved to live with her
husband. [no Monthly Meeting mentioned.]
1/6/1796 to New York Monthly Meeting for Unity Everham late
Pancoast, and her three minor children: Asa, Thomson and Hannah
Pancoast.
1/6/1796 to Philadelphia Northern District Monthly Meeting for
Caleb Shreve.
3/2/1796 to Chesterfield Monthly Meeting for Samuel Gaskill and
his wife, Sibilla and their three children: Rachel, Aaron and
Joseph Gaskill, all in their minority.
3/2/1796 to Philadelphia for Thomas Pope, son of Sarah Pope, a
minor, who is placed as an apprentice to Amos Taylor.
3/9/1796 to Chesterfield Monthly Meeting for Sarah Gaskill.
3/9/1796 to Rahway and Plainfield Monthly Meeting for Mary
Burnet.
3/9/1796 to Chesterfield Monthly Meeting for John and Samuel
Gaskill.
3/9/1796 to Philadelphia Northern District Monthly Meeting for
Elizabeth Newbold.
3/9/1796 to Rahway and Plainfield Monthly Meeting for Nathan
Robbins, and wife Joice, and Ann Nutt, a minor who lives with
them.
4/6/1796 to Fairfax Monthly Meeting, VA for Reuben Shreve and his
wife, Mary.
4/6/1796 to Chesterfield Monthly Meeting for Elizabeth Wright,

wife of David Wright.
4/6/1796 to Burlington Monthly Meeting for George Craft, his wife and dau., Ann and Joseph Ogborn, a minor who lives with them.
4/6/1796 to Fairfax Monthly Meeting, VA for Thomas Shreve.
5/4/1796 to Chesterfield Monthly Meeting for Sarah Curtis and two minor children, Tilton and Achsah.
5/4/1796 to Chesterfield Monthly Meeting for Samuel Decow.
5/4/1796 to Chesterfield Monthly Meeting for Samuel Rockhill, his wife, Hannah and their seven children: John, Aaron Sarah, Hannah, William, Samuel and Edward.
5/4/1796 to Chesterfield Monthly Meeting for William Wilson and his wife, Abigail and their minor son, Benjamin.
5/4/1796 to Philadelphia Northern District Monthly Meeting for Rhoda Dawson.
5/10/1796 to Burlington Monthly Meeting for David Ridgway.
6/3/1796 to Burlington Monthly Meeting for Amy Colly to live with her husband.
6/8/1796 to Chesterfield Monthly Meeting for Joshua Gibbs and his wife, Mary and their minor children: Hannah, Rebecca and Rheuben.
6/8/1796 to Burlington Monthly Meeting for Christian Black.
6/8/1796 to Evesham Monthly Meeting for Mary Pitman.
6/8/1796 to Evesham Monthly Meeting for Sylvanus Zilly.
6/8/1796 to Chesterfield Monthly Meeting for Abel and Robert Kirby.
6/8/1796 to Burlington Monthly Meeting for John Black, his wife, Mary and their three children: Jobe, Sarah and Elizabeth.
6/8/1796 to Chesterfield Monthly Meeting for Robert Kirby.
6/8/1796 to Philadelphia Monthly Meeting for Joseph Black, a minor, son of John and Mary Black.
8/3/1796 to Fairfax Monthly Meeting, VA for Isaac and William Furman.
8/3/1796 to Philadelphia Monthly Meeting for Titus Bennet.
8/3/1796 to Mt. Holly Monthly Meeting for Meriam Burtis, wife of William Burtis, Jr.
9/3/1796 to Chesterfield Monthly Meeting for Hudlah Chapman.
10/5/1796 to Philadelphia Northern District Monthly Meeting for Thomas Sykes.
11/4/1796 to Philadelphia Monthly Meeting for Mary Wright.
11/4/1796 to Burlington Monthly Meeting for Mary Newbold and her dau., Martha, a minor.
12/7/1796 to Philadelphia Northern District Monthly Meeting for Thomas Ridgway.
12/7/1796 to Philadelphia Northern District Monthly Meeting for Obediah Stockton.
12/17/1796 to Mt. Holly Monthly Meeting for Kedar Shinn.
3/1/1797 to Buckingham Monthly Meeting for Rachel Paxson, wife of Benjamin Paxson.
5/3/1797 to Chesterfield Monthly Meeting for Jerusha Rockhill, dau. of Samuel Rockhill.
5/3/1797 to Chesterfield Monthly Meeting for Isaac Decow, a minor, who is placed with Samuel Decow.
5/3/1797 to Burlington Monthly Meeting for Hannah Wright.
7/5/1797 to Chesterfield Monthly Meeting for Thomas Wardall.
7/5/1797 to Chesterfield Monthly Meeting for Sarah Wardall and

her dau., Elizabeth.
7/5/1797 to New York Monthly Meeting for George Newbold, son of Clayton Newbold, who is placed as an apprentice to Thomas Franklin.
4/4/1798 to Chesterfield Monthly Meeting for James Pancoast to marry.
6/6/1798 to Burlington Monthly Meeting for Benjamin and Hannah Sykes and their children: Rabbecah, Hannah, Ann and Elizabeth, all in their minority.
6/6/1798 to Salem Monthly Meeting for James and Margaret Stevenson.
7/4/1798 to Philadelphia Northern District Monthly Meeting for Elizabeth Ann Eyers to live with her parents.
10/3/1798 to Chesterfield Monthly Meeting for Rachel Kirby.
11/7/1798 to Chesterfield Monthly Meeting for Elijah Brown.
1/9/1799 to Chesterfield Monthly Meeting for Margaret Ivins.
1/9/1799 to Middletown Monthly Meeting, PA for Rebecca Richardson to live with her husband, Joseph.
1/9/1799 to Burlington Monthly Meeting for Sarah Pitman.
5/6/1799 to Chesterfield Monthly Meeting for Mary Wright.
5/8/1799 to Chesterfield Monthly Meeting for James Brown and Hannah his wife.
5/8/1799 to Salem Monthly Meeting for Rebecca Wright to live with her husband, George Wright.
6/5/1799 to Burlington Monthly Meeting for Abigail Antrim, a minor, dau. of John Antrim, who is placed with Daniel Zilly.
6/5/1799 to Burlington Monthly Meeting for Thomas Shinn.
6/5/1799 to Chesterfield Monthly Meeting for Elizabeth Wright, Jr.
6/5/1799 to Chesterfield Monthly Meeting for Elizabeth Wright, and her five minor children: John, Sarah, Elihu, Rebecca and Nathan.
6/5/1799 to Burlington Monthly Meeting for Hannah Cook Rockhill to live with her father, Nathan Rockhill.
9/4/1799 to Burlington Monthly Meeting for Benjamin Satterthwaite and his wife, Sarah and their minor children, Joel and Caleb.
10/9/1799 to Chesterfield Monthly Meeting for Stacy Decow.
10/9/1799 to Burlington Monthly Meeting for Joseph Sharpless.
11/6/1799 to Mt. Holly Monthly Meeting for Thomas Wilson and his wife, Ann and their four children: William, John, Joseph and Elizabeth.
12/4/1799 to Chesterfield Monthly Meeting for Elizabeth Bunting.
1/6/1800 to Philadelphia Monthly Meeting for Samuel Wright, a minor, who is placed under the care of John Folwell.
1/8/1800 to Mt. Holly Monthly Meeting for Ann, Sarah and Hannah Wilson, daus of Thomas Wilson.
1/8/1800 to Burlington Monthly Meeting for Sarah Newbold.
3/5/1800 to Burlington Monthly Meeting for Sarah Folwell, wife of Nathan Folwell.
4/9/1800 to Evesham for Benjamin Scattergood.
4/9/1800 to Philadelphia Northern District Monthly Meeting for Hannah Smith, wife of James Smith, to live with her husband.
5/7/1800 to Burlington Monthly Meeting for Caleb Gaskill.
5/7/1800 to Burlington Monthly Meeting for George Zilly.
5/7/1800 to Chesterfield Monthly Meeting for Martha Taylor, wife

of Thomas Taylor.
6/4/1800 to Wilmington Monthly Meeting, DE for John Platt and Alice his wife, and their four minor children: Elizabeth, William, Mary and George.
6/4/1800 to Pilesgrove Monthly Meeting for Charles Jones and his wife, Mary and their six minor children: Sarah, Elizabeth, Charity, Charles, and Mary. [only five children mentioned.]
7/1/1800 to Shrewsbury for Deborah Woodward, wife of Anthony Woodward.
7/9/1800 to Philadelphia Monthly Meeting for Tucker Earl.
7/9/1800 to Chesterfield Monthly Meeting for Asa Pointset.
8/1/1800 to Mt. Holly Monthly Meeting for Thomas Wilson, Jr.
9/3/1800 to Philadelphia Monthly Meeting for Joel Atkinson.
12/3/1800 to Philadelphia Northern District Monthly Meeting for Thomas Field, a minor who is placed with Arthur Donaldson.

MARRIAGES FROM UPPER SPRINGFIELD MONTHLY MEETING

Thomas Smith of the city and county of Burlington, NJ, son of Samuel and Tryphena Smith and Mary Rockhill, dau. of Edward and Elizabeth Rockhill of the twp of Chesterfield having consent of their parents m. 11th mo, 19th da, 1783.
Benjamin Poultney of the city of Philadelphia, PA, son of Thomas Poultney of said city and Eleanor, his wife, dec'd and Phebe Cook, dau. of William Cook of Shrewsbury, dec'd and Lydia his wife m. at Upper Springfield Monthyly Meeting having consent of their parents m. 12th da, 10th mo, 1783.
William Cook of the twp of Hanover, Burlington County, NJ and Diadamia Harrison of same place m. at Upper Springfield 1st mo, 15th da, 1784.
David Middleton of the twp of New Town, Gloucester County, NJ and Elizabeth Gaskill of Hanover, Burlington County, NJ m. at Upper Springfield 1st mo, 22nd da, 1784.
Benjamin Harrison, son of Thomas Harrison of the twp of Hanover, Burlington County, NJ and Miriam Allin, dau. of Ralph Allin, decd, of aforesaid twp and county having consent of parents m. 3rd mo, 11th da, 1784.
John Platt, son of Thomas Platt, dec'd, of New Hanover, Burlington County, and Alice Stevenson, dau. of William Stevenson of Upper Freehold, Monmouth, NJ having consent of parents m. 9th mo, 23rd da, 1784.
Joseph Earl, son of Tantom Earl and Mary, his wife, of Springfield twp, Burlington County, NJ and Theodosia Shreve, dau. of Joshua Shreve and his wife, Rebekah, of same place having consent of parents m. 12th mo, 14th da, 1785.
Benjamin Shreve, of the town of Alexandria, County of Fairfax, VA, son of Benjamin and Rebecca Shreve, late of Burlington County, NJ and Susanna Wood, dau. of John and Deborah Wood of Burlington County, NJ with consent of parents m. 4th mo, 6th da, 1786.
Thomas Westar [Wistar] of the city of Philadelphia, PA, a merchant, son of Richard Westar and Sarah his wife, late of said city, dec'd and Mary Waln, dau. of Richard and Elizabeth Waln of

Upper Freehold twp, Monmouth County, NJ having consent of
parents m. 5th mo, 24th da, 1786.
Cadwalader Foulke of Upper Freehold, Monmouth County, NJ and
Phebe Ellis of the aforesaid state having consent of parents m.
6th da, 21st day, 1786.
William Ridgway, son of Solomon Ridgway and Mary, his wife of the
twp of Willinborough, Burlington County, NJ and Mary Fowler,
dau. of Joseph Fowler and Meribah, his wife, of Hanover twp of
aforesaid county having consent of parents m. 11th mo, 23rd day,
1786.
Daniel Zelly, son of John Zelley, dec'd and Rachel, his wife of
the twp of Springfield, Burlington County, NJ and Penelope
Shrive, dau. of Caleb Shrieve, dec'd and Abigail, his wife of
Mansfield twp, aforesaid province, having consent of parents m.
1st mo, 10th da, 1787.
Israel Kirby, son of Robert and Amy Kirby of Hanover twp,
Burlington County, NJ and Rachel Shinn, dau. of Thomas and Sarah
Shinn, of Upper Freehold twp, Monmouth County, NJ having consent
of the parents m. 5th mo, 17th da, 1787.
Josiah Reeve of the twp of Alloways Creek, Salem County, NJ son
of Mark and Hannah Reeve and Martha Newbold, dau. of John
Newbold, dec'd, late of the twp of Chesterfield, Burlington
County, and Mary, his wife, having consent of the parents m.
10th mo, 17th da, 1787.
Charles Jones, son of Jeremiah Jones of Newton, Gloucester
County, and Mary Ivins, dau. of Samuel Ivins, dec'd, of
Chesterfield, Burlington County, NJ having consent of parents m.
11th mo, 22nd da, 1787.
Abner Woodward, son of Thomas Woodward, dec'd, and Susanna his
wife and Clemence Woodward, dau. of Anthony Woodward and
Increase his wife, both of the twp of Upper Freehold, Monmouth
County, NJ having consent of parents m. 7th da, 7th mo, 1787.
Samuel Rogers of the City and county of Burlington, NJ, son of
Samuel and Elizabeth Rogers, late within the limits of said
city, dec'd and Amy Rockhill, dau. of Edward and Elizabeth
Rockhill, of the twp of Chesterfield, Burlington County, NJ
having consent of the parents m. 11th mo, 19th da, 1788.
Jonathan Curtis, son of John and Mercy Curtis, dec'd, of
Springfield twp, Burlington county, NJ and Elizabeth Earl, dau.
of Tantom and Mary Earl of the same place having consent of the
parents m. 12th mo, 9th da, 1788.
Thomas Lawrie, son of James Lawrie and Mary, his wife of the twp
of Upper Freehold, Monmouth County, NJ and Ann Satterthwaite,
dau. of William Satterthwaite and Jane, his wife of twp of
Chesterfield, Burlington county, NJ having consent of the
parents m. 12th mo, 27th da, 1788.
Samuel Stevenson, son of William Stevenson and Mary, dec'd, of
Upper Freehold, County of Monmouth, and Catharine Minor, dau. of
Lawrence and Elizabeth Minor of Mansfield, Burlington County, NJ
having consent of the parents m. 1st mo, 21st da, 1789.
John Furman, son of Josiah Furman of Trenton, Hunterdon County,
NJ and Susanna Steward, dau. of Joseph and Bridget Steward of
Hanover twp, Burlington County, NJ, dec'd, having consent of the
parents m. 4th mo, 12th da, 1787.
Daniel Offley of the city of Philadelphia, Pa, an anchor smith,

son of Daniel Offley, late of the said city, dec'd, and Rachael his wife and Ann Newbold, dau. of John Newbold, late of the twp of Chesterfield, Burlington County, NJ, dec'd, and Mary his wife having consent of the parents m. 6th mo, 13th da, 1789.

Caleb Shreve, son of Caleb Shreve, dec'd, and Abigail his wife, of Mansfield, Burlington County, NJ and Charlotte Minor, dau. of Lawrence Minor and Elizabeth, his wife, of aforesaid county having consent of the parents m. 9th mo, 23rd da, 1789.

Joseph Murfin Lawrie, son of Thomas Lawrie, dec'd, and Ann Lawrie, of Nottingham twp, Burlington county, NJ and Edith Newbold, dau. of William and Susannah Newbold (Susannah being decd) of the twp of Springfield, of aforesaid county and state having consent of the parents m. 10th mo, 28th da, 1789.

Edward Robbins, son of Nathan Robbins of Mansfield, Burlington County, NJ and Amey Black, dau. of Ezra Black of Chesterfield of the aforesaid county and state having consent of the parents m. 4th mo, 21st da, 1789.

Nathan Rockhill, son of Edward Rockhill, dec'd, and Elizabeth, his wife of the twp of Chesterfield, Burlington County, NJ and Hannah Cook, dau. of William Cook, dec'd, and Lydia his wife, of the twp of Upper Freehold, Monmouth County having consent of the parents m. 5th mo, 12th da, 1790.

Uz Gaunt, son of Samuel and Hannah Gaunt of the twp of Springfield, Burlington County, NJ and Sarah Jones, dau. of Benjamin and Elizabeth Jones, of twp of New Hanover, of aforesaid county and state having consent of the parents m. 12th mo, 15th da, 1790.

William Chapman of the twp of Upper Freehold, Monmouth County, NJ, son of William Chapman and Rebecca, his wife and Sarah Ivins, of the twp of Chesterfield, Burlington County, NJ, dau. of Samuel Ivins, dec'd, and Sarah, his wife having consent of the parents m. 12th mo, 16th da, 1790.

Isaac Barton, son of Aaron Barton and Bathsheba, his wife, dec'd, and Sarah Gauntt, dau. of Samuel Gauntt, dec'd, and Hannah his wife, both of the twp of Springfield, Burlington County, NJ having consent of the parents m. 1st mo, 12th da, 1791.

Richard Burdsall, son of Stephen Burdsall, dec'd, of the twp of Stafford County, Monmouth, NJ and Elizabeth Nutt, widow of Levy Nutt, dec'd of twp of Mansfield, Burlington county, NJ having consent of the parents m. 4th mo, 7th da, 1791.

Clayton Brown, son of Samuel Brown, dec'd, and Ann his wife of the twp of Mansfield, Burlington county, NJ and Elizabeth Satterthwaite, dau. of Samuel Satterthwaite and Mary his wife, dec'd, of twp of Chesterfield, Burlington County, NJ having consent of the parents m. 4th mo, 13th da, 1791.

Joshua Gibbs, son of Joshua Gibbs and Hannah his wife, dec'd, and Mary Gaskil, dau. of Samuel and Sybilla Gaskill, both of the twp of Upper Freehold in the county of Monmouth, NJ having consent of the parents m. 4th mo, 14th da, 1791.

George O'Neal of the twp of Springfield, Burlington County, NJ and Sarah Bond, widow, dau. of Ralph Smith and Ann, his wife, of the twp of North Hampton, County aforesaid dec'd, having consent of the parents m. 12th mo, 14th da, 1791.

Alexander Shreve, son of Joshua Shreeve and Rebecca, his wife, of the twp of Hanover County, Burlington, NJ and Mary Earl, dau. of

Taunton Earl and Mary, his wife, of the twp of Springfield, aforesaid state, having consent of the parents m. 4th mo, 11th da, 1792.

Isacher Foulke, son of William Foulke and Priscilla, his wife, of twp of Richland, Bucks County, PA and Jane Barton, dau. of Aaron Barton of the twp of Springfield, Burlington County, NJ and Bathsheba, his wife, dec'd having consent of the parents m. 5th mo, 10th da, 1792.

Isaac Hutchins of the twp of Upper Freehold in the county of Monmouth, NJ, tanner, son of John Hutchins, dec'd, and Sarah, his widow, and Jane Satterthwaite, dau. of William and Jane Satterthwaite of the twp of Chesterfield, Burlington county, aforesaid state, having consent of the parents m. 4th mo, 10th da, 1792.

Joseph Sansom of the city of Philadelphia, PA, a merchant, son of Samuel Sansom of the same place and Hannah, his wife and Beulah Biddle, of twp of Springfield, Burlington County, NJ, dau. of Joseph Biddle, late of aforesaid twp, dec'd, and Sarah, his wife, having consent of the parents m. 11th mo, 1st da, 1792.

George Craft, son of Samuel and Hannah Craft of the twp of Mansfield, Burlington County, NJ and Elizabeth Ridgway, dau. of Jacob Ridgway of twp, county and state aforesaid, having consent of the parents m. 2nd mo, 13th da, 1793.

Joseph Forsyth of the twp of Chesterfield, Burlington County, NJ and Ann Gaunt, Jr. of the twp aforesaid, having consent of the parents m. 6th da, 12th mo, 1793.

Samuel Ellis, son of John and Lucy Ellis of the twp of Upper Freehold, Monmouth County, NJ and Elizabeth Henry, dau. of John and Susanna Henry, dec'd, of the twp of Mansfield, Burlington County, NJ, having consent of the parents m. 9th mo, 11th da, 1793.

Aaron Ivins of the Falls twp, Bucks County, PA, son of Aaron Ivins and Ann, his wife, and Miriam Middleton of the twp of Mansfield, Burlington County, NJ, dau. of George Middleton, dec'd, and Dinah, his wife, having consent of the parents m. 12th mo, 11th da, 1793.

Samuel Gaunt of the twp of Chesterfield in Burlington County, NJ, son of John Gaunt and Jane, his wife and Achsah Decow of the same place, dau. of John Taylor, dec'd, and Sarah, his wife, having consent of the parents m. 3rd mo, 12th da, 1794.

Joseph Tallman, Jr., son of Joseph Tallman and Sarah, his wife of the twp of Mansfield, Burlington County, NJ and Valeriah Woodward, dau. of Anthony Woodward and his, wife, Deborah of the twp of Upper Freehold, Monmouth County, NJ, having consent of the parents m. 4th mo, 17th da, 1794.

Amos Ellis, son of Peter Ellis and Miriam, his wife of the twp of Mansfield, Burlington County, NJ (he having consent of parents) and Mary Haines, dau. of Josiah Haines and Abigail, his wife of the twp of Burlington, NJ, dec'd, m. 1st mo, 14th da, 1795.

William Black, son of Edward Black of the twp of Ridley, in the County of Delaware, PA, a miller and Achsah Wright, dau. of Thomas Wright of the twp of New Hanover, Burlington County, NJ, having consent of the parents m. 4th mo, 17th da, 1795.

John Newbold of the city of Philadelphia, PA, a merchant, son of
William and Susanna Newbold, late of the twp of Chesterfield,
NJ, dec'd, and Elizabeth Lawrie, dau. of John and Achsah Lawrie
of the twp of New Hanover, Burlington County, NJ, having consent
of the parents m. 11th mo, 7th da, 1795.

Reuben Shreve, son of Caleb Shreve, dec'd, and Grace, his wife of
Mansfield, Burlington County, NJ and Mary Scattergood, Jr., dau.
of Caleb Sattergood, dec'd, and Mary, his wife, of the aforesaid
county and state, having consent of the parents m. 11th mo, 18th
da, 1795.

Joseph Richardson, son of William and Elizabeth Richardson of
Middletown, Bucks County, PA and Rebecca Newbold, dau. of
Clayton and Mary Newbold of Mansfield twp, Burlington County,
NJ, having consent of the parents m. 10th mo, 24th da, 1798.

Michael Earl, son of Thomas and Rebecca Earl of the twp of
Springfield, Burlington County, NJ and Rebecca Ridgway, dau. of
Job and Mary Ridgway of the twp and county aforesaid, dec'd,
having consent of the parents m. 10th mo, 12th da, 1796.

Benjamin Paxson of the twp of Solesbury, Bucks County, PA, son of
Thomas and Jane Paxson of aforesaid place, dec'd, and Rachel
Newbold of Springfield, Burlington County, NJ, m. 11th mo, 15th
da, 1797.

Asa Gibbs, son of Martin and Phebe Gibbs, of the twp of
Mansfield, Burlington County, NJ and Sarah Curtis, dau. of
Thomas and Alice Curtis of the aforesaid place, having consent
of the parents m. 12th mo, 12th da, 1798.

George Wright of Salem County, NJ, son of Benjamin and Ruth
Wright and Rebecca Minor of Burlington County, NJ, dau. of
Lawrence and Elizabeth Minor, having consent of the parents m.
12th mo, 19th da, 1798.

James Brown, son of Abraham Brown and Rebeckah, his wife and
Hannah Ivins, dau. of Barzillai Ivins, dec'd, and Margaret, his
wife, both of the twp of Hanover, Burlington County, NJ, having
consent of the parents m. 2nd mo, 14th da, 1799.

Nicholas Waln, son of Richard Waln and Elizabeth, his wife,
dec'd, and Sarah Ridgway, dau. of John Ridgway and Elizabeth,
his wife, both of the twp of Upper Freehold, Monmouth County, NJ
having consent of the parents m. 4th mo, 7th da, 1799.

Samuel Satterthwaite, son of William Satterthwaite and Jane, his
wife, all of the twp of Chesterfield, Burlington County, NJ and
Mary Decow, dau. of Joseph Decow, dec'd, and Achsah, his wife of
the aforesaid twp, having consent of the parents m. 10th mo,
16th da, 1799.

John Pope, son of Nathaniel Pope and Sarah, his wife, of twp of
Mansfield, Burlington County, NJ and Amy French of the aforesaid
twp and county, dau. of Jacob French and Elizabeth his wife, of
the twp of Waterford, Gloucester County, NJ, having consent of
the parents m. 11th da, 17th mo, 1799.

Thomas Taylor, son of James Taylor and Abigail, his wife of the
twp of Chesterfield, Burlington County, NJ and Martha
Satterthwaite, dau. of William Satterthwaite and Jane, his wife
of the aforesaid county and state, having consent of the parents
m. 11th mo, 13th da, 1799.

James Smith of the city of Philadelphia, a merchant, son of James and Rachel Smith of the county of Salem, dec'd, and Hannah Pancoast, dau. of Joseph Pancoast and Sarah his wife, Burlington County, NJ, having consent of the parents m. 2nd mo, 11th da, 1800.

MINUTES FROM UPPER SPRINGFIELD MONTHLY MEETING

5th mo, 7th da, 1783. Upper Springfield Monthly Meeting established.

6th mo, 4th da, 1783. Robert Emly appointed to provide a book and enter certificates.

7th mo, 7th da, 1783. Samuel Gaskill produced a certificate from Haddonfield Monthly Meeting for himself, his wife, Sybella, and children: John, Samuel, Aaron, Mary, Sarah and Rachel. Joseph Heritage produced a certificate from Haddonfield Monthly Meeting. A certificate produced from Haddonfield Monthly Meeting for Ruth and Elizabeth Gaskill. Meeting informed that Rebekuh Wright has been in England for some time, and has a certificate.

9th mo, 3rd da, 1783. Anthony Woodward, son of Anthony, reported for marrying one not a member, being guilty of gaming and has since left these parts in a disreputable manner. Nimrod Woodward reported for leaving these parts in a disreputable manner and being guilty of gaming. Isaac Woodward charged with committing fornication and leaving these parts in a disreputable manner.

10th mo, 10th da, 1783. Thomas Lawrence produced a certificate from Shrewsbury Monthly Meeting.

11th mo, 11th da, 1783. Richard Way Furman, his wife and children: Ann, George Middleton, Josiah and Ruth, all minors, produced a certificate from Burlington Monthly Meeting. Rachel Dawson produced a certificate from Evesham Monthly Meeting. Hannah Lloyd, wife of Levi Lloyd, produced a certificate from Shrewsbury Monthly Meeting.

12th mo, 3rd da, 1783. A certificate granted to Philadelphia Northern District Monthly Meeting for Benjamin Catheral, Sarah, his wife, and son, Benjamin.

1st mo, 7th da, 1784. David Middleton produced a certificate from Haddonfield Monthly Meeting.

2nd mo, 4th da, 1784. Susanna Wood received into membership. Thomas Steward granted a certificate to Chesterfield Monthly Meeting on account of marriage. Elizabeth Jones and her four children: Hester, Mary, Joseph and Israel received into membership. Sarah and Elizabeth Jones received into membership.

3rd mo, 3rd da, 1784. William Carslake acknowledged his having too early a familiarity with the woman he married, marrying a second cousin and marrying to a non-member of our society.

7th mo, 4th da, 1784. Susanna Ridgway received into membership. Ruth Stockton received into membership. Jacob Ridgway, Ells and Eli received into membership. John Platt received into membership.

5th mo, 5th da, 1784. Meribah Fowler, Jr. produced a certificate from Falls Monthly Meeting, PA.

6th da, 9th mo, 1784. Abraham Gaskill reported for enlisting as a soldier, going out in war, and neglecting meetings. Joshua Wright reported for not clearing himself of the charge of committing fornication. Moses Gaskill reported for marrying contrary to discipline and neglecting meeting. William Harris reported for marrying contrary to discipline to a first cousin and neglecting meetings. A certificate granted to Benjamin Pancoast, a minor, to Mt. Holly Monthly Meeting.

7th da, 7th mo, 1784. Aaron Gaskill reported for marrying contrary to discipline and neglecting meetings. John Ridgway, Jr. produced a certificate for himself and wife, Elizabeth, and children, Sarah and Caleb from Little Eggharbor Monthly Meeting. Mary Steward, wife of Thomas Steward, produced a certificate from Chesterfield Monthly Meeting. William Black, Jr. reported for being guilty of unchaste freedom before marriage, marrying contrary to discipline and neglecting meetings. Lydia Black late Newbold reported for marrying contrary to discipline to a non-member.

9th mo, 8th da, 1784. Margaret Shreve reported for marrying by a baptist preacher and to a man not in membership. Keziah Pattit received into membership. Mary Earl late Warren reported for marrying contrary to discipline. Elizabeth Nutt late Pope reported for marrying contrary to discipline to a man not of our society.

11th mo, 3rd da, 1784. Timothy Abbott, a minor, produced a certificate from Chesterfield Monthly Meeting. William Earl reported for neglecting meeting, marrying contrary to discipline and taking spirituous liquor to excess.

1st mo, 5th da, 1785. Samuel Smith reported for neglecting meeting and taking spirituous liquor to excess. Timothy Hance, an apprentice to William Cook, produced a certificate from Shrewsbury Monthly Meeting, read, approved and sent to Chesterfield Monthly Meeting with an endorsement.

2nd mo, 9th da, 1785. Elizabeth Ashton reported for being guilty of fornication, marrying contrary to discipline to a non-member by a baptist priest and neglecting meeting. Job Shreve produced a certificate for himself and wife, Elizabeth, from Salem Monthly Meeting. Samuel Wright recommended to meeting as a minister.

3rd mo, 9th da, 1785. Samuel Stockton produced an acknowledgement condemning his marrying contrary to discipline and before an hireling minister.

6th mo, 7th da, 1785. John Black reported for neglecting meeting and taking strong drink to excess. Lydia Bunting produced a certificate from Falls Monthly Meeting. Thomas Smith produced a certificate for himself, his wife, Deborah, and five children:

William, David, Ann, Lydia and Cowperthwaite from Haddonfield Monthly Meeting.

9th mo, 7th da, 1785. Hope Folwell reported for marrying contrary to discipline to a first cousin.

10th mo, 5th da, 1785. Jonathan Wright, his wife, Elizabeth, and their children: John, Mary, Hannah, Elizabeth and Sarah, (all minors) produced a certificate from Shrewsbury Monthly Meeting. John Wright produced an acknowledgement condemning his marrying contrary to discipline.

11th mo, 9th da, 1785. Esther Gaskill received into membership with her two children, Lydia and Elizabeth, minors. A certificate produced for Susanna Wood from Philadelphia Northern District Monthly Meeting. A certificate produced for Dinah Middleton and her dau., Patience, a minor, and one also for Miriam Middleton from Chesterfield Monthly Meeting.

1st mo, 7th da, 1786. Rhoda Middleton reported for committing fornication. Michel Rogers, Jr. and Phebe, his wife, reported for committing fornication and marrying contrary to discipline as being in relation as brother and sister by a former marriage. Mary Newbold requests to be released as elder.

2nd mo, 8th da, 1786. Testimony prepared against Richard Way Furman for committing fornication and taking spirituous liquor to excess. A certificate granted for Unity Pancoast to Mt. Holly Monthly Meeting. A certificate produced from Burlington Monthly Meeting Monthly Meeting for Sarah Pittman. Thomas Newbold produced an acknowledgement condemning his fornication. Joseph Willets produced an acknowledgement condemning his taking strong drink to exess.

3rd mo, 8th da, 1786. A certificate granted to Salem Monthly Meeting for Miles Gibbs, a minor. A certificate granted to Chesterfield Monthly Meeting for marriage for Joseph Williams. Benjamin Gibbs produced a certificate from Chesterfield Monthly Meeting for himself, his wife, Rebekah, and dau., Rebekah. Aaron Barton produced a certificate for himself and his wife, Sarah, from Burlington Monthly Meeting.

4th mo, 5th da, 1786. Benjamin Shreve produced a certificate from Fairfax Monthly Meeting. Joseph Ellis reported for being guilty of fornication and going with others in abusing a man. A certificate granted for Anthony Morris and Sarah, his wife, and children, Eliza and Anthony (minors), to Burlington Monthly Meeting. Stephen Wright and Priscilla, and their dau. Rebekah, a minor, requested a certificate to Salem Monthly Meeting. Thomas Gaskill appointed an elder. William White produced a certificate from Shrewsbury Monthly Meeting. A certificate produced for Jane Barton from Burlington Monthly Meeting, and one for Grace Shuff from Mt. Holly Monthly Meeting.

5th mo, 5th da, 1786. Thomas Wistar produced a certificate from

Philadelphia Monthly Meeting. Beulah Biddle received into
membership. Asa Ware reported for marrying contrary to discipline
and with the assistance of an hireling minister. Susanna Reeves
received into membership. Mary Newbold recommended as a minister.
Asa Branson produced a certificate from Woodbury Monthly Meeting.
Thomas Sykes produced a certificate from Philadelphia Northern
District Monthly Meeting.

6th mo, 7th da, 1786. A certificate granted for Susannah Shreve
to Fairfax Monthly Meeting, VA and a certificate for Elizabeth
Wright to Chesterfield Monthly Meeting. Charles Jones received
into membership. Antrim Conarroe produced a certificate from
Philadelphia Northern District Monthly Meeting. Cadwalader Foulke
produced a certificate from Horsham Monthly Meeting.

7th mo, 5th da, 1786. Keturah Boyd reported for marrying contrary
to discipline, marrying with the assistance of an hireling
minister and not keeping the plainness of dress and address.
Certificates granted for Hannah Newbold to Greenwich Monthly
Meeting and Tacy Harrison to Chesterfield Monthly Meeting.

8th mo, 9th da, 1786. William Black produced a certificate from
Haddonfield Monthly Meeting.

9th mo, 6th da, 1786. Joseph Willets produced an acknowledgement
condemning his taking strong drink to excess. Ann Wilson received
into membership. John Stevenson granted a certificate to
Chesterfield on account of marriage. William White, Jr. granted a
certificate to Burlington Monthly Meeting. Sarah Williams, wife
of Joseph, produced a certificate from Chesterfield Monthly
Meeting.

10th mo, 4th da, 1786. George Williams produced a certificate for
himself, his wife, Margaret, and children: Elizabeth, Lydia and
Phebe from Shrewsbury Monthly Meeting. Sarah Branson produced a
certificate from Woodbury Monthly Meeting.

11th mo, 8th da, 1786. Joseph Talman has complied with Friends to
emancipate two negroes he held in bondage. Peter Harvey's
acknowledgement condemning his going out in marriage accepted.
Emphson Kirby reported for not paying money he received in trust.
Constant Potter reported for being guilty of unchaste behavior,
marrying to a non-member and marrying contrary to discipline.
William Ridgway produced a certificate from Burlington monthly
meeting.

1st mo, 3rd da, 1787. Alice Curtice, wife of Thomas Curtice,
(Curtis) and children: Asa, Ann, Sarah and Mary received into
membership. Deborah Burnet, dau. of Joice Robins, received into
membership. Rebecca Pancoast former Forman reported for being
guilty of fornication with her brother-in-law, going out in
marriage to him by a priest, neglecting meeting and her dress and
address inconsistent with plainness. Joseph Bullock, Jr. produced
a certificate for himself, his wife, Lydia, and children, Mary
and Susanna. Isaac Barton produced a certificate from Evesham

Monthly Meeting. Daniel Zilly produced a certificate from Burlington Monthly Meeting.

2nd mo, 7th da, 1787. Mary Ridgway granted a certificate to Burlington Monthly Meeting.

3rd mo, 7th da, 1787. Joel Williams reported for unchaste behavior, going out in marriage, marrying by priest and neglecting meeting. Sarah Gibbs produced a certificate from Chesterfield Monthly Meeting.

4th mo, 4th da, 1787. John Forman produced a certificate from Chesterfield Monthly Meeting. Mary Shinn, wife of Caleb Shinn, and children: Thomas, Kedar and Sarah produced a certificate from Burlington Monthly Meeting.

5th mo, 9th da, 1787. Andrew Ware reported for taking strong drink to excess. Ruth Rogers, reported for going out in marriage, marrying by priest and neglecting meeting. Marriage of John Forman and Susanna Steward accomplished, they having parents' consent.

6th mo, 6th da, 1787. Abner Woodward acknowledged his guilt of taking strong drink to excess, unbecoming behavior and being present at a marriage accomplished contrary to discipline. Reuben Gibbs produced an acknowledgement condemning his taking strong drink to excess, attending places of diversion, horse racing and attending a marriage accomplished contrary to discipline. Ebenezer Gaskill produced a certificate from Mt. Holly Monthly Meeting. John Antram produced a certificate for himself and children: Charity, Isaac, Caleb, Ann and Abigail, all minors, from Burlington Monthly Meeting.

7th mo, 4th da, 1787. Alice Steward reported for going out in marriage by a priest. John Rockhill reported for neglecting meeting and going out in marriage. Theodosia Mount reported for going out in marriage by a priest, neglecting meeting and being inconsistent of dress and address. A certificate granted for Thomas Forman Jr. to Philadelphia Northern District Monthly Meeting returned as he has now moved back to the area. Charles Jones produced a certificate from Burlington Monthly Meeting.

8th mo, 8th da, 1787. A certificate produced for Elizabeth Woodward and her daus., Increase and Deborah, both minors, from Chesterfield Monthly Meeting. Joshua Gibbs, a minister, died 6th mo, 14th da, 1787. A certificate granted for Samuel Lipincott, his wife, Elizabeth, and children, Rebecca and Joseph, to Mt. Holly Monthly Meeting. A certificate granted for William Fox to Mt. Holly Monthly Meeting. A certificate granted for Achsash Warren to Mt. Holly Monthly Meeting. A certificate granted for Deborah Newbold to Greenwich Monthly Meeting. A certificate produced for Thomas Antram from Chesterfield Monthly Meeting.

9th mo, 5th da, 1787. Benjamin Woodward reported for striking a man in anger, going out in marriage, married by a priest and neglecting meeting. Sarah Harker late Branson reported for going out in marriage and married by a priest.

10th mo, 3rd da, 1787. Edith Howard's acknowledgement condemning her going out in marriage accepted. Elizabeth Ashton's acknowledgement condemning her guilt of fornication and going out in marriage by a priest accepted. Mary Horner late Rogers reported for going out in marriage. Josiah Reeve produced a certificate from Greenwich Monthly Meeting.

11th mo, 7th da, 1787. Phebe Jones produced an acknowledgement condemning her going out in marriage and attending a marriage of a Friend who went out in marriage. Sarah Garrison late Woodward reported for going out in marriage.

12th mo, 5th da, 1787. James Shinn reported for being guilty of unchaste behavior and going out in marriage. Sarah Jordan reported for going out in marriage, married by a priest, neglecting meeting and inconsistent in dress and address. George Holloway and family accepted into membership except two children who appear to be in Chesterfield Monthly Meeting.

1st mo, 9th da, 1788. John Harvey, Jr. reported for neglecting of meeting and going out in marriage. A certificate granted to Elizabeth Holloway, wife of George Holloway, and five children: William, Mary, Sarah, George and Thomas to Crooked Run Monthly Meeting VA. A certificate for Sary Fox received from New York Monthly Meeting. Elizabeth Donaldson produced a certificate from Philadelphia Monthly Meeting.

EXTRACTS FROM MINUTES OF QUARTERLY MEETING 8th mo, 27th da, 1787. [The quarterly meeting was not named.]
Joseph Morris condemns his becoming the father of an illegitimate child. John Gibbs reported for becoming the father of an illegitimate child and removing without a certificate. Elizabeth Warrick late Forman reported for being guilty of unchaste behavior, accomplishing marriage with the assistance of a priest, neglecting meeting and deviating from plainness in dress and address. Miles Gibbs produced a certificate from Haddonfield Monthly Meeting.

3rd mo, 5th da, 1788. A certificate produced for Aaron Irvins, Ann, his wife, and six children: Aaron, Isaac, Samuel, Ann, Mary and Berkley. A certificate produced for William Henry from Chesterfield Monthly Meeting.

4th mo, 9th da, 1788. Arthur Gaunt reported for going out in marriage. Keziah Shreve produced a certificate from Woodbury Monthly Meeting. Ann Gaunt produced a certificate from Haddonfield Monthly Meeting.

5th mo, 7th da, 1788. Sarah Fox reported for leaving Friends and joining another society. John Antrim reported for going out in marriage. Abigail Shreve produced a certificate from Burlington Monthly Meeting. Elizabeth Kerlin recommended as an a minister.

6th mo, 4th da, 1788. George O'Neal produced an acknowledgement condemning his taking strong drink to excess and using abusive language. Lawrence Minor, his wife, Elizabeth, and children: Catharine, Charlotte and Rebecca received as members. Sarah Harvey, wife of Peter Harvey, and dau., Mary, received as members. Joseph Green produced a certificate from Burlington Monthly Meeting.

7th mo, 9th da, 1788. Catharine Leonard received into membership. Mary Gaunt late Stockton reported for going out in marriage. John Thorn, Jr. and Tacy, his wife, and their two children, Abraham and Diadamia, produced a certificate.

8th mo, 6th da, 1788. Mary Stevenson, a minister, died 4th mo, 4th da, 1788. and Hannah Gibbs, an elder, died 3rd mo, 3rd da, 1788. Achsah Decow produced an acknowledgement condemning her taking spirituous liquor to excess. Sarah Aarons reported for going out in marriage. Titus Bennet produced a certificate from Concord Monthly Meeting. Mary Shinn produced a certificate from Chesterfield Monthly Meeting.

9th mo, 3rd da, 1788. Abigail Shreve, wife of John Shreve, requested that her son Joseph, an infant, be received into membership.

10th mo, 8th da, 1788. Samuel Ivins granted a certificate to Falls Monthly Meeting on account of marriage. George Holloway disowned for not taking proper care of his creditors.

11th mo, 5th da, 1788. Lettice Renior reported for being guilty of unchaste behavior, going out in marriage and neglecting meeting. Clayton Decow produced a certificate from Burlington Monthly Meeting. Jonathan Curtis informed meeting that a certificate will be brought at next meeting. Thomas Lawrie to present a certificate at the next month.

12th mo, 3rd da, 1788. Isaac Horner, his wife, and son, Joseph, received into membership. Caleb Ogborn and Ann, his wife, and children produced a certificate from Little Eggharbor Monthly Meeting. Jonathan Curtis produced a certificate from Mt. Holly Monthly Meeting. Thomas Lawrie produced a certificate from Chesterfield Monthly Meeting.

1st mo, 7th da, 1789. Thomas Wood reported for going out in marriage, married by a priest, neglecting meeting and being inconsistent with truth in his dress and address. Sarah Wardall, and her three children: Thomas, Antony and Elizabeth received into membership. A certificate requested for Thomas Newbold to Chesterfield Monthly Meeting.

2nd mo, 4th da, 1789. Job Harvey produced acknowledgment condemning his taking strong drink to excess. Caleb Shreve produced an acknowledgement condemning his keeping company with a young woman not of our society, leaving her without just cause and being inconsistent with truth in dress and address. Ann Elys produced an acknowledgment condemning her going out in marriage and married by a priest. Joseph Satterthwaite granted a certificate to Burlington Monthly Meeting on account of marriage. Edith Gaskill appointed as an elder. A certificate to John Forman to Middletown Monthly Meeting in Bucks County granted.

3rd mo, 4th da, 1789. Samuel Bunting reported for going out in marriage and married by a priest. Margaret Donaldson received into membership. A certificate produced for Ann Ivins, wife of Samuel Ivins, from Falls Monthly Meeting, PA, accepted.

4th mo, 8th da, 1789. John Black produced an acknowledgment condemning his making use of spirituous liquor to excess. John Haines produced a certificate from Little Eggharbor Monthly Meeting.

5th mo, 6th da, 1789. Daniel Offley produced a certificate from Philadelphia Southern District Monthly Meeting. Sarah Reeves granted a certificate to Mt. Holly Monthly Meeting. Samuel Fox reported for being the father of an illegitimate child and going out in marriage. A certificate produced for Thomas Lawrie and Mary Newbold, wife of Thomas Newbold, from Chesterfield Monthly Meeting. A certificate produced from Burlington Monthly Meeting for Elizabeth Satterthwaite, wife of Joseph Satterthwaite. A certificate for Achsah Warren from Mt. Holly Monthly Meeting.

6th mo, 3rd da, 1789. Isaac Davis reported for neglecting meeting, going out in marriage, taking spirituous drink to excess and using unbecoming language. A certificate granted for John Ely to Chesterfield Monthly Meeting. Reuben Gibbs granted a certificate to Fairfax Monthly Meeting, VA.

7th mo, 8th da, 1789. Joseph Parker reported for neglecting meeting and going out in marriage. Edward Parker reported for neglecting meeting, going out in marriage and married by a priest. A certificate produced for Charles Jones and Mary, his wife, from Evesham Monthly Meeting. A certificate produced for William Borden and Tacy, his wife, and their dau., Sarah from Chesterfield Monthly Meeting. Nicholas Buzby produced a certificate from Burlington Monthly Meeting.

8th mo, 5th da, 1789. John Cowperthwaite received into membership.

9th mo, 9th da, 1789. Jane Curtis reported for going out in marriage.

10th mo, 7th da, 1789. Job Ridgway reported for neglecting meeting, striking a man in anger and taking strong drink to excess. Joseph Murfin produced a certificate from Chesterfield Monthly Meeting.

11th mo, 4th da, 1789. Certificates granted for Keziah Shreve to West Monthly Meeting, and Joseph Morris to Burlington Monthly Meeting. A certificate granted for Joseph Bullock, Jr., his wife,

Lydia, and three children: Mary, Susannah and Lydia to
Chesterfield Monthly Meeting. A certificate produced for Mary
Tylor, dau. of Samuel Tylor, from Chesterfield Monthly Meeting
received. Joseph Green's acknowledgement accepted.

12th mo, 8th da, 1789. Sarah Folwell reported for going out in
marriage. A certificate produced for Mary Allen from New Yolk
Monthly Meeting. A certificate granted for Ann Kirby to Evesham
Monthly Meeting. A certificate granted for Thomas Antrim to
Chesterfield Monthly Meeting.

3rd mo, 2nd da, 1790 Isaac Bunting reported for going out in
marriage. Barzella Newbold Jr. reported for going out in
marriage. Edith Lawren granted a certificate to Chesterfield
Monthly Meeting.

3rd mo, 3rd da, 1790 A certificate granted for Joseph Green and
Ephraim Pittman, a minor, to Burlington Monthly Meeting. Joel
Gibbs reported for going out in marriage, striking a man in anger
and being inconsistent to truth in dress and address. John Corlis
produced a certificate from Shrewsbury Monthly Meeting.

6th mo, 9th da, 1790 Elizabeth Nutt and children, Edward and Ann,
received into membership. Deborah Harrison reported for
neglecting meeting and having an illegitimate child. Eliakim
Willets produced a certificate for himself and Phebe, his wife,
and three children: David, Elizabeth and Mary from Burlington
Monthly Meeting. Certificates produced for Christian Wilson,
Abigail Wilson and Sarah Haines from Burlington Monthly Meeting.
A certificate produced for Hannah Dawson from Chesterfield
Monthly Meeting.

7th mo, 7th da, 1790 A certificate produced for Huldah Chapman
from Chesterfield Monthly Meeting.

8th da, 8th mo, 1790 Samuel Satterthwaite elder, died 9th mo,
20th da, 1789. and Mary Newbold, elder died 10th mo, 20th da,
1789. Rebekah Perkins reported for going out in marriage. A
certificate produced for Lydia William from Burlington Monthly
Meeting.

9th mo, 8th da, 1790. Amos Ellis received into membership.
Elizabeth Taylor, wife of John Taylor, received into membership
with her three children: Daniel, Robert and Charles. A
certificate produced for Amy Colley, wife of Samuel Colley, from
Chesterfield Monthly Meeting.

11th mo, 3rd da, 1790. Leah Burr's acknowledgement accepted.

12th mo, 10th da, 1790. William Chapman produced a certificate
from Chesterfield Monthly Meeting.

5th mo, 1st da, 1791. John Taylor produced a certificate from
Chesterfield Monthly Meeting.

3rd mo, 9th da, 1791. Job Kirby produced an acknowledgment condemning his marrying contrary to Friends. Caleb Sattergood reported for being guilty of fornication, horse racing and keeping unprofitable company. Sarah Gibbs produced a certificate from Haddonfield Monthly Meeting. A certificate granted for Mary Shinn to Chesterfield Monthly Meeting. Richard Burdsall and Elizabeth Nutt declare their intentions of marriage; but, he not having a certificate from the Monthly Meeting he belongs, the case is referred to the yearly meeting.

4th mo, 6th da, 1791. John Wright, his wife, Achsah, and three children: John, Mary and Elisha received into membership. Joseph Stockton reported for going out in marriage. Taunt Gibbs granted a certificate to Evesham Monthly Meetingon account of marriage. William Newbold granted a certificate to Middletown Monthly Meeting on account of marriage. Richard Burdsall and Elizabeth Nutt again declare their intentions of marriage, his mother, being present consenting. Richard Burdsall produced a certificate from Little Eggharbor Monthly Meeting.

5th mo, 4th da, 1791. Edward Robbins and wife's acknowledgment condemning their becoming parents of a child too soon after marriage accepted. William Lawrie reported for being the father of a illegitimate child and going out in marriage with another woman. Josiah Woodward reported for being guilty of fornication and neglecting meeting. Rachel and Ann Wilson received into membership. Samuel Warren produced an acknowledgement condemning his marrying by a priest. Marriage of Richard Burdall and Elizabeth Nutt accomplished.

6th mo, 8th da, 1791. A certificate produced for Hannah Ridgway from Mt. Holly Monthly Meeting. Gersham Shreve reported for taking spirituous drink to excess, unnecessary frequenting of taverns and keeping unprofitable company. John Black and Mary, his wife, received into membership.

7th mo, 6th da, 1791. Thomas Wilson and his six children: Thomas, Sarah, Hannah, William, Lydia and Elizabeth received into membership.

8th mo, 3rd da, 1791. John Rogers and Catharine, his wife, reported for going out in marriage, she being his former wife's brother's widow. A certificate granted for Samuel Newbold to Burlington Monthly Meeting on account of marriage. A certificate produced for Hannah Newbold and John Furman from Middletown Monthly Meeting. A certificate produced for Daniel Ridgway from Burlington Monthly Meeting.

9th mo, 7th da, 1791. Joseph Brown reported for going out in marriage and neglecting meeting. Asher Brown reported going out in marriage, neglecting meeting, concerned in military services and marrying a second wife while the first is living.

10th mo, 5th da, 1791. Sarah Clevenger and Sarah Bond received into membership.

11th mo, 9th da, 1791. Testimony prepared for Sarah Scattergood late Antrim for going out in marriage. Certificates produced for Mary Newbold, wife of Samuel, and Silvanus Zilly from Burlington Monthly Meeting.

12th mo, 7th da, 1791. Mercy Horner produced acknowledgment condemning her going out in marriage.

1st mo, 4th da, 1792. Thomas Forman reported for going out in marriage. A certificate granted for Elizabeth Woodward, dau. Deborah, a minor, and Increase Woodward, Jr. to Chesterfield Monthly Meeting.

2nd mo, 8th da, 1792. Joseph Newbold produced an acknowledgment condemning his going out in marriage, accepted. Antrim Conaroe reported for going out in marriage. Caleb Rockhill reported for taking spirituous liquors to excess, neglecting meeting, using profane language and being concerned in horse racing.

3rd mo, 7th da, 1792. Reuben Gauntt reported for fighting and neglecting meeting. Sarah Bowne reported for going out in marriage.

5th mo, 9th da, 1792. Isaac Hutchin produced a certificate from Chesterfield Monthly Meeting. Isacher Foulke produced a certificate from Richland Monthly Meeting.

7th mo, 4th da, 1792. Anthony Sykes reported for neglecting meeting and taking spirituous liquors to excess. A certificate granted for William Henry to Falls Monthly Meeting, PA. Ebenezer Gaskill produced a certificate on behalf of himself, Esther, his wife, and two minor children, Lydia and Elizabeth, from Evesham Monthly Meeting. Peter Shin produced a certificate for himself, Grace, his wife, and four minor children: David, Hannah, Rachel and John from Mt. Holly Monthly Meeting.

8th mo, 8th da, 1792. Job Stockton reported for neglecting meeting and marrying contrary to discipline. Susannah Lishmael reported for marrying first cousin. Tallman Pimmock reported for committing fornication with his first cousin, neglecting meeting, keeping unprofitable company, deviating in dress from the discipline, frequenting places of diversion and following vain amusements. Penelope Fortenburg reported for marrying a man not in membership, he being her first cousin.

11th mo, 7th da, 1792. Elizabeth Aarons reported for going out in marriage. A certificate granted for Aaron Ivins, Ann, his wife, and four minor children: Samuel, Ann, Mary and Berkly to the Falls Monthly Meeting, PA. Mary Wright produced a certificate from Evesham Monthly Meeting.

12th mo, 5th da, 1792. Joseph Lamb, Jr. reported for neglecting meeting and suing a Friend at law. Mary Rockhill late Davis reported for neglecting meeting and going out in marriage. Caleb Shreve granted a certificate to Horsham Monthly Meeting.

1st mo, 9th da, 1793. Margaret Lawrence reported for neglecting meeting and going out in marriage.

2nd mo, 6th da, 1793. George Craft produced a certificate from Burlington Monthly Meeting.

3rd mo, 6th da, 1793. Elizabeth Henry produced a certificate from Chesterfield Monthly Meeting. Joseph Green produced a certificate from Burlington Monthly Meeting. James Stevenson produced an acknowledgement condemning his striking a man in anger.

4th mo, 5th da, 1793. Ann Gauntt produced a certificate from Eggharbor Monthly Meeting. John Gauntt and Jane, his wife, Mary Gaunt, Phebe Gaunt and Samuel Gauntt all produced certificates from Eggharbor Monthly Meeting. Joseph Sharpless produced a certificate from Philadelphia Northern District and George Craft produced one from Burlington Monthly Meeting.

5th mo, 8th da, 1793. Isaac and William Gaskill reported for having unchaste behavior with ones who are now their wives. a certificate produced Achsah Decow and children: Mary, Joseph and Clayton from Chesterfield Monthly Meeting. A certificate produced for Sarah Curtis and children, Tilton and Achsah, from Chesterfield Monthly Meeting.

6th mo, 5th da, 1793. A certificate produced for Joseph Southwich and Phebe, his wife, and three children: Mary, Samuel and Peter from Mt. Holly Monthly Meeting. Taunton Gibbs reported for unchaste behavior with a woman that is now his wife and neglecting meeting. Joseph Forsyth produced a certificate from Chesterfield Monthly Meeting. Meribah Branson late Davis reported for going out in marriage. John Wright produced and condemning his taking drink to excess and striking a man in anger.

7th mo, 5th da, 1793. William Borden reported for neglecting meeting and using profane language. William Wilson, Jr. reported for neglecting meeting, using profane language, horse racing and leaving his father's house in a disreputable manner, he being a minor. Deborah Watkins reported for going out in marriage. Frances Pitman produced a certificate from Evesham Monthly Meeting. Abraham Tilton produced a certificate from Chesterfield Monthly Meeting.

9th mo, 4th da, 1793. Thomas Parker produced a certificate from Ulwchland Monthly Meeting. Rachel Lund produced a certificate from Wilmington Monthly Meeting.

10th mo, 9th da, 1793. William Elis produced an acknowledgement condemning his guilt of fornication.

11th mo, 6th da, 1793. Caleb Newbold reported for being guilty of fornication and neglecting meeting.

1st mo, 8th da, 1793. Sarah Shinn reported for having an unlawful child. Mary Shinn, wife of Caleb Shinn, requested membership.

Joshua Scattergood reported for frequenting taverns. Barzailla Barton reported for frequenting taverns, horse racing, fox hunting and attending a place of training for military service. Stacy Lipincott produced an acknowledgement of guilt of unchaste behavior and marrying contrary to discipline.

2nd mo, 5th da, 1794. Charlotte Biddle, wife of Thomas Biddle, produced a certificate.

3rd mo, 5th da, 1794. Mary Shinn received into membership. Caleb Shinn produced a certificate from Burlington Monthly Meeting.

4th mo, 9th da, 1794. Joshua Scattergood reported for frequenting taverns, attending horse racing, foxhunting and, at times, taking strong drink to excess. Abraham Wilson reported for marrying contrary to a woman not in membership and having a child too soon after marriage. Marriage of Benjamin Satterthwaite and Sarah Haines accomplished. John English requested a certificate to Burlington Monthly Meeting. Rebecca Moon late Brown reported for having an unlawful child, marrying to a man not in membership with us and neglecting meeting.

4th mo, 7th da, 1794. Mary Haines produced a certificate from Haddonfield Monthly Meeting. Joseph Allen testified against for fighting unnecessarily, frequenting a tavern and being inconsistent in religious principals; disowned.

6th mo, 4th da, 1794. Hannah Van late Ridgway reported for marrying to a man not in membership with us and having a child too soon after marriage.

7th mo, 9th da, 1794. Joseph Ogborn, a minor, received by a certificate from Little Eggharbor Monthly Meeting. Caleb Shreve produced a certificate from Horsham Monthly Meeting. Joseph Willets reported for neglecting meeting, keeping unprofitable company and taking strong drink to excess. Huldah Chapman complains of Isaac Wright for neglecting to fulfill his contract; he has since moved from the limit of our meeting without applying for a certificate.

8th mo, 6th da, 1794. Henry Ridgway, Mary, his wife and six children: Samuel, Solomon, Elizabeth, Mary, Sarah and Rebecca produced a certificate from Burlington Monthly Meeting. Eben Decow reported for neglecting meeting, keeping unprofitable company, frequenting taverns and attending a place of training for military.

9th mo, 3rd da, 1794. Joseph Willits reported for neglecting meeting, keeping unprofitable company and taking strong drink to excess. Thomas Ridgway produced a certificate from Evesham

Monthly Meeting. Joshua Gibbs, Mary, his wife, and children, Hannah and Rebecca, produced a certificate from Burlington Monthly Meeting. Ann Sherod late Curtis reported for going out in marriage to one not a Friend. Unity Meirs late Shinn produced an acknowledgement condemning her marrying contrary to discipline.

10th mo, 8th da, 1794. John Forman and Ruth formerly Gaskill, his wife, reported for marrying contrary to discipline, having a child too soon after marriage, deviating from friends principles and neglecting meeting. Asa Branson reported for neglecting meeting and marrying contrary to discipline to a woman who is a distant relation.

11th mo, 5th da, 1794. Miriam Woodmancy produced a certificate for herself and three children: William, Sille and Anne from Shrewsbury Monthly Meeting. Sarah Scattergood late Forman reported for accomplishing marriage by an hireling minister, neglecting meeting and inconsistent dress and address with our principles.

12th mo, 3rd da, 1794. Israel Jones reported for neglecting meeting, being concerned with horse racing and marrying out to a woman not a Friend. Rhoda Dawson produced a certificate from Chesterfield Monthly Meeting.

2nd mo, 4th da, 1795. Ann Kirby, wife of Empson Kirby, reported for neglecting meeting and joining another society. Achsah Tolhamous late Kirby reported for going out in marriage to a man not of us and marrying by a hireling preacher.

6th mo, 5th da, 1795. A certificate produced for Elizabeth English from Mt. Holly Monthly Meeting.

6th mo, 3rd da, 1795. Frances Wright produced a certificate from Evesham Monthly Meeting. Edward Rockhill requested a certificate for himself and wife, Grace, to Burlington Monthly Meeting. Sarah Decow requested a certificate for her son, William Decow, a minor, to Monthly Meeting of New York. A certificate granted for William French, his wife, Rachel, and children: John, William, Mahlon, Amos and Rachel to Philadelphia Northern District Monthly Meeting.

5th mo, 6th da, 1795. Isaac Wright expressed sorrow for his breach of good order in removing without a certificate now requested a certificate to Chesterfield Monthly Meeting. Ann Kirby, wife of Empson Kirby, disowned for joining another society. Susannah Clayton produced an acknowledgement condemning her going out in marriage with a man not in membership.

6th mo, 3rd da, 1795. Joshua Woodward reported for neglecting meeting, training in a military way and fighting. A certificate produced for Frances Wright from Evesham Monthly Meeting.

7th mo, 8th da, 1795. William Decow granted a certificate to New York Monthly Meeting. Jonathan Steward reported for neglecting meeting and marrying to a woman not of our religious society. Rebecca Wright produced a certificate from Evesham Monthly Meeting. Job Shreve, Elizabeth, his wife, and four children: Abigail, Job, Elizabeth and Thomas produced a certificate from Salem Monthly Meeting. Unity Everham produced a certificate from Mt. Holly Monthly Meeting.

8th mo, 5th da, 1795. Hannah Gaunt died 6th mo, 13th da, 1794. age nearly age 69. Thompson Wright granted a certificate to Rahway Monthly Meeting. Joseph English produced an acknowledgement condemning his being in the practice of frequenting taverns, fox hunting and horse racing.

9th mo, 9th da, 1795. David Branson Jr., wife, Sarah, and two sons, Stacy and Samuel, produced a certificate from Haddonfield Monthly Meeting. Caleb Shreve Sr. granted a certificate to marry Margaret Donaldson of Philadelphia Southern District Monthly Meeting. Rebecca Hall late Harrison reported for marrying a man not in membership with us. Mariam Burtis late Shinn reported marrying a man not in membership with us and going out in marriage. Achsah Stevenson late Branson reported same as Mariam Burtis.

10th mo, 7th da, 1795. Anne Carter produced a certificate from Mt. Holly Monthly Meeting.

11th mo, 5th da, 1795. Jonathan Steward reported for neglecting meeting and marrying contrary to discipline. The daughter, an infant, of Unity Everham received into membership. John Woodward requested a certificate on account of marriage to Mt. Holly Monthly Meeting. John Newbold produced a certificate from Philadelphia Monthly Meeting. Henry Ridgway reported for neglecting meeting, fighting and voluntarily paying a tax in lieu of personal service in the militia.

12th mo, 9th da, 1795. Caleb Newbold produced an acknowledgement condemning his guilt of fornication and neglecting meeting. Jethro Woodward reported for fighting, attending a place of training for military service and neglecting meeting; disowned. Rebecca Hall reported for marrying contrary to discipline. John E. Wood granted a certificate on account of marriage to Mt. Holly. Phebe Dennis late Woodward reported going out in marriage with a man not a member, being a first cousin.

1st mo, 6th da, 1796. Caleb Shreve granted a certificate to Philadelphia Northern District Monthly Meeting.

2nd mo, 3rd da, 1796. Margaret Lawrence late Shinn reported for marrying a man not of our society. Henry Ridgway reported for neglecting meeting, fighting and paying a tax in lieu of personal service.

3rd mo, 9th da, 1796. Elizabeth Newbold, wife of John Newbold, granted a certificate to Philadelphia Northern District Monthly Meeting. Sarah Gaskill granted a certificate to Chesterfield

Monthly Meeting. Silvenus Zilly granted a certificate to Mt. Holly Monthly Meeting on account of marriage. Edward Bullock produced a certificate from Falls Monthly Meeting. Thomas Sykes requested to be released from the station of an overseer, granted.

4th mo, 6th da, 1796. John Barton reported for neglecting meeting and marrying a woman not in membership. Susanna Brown late Stevenson reported for being guilty of fornication and marrying a man not a member of our society.

5th mo, 4th da, 1796. Testimony presented against Susanna Brown for being guilty of fornication with a man she has since married who is not a member of our society. Joseph Pope reported for removing without a certificate, accomplishing his marriage contrary to discipline and unchaste freedom before marriage with the woman now his wife. Richard Waln, the recorder, appointed to record all births and burials. Rebecca Harrison late Waln reported for marrying a man not of our society by the assistance of an hireling teacher, being inconsistent in her dress and address and neglecting meeting. Hannah Heatton late Dawson reported for neglecting meetings. Leah English late Elis reported for marrying contrary to discipline. A certificate granted for Elizabeth Wright, wife of David Wright, and her dau., Mary, a minor, to Chesterfield Monthly Meeting. Jonathan Wright appointed to the station of an elder.

6th mo, 8th da, 1796. Aaron Barton produced an acknowledgement condemning his paying a tax in lieu of personal service in the militia. Testimony against John Barton for neglecting meeting and marrying a woman not of our society was approved. A certificate produced for Amy French from Haddonfield Monthly Meeting. A certificate was produced for Ann Forsythe and her dau., Ann, a minor, from Chesterfield Monthly Meeting. A certificate was produced for Rebecca Woodward from Mt. Holly Monthly Meeting.

7th mo, 6th da, 1796. Joseph Pope reported for marrying contrary to discipline and unchaste freedom before marriage with the woman now his wife. Titus Bennett produced an acknowledgement condemning his paying a tax or fine in lieu of personal military service. Sarah Middleton late Shinn reported for accomplishing her marriage contrary to discipline and becoming a mother sooner than was reputable after marriage. A certificate was produced for Rebecca Kirby from Chesterfield Monthly Meeting.

8th mo, 3rd da, 1796. Uz Gaunt produced an acknowledgement condemning his deviating from our religious principles in paying a fine in lieu of personal military service. A certificate was produced for John Emly and Hannah, his wife, from the Kingwood Monthly Meeting. Samuel Stockton reported for neglecting meeting, taking strong drink to excess and paying a tax in lieu of service in the military.

9th mo, 7th da, 1796. Esasias Lamb reported for taking strong drink to excess, neglecting meeting and marrying contrary to discipline. Susanna Lamb late Warren reported for accomplishing her marriage contrary to discipline. Thomas Sykes requested a certificate to Philadelphia Monthly Meeting. Asa Pointsit requested to be joined in membership. Isaac Barton produced an acknowledgment not being satisfactory to meeting returned to him. Abigail Haines produced a certificate from Mt. Holly Monthly Meeting. Elizabeth Saxton late Shinn reported for accomplishing her marriage by the assistance of an hireling teacher. Elizabeth Lamb late Gibbs reported for marrying the man that was formerly her half sister's husband.

10th mo, 5th da, 1796. A certificate was granted for Daniel Ridgway to Burlington Monthly Meeting. Susanna Antrim produced a certificate from Chesterfield Monthly Meeting. William Newbold appointed as overseer.

11th mo, 9th da, 1796. William Forman informs the meeting that he declined having a certificate and acknowledged he expected shortly to marry a woman not of our society. A certificate was produced for Rachel Kerby from Chesterfield Monthly Meeting. A certificate was produced for Edward Rockhill and wife, Grace, from Burlington Monthly Meeting. John Corlass reported for leaving his master's service before the expiration of his apprenticeship, without sufficient reason and in a disreputable manner.

1st mo, 4th da, 1797. A certificate was produced for Elizabeth Bunting from Chesterfield Monthly Meeting. A certificate was granted for Mahlon Wright to Philadelphia Monthly Meeting.

2nd mo, 8th da, 1797. Samuel Stockton, Jr. reported for neglecting meeting, marrying contrary to discipline, paying a military fine in lieu of personal service and taking strong drink to excess. Joseph Harris reported for neglecting meeting and marrying contrary to discipline. A certificate was produced for Ann Stewart from Pilesgrove Monthly Meeting which was not quite explicit nor satisfactory.

3rd mo, 8th da, 1797. Samuel Stockton and wife disowned. Ann Stewart's certificate accepted. A certificate was produced for James Brown and Elijah Brown, a minor, from Chesterfield Monthly Meeting.

4th mo, 5th da, 1797. Testimony against Joseph Harris and wife to be prepared. Nathan Rockhill reported for accomplishing his marriage contrary to discipline and taking strong drink to excess. Memorial prepared for Friend, Ann Gaunt, dec'd, along with one from Little Eggharbor Monthly Meeting to be forwarded to the quarterly meeting. A certificate was produced for Eliakim Willets, Phebe, his wife, and five children: David, Elizabeth, Mary, Sarah and Ann from Burlington Monthly Meeting. A certificate was produced for Elizabeth Stewart from Pilesgrove Monthly Meeting. Isaac Forman, Jr. returned the certificate granted to Fairfax Monthly Meeting, VA without any endorsement.

5th mo, 3rd da, 1797. A certificate produced for Barzillai Gaskill from Burlington Monthly Meeting. Obediah Stockton reported for marrying contrary to discipline and is inconsistent with his dress and address with our religious profession; disowned.

6th mo, 4th da, 1797. A certificate produced for Daniel Gauntt from Chesterfield Monthly Meeting.

7th mo, 5th da, 1797. Forman Woodward produced an acknowledgment condemning his being guilty of gaming, taking strong drink to excess and marrying contrary to discipline. John Lawrie reported for neglecting meeting, using profane language and laying hold of a man in anger. Elizabeth and Hannah Waln reported for neglecting meeting, are inconsistent with dress and address in plainness and attending a marriage accomplished by an hireling teacher; both disowned. A certificate was produced for Sarah Curtis and her two children, Tilton and Achsah, from Chesterfield Monthly Meeting.

8th mo, 9th da, 1797. John Fellow received into membership. A certificate granted for Miriam Burtis to Mt. Holly Monthly Meeting returned since she intends to return to this meeting. Sara Pope appointed as minister; Joseph Saterthwaite, Elizabeth Saterthwaite and William Newbold appointed as elders. Thomas Middleton, Jr. reported for keeping unprofitable company and being guilty of fornication; disowned. A certificate was produced for James Pancoast from Philadelphia Monthly Meeting.

9th mo, 6th da, 1797. Certificates were produced for Heziah Johnson and Asa Johnson, minors, from New York Monthly Meeting. Samuel Ridgway reported for having married contrary to discipline to a woman not a member. Hudson Gaskill reported for neglecting meeting and is charged with committing fornication. Martha Scott late Scattergood reported for marrying a man not in membership with Friends; disowned. Abigail Civil late Wilson reported for accomplishing her marriage contrary to discipline and neglecting meeting.

10th mo, 4th da, 1797. William Newbold appointed clerk for the meeting and Isaac Bullock to be his assistant. A certificate was produced for William Stokes, a minor, from Burlington Monthly Meeting, information being obtained that he is placed as an apprentice to a non member.

11th mo, 8th da, 1797. Benjamin Paxson produced a certificate from Buckingham Monthly Meeting, PA.

12th mo, 6th da, 1797. Martha Scott disowned. Mary Beck requested to be received into membership. Testimony against Hudson Gaskill was read and approved. Testimony against Thomas Havens for marrying contrary to discipline to a non member of our society was approved. A certificate for John Pancoast to Chesterfield Monthly Meeting to marry Ann Abbott was granted.

1st mo, 3rd da, 1798. A certificate granted for Rachel Paxson, wife of Benjamin Paxson, to Buckingham Monthly Meeting. John Lawrie reported for neglecting meeting, using profane language and laying hold of a man in anger; disowned. A certificate produced for Samuel Taylor, a minor, from Chesterfield Monthly Meeting.

2nd mo, 7th da, 1798. Mary Beck received into membership. Elizabeth Ann Eyers requested membership.

7th mo, 3rd da, 1798. James Cooper produced a certificate from Evesham Monthly Meeting. Anthony Bullock requested a certificate on account of marriage to Chesterfield Monthly Meeting.

4th mo, 4th da, 1798. Elizabeth Ann Eyre received into membership. Robert Johnston & Co. of Philadelphia proposed printing the memoirs of the life of Catharine Phillips.

5th mo, 9th da, 1798. Samuel Pancoast reported for marrying contrary to discipline and having a child too soon after marriage than is reputable. William Wilson, his wife, Abigail and their son, Benjamin, produced a certificate from Chesterfield Monthly Meeting. William Henry produced a certificate from the Falls Monthly Meeting, PA. Rebecca Ivins late Gibbs reported for going out from amongst Friends in marriage; disowned. Ann Starkey late Nutt reported for marrying a man not of our society; disowned.

6th mo, 6th da, 1798. Samuel Clevenger produced a certificate from Chesterfield Monthly Meeting for himself, his wife and their eight minor children: Zachariah, Thomas, Urcilla, John, Rhoda, Sarah, Huldah and Samuel. Rebecca Clevenger produced a certificate from Chesterfield. Charity Cook late Antrum reported for going out in marriage to a man not in our society and neglecting meeting; disowned.

7th mo, 4th da, 1798. Thomas Shinn, Jr. reported for having married a woman not in membership with us. Solomon Shinn reported for having married a woman not in membership with us. Jonathan Davis reported for neglecting meeting and having struck a man in anger. A certificate was produced for John Field, Mercy, his wife, and their infant son, William, from Philadelphia Northern District Monthly Meeting. Ann Pancoast, wife of John Pancoast, produced a certificate from Chesterfield Monthly Meeting.

5th mo, 8th da, 1798. Jonathan Wright, an elder died 5th mo, 1st da, 1798. age 55. Thomas Shinn, Jr. produced an acknowledgement condemning his misconduct. John Gibbs reported for having married a woman not in membership with us. John Earl, Jr. reported for having attended a marriage of those in membership marrying contrary to discipline. Daniel Earl is reported for being guilty of fornication with the woman he is now married to and marrying to one not of our society. Samuel Wright reported for having deviating from our profession in administering oaths, he being a magistrate, and hath joined in marriage those that are members of our religious society; disowned.

9th mo, 5th da, 1798. Solomon Shinn produced an acknowledgement condemning his marrying out to a woman not in our membership.

10th mo, 3rd da, 1798. William Newbold appointed as clerk and Isaac Bullock appointed his assistant. Joseph Richardson produced a certificate from Middletown Monthly Meeting, PA.

11th mo, 7th da, 1798. Samuel Newbold granted a certificate to Mt. Holly Monthly Meeting on account of marriage. William Saterthwaite produced a certificate from Red Stone Monthly Meeting.

12th mo, 5th da, 1798. William Wright reported for neglecting meeting, taking spirituous liquors to excess, attending horse racing and unnecessary frequents taverns, disowned. Thomas Decow reported for neglecting meetings, taking spirituous liquors to excess, attending horse racing and concerned in military training. George Wright produced a certificate from Salem Monthly Meeting.

1st mo, 9th da, 1799. William Ellis reported for marrying contrary to discipline and being concerned with horse racing. William Black appointed to draw [record] marriage certificates within the meeting.

2nd mo, 6th da, 1799. Thomas Harris and Christian, his wife, reported for marrying contrary to discipline and neglecting meeting; disowned. Caleb Newbold granted a certificate to marry with Sarah Green at the New York Monthly Meeting.

3rd mo, 7th da, 1799. Caleb Scattergood produced an acknowledgment condemning his misconduct. Benjamin Scattergood produced an acknowledgement condemning his neglecting meeting and marrying contrary to discipline. A certificate produced for George Zilly from Burlington Monthly Meeting.

4th mo, 3rd da, 1799. The certificate for Elijah Brown has been lost before its delivery to the meeting it was directed. Abner Woodward reported for neglecting meeting, holding slaves, attending places of training for the military, horse racing and using profane language.

5th mo, 8th da, 1799. Clayton Earl reported for having married a person not of our society.

6th mo, 5th da, 1799. Samuel Stevenson produced a certificate for himself, wife, Catharine, and three minor children: Thomas M., Rebecca M. and Samuel from Chesterfield Monthly Meeting. Joseph Craft produced a certificate for himself, Hester, his wife, and their six minor children: Job, John, Thomas, Ridgway, Jesse and Elizabeth from Burlington Monthly Meeting. Abigail Earl reported for having married to her first cousin. Sarah Folwell produced an acknowledgment condemning her marrying contrary to discipline. Anna Brown reported for having an unlawful child and neglecting meeting. Sarah Scattergood produced an acknowledgement condemning her misconduct in marrying contrary to discipline. Mary Newbold, wife of Samuel Newbold, produced a certificate from Mt. Holly Monthly Meeting. Sarah Newbold, wife of Caleb Newbold, produced a certificate from New York Monthly Meeting.

2nd mo, 7th da, 1799. Christian Black produced a certificate from Evesham Monthly Meeting.

9th mo, 4th da, 1799. Joseph Williams reported for neglecting meeting and is charged by his bound girl as being the father of her unlawful child; disowned.

10th mo, ? da, 1799. Stacy Decow granted a certificate to Chesterfield Monthly Meeting. Joseph Sharpless granted a certificate to Burlington Monthly Meeting. Meribah Fowler, Jr. produced a certificate from Chesterfield Monthly Meeting. Thomas Wilson requested a certificate to Mt. Holly Monthly Meeting for himself, his wife, Ann, and three minor children.

12th mo, 3rd da, 1799. William Newbold to continue as clerk and Isaac Bullock to continue as his assistant. John Pancoast appointed treasurer; Joseph Pancoast being released as treasurer. Mathew Forsythe produced a certificate from Chesterfield Monthly Meeting. A certificate was granted for Elizabeth Bunting to Chesterfield Monthly Meeting.

1st mo, 1st da, 1800. Clayton Earl disowned. Hope Rockhill produced a certificate from Mt. Holly Monthly Meeting. Samuel Lamb reported for marrying contrary to discipline to a non-member.

UPPER EVESHAM MONTHLY MEETING
BIRTHS/DEATHS/MARRIAGES/CERTIFICATES

Children of Thomas Evans, son of William and Elizabeth Evans, b. 12th mo, 12th da, 1693, d. 2nd mo, 1788 and Esther Evans, his wife, dau. of John and Esther Haines, b. 1699, d. 12th mo, 22nd da, 1728: William Evans, b. 7th mo, 6th da, 1716, d. 5th mo, 25th da, 1761; Elizabeth Evans, b. 1st mo, 8th da, 1718; Isaac Evans, b. 11th mo, 21st da, 1720; Isaac Evans, b. 2nd mo, 18th da, 1721; Esther Evans, b. 10th mo, 6th da, 1723; Jacob Evans, b. 1st mo, 14th da, 1725; Nathan Evans, b. 2nd mo, 1727.
Children of Thomas Evans and Rebecca Evans, his second wife: Joshua Evans, b. 7th mo, 23rd da, 1731, d. 8th mo, 24th da, 1798; Cabel Evans, b. 6th mo, 26th da, 1733, d. 10th mo, 24th da, 1733; 2nd Cabel Evans, b. 12th mo, 2nd da, 1736; Jamima Evans, b. 4th mo, 1st da, 1738; Martha Evans, b. 9th mo, 16th da, 1742, d. 1st mo, 1799.

Rebecca Evans, d. 12th mo, 20th da, 1773.
William Evans m. Sarah Roberts 3rd mo, 8th da, 1730.

Jacob Borton, son of Isaac and Mary Borton, b. 6th mo, 5th da, 1777 and Jemima Borton, dau. of Isaac and Hannah Hay, b. 9th mo, 3rd da, 1782, d. 3rd mo, 2nd da, 1803 at Cropwell.

Child of Jacob Collins, son of Frances and Ann Collins, b. 6th mo, 13th da, 1752 and Mary, his first wife, dau. of Jonathan and Hannah Haines, b. 9th mo, 27th da, 1752: Sarah Collins, b. 11th mo, 15th da, 1774.
Children of Job Collins and Elizabeth, his second wife, dau. of Joshua and Naomi Ballinger, b. 11th mo, 15th da, 1755: Mary Collins, b. 8th mo, 19th da, 1780; John Collins, b. 5th mo, 31st da, 1782; Naomi Collins, b. 4th mo, 26th da, 1784; Elizabeth Collins, b. 2nd mo, 9th da, 1786, d. 9th mo, 30th da, 1796; Lydia Collins, b. 11th mo, 17th da, 1787; Josiah Collins, b. 6th mo, 18th da, 1789, d. 6th mo, 1st da, 1790; Hannah Collins, b. 9th mo, 5th da, 1792, d. 10th mo, 22nd da, 1795; Hope Collins, b. 10th mo, 7th da, 1794, d. 9th mo, 28th da, 1795; Isaac Collins, b. 7th mo, 4th da, 1797, d. 1st mo, 27th da, 1798; Ezra Collins, b. 2nd mo, 12th da, 1801, d. 8th mo, 11th da, 1825.

Sarah Collins, dau. of Job and Mary Collins, m. 3rd mo, 12th da, 1794. Samuel Thorn, removed to Haddonfield 5th mo, 10th da, 1794. Mary Collins, 1st wife of Job Collins d. 4th mo, 27th da, 1776. Job Collins and Mary Haines m. 3rd mo, 17th da, 1774. Job Collins and Elizabeth Ballinger m. 5th mo, 14th da, 1778. Mary Collins, dau. of Job and Elizabeth Collins, m. Uriah Borton, 9th mo, 12th da, 1798; removed to Evesham Monthly Meeting 12th mo, 6th da, 1798. Naomi Collins, dau. of Job and Elizabeth Collins, m. Isaac Roberts. Lydia Collins, dau. of Job and Elizabeth Collins, m. Isaac Stokes, 10th mo, 18th da, 1809. Elizabeth Collins, 2nd wife of Job Collins, d. 2nd mo, 1st da, 1831 at Upper Evesham.

Children of Thomas Lippincott, son of Caleb and Hannah Lippincott, b. 3rd mo, 24th da, 1754, d. 6th mo, 24th da, 1826 at Cropwell, and Rachel, his wife, dau. of John and Mary Haines, b. 5th mo, 13th da, 1759, d. 9th mo, 9th da, 1817 at Cropwell: Joshua Lippincott, b. 7th mo, 24th da, 1780; Ahab Lippincott, b. 2nd mo, 26th da, 1782; Hannah Lippincott, b. 3rd mo, 8th da, 1784; Mary Lippincott, b. 3rd mo, 29th da, 1786; Beulah Lippincott, b. 10th mo, 16th da, 1788; Hope Lippincott, 10th mo, 16th da, 1788; Esther Lippincott, b. 2nd mo, 19th da, 1792; Thomas Lippincott, b. 8th mo, 9th da, 1794; Caleb Lippincott, b. 10th mo, 24th da, 1801.

Ahab Lippincott m. Mary Wills; Hannah Lippincott m. John Collins; Beulah Lippincott m. Mahlon Stacy Atkinson; Hope Lippincott m. Caleb Haines of Chesterfield Monthly Meeting.

Children of Jonathan Jones, son of William and Elizabeth Jones, b. 3rd mo, 25th da, 1749. Mary Jones, wife of Jonathan Jones, dau. of Rowland and Prudence Owen, b. 9th mo, 8th da, 1756: William Jones, b. 5th mo, 17th da, 1776; Elizabeth Jones, b. 10th mo, 4th da, 1780; Jesse Jones, b. 10th mo, 6th da, 1782; Owen Jones, b. 2nd mo, 4th da, 1787; Sarah Jones, b. 5th mo, 27th da, 1789; Hannah Jones, b. 5th mo, 27th da, 1797.

Elizabeth Jones m. Caleb Clothier 3rd mo, 13th da, 1800. Jonathan and Mary Jones removed to Maurice River Monthly Meeting 4th mo, 8th da, 1809; Elizabeth Jones removed to Mount Holly Monthly Meeting 8th mo, 10th da, 1800; Jesse Jones removed to Haddonfield Monthly Meeting 8th mo, 3rd da, 1794; Owen Jones removed to Greenwich Monthly Meeting 5th mo, 7th da, 1803; Hannah Jones removed to Maurice Monthly Meeting 4th mo, 8th da, 1809. William Jones disowned 4th mo, 12th da, 1800.

Children of John Haines, Jr., son of John and Mary Haines, b. 11th mo, 26th da, 1765, d. 10th mo, 4th da, 1822 at Cropwell Monthly Meeting and Elizabeth, his wife, dau. of Benjamin and Mary Moore, b. 5th mo, 2nd da, 1767: Benjamin Haines, b. 9th mo, 22nd da, 1793; Keturah Haines, b. 2nd mo, 1st da, 1795; Reuben Haines, b. 12th mo, 13th da, 1796; Mary Haines, b. 10th mo, 25th da, 1798; Rachel Haines, b. 10th mo, 16th da, 1800; John M. Haines, b. 9th mo, 14th da, 1802; Bethuel Haines, b. 5th mo, 14th da, 1815; Rebecca and Chalkley Haines, twins, b. 7th mo, 7th da, 1808.

John Haines and Elizabeth Moore m. 1st mo, 17th da, 1793. Rachel Haines m. Reuben Roberts; John M. Haines m. Sarah Evans.

Children of William Evans, son of Thomas and Esther Evans, b. 7th mo, 6th da, 1716, d. 5th mo, 25th da, 1761 and Sarah Evans, formerly Roberts, b. 11th mo, 2nd da, 1719: John Evans, b. 2nd mo, 8th da, 1739; Hannah Evans, b. 3rd mo, 30th da, 1740; Enoch Evans, b. 2nd mo, 27th da, 1743; Esther Evans, b. 1st mo, 12th da, 1745; Mary Evans, b. 2nd mo, 24th da, 1748; Rebecca Evans, b. 6th mo, 19th da, 1753; Deborah Evans, b. 11th mo, 13th da, 1755; Sarah Evans, b. 3rd mo, 23rd da, 1758; William Evans, b.

10th mo, 5th da, 1760.

Hannah Evans, m. James Eldrdige; Enoch Evans m. Mary Wilcox; Esther Evans m. Thomas Wilkins; Mary Evans m. Joseph Morgan; Rebecca Evans m. Isaac Andrews; Sarah Evans m. Jabez Buzby; William Evans m. Rachel Ballinger.

Children of Enoch Evans, son of William and Sarah Evans, b. 2nd mo, 27th da, 1743 and Mary Evans, dau. of Joseph and Sarah Wilcox, b. 8th mo, 29th da, 1753, d. 3rd mo, 21st da, 1785: Joseph Evans, b. 12th mo, 7th da, 1770, d. 12th mo, 17th da, 1770; John Evans, b. 2nd mo, 17th da, 1774; Lydia Evans, b. 11th mo, 17th da, 1777; Joel Evans, b. 2nd mo, 16th da, 1780; Thomas Evans, b. 3rd mo, 6th da, 1783; Elizabeth Evans, no date.

Enoch Evans and Mary Wilcox m. 11th mo, 16th da, 1769; John Evans m. Rebecca Cowperthwaite, 2nd mo, 12th da, 1799; Lydia Evans m. Joshua Stokes; Thomas Evans m. Abigail Bispham, removed to Haddonfield Monthly Meeting; Elizabeth Evans, 2nd wife m. Enoch Evans 4th mo, 12th da, 1787.

Children of Solomon Haines, son of Carlisle and Sarah Haines, b. 1st mo, 25th da, 1728 and Rebecca Haines, fist wife, dau. of William and Rebecca Sharp, b. 9th mo, 2nd da, 1730, d. 8th mo, 17th da, 1781: Rachel Haines, b. 4th mo, 16th da, 1750, d. 5th mo, 6th mo, 1771; Levi Haines, b. 8th mo, 4th da, 1752; Rebecca Haines, b. 7th mo, 30th da, 1754, d. 8th mo, 15th da, 1789; Solomon Haines, b. 11th mo, 13th da, 1756, d. 9th mo, 1760; Phebe Haines, b. 5th mo, 26th da, 1759; Jesse Haines, b. 8th mo, 21st da, 1761; Ruth Haines, b. 12th mo, 7th da, 1764, d. 7th mo, 23rd da, 1766; Jane Haines, b. 12th mo, 7th da, 1767; Carlisle Haines, b. 5th mo, 14th da, 1767; William Haines, b. 10th mo, 4th da, 1772, d. 11th mo, 15th da, 1783; Sarah Haines, b. 8th mo, 18th da, 1776.

Child of Solomon and Mercy Haines, his second wife, formerly Collins: Elizabeth Haines; b. 9th mo, 2nd da, 1783.

Solomon Haines and Rachel, dau. of Jonathan and Jane Gaskill, his third wife, b. 11th mo, 18th da, 1739 m. in 12th mo, 13th da, 1797. Mercy Haines, formerly Collins m. 9th mo, 1782. Rachel Haines, dau. of Jonathan and Jane Gaskill, m. 12th mo, 13th da, 1797. Mercy Haines, wife of Solomon Haines, d. 9th mo, 24th da, 1793 at Upper Evesham. Rachel Haines, wife of Solomon Haines, d. 2nd mo, 27th da, 1812 at Upper Evesham Monthly Meeting. Jane Haines m. Joshua Sharp at Evesham Monthly Meeting. Sarah Haines m. Josiah Austin at Evesham Monthly Meeting.

John Haines, son of Carlisle and Sarah Haines, b. 9th mo, 15th da, 1742 married to Martha Haines, dau. of Habakkuk and Mary Eyre, b. 9th mo, 19th da, 1748: Mary Haines, b. 10th mo, 27th da, 1767; Esther Haines, b. 6th mo, 24th da, 1781.

Mary Haines m. Core Haines. Esther Haines m. Isaac Ballinger 5th mo, 22nd da, 1799 at Evesham.

Children of Josiah Foster, Sr., son of William and Hannah Foster, b. 5th mo, 20th da, 1743, and Rachel Foster, dau. of Henry and Marge Burr, b. 6th mo, 6th da, 1743: Hannah Foster, b. 8th mo, 7th da, 1768; Mary Foster, b. 8th mo, 17th da, 1770; Rebecca Foster, b. 11th mo, 24th da, 1772; Lydia Foster, b. 11th mo, 17th da, 1775; Rachel Foster, b. 12th mo, 9th da, 1778.

Hannah Foster m. Edmund Hollingshead at Evesham Monthly Meeting. Mary Foster m. Samuel Clements, at Haddonfield Monthly Meeting. Rebecca Foster m. David Jones, 9th mo, 13th da, 1797, removed to Northern District Philadelphia Monthly Meeting 11th mo, 11th da, 1797. Lydia Foster m. Richard Sheppard, 10th mo, 11th da, 1797, removed to Greenwich 2nd mo, 10th da, 1798.

Children of Job Prickett, b. 6th mo, 24th da, 1744, d. and Ann, his wife, dau. of Thomas and Elizabeth Smith, b. 2nd mo, 27th da, 1749: Rachel Prickett, b. 11th mo, 5th da, 1770; Sabillah Prickett, b. 9th mo, 9th da, 1772; Josiah Prickett, b. 9th mo, 29th da, 1775, d. 7th mo, 10th da, 1778; Job Prickett, b. 7th mo, 9th da, 1777; Josiah Prickett, b. 2nd mo, 25th da, 1779; Barzillai Prickett, b. 2nd mo, 20th da, 1781; Ann Prickett, b. 2nd mo, 13th da, 1782; Zachariah Prickett, b. 1st mo, 4th da, 1784; Stacy Prickett, b. 10th mo, 14th da, 1785; John Prickett, b. 5th mo, 28th da, 1787; Elizabeth Prickett, b. 7th mo, 9th da, 1789, d. 1st mo, 26th da, 1789 at Upper Evesham.

Job Prickett and Ann Smith, m. 3rd mo, 30th da, 1769; Sabillah Prickett m. James Allen; Josiah Prickett m. Ann Huff, disowned 6th mo, 8th da, 1799; Barzillai Prickett m. Ann Sharpe, disowned;. Zachariah Prickett m. Martha Haines, removed; Ann Prickett m. Allen Joyce.

Children of Jonathan Stratton, son of Daniel and Mary Stratton, b. 3rd mo, 6th da, 1741 and Sarah, his wife, dau. of Rowland and Prudence Arren, b. 3rd mo, 14th da, 1742, m. 11th mo, 16th da, 1763: Job Stratton, b. 3rd mo, 9th da, 1765; Eber Stratton, b. 9th mo, 10th da, 1766, d. 8th mo, 17th da, 1777 at Upper Eve; Aaren Stratton, b. 5th mo, 16th da, 1769; Noah Stratton, b. 10th mo, 25th da, 1770, disowned 10th mo, 10th da, 1795; Eli Stratton, b. 12th mo, 20th da, 1772; Jonathan Stratton, b. 11th mo, 14th da, 1775; Prudence Stratton, b. 10th mo, 25th da, 1778; Caleb Stratton, b. 7th mo, 10th da, 1781; William Stratton, b. 6th mo, 19th da, 1783; Naomi Stratton, b. 3rd mo, 18th da, 1786.

Eli Stratton removed to Greenwich, 12th mo, 10th da, 1796.

Joshua Peacock, son of John and Susannah Peacock, b. 11th mo, 22nd da, 1758 and Ann Peacock, his 1st wife, dau. of Amos and Deborah Sharp, b. 8th mo, 26th da, 1754, d. 5th mo, 31st da, 1786, m. at Haddonfield 1st mo, 14th da, 1784. Joshua Peacock and Hannah Griffin m. 1st mo, 13th da, 1788 at Haddonfield.

Child of Joshua and Ann Peacock: Joseph Peacock, b. 8th mo, 23rd da, 1784.

Hannah Peacock, 2nd wife of Joshua Peacock, dau. of Jonathan and Hannah Griffin, b. 7th mo, 7th da, 1762: William Peacock, b. 12th mo, 17th da, 1788; Susannah Peacock, b. 6th mo, 19th da, 1791, d. 5th mo, 23rd da, 1797; Ann Peacock, b. 3rd mo, 26th da, 1793, d. 5th mo, 23rd da, 1797; Elizabeth Peacock, b. 1st mo, 8th da, 1797; Anna Peacock, b. 12th mo, 30th da, 1802.

Children of Joshua Stratton, son of Daniel and Mary, b. 11th mo, 28th da, 1739 and Elizabeth Stratton, dau. of Michael and Elizabeth Branin, b. 10th mo, 8th da, 1735: Lydia Stratton, b. 1st mo, 9th da, 1762; Phebe Stratton, b. 2nd mo, 12th da, 1763; Aaron Stratton, b. 9th mo, 16th da, 1764; Michael Stratton, b. 1st mo, 6th da, 1766; Ann Stratton, b. 2nd mo, 19th da, 1768; Asa Stratton, b. 11th mo, 16th da, 1769; Daniel Stratton, b. 7th mo, 29th da, 1771; Mary Stratton, b. 12th mo, 21st da, 1772; Stacy Stratton, b. 9th mo, 3rd da, 1774; Elizabeth Stratton, b. 9th mo, 21st da, 1776; John Stratton, b. 11th mo, 17th da, 1778.

Asa Stratton d. 9th mo, 21st da, 1770. Mary Stratton removed from Evesham. Stacy Stratton disowned 2nd mo, 6th da, 1796. Elizabeth Stratton removed to Eggharbor and Cape May Monthly Meeting. John Stratton, d. 11th mo, 1778.

Enoch Stratton, son of John and Ann Stratton, b. 1st mo, 3rd da, 1763 and Hannah Stratton, dau. of John and Jane Branin, b. 1st mo, 9th da, 1761 m. 4th mo, 11th da, 1792.

Children of Enoch and Hannah Stratton: Dorothy Stratton, b. 1st mo, 28th da, 1793; Abi Stratton, b. 12th mo, 16th da, 1794; John Stratton, b. 10th mo, 6th da, 1796; Achsah Stratton, b. 12th mo, 20th da, 1798; Enoch Stratton, b. 9th mo,. 16th da, 1800; William Stratton, b. 7th mo, 28th da, 1804.

Lydia Stratton d. 3rd mo, 27th da, 1785. Dorothy Stratton m. Daniel Zelly. Achsah Stratton, m. Samuel Reeves.

Children of Joshua Lippincott, son of Freedom and Elizabeth Lippincott, b. 7th mo, 2nd da, 1732 and Rachel Lippincott, dau. of Francis and Rachel Dudley, b. 6th mo, 31st da, 1736, d. 4th mo, 29th da, 1795, m. 6th mo, 3rd da, 1756: Nathan Lippincott, b. 3rd mo, 24th da, 1756; Mary Lippincott, b. ? mo, 22nd da, 1762; Hannah Lippincott, b. ? mo, 3rd da, 1766; Elizabeth Lippincott, b. 8th mo, 19th da, 1765; Rachel Lippincott, b. 7th mo, 5th da, 1771; Rebecca Lippincott, b. 7th mo, 3rd da, 1774.

Mary Lippincott, d. 5th mo, 31st da, 1776. Elizabeth Lippincott, d. 4th mo, 2nd da, 1785.

Children of Samuel Burrough, son of Samuel and Ann Burrough, b. 5th mo, 4th da, 1742, d. 4th mo, 29th da, 1793 and Sarah Burrough, dau. of Jacob and Lydia Lamb, b. 7th mo, 27th da, 1751, m. 11th mo, 27th da, 1756: Abel Burrough, b. 3rd mo, 31st da, 1769, d. 2nd mo, 8th da, 1775; Samuel Burrough, b. 7th mo, 10th mo, 1772, d. 7th mo, 5th da, 1778; Eber Burrough, b. 4th mo, 19th da, 1775, d. 7th mo, 12th da, 1778; Thomas Burrough, b.

5th mo, 1st da, 1779, d. 6th mo, 25th da, 1784; Lydia Burrough, b. 12th mo, 16th da, 1781; Sarah Burrough, b. 9th mo, 29th da, 1784; Samuel Burrough, b. 8th mo, 4th da, 1787.

Lydia Burrough m. Solomon Saunders, 12th mo, 12th da, 1800. Sarah Burrough m. Thomas Evens. Samuel Burrough m. Priscilla Moore.

Children of Benjamin Cooper, son of James and Deborah Cooper, b. 11th mo, 15th da, 1748 and Ann Cooper, dau. of William and Mary Black, b. 11th mo, 3rd da, 1755, both born at Evesham, m. 5th mo, 12th da, 1798: Mary Cooper, b. 12th mo, 6th da, 1773 at Evesham, d. 11th mo, 15th da, 1774, James Cooper, b. 2nd mo, 17th da, 1775 at Upper Springfield; William Cooper, b. 8th mo, 16th da, 1776 at Evesham ; Deborah Cooper, b. 10th mo, 30th da, 1778; Samuel Cooper, b. 11th mo, 8th da, 1780, d. 4th mo, 8th da, 1782; Mary Cooper, b. 3rd mo, 19th da, 1783; Rebecca Cooper, b. 3rd mo, 28th da, 1785; Ann Cooper, b. 4th mo, 16th da, 1787; Achsah Cooper, b. 10th mo, 17th da, 1789, d. 3rd mo, 4th da, 1791; Benjamin C. Cooper, b. 12th mo, 20th da, 1791; Matilda and Samuel Cooper, b. 2nd mo, 4th da, 1795. Matilda Cooper d. 9th mo, 12th da, 1796.

Solomon L. Saunders, son of John and Elizabeth Saunders, b. 1st mo, 30th da, 1777 married to Lydia Saunders, dau. of Samuel and Sarah Burrough, b. 12th mo, 16th da, 1781.

Children of Isaac Haines, son of Jonathan and Hannah Haines, b. 9th mo, 14th da, 1742, d. 10th mo, 12th da, 1804 at Upper Evesham and Mary Haines, dau. of Thomas and Mary Wilkins, b. 11th mo, 10th da, 1743, d. 3rd mo, 3rd da, 1793 at Upper Evesham: Jonathan Haines, b. 6th mo, 6th da, 1764, d. 8th mo, 17th da, 1774; Hephzibah Haines, b. 3rd mo, 17th da, 1766, d. 10th mo, 6th da, 1766; Job Haines, b. 8th mo, 29th da, 1768; Esther Haines, b. 4th mo, 22nd da, 1770; Isaac Haines, b. 4th mo, 12th da, 1772, d. 10th mo, 12th da, 1774; Josiah Haines, b. 5th mo, 18th da, 1774; Jonathan Haines, b. 9th mo, 6th da, 1776; Isaac Haines, b. 12th mo, 26th da, 1778; Mary Haines, b. 2nd mo, 21st da, 1782.
Children of Isaac Haines and his second wife, Elizabeth, dau. of Aaron and Elizabeth Lippincott, b. 9th mo, 14th da, 1762: Elizabeth Haines, b. 12th mo, 31st da, 1794, d. 4th mo, 11th da, 1797 at Upper Evesham; Ephraim Haines, b. 3rd mo, 20th da, 1797; Elizabeth Haines, b. 1st mo, 9th da, 1800.

Job Haines m. Martha Ballinger. Esther Haines m. Josiah Costlow. Josiah Haines m. Rebecca Lippincott. Jonathan Haines m. Mary Haines. Isaac Haines m. Elizabeth Austin. Mary Haines m. Francis Shinn. Mary Haines disowned 12th mo, 12th da, 1799.
Isaac Haines and Elizabeth Lippincott, his second wife m. 3rd mo, 19th da, 1794.

Children of Joseph and Elizabeth Butcher: Prudence Butcher, b. 6th mo, 7th da, 1782; Samuel Butcher, b. 12th mo, 28th da, 1784 at Haddonfield; Sarah Butcher, b. 2nd mo, 4th da, 1788 at Haddonfield; Joseph Butcher, b. 5th mo, 24th da, 1791.

Children of Jonathan Haines, son of Jonathan and Mary Haines and
Hannah his wife, b. 1st mo, 27th da, 1721, dau. of William
Sharp: Isaac Haines, 9th mo, 14th da, 1742; Jacob Haines, b. 8th
mo, 24th da, 1745; Josiah Haines, b. 8th mo, 13th da, 1748; Mary
Haines, b. 9th mo, 27th da, 1752; Nehemiah Haines, b. 1st mo,
23rd da, 1755; Hannah Haines, b. 4th mo, 11th da, 1762.

Isaac Haines m. Mary Wilkins. Jacob Haines m. Sarah Austin.
Josiah Haines m. Rebecca Austin. Mary Haines m. Job Collins 3rd
mo, 17th da, 1774. Nehemiah Haines m. Abigail Haines. Hannah
Haines m. Jophet Garwood. Jonathan Haines, son of Jonathan and
Mary Haines d. 4th mo, 16th da, 1785. Hannah Haines, wife of
Jonathan Haines d. 8th mo, 23rd da, 1784. Mary Haines d. 4th mo,
27th da, 1776 at Upper Evesham.

Children of Nehemiah Haines, son of Jonathan and Hannah Haines,
b. 1st mo, 23rd da, 1755 and wife, Abigail Haines, b. 17th mo,
29th da, 1762, dau. of Noah and Hannah Haines: Sarah Haines, b.
9th mo, 15th da, 1785; Joseph Haines, b. 2nd mo, 1st da, 1786;
Charles Haines, b. 1st mo, 19th da, 1788; Hannah Haines, 3rd
mo, 2nd da, 1790; Clayton Haines, b. 2nd mo, 7th da, 1792; David
Haines, b. 3rd mo, 18th da, 1794; Rachel Haines , b. 3rd mo,
20th da, 1796; George Haines, b. 6th mo, 13th da, 1798; Lydia
Haines, b. 6th mo, 13th da, 1798; Abigail, b. 11th mo, 8th da,
1800.
Children of Enoch Stratton, son of Mark Stratton, b. 9th mo, 8th
da, 1720, d. 7th mo, 1st da, 1781 and Amy Stratton, dau. of
Joseph Elkinton, b. 1st mo, 13th da, 1724: Isaiah Stratton, b.
4th mo, 23rd da, 1748, d. 12th mo, 26th da, 1781; Anner
Stratton, b. 12th mo, 24th da, 1794, d. 10th mo, 26th da, 1781;
Josiah Stratton, b. 6th mo, 18th da, 1752, d. 1st mo, 28th da,
1789; Elizabeth Stratton, b. 2nd mo, 13th da, 1754; Alice
Stratton, b. 1st mo, 3rd mo, 1756; Ruth Stratton, b. 3rd mo,
16th da, 1758, d. 10th mo, 16th da, 1790; Hope Stratton, b. 11th
mo, 23rd da, 1760; Abigail Stratton, b. 3rd mo, 6th da, 1763, d.
8th mo, 18th da, 1828 at Upper Evesham; Levi Stratton, b. 12th
mo, 9th da, 1765.
Anner Stratton m. Joshua Shreve. Elizabeth Stratton m. Isaiah
Hunt. Ruth Stratton m. Thomas Sharp. Hope Stratton m. Joshua
Shreeve. Abigail Stratton m. John Bates. Elizabeth Stratton,
Hope Stratton, and Levi Stratton all disowned.

Children of Jacob Prickitt, son of Jacob and Hannah Prickitt, b.
11th mo, 18th da, 1735 and Elizabeth Prickitt, dau. of Peter and
Sarah Phillips, b. 2nd mo, 23rd da, 1732: Hepehzibah Prickitt,
b. 2nd mo, 11th da, 1759, d. 7th mo, 9th da, 1768; John
Prickitt, b. 3rd mo, 3rd da, 1761; Aaron Prickitt, b. 5th mo,
16th da, 1763; Samuel Prickitt, b. 9th mo, 7th da, 1765;
Elizabeth Prickitt, b. 11th mo, 28th da, 1770.
John Prickitt m. Sabillah Hammit, dau. of Samuel and Elizabeth
Hammit, b. 12th mo, 25th da, 1765.

Children of Ephraim Stratton, b. 12th mo, 17th da, 1747, son of
John and Ann Stratton, and Margaret Stratton, dau. of Stephen
Minion, b. no date, d. 8th mo, 24th da, 1780 Upper Evesham

Monthly Meeting: Reuben, b. 1st mo, 29th da, 1776; John, b. 4th mo, 26th da, 1777; Alice, b. 6th mo, 26th da, 1779.

Ephraim Stratton married to his second wife, Rachel, b. 3rd mo, 1st da, 1758, d. 5th mo, 15th da, 1798, dau. of John Shinn, second wife: Lydia, b. 8th mo, 20th da, 1786.
Ephraim Stratton and Hannah, his third wife, b. 1st mo, 3rd da, 1755, dau. of Jonathan and Ann Palmer.
Alice Stratton m. Edward Boulton, 10th mo, 25th da, 1797. Lydia Stratton, m. John Sleeper, removed to Philadelphia Monthly Meeting.

Children of Samuel Lippincott, son of Samuel and Theodosia Lippincott, b. 11th mo, 10th da, 1770 and Anner Lippincott, dau. of John and Mary Haines, b. 3rd mo, 3rd da, 1774. Samuel Lippincott and Anner Haines m. 1st mo, 14th da, 1791: Theodosia Lippincott, b. 10th mo, 16th da, 1791, d. 11th mo, 18th da, 1796; Samuel Lippincott, b. 4th mo, 16th da, 1793; Charles Lippincott, b. 2nd mo, 26th da, 1795; Clayton Lippincott, b. 6th mo, 14th da, 1797; Nathan Lippincott, b. 1st mo, 7th da, 1800; John H. Lippincott, b. 6th mo, 6th da, 1802; Lydia Lippincott, b. 3rd mo, 14th da, 1806; Mark Lippincott, b. 2nd mo, 16th da, 1812; William Cooper Lippincott, b. 3rd mo, 4th da, 1814; Agneys Lippincott, b. 5th mo, 17th da, 1816.

Hope Lippincott, dau. of Samuel and Theodosia, b. 5th mo, 28th da, 1774. Theodosia Lippincott, b. 6th mo, 10th da, 1776 dau. of Samuel and Theodosia Lippincott m. Jacob Wilkins.

Children of Rehobram Braddock, son of Robert Braddock, b. 2nd mo, 14th da, 1742 and Jemima Braddock, dau. of John and Hannah Darnel, b. 10th mo, 6th da, 1744, m. 3rd mo, 31st da, 1763: Job Braddock, no date, Elizabeth Braddock, b. 10th mo, 12th da, 1767; Bathsheba Braddock, b. 2nd mo, 22nd da, 1770; Hannah Braddock, b. 9th mo, 13th da, 1772; Phebe Braddock, b. 12th mo, 25th da, 1774; Darnel Braddock, b. 4th mo, 18th da, 1777; William Braddock, b. 10th mo, 24th da, 1779; Jemima Braddock, b. 3rd mo, 28th da, 1782; Rachel Braddock, b. 4th mo, 10th da, 1784.

Job Braddock m. Hannah Snowden; Elizabeth Braddock m. Noah Sharp, removed; Bathsheba Braddock m. Daniel Zilla, removed; Hannah Braddock m. William Gifford, removed; Phebe Braddock m. Joseph Haines, removed to Mt. Holly Monthly Meeting; Darnel Braddock m. Sarah Rogers; William Braddock m. Ann Rogers; Jemima Braddock m. John Borton, 5th mo, 14th da, 1800, removed to Evesham Monthly Meeting; Rachel Braddock m. John Dudley, removed to Chester Monthly Meeting; Mary Braddock m. Edward Borton, removed to Evesham Monthly Meeting.

Jacob Borton, son of Isaac and Mary Borton, b. 6th mo, 5th da, 1777 married to Jemima Borton, dau. of Isaac and Hannah Kay, b. 9th mo, 3rd da, 1782.
Children of Isaac Borton, b. 9th mo, 12th da, 1736 married to Mary Borton, formerly Hutten, b. 6th mo, 17th da, 1741: Ann

Borton, b. 4th mo, 3rd da, 1762; d. 7th mo, 21st da, 1799; John
Borton, b. 3rd mo, 14th da, 1764, d. 9th mo, 8th da, 1786;
Elizabeth Borton, b. 7th mo, 9th da, 1766, d. 10th mo, 16th da,
1767; Mary Borton, b. 11th mo, 27th da, 1769; Hope Borton, b.
1st mo, 30th da, 1772; Elizabeth Borton, b. 11th mo, 19th da,
1774; Jacob Borton, b. 6th mo, 5th da, 1777; Sarah Borton, b.
1st mo, 1st da, 4th da, 1779.

Hope Borton m. Josiah Stokes 12th mo, 12th da, 1794 removed to
Woodbury; Jacob Borton m. Jemima Kay; Sarah Borton m. Aquila
Stokes, removed to Haddonfield; Jacob Borton disowned. Elizabeth
Borton disowned.

Children of Jacob Evans, son of Nathan and Syllania Evans, b. 9th
mo, 25th da, 1762 and Deborah Evans, his first wife, dau. of
William and Esther Troth, b. 12th mo, 28th da, 1759, d. 7th mo,
31st da, 1791: Esther Evans, b. 2nd mo, 24th da, 1785; George
Evans, b. 12th mo, 13th da, 1787, d. 7th mo, 20th da, 1791; Ruth
Evans, b. 2nd mo, 15th da, 1790, d. 5th mo, 7th da, 1790; Joab
Evans, b. 5th mo, 31st da, 1791.
Children of Jacob Evans and Rachel Evans, his second wife, dau.
of Abraham and Rachel Borton, b. 8th mo, 26th da, 1774 m. 3rd
mo, 7th da, 1795 at Evesham: Abraham Evans, b. 12th mo, 14th da,
1795; Amos Evans, b. 6th mo, 2nd da, 3rd da, 1797; Syllania
Evans, b. 10th mo, 6th da, 1799; Uriah Evans, b. 10th mo, 10th
da, 1801; Rachel B. Evans, b. 7th mo, 28th da, 1803, d. 11th mo,
2nd da, 1869; Jacob Evans, b. 6th mo, 1st da, 1805; Carlton
Evans, b. 5th mo, 2nd da, 1807, d. 11th mo, 22nd da, 1807;
Joseph B. Evans, b. 9th mo, 7th da, 1811; Hannah Evans, b. 12th
mo, 6th da, 1813.

Joshua Stokes, son of Joseph and Atlantick Stokes, b. 7th mo,
29th da, 1762 and Deborah, his first wife, dau. of Thomas and
Bathsheba Hooton, b. 10th mo, 16th da, 1764, d. 6th mo, 30th da,
1796 at Upper Evesham.

Children of Joshua and Deborah Stokes: Atlantick Stokes, b. 10th
mo, 23rd da, 1788, d. 11th mo, 21st da, 1801 at Upper Evesham;
Joseph Stokes, b. 11th mo, 4th da, 1790, d. 5th mo, 8th da, 1796
at Upper Evesham; Mary Stokes, b. 3rd mo, 23rd da, 1793; Thomas
Stokes, b. 9th mo, 7th da, 1795.
Joshua Stokes married to his second wife, Rebecca, dau. of
Abraham and Eliza Matlack: Abraham M. Stokes, b. 3rd mo, 7th da,
1801, d. 11th mo, 4th da, 1801 at Upper Evesham.
Joshua Stokes married to his third wife, Lydia, dau. of Enoch and
Mary Evans, b. 11th mo, 17th da, 1777.

Rebecca Stokes, wife of Joshua Stokes died 10th mo, 8th da, 1801.
Rebecca Matlack received by certificate from Evesham 4th mo, 6th
da, 1799.
Joshua Stokes and Lydia Evans m. 3rd mo, 16th da, 1804.

William Rogers, son of William and Grace Rogers b. 2nd mo, 12th
da, 1768 and Mary Rogers, dau. of David and Martha Davis, b. 3rd
mo, 1st da, 1768 m. 2nd mo, 26th da, 1789.

Children of William and Mary Rogers: Martha Rogers, b. 1st mo, 26th da, 1790, d. 7th mo, 20th da, 1795 at Upper Evesham; Rachel Rogers, b. 2nd mo, 27th da, 1791; Grace Rogers, b. 6th mo, 21st da, 1793; Josiah Rogers, b. 1st mo, 9th da, 1795; David Rogers, b. 1st mo, 4th da, 1797; Mary Rogers, b. 2nd mo, 11th da, 1799; Ann Rogers, b. 5th mo, 21st da, 1801; Allen Rogers, b. 5th mo, 14th da, 1803; Joseph Rogers, b. 5th mo, 14th da, 1815; William D. Rogers, b. 10th mo, 2nd da, 1807.

William Rogers and wife, Mary and Children, Rachel, Grace, Josiah, David, Mary, Ann, Allen, Joseph and William D. removed to Evesham Monthly Meeting 3rd mo, 12th da, 1808.

Joseph Rogers, son of William and Grace Rogers, b. 1st mo, 16th da, 1770, and Sarah his wife, dau. of Bethuel and Martha Moore,. 9th mo, 23rd da, 1771, m. 12th mo, 22nd da, 1791.

Children of Joseph and Sarah Rogers: William Rogers, b. 9th mo, 12th da, 1792; Martha Rogers, b. 1st mo, 21st da, 1807. Martha Rogers m. Izvy Roberts.

Children of Amos and Lydia Ashead: John Ashead, b. 4th mo, 12th da, 1768; Mary Ashead, b. 5th mo, 28th da, 1770, d. 5th mo, 29th da, 1770; Abel Ashead, b. 9th mo, 14th da, 1772; Eleanor Ashead, b. 5th mo, 20th da, 1779; Amos Ashead, b. 2nd mo, 4th da, 1786; Moses Ashead, b. 10th mo, 6th da, 1789.

Amos and Lydia Ashead, and children: Elanor, Amos and Moses received by certificate from Haddonfield Monthly Meeting 6th mo, 6th da, 1795.

Daniel Garwood, son of Thomas and Margaret Garwood, b. 4th mo, 15th da, 1710, d. 4th mo, 8th da, 1784 at Upper Evesham married to Susannah, dau. of John and Ruth Collins, b. 5th mo, 11th mo, 1718, d. 12th mo, 14th da, 1809.

Jopheth Garwood, son of Daniel and Susannah b. 6th mo, 26th da, 1750 and Hannah Garwood, b. 4th mo, 11th da, 1762, d. 12th mo, 23rd da, 1786.

Child of Japheth and Hannah Garwood: Hannah b. 12th mo, 20th da, 1786.

Children of Japheth and Elizabeth Garwood, his second wife, b. 1st mo, 2nd da, 1757: Sarah Garwood, b. 2nd mo, 22nd da, 1792; Hope Garwood, b. 1st mo, 11th da, 1796; Rachel Garwood, b. 11th mo, 16th da, 1797, d. 12th mo, 22nd da, 1815; Daniel Garwood, b. 3rd mo, 20th da, 1800.

Children of Robert Braddock, b. 2nd mo, 18th da, 1712, d. 6th mo, 4th da, 1767 and wife Francis, b. 2nd mo, 25th da, 1722, d. 3rd mo, 23rd da, 1800: John Braddock, b. 3rd mo, 9th da, 1751/2; Daniel Braddock, b. 4th mo, 29th da, 1753, 4th da, 8th da, 1807; Hannah Braddock, b. 3rd mo, 14th da, 1755, 10th mo, 2nd da, 1758; Mary Braddock, b. 4th mo, 23rd da, 1756, d. 9th mo, 26th da, 1758; Barzillai Braddock, b. 11th mo, 29th da, 1757, 11th mo, 3rd da, 1823; Robert Braddock, b. 8th mo, 28th da, 1759, d. 1st mo, 12th da, 1842; Elizabeth Braddock, b. 12th mo, 19th da, 1761, d. 9th mo, 5th da, 1766; Jerusha Braddock, b. 3rd mo, 4th mo, 1765, d. 8th mo, 31st da, 1766.

Children of Robert Braddock, son of Robert and Francis, b. 8th
mo, 28th da, 1759 and Sarah, dau. of Elijah and Mary Birdsill,
b. 2nd mo, 17th da, 1768: Frances Braddock, b. 12th mo, 9th da,
1790; Robert Braddock, b. 9th mo, 21st da, 1793, d. 9th mo, 8th
da, 1795.

John Brown, son of Samuel and Ann Brown, b. 8th mo, 19th da,
1752, d. 8th mo, 5th da, 1800 at Hopewell and wife, Virgin
Brown, dau. of Joseph and Grace Gaskill, b. 3rd mo, 1751.
Children of John and Virgin Brown: Joseph Brown, b. 7th mo, 17th
da, 1775; Abraham Brown, b. 9th mo, 21st da, 1777; John Brown,
b. 9th mo, 21st da, 1777; Mahlon Brown, b. 9th mo, 26th da,
1779; Clayton Brown, b. 10th mo, 3rd da, 1781; Samuel Brown, b.
4th mo, 22nd da, 1785; Beulah Brown, b. 2nd mo, 17th da, 1787;
Mary Brown, b. 7th mo, 17th da, 1788; William Brown, b. 1st mo,
26th da, 1792.
Mahlon Brown, son of John and Virgin Brown, b. 9th mo, 26th da,
1779 married to Alice Brown, dau. of Thomas and Ann Brown, b.
1st mo, 16th da, 1785.
John Shinn, son of Caleb and Mehatable Shinn and Sarah Shinn,
dau. of Benjamin and Elizabeth Jones, b. 11th mo, 24th da, 1747.
Isaac Andrew, son of Isaac and Elizabeth Andrew, b. 9th mo, 21st
da, 1749 married to Rebecca Andrew, dau. of William and Sarah
Evans, b. 6th mo, 19th da, 1753.

Child of John and Sarah Shinn: Benjamin Shinn, b. 10th mo, 18th
da, 1786. John Shinn, wife, Sarah and son, Benjamin received by
certificate from Mt. Holly Monthly Meeting 6th mo, 9th da, 1798.
Children of Isaac and Rebecca Andrew: Sarah Andrew, b. 12th mo,
6th da, 1772; William Andrew, b. 4th mo, 22nd da, 1776;
Elizabeth Andrew, b. 11th mo, 30th da, 1778; Rebecca Andrew, b.
5th mo, 12th da, 1781; Hannah Andrew, b. 11th mo, 18th da, 1784;
Esther Andrew, b. 11th mo, 18th da, 1784; Mary Andrew, b. 9th
mo, 18th da, 1791; Lydia Andrew, b. 10th mo, 8th da, 1798.

Lydia Andrew m. Samuel Braxenton. Sarah Andrew removed to Evesham
Monthly Meeting. William removed to Mt. Holly Monthly Meeting,
1st mo, 6th da, 1796. Isaac Andrew and Rebecca Evans m. 11th mo,
14th da, 1741.
Abner Watson, b. 10th mo, 2nd da, 1766, son of Mark and Mary
Watson married to Elizabeth Borton, dau. of William and Hannah
Borton, b. 6th mo, 10th da, 1767. Elizabeth Watson received by
certificate from Falls Monthly Meeting, PA, 2nd mo, 10th da,
1798.

Children of Abner and Elizabeth Watson: Mary Watson, b. 5th mo,
17th da, 1793; Mark Watson, b. 6th mo, 17th da, 1796, d. 10th
mo, 20th da, 1797; Hannah Watson, b. 3rd mo, 23rd da, 1798;
William Watson, b. 2nd mo, 17th da, 1800; Deborah Watson, b. 1st
mo, 23rd da, 1802; Phebe Watson, b. 1st mo, 9th da, 1804; Ann
Watson, b. 4th mo, 11th da, 1807; Mark Watson, b. 5th mo, 7th
da, 1810.

Abner Watson, wife Elizabeth and children: Mary, Hannah, William,
Deborah, Phebe, Ann and Mark removed to Goshen Monthly Meeting,

PA.
Nicholas Hoile, son of Andrew and Elizabeth Hoile, b. 1st mo, 11th da, 1755, d. 12th mo, 3rd da, 1820 and Priscilla Bell, dau. of James and Elizabeth Bell, b. 4th mo, 24th da, 1758, d. 11th mo, 23rd da, 1795.

Children of Nicholas and Priscilla Hoile: Hannah Hoile, b. 8th mo, 12th da, 1779, d. 12th mo, 8th da, 1779; Elizabeth Hoile, b. 11th mo, 12th da, 1781; Levi Hoile, b. 12th mo, 8th da, 1782; Joshua Hoile, b. 11th mo, 23rd da, 1784; Enoch Hoile, b. 11th mo, 23rd da, 1784; Joseph Hoile, b. 10th mo, 14th da, 1784; Martha Hoile, b. 5th mo, 20th da, 1790; Margaret Hoile, b. 11th mo, 25th da, 1792; James Hoile, b. 10th mo, 26th da, 1794.

Phebe Hoile, b. 9th mo, 8th da, 1771, dau. of John Gant, received by certificate from Mt. Holly Monthly Meeting.
Reuben Braddock, son of Reuben and Abigail Braddock, b. 12th mo, 21st da, 1770 married to Elizabeth Stokes, dau. of Thomas and Sarah Stokes, b. 8th mo, 24th da, 1774. Reuben Braddock and Elizabeth Stokes m. 5th mo, 6th da, 1796 at Haddonfield.

Children of Reuben and Elizabeth Braddock: Samuel Braddock, b. 3rd mo, 25th da, 1799; Sarah Braddock, b. 11th mo, 26th da, 1800; Abigail Braddock, b. 6th mo, 14th da, 1802; Lydia Braddock, b. 11th mo, 16th da, 1804; Thomas Braddock, b. 12th mo, 11th da, 1806.

Elizabeth Braddock and children: Samuel, Sarah, Lydia and Thomas removed to Woodbury Monthly Meeting. Abigail Braddock removed to Philadelphia Monthly Meeting.

William Troth, son of Paul and Deborah Troth, b. 6th mo, 21st da, 1735 and Esther Borton, dau. of William and Deborah Borton, b. 1st mo, 24th da, 1738, received by certificate from Evesham Monthly Meeting, 4th mo, 8th da, 1796.

Children of William and Esther Troth: Paul Troth, b. 1st mo, 3rd da, 1758; Deborah Troth, b. 12th mo, 28th da, 1759; Isaac Troth, b. 11th mo, 14th da, 1762; Jacob Troth, b. 1st mo, 15th da, 1764, d. 8th mo, 1764; John Troth, b. 11th mo, 13th da, 1767; Esther Troth, b. 2nd mo, 18th da, 1771.

Deborah Troth m. Jacob Evans. John Troth m. Ann Engle. Esther Troth m. Aaron Engle, removed to Haddonfield Monthly Meeting. Paul Troth removed to Woodbury 5th mo, 9th da, 1801.

Children of John Troth, son of William and Esther, b. 11th mo, 13th da, 1767, and Ann Engle, dau. of Joseph and Mary Engle, b. 3rd mo, 5th mo, 1774, received from Evesham Monthly Meeting 4th mo, 8th da, 1796: Mary Troth, b. 3rd mo, 22nd da, 1795; Charles Troth, b. 2nd mo, 14th da, 1797; Deborah Troth, b. 9th mo, 28th da, 1798; Susannah Troth, b. 10th mo, 22nd da, 1800; Huldah Troth, b. 11th mo, 2nd da, 1802, d. 9th mo, 8th da, 1805; Esther Troth, b. 9th mo, 16th da, 1804; Lucy Ann Troth, b. 4th mo, 2nd da, 1807; John Troth, b. no date.

John Evans, b. 2nd mo, 17th da, 1774, d. 3rd mo, 18th da, 1841 at
Cropwell, son of Enoch and Mary Evans and Rebecca, dau. of Hugh
and Rebecca Cowperthwaite, b. 8th mo, 22nd da, 1778, d. 4th mo,
15th da, 1861 at Cropwell, m. 12th mo, 2nd da, 1799.
Thomas Evans, son of Enoch and Mary Evans, b. 3rd mo, 5th mo,
1785 and Abigail Bispham, dau. of Thomas and Hannah Bispham, b.
10th mo, 6th da, 1785, m. 12th mo, 20th da, 1784. Abigail Evans
formerly Bispham received by certificate from Chester Monthly
Meeting.

Children of John Roberts, Jr., son of John and Phebe Roberts, b.
12th mo, 12th da, 1771 and his wife, Esther, dau. of Jacob and
Mary Evans, b. 9th mo, 29th da, 1777: Jacob Roberts, b. 11th mo,
27th da, 1798; Reuben Roberts, b. 3rd mo, 4th da, 1800; Thomas
E. Roberts, b. 4th mo, 13th da, 1803; Mary Roberts, b. 10th mo,
23rd da, 1807; John E. Roberts, b. no date.
Children of Joseph Evans, son of Thomas and Mary Evans, b. 6th
mo, 28th da, 1775 and wife, Rebecca, dau. of Joseph and Susan
Roberts, b. 4th mo, 22nd da, 1775: Ann Evans, b. 12th mo, 14th
da, 1799; Mary Evans, b. 12th mo, 21st da, 1801; Sarah Evans, b.
3rd mo, 3rd da, 1804; Thomas Evans, b. 7th mo, 11th da, 1805;
Susanna Evans, b. 4th mo, 30th da, 1808; Rebecca Evans, b. 10th
mo, 18th da, 1810; Martha Evans, b. 10th mo, 26th da, 1812.

Joseph Evans and Rebecca Roberts m. 3rd mo, 12th da, 1799; Ann
Evans m. Jacob Roberts; Sarah Evans m. John Haines; Thomas Evans
m. Mary Barton; Susanna Evans m. William Evans; Rebecca Evans m.
William Matlock at Chester Monthly Meeting.

Children of Moses Lippincott, son of Aaron and Elizabeth
Lippincott, b. 4th mo, 14th da, 1755 and wife, Mary, dau. of
Jonathan and Elizabeth Hewlings, b. 5th mo, 15th da, 1760:
Elizabeth Lippincott, b. 2nd mo, 2nd da, 1781; Sarah Lippincott,
b. 12th mo, 9th da, 1783; Benjamin Lippincott, b. 12th mo, 23rd
da, 1785; Dorothy Lippincott, b. 8th mo, 31st da, 1788; Joseph
Lippincott, b. 6th mo, 12th da, 1792; Mary Lippincott, b. 11th
mo, 22nd da, 1794.

Moses Lippincott, wife, Mary, and children: Elizabeth, Sarah,
Benjamin and Dorothy received by certificate 8th mo, 8th da,
1795.

Elizabeth Lippincott, m. William Austin; Benjamin Lippincott m.
Elizabeth Wilkins; Dorothy Lippincott m. Joseph Matlock; Moses
Lippincott and wife, Mary removed by certificate to Haddonfield
Monthly Meeting.
Mary Lippincott, wife of Moses Lippincott d. 11th mo, 28th da,
1794. Elizabeth Lippincott removed by certificate to Evesham
Monthly Meeting; Sarah Lippincott removed by certificate to
Evesham Monthly Meeting; Benjamin Lippincott removed by
certificate to Evesham Monthly Meeting; Dorothy Lippincott
removed by certificate to Evesham Monthly Meeting.

Children of Sarah Lippincott, dau. of David and Rebecca Stratton,
b. 5th da, 1st da, 1792: John Lippincott, b. 5th mo, 19th da,

1797; Mary Lippincott, b. 8th mo, 25th da, 1799; Eliz. S. Lippincott, b. 9th mo, 30th da, 1809.

Sarah Lippincott, and children: John, Mary and Sarah removed by certificate to Haddonfield Monthly Meeting.

Children of Edward Boulton, son of William and Hannah Boulton, b. 1st mo, 26th da, 1771, and wife, Alice, dau. of Ephraim and Mary Stratton: Reuben Boulton, b. 10th mo, 30th da, 1798; Lydia Boulton, b. 3rd mo, 19th da, 1800; Phebe Boulton, b. 3rd mo, 19th da, 1801.
Children of Core Haines, son of Isaiah and Sarah Haines, b. 8th mo, 6th da, 1766, d. 3rd mo, 1st da, 1801 at Upper Evesham and wife, Mary, dau. of John and Martha Haines, b. 10th mo, 27th da, 1767: Ann Haines, b. 9th mo, 17th da, 1795; John Haines, b. 4th mo, 9th da, 1797, d. 2nd mo, 3rd da, 1798; Grace Haines, b. 5th mo, 6th da, 1798; Ruth Haines, b. 10th mo, 13th da, 1811; Mark Haines, b. 1st mo, 2nd da, 1807.

Core Haines and Mary Haines, and Ann received by certificate from Evesham Monthly Meeting 5th mo, 7th da, 179?. Core Haines and Mary Haines m. 12th mo, 10th da, 1794. Ruth Haines m. Joshua Ballinger.

Children of Isaac Wilson, son of John and Mary Wilson, b. 12th mo, 16th da, 1767, and wife, Phebe, dau. of Samuel and Ann Middleton, b. 8th mo, 8th da, 1773: Anna Wilson, b. 7th mo, 21st da, 1794; Mary Wilson, b. 2nd mo, 4th da, 1796, d. 11th mo, 15th da, 1796; Samuel Wilson, b. 10th mo, 2nd da, 1797; John Wilson, b. 6th mo, 22nd da, 1797 (?); William Wilson, b. 6th mo, 13th da, 1811; Abigail Wilson, b. 1st mo, 25th da, 1803; Rebecca Wilson, b. 3rd mo, 26th da, 1805; Mordecai Wilson, b. 12th mo, 9th da, 1808; Ira Wilson, b. 7th mo, 22nd da, 1811; Isaac Wilson, b. 9th mo, 13th da, 1813; Nathan W. Wilson, b. 8th mo, 24th da, 1814.

Isaac Wilson, wife Phebe and dau., Anna received by certificate from Philadelphia Monthly Meeting 8th mo, 6th da, 1796. Anna Wilson m. William Stokes.

Children of Josiah Reeve, son of Mark and Hannah Reeve, b. 9th mo, 23rd da, 1762, d. 11th mo, 10th da, 1840 at Upper Evesham and Martha, his first wife, dau. of John and Mary Newbold, b. 8th mo, 22nd da, 1761, d. 3rd mo, 24th da, 1791 at Salem: John N. Reeve, b. 8th mo, 6th da, 1789; Martha Reeve, b. 3rd mo, 7th da, 1791.
Josiah Reeve married to his second wife, Elizabeth, dau. of William and Elizabeth Richardson, b. 1st mo, 31st da, 1770.
Elizabeth Reeve, 2nd wife of Josiah received by certificate from Middletown Monthly Meeting, PA.
James Cooper, son of Benjamin and Ann Cooper, b. 2nd mo, 17th da, 1775 married to wife, Elizabeth, dau. of Nicholas and Priscilla Hoile, b. 11th mo, 12th da, 1780.

Children of Mark Reeve, son of Josiah and Hannah Reeve, b. 8th

mo, 30th da, 1765 and wife, Hannah, dau. of Job and Sarah
Whitall, b. 9th mo, 26th da, 1775: Job Reeve, b. 9th mo, 1st da,
1796, d. 7th mo, 15th da, 1797 at Upper Evesham; Casper Reeve,
b. 1st mo, 3rd da, 1798; Robert Reeve, b. 7th mo, 1st da, 1799;
Job Whitall Reeve, b. 12th mo, 30th da, 1800; Clayton Reeve, b.
11th mo, 12th da, 1802; Hannah Ann Reeve, b. 3rd mo, 31st da,
1806; Sarah Whitall Reeve, b. 2nd mo, 22nd da, 1808; Rebecca
Reeve, b. 11th mo, 19th da, 1810; Franklin Reeve, b. 11th mo,
9th da, 1811.

Clayton Haines, son of Benjamin and Sarah Haines, b. 5th mo, 20th
da, 1780, d. 11th mo, 16th da, 1876 married to Rebecca Haines,
dau. of Zebedoe and Priscilla Wills, b. 11th mo, 17th da, 1784.

Children of Peter Shinn, son of Clement and Elizabeth Shinn, b.
10th mo, 20th da, 1744 and Grace, dau. of Joseph and Grace
Gaskill, b. 9th mo, 12th da, 1755: Elizabeth Shinn, b. 5th mo,
14th da, 1780, d. 2nd mo, 19th da, 1789 at Springfield; David
Shinn, b. 10th mo, 13th da, 1782; Hannah Shinn, b. 3rd mo, 24th
da, 1785; Joseph Shinn, b. 1st mo, 29th da, 1787; Rachel Shinn,
b. 3rd mo, 28th da, 1789; John Shinn, b. 3rd mo, 19th da, 1791;
Mahlon Shinn, b. 11th mo, 1st da, 1794; Abraham Shinn, b. 3rd
mo, 19th da, 1798.

Peter Shinn, wife Grace and children: Elizabeth Shinn, David
Shinn, Hannah Shinn received by certificate from Mt. Holly 5th
mo, 6th da, 1798. Peter Shinn and Grace Gaskill m. 5th mo, 1779.

Children of Aaron Engle, son of Joseph and Marg Engle, b. 11th
mo, 6th da, 1764 and Esther, dau. of William and Esther Smith,
b. 2nd mo, 15th da, 1777: Deborah Engle, b. 1st mo, 5th mo,
1793; Paul Engle, b. 10th mo, 22nd da, 1797, d. 5th mo, 25th da,
1849; Elizabeth Engle, b. 9th mo, 17th da, 1807; Esther T.
Engle, b. 9th mo, 2nd da, 1813; Maryann Engle, b. 9th mo, 28th
da, 1816.

Aaron Engle and Esther Smith m. 12th mo, 15th da, 1792. Aaron
Engle, wife, Esther and child: Deborah Engle received by
certificate from Chester Monthly Meeting.

Children of Benjamin Haines, son of Benjamin and Elizabeth
Haines, b. 6th mo, 18th da, 1765 and wife Elizabeth, dau. of
Benjamin and Rachel Hurley, b. 9th mo, 20th da, 1774: Empson
Haines, b. 2nd mo, 23rd da, 1796; Benjamin Haines, b. 6th mo,
17th da, 1797; Nathan Haines, b. 5th mo, 1st da, 1799; Rachel
Haines, b. 7th mo, 14th da, 1801; Elizabeth Haines, b. 10th mo,
23rd da, 1803; Abraham Haines, b. 12th mo, 2nd da, 1805; Mary
Haines, b. 10th mo, 11th da, 1807; Clayton Haines, b. 11th mo,
9th da, 1809; Rebecca Haines, b. 12th mo, 21st da, 1811; William
Haines, b. 12th mo, 24th da, 1813; Samuel Haines, b. 7th mo,
19th da, 1816.

Benjamin Haines, wife, Elizabeth, and children: Empson, Benjamin,
Nathan, Rachel, Elizabeth, Abraham, Mary, Clayton, Rebecca and
William removed by certificate to Pilesgrove Monthly Meeting.

Children of Samuel Haines, son of Jonathan and Mary Haines, b.
11th mo, 15th da, 1765 wife, Elizabeth, dau. of Isaac and Hannah
?, b. 4th mo, 31st da, 1772: Hannah Haines, b. 8th mo, 12th da,
1799, d. 5th mo, 21st da, 1838 at Cropwell; Charles Haines, b.
1st mo, 24th da, 1801; Isaac Haines, b. 1st mo, 28th da, 1803;
Elizabeth Haines, b. 9th mo, 24th da, 1809.
Children of John Stokes, son of Jacob and Amy Stokes, b. 7th mo,
3rd da, 1758 and wife, Beulah, dau. of Elisha and Mary Haines,
b. 11th mo, 17th da, 1762: Caleb Stokes, b. 7th da, 21st da,
1752; Samuel Stokes, b. 11th mo, 10th da, 1784; Isaac Stokes, b.
4th mo, 10th da, 1787; William Stokes, b. 6th mo, 29th da, 1790;
Mary Stokes, b. 5th mo, 13th da, 1792; Atlanlick Stokes, b. 10th
mo, 10th da, 1794; Rachel Stokes, b. 3rd mo, 4th da, 1797.
Children of William Page, son of Thomas and Alice Page, b. 7th
mo, 9th da, 1770 and wife, Agness, dau. of Hugh and Elanor
Hollingsworth, b. 8th mo, 6th da, 1776: Thomas Page, b. 6th mo,
8th da, 1798; William Page, b. 11th mo, 8th da, 1801; Elanor
Page, b. 1st mo, 16th da, 1808; Agness Page, b. 1st mo, 22nd da,
1813; Clayton H. Page, b. 2nd mo, 6th da, 1814; Sarah Page, b.
4th mo, 10th da, 1818; Elizabeth Page, b. 7th mo, 1st da, 1821;
Abigail Page, b. 1st mo, 30th da, 1825.
Children of William Vennable, son of Thomas and Esther Vennable,
b. 8th mo, 23rd da, 1765 and Rachel, dau. of Thomas Crusher, b.
4th da,1771: John Vennable, b. 7th mo, 2nd da, 1789; Mary Ann
Vennable, b. 7th mo, 20th da, 1791; Joseph Vennable, b. 6th mo,
5th mo, 1793; Arthur Vennable, b. 10th mo, 24th da, 1795;
William Vennable, b. 2nd mo, 18th da, 1798; Charles Vennable, b.
10th mo, 27th da, 1800; Martha Vennable, b. 3rd mo, 28th da,
1803; Thomas Vennable, b. 9th mo, 28th da, 1805; Rachel
Vennable, b. no date.

Samuel Reeves, son of Samuel and Hannah Reeves, b. 10th mo, 27th
da, 1752 and wife, Elizabeth, dau. of John and Martha Wright, b.
3rd mo, 9th da, 1751: Thomas Reeves, b. 4th mo, 12th da, 1789;
Samuel Reeves, b. 7th mo, 6th da, 1791; Mahlon Reeves, b. 7th
mo, 4th da, 1793; Elizabeth Reeves, b. 5th mo, 19th da, 1795;
Martha Reeves, b. 5th mo, 18th da, 1798.

Samuel Reeves, and children: Thomas, Samuel, Mahlon, Elizabeth
and Martha received by certificate. Elizabeth Reeves received by
certificate 6th mo, 7th da, 1800.
Samuel Reeves m Ann Reeves, his second wife, 1st mo, 13th da,
1808.

Child of Samuel Reeves and Ann: Amirah Ann Reeves, b. no date.
Children of Job Haines, son of Isaac and Mary Haines, b. 8th mo,
29th da, 1769 and wife, Martha, dau. of Thomas and Susan
Ballinger, b. 5th mo, 26th da, 1776: Mary Haines, b. 2nd mo,
24th da, 1795; Thomas Haines, b. 1st mo, 17th da, 1797, d. 7th
mo, 10th da, 1800 at Upper Evesham; Joshua Haines, b. 12th mo,
7th da, 1798, d. 9th mo, 24th da, 1826; Nathan Haines, b. 11th
mo, 3rd da, 1801; Ira Haines, b. 1st mo, 3rd da, 1804; Esther
Haines, b. 11th mo, 18th da, 1805; Anna Haines, b. 11th mo, 20th
da, 1807; Isaac B. Haines, b. 11th mo, 28th da, 1809; Jacob
Haines, b. 9th mo, 4th da, 1811, d. 8th mo, 30th da, 1834 at

Upper Evesham; Martha Haines, b. 9th mo, 7th da, 1813; Job
Haines, b. 3rd mo, 25th da, 1815; Thomas Haines, b. 2nd mo, 3rd
da, 1821, d. 7th mo, 1st da, 1821.

Job Haines m. Martha Ballinger 5th mo, 14th da, 1794.

Laurance Webster, son of Thomas and Sarah Webster, b. 10th mo,
12th da, 1737 and wife, Hannah, dau. of Daniel and Mary Wills,
b. 12th mo, 7th mo, 1737, d. 3rd mo, 11th da, 1803 at Upper
Evesham: Levi Webster, b. 6th mo, 14th da, 1764; William
Webster, b. 11th mo, 1st da, 1765; Laurance Webster, b. 11th mo,
12th da, 1767; Hannah Webster, b. 11th mo, 7th da, 1771; Samuel
Webster, b. 5th mo, 15th da, 1774; Sarah Webster, b. 3rd mo,
22nd da, 1776; Daniel Webster, b. 10th mo, 5th da, 1778, d. 10th
mo, 4th da, 1795.

Levi Webster m. Lydia Cox; William Webster m. Hannah Read;
Laurance Webster m. Ann Birdsill; Hannah Webster m. Benjamin
Butter; Sarah Webster m. William Jones. Levi Webster disowned
5th mo, 9th da, 1795.

Children of Hugh Sharp, b. 11th mo, 15th da, 1724, d. 12th mo,
10th da, 1805 at Upper Evesham and wife, Sibillah: Sibillah
Sharp, b. 4th mo, 23rd da, 1755; Hannah Sharp, b. 5th mo, 24th
da, 1757; Thomas Sharp, b. 8th mo, 1st da, 1759; Job Sharp, b.
10th mo, 21st da, 1761; William Sharp, b. 3rd mo, 10th da, 1770.

Sibillah, Hannah and Thomas Sharp all disowned, no dates; William
Sharp disowned 3rd mo, 12th da, 1796.
Josiah Foster, Jr., son of William and Agness Foster, b. 11th mo,
21st da, 1774 and wife, Elizabeth, dau. of James and Anna
Wilkins, b. 9th da, 18th da, 1779.
Charles Foster, son of William and Agness Foster, b. 7th mo, 20th
da, 1782 married to wife, Mary, dau. of James and Anna Wilkins,
b. 12th mo, 10th da, 1780.

Children of James and Anna Wilkins: Anna Wilkins b. 10th mo, 13th
da, 1786, removed to Philadelphia Monthly Meeting; Esther
Wilkins, 5th mo, 26th da, 1791.

Jonathan Haines, son of Isaac and Mary Haines, b. 9th mo, 6th da,
1776 married to wife, Mary, dau. of William and Mary Haines, b.
1st mo, 6th da, 1783.
Isaac Haines, son of Isaac and Mary Haines, b. 12th mo, 25th da,
1778 married to wife, Elizabeth, dau. of Jonathan and Rek
Austin, b. 8th mo, 7th da, 1773.
Benjamin Davis, son of David and Martha Davis, b. 11th mo, 28th
da, 1776.
Samuel Cole Davis, son of Samuel C. and Ann Davis, b. 10th mo,
11th da, 1794.

Children of Elijah Burdsall, b. 1st mo, 10th mo, 1739 and Mary,
his wife, b. 11th mo, 18th da, 1749: Heziah Burdsall, b. 2nd mo,
20th da, 1766, d. 4th mo, 29th da, 1793; Sarah Burdsall, b. 2nd
mo, 17th da, 1768; Lydia Burdsall, b. 4th mo, 11th da, 1770;

Wills Burdsall, b. 5th mo, 10th da, 1773; Anna Burdsall, b. 11th mo, 9th da, 1775, d. 7th mo, 6th da, 1820; Elijah Burdsall, b. 11th mo, 7th da, 1778; William Burdsall, b. 7th mo, 27th da, 1781, d. 12th mo, 13th da, 1827 at Upper Evesham; John Burdsall, b. 3rd mo, 7th da, 1784; Mary Burdsall, b. 1st mo, 16th da, 1787; Charles Burdsall, b. 8th mo, 5th da, 1789, d. 1st mo, 1st da, 1791; Heturah Burdsall, b. 4th mo, 25th da, 1792.

Sarah Burdsall m. Robert Braddock; Anna Burdsall m. Laurance Webster; Mary Burdsall m. John Mullin; Heturah Burdsall m. John Shinn. Lydia Burdsall disowned 7th mo, 9th da, 1796; Anna Burdsall disowned 11th mo, 8th da, 1794; Elijah Burdsall disowned 7th mo, 9th da, 1796; John Burdsall disowned; Mary Burdsall disowned.

Hezekiah Stokes, son of Samuel and Hope Stokes married to Frances Stokes, dau. of Hubert and Sarah Braddock, b. 12th mo, 9th da, 1790.

Simeon Wiltse, b. 7th mo, 10th da, 1763 married to Elizabeth, b. 4th mo, 30th da, 1787.

Simeon Wiltse received by request 7th mo, 6th da, 1799. Simeon Wiltse, wife Elizabeth and children: Henry, Simeon, William, John C. and Martin removed by certificate to Miami Monthly Meeting.

Children of David Stratton and wife, Rebecca: Martha Stratton, b. 8th mo, 10th da, 1770; Sarah Stratton, b. 5th mo, 1st da, 1772; John Stratton, b. 9th mo, 23rd da, 1773; Joseph Stratton, b. 8th mo, 21st da, 1775; Hephzibah Stratton, b. 8th mo, 17th da, 1777; Beulah Stratton, b. 7th mo, 6th da, 1779; Samuel Stratton, b. 10th mo, 13th da, 1781; Rebecca Stratton, b. 1st mo, 30th da, 1785.

Martha Stratton m. William Cowperthwaite; Sarah Stratton m. Moses Lippincott. John Stratton removed to Morris River Monthly Meeting; Joseph Stratton removed; Rebecca Stratton removed to Evesham Monthly Meeting. Joseph Stratton disowned; Hephzibah Stratton disowned 9th mo, 8th da, 1799; Beulah Stratton disowned 5th mo, 7th da, 1796.

Mahlon Stacy Atkinson, son of ? and Mary Atkinson married to Beulah dau. of Thomas and Rachel Lippincott, b. 10th mo, 16th da, 1788.

David Shinn, son of Peter and Grace Shinn, b. 10th mo, 13th da, 1782 married to Hannah, dau. of Thomas and Elizabeth Wilson, b. 7th mo, 15th da, 1781.

Ann Bates, dau. of ? and Catharine Lynch b. 4th mo, 6th da, 1767.

Elizabeth Leeds, dau. of John and Rebecca Eayre, b. 11th mo, 30th da, 1759.

Margaret Phillips dau. of Leland and Prudence Orsen, b. 4th mo, 24th da, 1754.

Mary Newton dau. of ? and Hannah Stokes, b. 8th mo, 15th da, 1745.

Rachel Holmes b. 4th mo, 7th da, 1769.

Hannah Boulton b. 3rd mo, 24th da, 1742.

Beulah Lippincott dau. of Daniel and Sarah Wills, b. 2nd mo, 2nd da, 1754.
Elizabeth Armstrong dau. of Jonas and Ruth Shinn b. 3rd mo, 5th da, 1748.
Sarah Braddock, dau. of William Rogers, b. 3rd mo, 15th da, 1776, m. Darnel Braddock.
Thomas White, son of Samuel and Hannah White, b. 11th mo, 29th da, 1766 and wife, Sabilla removed to Middletown, OH Monthly Meeting.
Elizabeth Collins, b. 1743, d. 2nd mo, 4th da, 1811 at Upper Evesham.
Sarah Lippincott b. 3rd mo, 4th da, 1758 received by certificate from Haddonfield, removed by certificate to Haddonfield Monthly Meeting.

John Collins, son of ? and Elizabeth Collins, b. 5th mo, 31st da, 1782 married to his 1st wife, Esther, dau. of Jonathan and Hannah Borton, b. 1st mo, 3rd mo, 1785.
John Collins married to his 2nd wife, Hannah, dau. of Thomas and Rachel Lippincott, b. 3rd mo, 8th da, 1784.
John Collins married to his 3rd wife, Sarah, dau. of Job and Sarah Haines.
Caleb Stokes, son of John and Beulah Stokes, b. 7th mo, 21st da, 1782 married to his wife, Ruth, b. 8th mo, 22nd da, 1779, dau. of Levi and Hannah Shinn.

Children of William Reeve, son of Mark and Hannah, b. 12th mo, 11th da, 1766 and wife, Leatitia, dau. of Josiah and Leatitia Miller, b. 6th mo, 1st da, 1769: Josiah Miller Reeve, b. 3rd mo, 13th da, 1791; Ann Reeve, b. 3rd mo, 31st da, 1793; Elizabeth Reeve, b. 11th mo, 18th da, 1796; Leatitia Reeve, b. 8th mo, 1st da, 1799; William F. Reeve, b. 6th mo, 7th da, 1802; Mark Reeve, b. 4th mo, 6th da, 1804; Priscilla Reeve, b. 11th mo, 28th da, 1806; Richard Miller Reeve, b. 3rd mo, 24th da, 1809; Emmor Reeve, no date.

William Reeve, wife Leatitia and children: Josiah Miller and Ann received by certificate from Greenwich 7th mo, 9th da, 1796.

Joshua Haines, son of John and Mary Haines, b. 9th mo, 16th da, 1776 married to Mary, dau. of John and Rachel Pine, b. 9th mo, 12th da, 1778.
John Hincham, b. 8th mo, 22nd da, 1788 removed to Philadelphia by certificate.

Children of Isaac Stokes, son of John and Beulah Stokes, b. 4th mo, 10th da, 1787 married to Lydia, dau. of Job and Elizabeth Collins, b. 11th mo, 17th da, 1787.
Children of William Branin, son of Michael and Elizabeth, b. 2nd mo, 15th da, 1750 and wife, Elizabeth Branin formerly Brooks, b. 1750, d. 11th mo, 12th da, 1776: William Branin, b. 9th mo, 15th da, 1772; Thomas Branin, b. 5th mo, 2nd da, 1774; Michael Branin, b. 1st mo, 28th da, 1776.
Children of William Branin and 2nd wife, Abigail, dau. of Abner and Hope Rogers, b. 10th mo, 5th da, 1755, d. 9th mo, 17th da,

1796; Abner Branin, b. 11th mo, 12th da, 1779, d. 11th mo, 1780;
Hope Branin, b. 4th mo, 14th da, 1781; Abijah Branin, b. 5th mo,
9th da, 1783; Elizabeth Branin, b. 2nd mo, 9th da, 1786; Ezra
Branin, b. 10th mo, 9th mo, 1788; Nathaniel Branin, b. 5th mo,
6th da, 1791.
Children of Isaac Garwood, son of Isaiah and Mary Garwood, b.
10th mo, 25th da, 1780 married to Alice, dau. of Levi and Hannah
Shinn.
Children of Samuel Butcher, son of Joseph and Elizabeth Butcher,
b. 12th mo, 28th da, 1784 married to Mary, dau. of Stephen and
Bathsheba Morris.

Beulah Wills b. 2nd mo, 2nd da, 1754. Sarah Lippincott, b. 3rd
mo, 4th da, 1758.
Job Engle, son of John and Patience Engle, b. 2nd mo, 18th da,
1780 married to wife, Sarah, dau. of Josiah and Rek Borton, b.
7th mo, 25th da, 1782.
John Sleeper, son of ? and Jane Sleeper married to Lydia, b. 8th
mo, 20th da, 1786.
Joseph F. Ogborn, b. 11th mo, 3rd da, 1785 married to Elizabeth,
dau. of Isaac and Rebecca Andrews, b. 11th mo, 30th da, 1778.
Samuel Ogborn, b. 3rd mo, 14th da, 1788 married to Esther, dau.
of Isaac and Rebecca Andrews, b. 11th mo, 18th da, 1784.
Amos Ashead, b. 2nd mo, 4th da, 1786 married to Sarah Ashead, b.
2nd mo, 4th da, 1788.
Ezra Branin, b. 10th mo, 9th da, 1788, son of William and Abigail
Branin married to Rachel, dau. of Laber? and Grace Shinn, b. 3rd
mo, 28th da, 1789.

Children of John Brown, b. 9th mo, 1st da, 1777, son of ? and
Virgin Brown married to Elizabeth, dau. of ? and Hannah ?, b.
4th mo, 12th da, 1808.
Child of Samuel R. Smith, b. 5th mo, 8th da, 1788 son of Thomas
and Meribah Smith and wife, Esther, dau. of John and Susanna
Brooks, b. 10th mo, 2nd da, 1790: Rebekah Smith, no date.

John Brown, b. 9th mo, 21st da, 1777, son of ? Brown and
Elizabeth his 1st wife, b. 4th mo, 12th da, 1800.
John Brown and Sarah, dau. of ? married to Ruth Morre, b. 6th mo,
29th da, 1786.

Children of John Shinn, son of Levi and Grace Shinn, b. 3rd mo,
19th da, 1791 married to Sabillah Shinn formerly Collins.
Children of Abraham Haines, son of ? and Sarah Haines, b. 5th mo,
7th da, 1776 married to Sarah, dau. of ? and Theodocia Haines,
b. 12th mo, 20th da, 1784.
William Stokes, son of John and Beulah Stokes, b. 6th mo, 29th
da, 1798 married to Ann, b. 7th mo, 21st da, 1794.
Joseph Haines, son of Nehemiah and Abigail Haines, b. 2nd mo, 1st
da, 1786 married to Deborah E. dau. of Aaron and Esther Engle,
b. 1st mo, 5th da, 1793.
Zebidee M. Mills, son of ? and Priscilla Mills, b. 9th mo, 9th
da, 1791 and wife, Rachel, dau. of ? married to Mary Rogers, b.
2nd mo, 27th da, 1791.
Amaziel Lippincott, b. 1st mo, 17th da, 1745.

Rebecca Ballinger b. 2nd mo, 22nd da, 1770.

Children of Joshua Lippincott, son of Nathan and Sarah
Lippincott, b. 12th mo, 1st da, 1790, d. 8th mo, 26th da, 1822
and Sarah Lipincot, dau. of Jeboz and Sarah Buzby, b. 4th mo,
17th da, 1797.

Joshua Lippincott, wife Sarah received by certificate from
Haddonfield Monthly Meeting 4th mo, 8th da, 1796.
Thomas Evans, son of Thomas and Mary Evans, b. 11th mo, 4th mo,
1792 married to Sarah, dau. of Samuel and Sarah Burrough, b. 9th
mo, 29th da, 1784.
Joseph Matlack, son of ? and Sarah Matlack, b. 11th mo, 2nd da,
1789 married to Dorothy Matlack formerly Lippincott, b. 8th mo,
31st da, 1789.
George Haines son of Nehemiah and Abigail Haines, b. 6th mo, 13th
da, 1798 married to Sarah W. dau. of ? and Priscilla Wills, b.
3rd mo, 30th da, 1802.
John W. Reeve, son of Josiah and Martha Reeve, b. 8th mo, 6th da,
1789 Priscilla W., dau. of John and Mary Sheppard, b. 5th mo,
15th da, 1800.
Job Lippincott, b. 5th mo, 12th da, 1791 married to Mary, dau. of
John and Beulah Stokes, b. 5th mo, 13th da, 1792.
Daniel Zillah married to Dorothy, dau. of Enoch and Hannah
Stratton, b. 1st mo, 28th da, 1793.
John Gardiner, b. 7th mo, 27th da, 1793 son of Joseph and Mary
Gardiner married to Hannah, dau. of ? and Priscilla Wills, b.
1st mo, 22nd da, 1799.
Isaac Brown, b. 1st mo, 21st da, 1787 married to Sarah formerly
Lippincott, b. 1st mo, 23rd da, 1790.
Clayton Roberts, b. 4th mo, 2nd da, 1797 son of Joshua Roberts
married to and Elizabeth, dau. of John and Elizabeth Pope, b.
3rd mo, 2nd da, 1803.
Thomas Page, son of William and Agnes Page, b. 6th mo, 8th da,
1798 married to Elizabeth, b. 10th mo, 4th da, 1804
Amos Evans, son of Jacob and Rachel Evans, b. 6th mo, 23rd da,
1797 and Elizabeth.

Children of Jacob Roberts, son of John and Esther Roberts, b.
11th mo, 27th da, 1798, d. 6th mo, 1855 married to Syllania
formerly Evans, b. 10th mo, 6th da, 1799, d. 9th mo, 30th da,
1830.

Jacob Roberts m. Ann Evans, dau. of Joseph and to Rebecca Evans.
Charles Haines, son of Nehemiah and Abigail Haines, b. 1st mo,
19th da, 1788 married to wife, Mary dau. of John and Ann Troth,
b. 3rd mo, 22nd da, 1795.

UPPER EVESHAM MONTHLY MEETING MINUTES
1794-1800

2nd mo, 8th da, 1794. Samuel Thorn, son of Thomas, to present a certificate from Haddonfield Monthly Meeting to marry. A certificate requested for Joseph Boulton to Burlington Monthly Meeting in order to marry. Jonathan Jones requested a certificate for his son, Jesse, a minor, to Haddonfield Monthly Meeting. Lawrence Webster reported for neglecting to pay his debts.

3rd mo, 8th da, 1794. Hannah Jenkinson to receive her maintenance from this meeting. Joshua Owen requested to be released from the station of an overseer. A committee appointed to have the care of poor Friends within the compass of this Monthly Meeting: Nehemiah Haines, William Brannen, Joshua Stokes, Jacob Evans, Joseph Thorn and Nehemiah Hains. William Rogers is appointed to record marriage certificates. A certificate requested for Job Hains to marry a Friend of Evesham Monthly Meeting.

4th mo, 12th da, 1794. Marriage of Isaac Hains and Elizabeth Butcher accomplished, rights of her children taken care of. Marriage of Samuel Thorn and Sarah Collins accomplished, parents present consenting. Jonathan Evans reported for neglecting meetings and for being charged with being the father of a bastard child. Joshua Lippincott requested a certificate to Burlington Monthly Meeting. Sarah Thorn requested a certificate to Haddonfield Monthly Meeting and Ruth Kimble requested a certificate to Greenwich Monthly Meeting.

5th mo, 10th da, 1794. Laurence Webster has not settled his affairs to satisfaction. James Kettle produced a certificate to this meeting for himself, wife, Deborah and their dau., Ann, from Mt. Holly Monthly Meeting. Ann Kirby requested a certificate to Chesterfield Monthly Meeting; Anna Thomas requested a certificate to Burlington Monthly Meeting. A certificate requested for James Griffith to Evesham Monthly Meeting. A certificate produced for Azuba Boulton from Burlington Monthly Meeting. A certificate produced for Caleb Shrieve, a minor, from Haddonfield Monthly Meeting.

7th mo, 12th da, 1794. Aaron Tomlinson Lippincott produced a certificate Evesham Monthly Meeting. Ester Middleton requested a certificate to Woodbury Monthly Meeting.

8th mo, 9th da, 1794. Whereas Jonathan Evans who hath had a birthright, charged with neglecting meeting and is the father of a bastard child; disowned. John Atkinson produced a certificate from Mt. Holly Monthly Meeting. A certificate requested for Isaac Griffith to Salem Monthly Meeting; James Allinson, a minor, requested a certificate to Monthly Meeting of Northern District Philadelphia. A certificate produced for Susannah Reeves from Mt. Holly Monthly Meeting. Beulah Halbert late Stratton reported for having gone out in marriage; disowned. Rachel Peacock treated with for being the mother of an illegitimate child; disowned.

9th mo, 6th da, 1794. A certificate produced for Elizabeth Leeds
from Mt. Holly Monthly Meeting.

11th mo, 8th da, 1794. Samuel Hains acknowledged his marriage
contrary to discipline [before a magistrate]. A certificate
requested for Jacob Evans to marry a friend of Evesham Monthly
Meeting. Paul Troth produced a certificate from Haddonfield
Monthly Meeting for himself and four children: William, James,
Jacob and Elizabeth. A certificate produced from Evesham Monthly
Meeting for Selany Crispin. Core Haines, son of Isaiah and Mary
Haines, produced a certificate from another Monthly Meeting
[Evesham Monthly Meeting] to marry. Josiah Stokes, son of Thomas
Stokes, produced a certificate from Haddonfield Monthly Meeting.
Ann Webster treated with for accomplishing her marriage contrary
to the rules of Friends; disowned.

12th mo, 6th da, 1794. A certificate produced for Hope, wife of
James Cattle, and their two daus., Jane and Rachel, from Evesham
Monthly Meeting.

1st mo, 10th da, 1795. Marriage of Core Haines and Mary Hains
accomplished, parents consenting. Marriage of Josiah Stokes and
Hope Bourton accomplished, parents consenting. A certificate
produced for Hannah Wills from Salem Monthly Meeting.

2nd mo, 7th da, 1795. Job Hains requested to be released from
station of overseer.

3rd mo, 7th da, 1795. A certificate produced for Rachel Evans
from Evesham Monthly Meeting. Certificates granted for Mary Hains
to Evesham Monthly Meeting and for Sidney and Rachel Owen to
Pilesgrove Monthly Meeting.

4th mo, 11th da, 1795. A certificate granted for Joshua Owen and
wife with their nine minor children: Jesse, Sarah, Prudence,
David, Joshua, Joseph, Elizabeth, Benjamin and Roland to
Pilesgrove Monthly Meeting. Levi Webster stands charged with
being the father of a bastard child which he did not deny. Martin
Moody requested to join the society. A certificate requested for
Joshua Hains, a minor, to Philadelphia Monthly Meeting.

5th mo, 9th da, 1795. A certificate granted for James Cattle,
Jr., his wife, Deborah, and dau., Ann to Burlington Monthly
Meeting. A certificate produced for Martha, wife of Job Hains,
from Evesham Monthly Meeting. Isabel Brannin treated for being
the mother of a bastard child. Jacob Ballenger, Jr., requested a
certificate to Philadelphia Monthly Meeting.

6th mo, 6th da, 1795. A certificate granted for William Vinnacomb
to Mt. Holly Monthly Meeting. Moses Lippincott requested his four
children: Elizabeth, Sarah, Benjamin, and Dorothy be joined in
membership. A certificate produced for Amos Ashead, his wife,
Lydia, and their children: Ellenor, Amos and Moses from
Haddonfield Monthly Meeting. A certificate produced for Daniel
Zilly, Bathsheba, his wife, and their children, Job, Daniel and

William Braddock from Haddonfield Monthly Meeting. Webster Thomas has been treated with for neglecting meetings, paying a fine in lieu of military service and exercising among the militia. A certificate requested for Samuel Webster, Jr. to Woodbury Monthly Meeting. John Torr requested a certificate for his children, John to Mt. Holly Monthly Meeting and Josiah to Burlington Monthly Meeting, but there is some uneasiness with their being placed with persons not in membership with Friends.

7th mo, 11th da, 1795. A certificate produced for Hannah Stokes from Haddonfield Monthly Meeting, also one for Abigail Bates from Evesham Monthly Meeting. Sarah Allen of Cropwell Monthly Meeting requested her son, Nathan Allen, be taken into membership. Solomon Hains requested a certificate for his dau., Elizabeth, to Evesham Monthly Meeting. John Atkinson appointed to record births and burials.

8th mo, 8th da, 1795. Mark Stratton condemns his striking a person in anger. John Haines, Jr. to serve in the station of an overseer. Elizabeth Taylor late Peacock treated with for going out in marriage; disowned. Lydia Durell requested to join in membership. Susanna Reeves requested a certificate to Mt. Holly Monthly Meeting; and, Sarah Lippincott, a minor, requested a certificte to Haddonfield Monthly Meeting.

9th mo, 12th da, 1795. Certificates granted for John Torr, a minor, to Burlington Monthly Meeting and one for Josiah Torr to Mt. Holly Monthly Meeting. Stacy Stratton has been treated with for striking his fellow men in anger. Noah Stratton treated with for taking strong drink to excess and using profane language.

10th mo, 10th da, 1795. William Hains, Jr., produced a certificate from Mt. Holly Monthly Meeting.

11th mo, 7th da, 1795. John Evans condemns his falling into unprofitable company at which time he took strong drink to excess and gave provoking language to one of his fellow men.

12th mo, 12th da, 1795. Tacy Worster treated with for accomplishing her marriage contrary to Friends rules. Hope Kettle [Cattle] and her two daus., Jane and Rachel, requested a certificate to Burlington Monthly Meeting.

1st mo, 9th da, 1796. John Torr requested a certificate for his son, Jaboel, a minor, to Burlington Monthly Meeting. A certificate requested for William Foster, a minor, to Philadelphia Monthly Meeting.

2nd mo, 6th da, 1796. William Sharp treated with for going out in marriage and complying with military requisitions so far as to pay a fine.

3rd mo, 12th da, 1796. Elizabeth Hains acknowledged her going out in marriage. Josiah Stokes produced a certificate from Haddonfield Monthly Meeting.

4th mo, 9th da, 1796. A certificate granted for William Davidson, his wife, Elizabeth, and their children, Mary and William to Pilesgrove Monthly Meeting. Joseph Thorn acknowledged paying a military fine. Eli Evans treated with for neglecting meetings, taking undue liberty in dress and taking spirituous liquors to excess. Samuel Eves treated with for neglecting meetings and paying a military fine. John Evans is appointed in the room of William Rogers to record marriage certificates. Certificates requested for Charity Middleton to Pilesgrove Monthly Meeting and one for Elizabeth Stratton, Jr. to Eggharbor and Cape May Monthly Meeting.

5th mo, 7th mo, 1796. Marriage of Benjamin Butler, son of John Butler, and Hannah Webster, dau. of Laurence Webster, accomplished; he produced his father's consent in writing and her parents present consenting. A certificate produced by Core Hains for himself, his wife, Mary, and their dau., Ann, from Evesham Monthly Meeting. Stacy Shreeve produced a certificate from Haddonfield Monthly Meeting. A committee appointed to nominate an elder: Job Collins, Barzillai Braddock, Samuel Shinn, Thomas Lippincott, Joshua Lippincott and Enoch Evans. Lydia Wolston condemns her going out in marriage. Hipseba Willits reported that she is the mother of a bastard child; disowned. Beulah Rogers late Stratton treated with her going out in marriage.

6th mo, 11th da, 1796. John Shinn, Sr., produced a certificate from Mt. Holly Monthly Meeting. Hugh Sharp treated with for neglecting meetings and disregarding the company and advice of the Friends. Josiah Foster, Jr. has been treated with for neglecting meetings, complying with military requisitions and being the father of a bastard child. Elijah Rundall Jr., has been treated with for going out in marriage and unchaste behavior before marriage with her that is now his wife. Martin Moody informed this meeting that he had a prospect of visiting his relations in his native land in the state of Connecticut and requested a few lines to take with him.

7th mo, 9th da, 1796. Elijah Burdsall, Jr.; disowned. A certificate for Daniel Zilly, Bathsheba, his wife, and their four children: Job, Daniel, William Braddock and Jemima granted to Burlington Monthly Meeting. Certificates produced for Thomas White from Evesham Monthly Meeting; for William Reeves, his wife, Leatitia, and their children, Josiah and Ann from Greenwich Monthly Meeting; and for Rachel Curtis, Jonathan Curtis and Hepsiba Stratton from Mt. Holly Monthly Meeting.

8th mo, 6th da, 1796. Isaac Wilson produced a certificate from Philadelphia Monthly Meeting, with Phebe, his wife, and their two minor children, Ann and Mary. John Middleton, Jr. granted a certificate, he being placed as an apprentice to a Friend in Philadelphia Monthly Meeting. A certificate granted for Sarah Lippincott, a minor, to Evesham Monthly Meeting.

10th mo, 8th da, 1796. Thomas Ballenger, Jr. treated with for neglecting meetings. A certificate granted for Thomas Bond to

Evesham Monthly Meeting.

11th mo, 12th da, 1796. A certificate granted for Reuben Braddock to Haddonfield Monthly Meeting to marry with a Friend of that meeting. A certificate granted for Eli Stratton to Greenwich Monthly Meeting. Sybilla Durel requested to join in membership.

1st mo, 7th da, 1797. Wills Burdsall treated with for marrying with one not in membership.

2nd mo, 11th da, 1797. Jonathan Jones granted a certificate for his son, William, to Greenwich Monthly Meeting.

3rd mo, 11th da, 1797. Gersham Penquite produced a paper condemning his deviation from Friends principles in paying a military fine.

4th mo, 8th da, 1797. William Jones returned the certificate granted last month for Greenwich Monthly Meeting. William Troth produced a certificate for himself and his wife, Esther, from Evesham Monthly Meeting. John Troth produced a certificate from same meeting for himself, his wife, Ann, and their infant dau., Mary, and one infant son born since the date of the certificate (10th mo, 3rd da, 1797). Jane Shinn, wife of Thomas Shinn, requested to join in membership. George Sharp treated with for neglecting meetings.

5th mo, 6th da, 1797. A certificate produced for Elizabeth Braddock from Haddonfield Monthly Meeting and one for Frances Elkaton (Elhaton?) from Mt. Holly Monthly Meeting. Benjamin Butler granted a certificate for himself, and his wife, Hannah, to Haddonfield Monthly Meeting. Peter Shinn produced a certificate from Mt. Holly Monthly Meeting for himself, his wife, Grace, and their children: David, Rachel, John and Maylon. A certificate granted for Elizabeth Torr to Haddonfield Monthly Meeting.

6th mo, 10th da, 1797. Joseph Stratton produced a certificate from Mt. Holly. Jacob Ridgway granted a certificate for his son, Ellis, to Philadelphia Monthly Meeting.

7th mo, 8th da, 1797. Martha Allinson granted a certificate for her son Samuel, a minor, to Burlington Monthly Meeting.

8th mo, 12th da, 1797. Moses Lippincott and Sarah, his wife, treated with for his unchaste behavior before marriage with her that is now his wife and accomplishing his marriage contrary to the rules of discipline; disowned.

9th mo, 9th da, 1797. Martha Coperthwait, formerly Stratten, acknowledged her going out in marriage.

10th mo, 7th da, 1797. Marriage of David Jones, son of David Jones, dec'd, and Rebecca Foster, dau. of Josiah Foster, accomplished, parents present consenting, he being from

Philadelphia Monthly Meeting. Esteemed Friend Jervas Johnson
attended this meeting and produced a certificate from Monthly
Meeting of Antrim in Ireland.

11th mo, 11th da, 1797. Marriage of Richard Sheppard, son of John
Sheppard, and Lydia Foster, dau. of Josiah Foster, accomplished.
Marriage of Edward Boulton, son of William Boulton, and Alce
Stratten, dau. of Ephraim Stratten, accomplished, parents present
consenting. Elizabeth Robinson requested to join in membership.
Certificates granted for Rebecca Jones to Northern District
Philadelphia Monthly Meeting and one for Lydia Sheppard to
Greenwich Monthly Meeting.

12th mo, 9th da, 1797. Jacob Lippincott has been treated with for
being the father of a bastard child and afterwards accomplishing
his marriage with another woman before a magistrate. Elizabeth
Hains and her husband, Samuel, requested membership for their
infant dau., Hannah.

1st mo, 1st da, 1798. Marriage of Solomon Hains and Rachel Curtes
accomplished, rights of her children settled. A certificate
requested for John Atkinson to Evesham Monthly Meeting to marry.
Elizabeth Shreve treated with for being the mother of a child, in
an unmarried state.

2nd mo, 10th da, 1798. Abner Watson produced a certificate for
himself, his wife, Elizabeth, and their infant dau., Mary, from
Falls Monthly Meeting, Bucks County, PA. Joseph Boulton requested
a certificate for himself, his wife and child to Eggharbour and
Cape May Monthly Meeting.

3rd mo, 10th da, 1798. A certificate granted for Joseph Boulton,
Azubah, his wife, and their infant dau., Margaret. A certificate
granted for Margaret Hiles, a minor, to Haddonfield Monthly
Meeting. Martha Allinson requested a certificate for herself and
her children, Margaret and John, to Burlington Monthly Meeting.

4th mo, 7th da, 1798. A certificate granted for Jane Siddens,
Mary, Elizabeth and Sybil Allinson, to Burlington Monthly
Meeting. Heziah Long requested that she be joined in membership.

5th mo, 12th da, 1798. A certificate granted for Aaron
Lippincott, a minor, to Woodbury Monthly Meeting. A certificate
produced for Benjamin Cooper and his wife, Ann, and their
children: Deborah, Rebecca, Ann, Benjamin and Samuel; a
certificate for John Roberts and his wife, Esther; a certificate
for Elizabeth Atkinson and a certificate for Elizabeth Hains; all
from Evesham Monthly Meeting. Nev Braddock treated for marrying
his first cousin, Selany; disowned.

6th mo, 9th da, 1798. Caleb Bourton, Jr., guilty of copying a
propaganda piece of poetry to the trouble of his friends, taking
strong drink to excess and associating with unprofitable company.
A certificate produced for Elizabeth Collins from Haddonfield
Monthly Meeting; and a certificate produced for Hope Oliphent

from Mt. Holly Monthly Meeting. John Shinn produced a certificate for himself, Sarah, his wife, and their son, Benjamin, from Mt. Holly Monthly Meeting; and a certificate produced from same meeting for Jane Steepens (Sleepers?) and her minor children: Sarah, John and Benjamin. Abel Ashead condemns his conduct in paying military demands and suffering his horse to run a race. William Andrews has been treated with for going out in marriage with a person not in membership. Nicholas Hiles requested a certificate for his son Joseph, a minor, to Evesham Monthly Meeting. Hannah Jenkinson, a poor friend of this meeting, has had some property fall to her by heirship from the estate of Abednego Wright, dec'd.

7th mo, 7th da, 1798. William Jones condemns his conduct in drinking to excess, using profane languange and paying a military fine.

11th mo, 8th mo, 1798. William Cooper produced a certificate for himself and his wife, Hannah, from Evesham Monthly Meeting. Sarah, wife of William Salter, requested to join into membership.

9th mo, 8th mo, 1798. Eli Field, Jr. produced a certificate from Falls Monthly Meeting of Bucks County. Uriah Bourton produced a certificate from Evesham Monthly Meeting.

10th mo, 6th da, 1798. Marriage of Uriah Bourton, son of Abraham Bourton, dec'd. and Mary Collins, dau. of Job Collins, accomplished, with the young woman's parents being present consenting. Eli Field produced a certificate for himself, his wife, Hannah, and their dau., Martha, from Falls Monthly Meeting, Bucks County, PA. Joseph Pierce produced a certificate from Burlington Monthly Meeting for himself, his wife, Mary, and their children: Susanna, Mary, Hannah and Rachel. Prudence Austin treated for going out in marriage and unchaste behavior before marriage.

11th mo, 10th da, 1798. Elizabeth Hains, wife of Jno. Hains, appointed Elder. Abel Ashead requested a certificate to Haddonfield Monthly Meeting to marry. David Allinson requested a certificate to Woodbury Monthly Meeting.

12th mo, 6th da, 1798. Marriage of David Davis, son of David Davis, and Mary Hains, dau. of John Haines, accomplished, their parents present consenting. David Davis to produce a certificate from the Monthly Meeting where he belongs. Edmond Hains produced a certificate from Evesham Monthly Meeting for himself, his wife, Charlotte, and their children: Reuben, Deborah and Leeds. A certificate granted for Mary Bourton to Evesham Monthly Meeting. Hannah Braddock requested a certificate for herself and her children: Charlotte, Mariah and Job to Evesham Monthly Meeting. A certificate granted for Mary Bourton to Evesham Monthly Meeting. John Evans requested a certificate to Evesham Monthly Meeting to marry.

1st mo, 12th da, 1799. Michael Brannen has been treated for

neglecting meetings and committing fornication with one who is now his wife. Theodocia Gibs has been treated for going out in marriage.

2nd mo, 9th da, 1799. Benjamin Willits has been treated for neglecting meetings and going out in marriage. Joseph Thorn granted a certificate to Burlington Monthly Meeting. Rebecca Wright treated for going out in marriage.

3rd mo, 9th da, 1799. Memorial being produced for deceased Friend, Martin Moody. Joseph Thorn acknowledged his attending a marriage consummated contrary to the rules of our discipline. Marriage of Paul Troth and Sybilla Ballenger accomplished, their surviving parents consenting. A certificate granted for William Andrews to Mt. Holly Monthly Meeting. A certificate granted for Joshua Stokes to Evesham Monthly Meeting to marry.

4th mo, 6th da, 1799. Certificates granted for Elizabeth Lippincott to Evesham Monthly Meeting and one for Keziah Long to Woodbury Monthly Meeting. A certificate produced for Anna Ashead from Haddonfield Monthly Meeting. A certificate produced for Anna Hains from Chesterfield Monthly Meeting.

5th mo, 11th da, 1799. Jonathan Artes, Jr. condemning his deviation in accomplishing his marriage contrary to the rules of Friends. Job Pricket, Jr. treated for accomplishing his marriage contrary to rules of Friends, marrying with one not in membership and by the assistance of a Baptist minister. A certificate granted for Lydia Durel and Mary Davis to Evesham Monthly Meeting. Caleb Bourton, Jr. granted a certificate to Evesham Monthly Meeting.

6th mo, 8th da, 1799. Marriage of Isaac Ballenger, son of Thomas Ballenger and Esther Hains, dau. of John Haines, accomplished with consent of parents. Isaac Ballenger, the young man being from another Monthly Meeting [Evesham]. Simeon Wilsey has requested to join in membership. A certificate produced for Rebecca Evans from Evesham Monthly Meeting. Jonathan Curtis granted a certificate to Salem Monthly Meeting.

7th mo, 6th da, 1799. A certificate produced for Rebecca Stokes from Evesham Monthly Meeting; a certificate produced for Beulah Atkinson, a minor, from Woodbury Monthly Meeting; and a certificate produced for Isaac Person Rodman, a minor, from Burlington Monthly Meeting.

9th mo, 3rd da, 1799. An essay of a certificate for Elizabeth Collins produced. A certificate produced for Theodocia Wilkins from Evesham Monthly Meeting.

10th mo, 12th da, 1799. A certificate produced for Joseph Taylor from Bradford Monthly Meeting, PA.

12th mo, 7th da, 1799. Josiah Hains, Jr., condemns his going out in marriage with one not in membership. Daniel Braddock condemns his conduct in accomplishing marriage contrary to the rules. A certificate granted for Esther Ballenger to Evesham Monthly Meeting. A certificate produced from Evesham Monthly Meeting for Hannah Shinn.

1st mo, 11th da, 1800. A certificate produced from Chesterfield Monthly Meeting for Lydia Williams. William Jones treated for neglecting meetings. John Brown requested to be released from station of overseer. Job Pricket, Jr. has been treated for paying military demands. A certificate produced for Samuel Butcher, a minor, from Haddonfield Monthly Meeting.

2nd mo, 8th da, 1800. John Brown, Jr. condemns his accomplishing his marriage contrary to rules of Friends with one not in membership. Japhit Garwood produced a certificate from Evesham Monthly Meeting.

3rd mo, 8th da, 1800. A certificate granted Jacob Ridgway, his wife, Susannah, and their minor children: Eli, Elizabeth, Jacob, Aaron, Lydia, and Sarah to Pilesgrove Monthly Meeting. A certificate produced from Mt. Holly Monthly Meeting for Sarah Braddock and Mary Lippincott, a minor.

4th mo, 12th da, 1800. Marriage of Caleb Clothier, son of James Clothier, and Elizabeth Jones, dau. of Jonathan Jones, accomplished, their surviving parents consenting. The young man being from another Monthly Meeting [Mt. Holly]. Aaron Lippincott granted a certificate to Evesham Monthly Meeting.

5th mo, 10th da, 1800. William Brannin condemns his going out in marriage. Elizabeth Reeve, wife of Samuel Reeve, requested to join in membership. Sarah Salter, wife of Wm. Salter, requested that her two minor daus., Sarah and Mary, be received into membership. A certificate for Elizabeth Clothier to Mt. Holly Monthly Meeting granted.

6th mo, 7th da, 1800. Marriage of John Bourton of Evesham Monthly Meeting, son of John Bourton, dec'd, and Jemima Braddock, dau. of Rehoboam Braddock, accomplished, her surviving parents consenting. Mark Reeve produced a certificate from Philadelphia Monthly Meeting Northern District for himself, his wife, Hannah, and their children, Casper and Robert. A certificate produced from Mt. Holly Monthly Meeting for Jemima Bourton.

8th mo, 18th da, 1800. A certificate requested for Jacob Bourton to Mt. Holly Monthly Meeting to marry. John Brown requested a certificate for his son, Clayton, a minor, to Woodbury Monthly Meeting.

9th mo, 8th da, 1800. Friend John Brown being removed by death since last meeting; Edward Boulton is appointed in his room to the oversee the meetings at New Hopewell. A certificate granted for John Brown, Jr., to Woodbury Monthly Meeting.

6th mo, 9th da, 1800. John Stratton, Jr. has been treated for neglecting meetings and complying with military services. A certificate produced from Evesham Monthly Meeting for Sarah Bourton.

11th mo, 10th da, 1800. Edward Hains has been treated for neglecting meetings and taking strong drink to excess. Elizabeth Mullen formerly Hains has been treated with for going out in marriage.

8th mo, 11th da, 1800. A certificate granted for Mary Pierce, a minor, to Evesham Monthly Meeting. Hepziba Pricket late Stratton has been treated for unchaste conduct before marriage with him that is now her husband.

6th mo, 12th da, 1800. Marriage of Richard Bourton, son of Caleb Bourton, and Rachel Braddock, dau. of Reuben Braddock, dec'd., accomplished, their surviving parents consenting, the young man being from another Monthly Meeting. Sabylla Pricket, wife of John Pricket, requested to join; also Abigail Bates, wife of John Bates, requested that her two minor daus., Elizabeth and Amy, be taken under the care of Friends. Solomon Saunders, son of John Saunders, dec'd., and Lydia Borough, dec'd., to marry.

BURLINGTON COUNTY BIRTH RECORDS

Note: The foregoing birth record was kept by a Quaker physician in Burlington county, NJ. I purchased it from a dealer in antiques in Philadelphia, who secured it with other material from the attick [attic] of an old house which was being torn down near Crosswicks, New Jersey. Inquiry failed to develop the name of the writer. The name of Joseph Reckless on the inside cover led to inquires in that family, but without finding any physician in that family. H. E. Deats. Published in the New Jersey Historical Society Bulletin, Vol. III, 1918. No. 1.

A dau. was born to Sarah Beck on Jan 3, 1770.
A dau. was born to Peter Curtiss and his wife on Jan 10, 1770.
A dau. was born to Asa Shin and his wife on Jan 10, 1770.
A dau. was born to John Woodward and his wife on Jan 11, 1770.
A dau. was born to Joseph Woodward and Hannorah on Jan 19, 1770.
A dau. was born to Richard Potts and his wife on Jan 23, 1770.
A son was born to John Martin and his wife on Jan 27, 1770.
A dau. was born to Jos: Pancoast's negro Jack and his wife, Pleasant on Jan 27, 1770.
A dau. was born to Anthony Taylor on Jan 29, 1770.
A dau. was born to Rebeckah Willard on Jan 31, 1770.
A son was born to James Hulse on Feb 1, 1770.
A dau. was born to Andrew Martin on Feb 3, 1770.
A dau. was born to Joseph Kirby and his wife on Feb 22, 1770.
A son was born to James Kobson and his wife on Feb 23, 1770.
A son was born to James Bunting and his wife on Mar 15, 1770.
A son was born to Thomas Leyland and his wife on Mar 17, 1770.
A dau. was born to Thomas Cassaday and his wife on Mar 18, 1770.
A dau. was born to William Woodward and his wife, Rebeckah on Apr 1, 1770.
A dau. was born to Andrew Taylor's black Tom on Apr 3, 1770.
A dau. was born to Elizabeth Martin, a bastard born in Mansfield.
A son was born to Solomon Rockhill and his wife on Apr 27, 1770.
A dau. was born to Marggrett Brady in Mansfield May 3, 1770 said to be Joseph Cogill's.
A dau. was born to Richard Buffin and his wife on Jun 17, 1770.
A dau. was born to Samuel Quickfall and his wife on Jul 2, 1770.
A son was born to Thomas Merrit and his wife on Jul 8, 1770.
A dau. was born to John Herd and his wife on Aug 8, 1770.
A son was born to John Leonard and his wife on Aug 11, 1770.
A son was born to Anthony Woodward and Cressy on Aug 11, 1770.
A son was born to David Allen and his wife on Aug 17, 1770.
A son was born to William Newbold's wench Dinah on Sep 8, 1770.
A dau. was born to Jacob Gibson and his wife on Sep 10, 1770.
A son was born to Joseph Ashton and his wife on Oct 18, 1770.
A dau. was born to Joseph Bussom and his wife on Oct 29, 1770.
A dau. was born to Sophia Bunting's wench Sabeak on Nov 18, 1770.
A dau. was born to John Adams and his wife on Dec 3, 1770.
A dau. was born to Thomas Newbold and his wife on Dec 17, 1770.
A dau. was born to Abel Starkey and his wife on Dec 21, 1770.
A son was born to Joseph Chapman and his wife on Dec 21, 1770.
A son was born to John Steward and his wife on Dec 22, 1770.

A dau. was born to Abraham Rakeltran and his wife on Dec 23, 1770.
A dau. was born to Daniel Randolph and his wife on Jan 6, 1771.
A son was born to William Wheatley on Jan 14, 1771.
A son was born to David Antram on Jan 20, 1771.
A son was born to John Wood and his wife on Jan 20, 1771.
A dau. was born to William Hay and his wife on Jan 27, 1771.
A dau. was born to Joseph Borden and his Sarah on Jan 30, 1771.
A dau. was born to James Saxton and his wife on Feb 1, 1771.
A dau. was born to Nathaniel Pope and his wife on Feb 3, 1771.
A son was born to Mary Martin on Feb 17, 17771 at John Newells in Chesterfield.
A dau. was born to John Ogburn and his wife on Mar 5, 1771.
A dau. was born to Abraham Chapman and his wife on Mar 11, 1771.
A dau. was born to Edward Wheatcraft on Mar 13, 1771.
A dau. was born to Edmond Beakes on Mar 15, 1771.
A dau. was born to Sophua Gibbs on Mar 22, 1771.
A dau. was born to David Thomas on Mar 23, 1771.
A dau. was born to John Mim on Mar 24, 1771.
A dau. was born to Joshua Bunting on Mar 26, 1771.
A dau. was born to Isaac Marshall on Mar 26, 1771.
A dau. was born to Edward Page on Apr 5, 1771.
A dau. was born to Philip Dennis on Apr 16, 1771.
A dau. was born to John Parker on May 14, 1771.
A son was born to Samuel Rogers on May 26, 1771.
A son was born to William Cooke on May 28, 1771.
A son was born to Joseph Pancoast and Unity on Jun 10, 1771.
A dau. was born to Robert Frasher on Jun 5, 1771.
A dau. was born to Frederick Muskott on Jun 11, 1771.
A son was born to Jacob Lawrence on Jun 14, 1771.
A son was born to Jerusa Clevenger on Jun 15, 1771 at William Wheatley's, a bastard.
A son was born to Joseph Dugless and his wife on Jun 29, 1771.
A dau. was born to Sollomon Jevins and Susannah on Jul 7, 1771.
A dau. was born to Samuell Shreve and his wife on Jul 7, 1771.
A son was born to Amos Thorn and his wife on Jul 16, 1771.
A dau. was born to Barzilla Gaskin and his wife on Jul 21, 1771.
A son was born to Joseph Pancoast and Sarah on Jul 22, 1771.
A son was born to Thomas Parent and his wife on Jul 29, 1771.
A dau. was born to Jane Nevell on Jul 30, 1771 said to be Jonathan Middleton's.
A son was born to Jacob Lawrence's negro wench Tamar on Jul 27, 1771.

BURLINGTON COUNTY MARRIAGES

From the Docket of Josiah Foster, Justice of the Peace
Note:The entries with an asterick are by Governor's license.

Dec 25, 1782 -Isaac Stratton and Mary Bullen. *.
Dec 31, 1786 -Samuel Clement, Jr. and Mary Foster.
Aug 8, 1786 -Uriah Foster and Phoebe Stratton.
Apr 7, 1787 -John Bishop and Rachel Snuffin.*
Jan 11, 1787 -John Allen and Amy Miller.
Nov 9, 1788 -Jonathan Morse and Grace Stratton.
Nov 20, 1788 -Barzilla Ridgway and Rachel Murrell.
Dec 17, 1788 -James Allen and Rachel Prickett.
Dec 25, 1788 -James Budden and Elizabeth Anderson.
Mar 1, 1789 -John Williams and Rebecca Roy.
Apr 30, 1789 -Wm. Salter and Sarah Robinson.
May 6, 1789 -Seth Crispin and Hope Thomas.
Dec 17, 1789 -John Savage and Elizabeth Devit.
--- -- 1789 -Solomon Parker and Sarah Clear.
--- -- 1789 -Peter Allen, Jr. and Abigail Wilshear.
Dec 24, 1789 -William Mason and Hope Austin.
Mar 3, 1790 -William Garwood and Ann Irwin.
Apr 27, 1790 -Eber Talor and Tamson Tomlin.
Mar 9, 1790 -Benjamin Sever and Mary Musgrave.
Jun 28 1790 -Benjamin Pine and Sarah Moore, widow.*
Mar 10, 1790 -George Monrow and Hannah Ellis.
May 10, 1790 -Thomas Taylor and Catennor Jackson.
Sep 28, 1790 -Burzilla Branin and Susannah Stratton.
Oct 8, 1791 -Thos. Gallifer and Mary Sharp, dau. of John, dec'd.
Nov 9, 1791 -George Betzler and Elizabeth Brooks.
Jan 4, 1792 -John King and Margaret Mingin.
Jan 14, 1792 -Joshua Lord and Mary Sleeper.
Jan 29, 1792 -Ephraim Cline, Jr. and Rachel Salter, dau. of Joseph.
Mar 8, 1792 -Aaron Sharp and Rachel Cox.
Apr 5, 1792 -Jonathan Sleeper and Edith Peddle.
May 29, 1792 -Thomas Lester and Abigail Cattle, widow.
Jul --, 1792 -Wm. Nixon and Phoebe Goslin.
Jan 2, 1793 -Enoch Sharp and Sarah Philips.
Jan 2, 1793 -Samuel Goforth and Mary Brown.
Jan 10, 1793 -Joseph Hugg, Jr. and Deborah Matlock, dau of Abram.
Feb 14, 1793 -Caleb Haines and Rebecca Haines.
Apr 1, 1793 -Joseph Garwood and Rachel Shivers.
May 28, 1793 -Amos Springer and Sarah Harber.
Jun 27, 1793 -Jonathan Atkinson and Rebecca Cohean.
--- -- 1793 -Samuel Jones and Drucilla Wallins.
--- -- 1793 -Josiah Lippincott and Mary Philipps.
Dec 14, 1793 -Joshua Holbert and Beulah Stratton.
Dec 23, 1793 -Peter Budey and Abigail Smith.
Feb 25, 1794 -Job Lippincott and Barsheba Evans, dau of S. Evans.
Mar 5, 1794 -John Middleton, weaver, and Deborah Sharp.
Mar 8, 1794 -Abraham Witcraft and Mary Addoms.
Mar --, 1794 -Timothy Sharp and Elizabeth Myoveria, widow.

BURLINGTON COUNTY, NEW JERSEY MARRIAGE LICENSES

Mar 29, 1727, Andrew Conerow of Burlington County and Rebecca Arnold of the same county, spinster.
Apr 12, 1727, Samuel Waterman, Burlington County, yeoman, and Mary Godfrey of same, spinster.
May 30, 1727, Joseph Woodward, Burlington County, yeoman, and Hannah Warner of same, spinster.
May 5, 1727, John Ridgway, Burlington County, yeoman, and Hannah Brown of same, spinster.
May 5, 1727, Patrick Byrne, Burlington County, and Mary Ballenger of same, spinster.
Jun 21, 1727, Roger Heartly, Province of Pennsylvania, yeoman, and Rebecca Parker of Burlington County, spinster.
Jul 19, 1727, James Burnside, Burlington County, yeoman, and Mary Hendricks of same, spinster.
Jul 21, 1727, James Kemings, Burlington County, yeoman, and Anne Hodson of same, spinster.
Aug 19, 1727, Robert Bishop, Evesham Twp., Burlington County, yeoman, and Mary Hall of same, spinster.
Jun 20, 1727, George Satterthwaite, Burlington, glazier, and Rebecca Pattison of same, widow.
Aug 31, 1727, James Siddel, Burlington County, weaver, and Sarah Bolton of same, spinster.
Sep 14, 1727, James Scholey, Burlington, weaver, and Mary Willson of same, spinster.
Oct 5, 1727, Bartho. West, Monmouth County, weaver, and Susannah Shinn of Burlington County, spinster.
Dec 6, 1727, William Follwell, Burlington County, yeoman, and Anne Potts of same, spinster.
Jan 4, 1727, John Lee, Town and county of Burlington, brickmaker, and Johanna Fort of Springfield, Burlington County, spinster.
Feb 1, 1727, Ezekiah Willson, Springfield, Burlington County, yeoman, and Christian Atkinson of Northampton, same county, spinster.
Feb 3, 1727, Joseph Morton, Northampton, Burlington County, yeoman, and Anne Cozens of same, spinster.
Feb 9, 1727, Samuel Horseman, Freehold, Monmouth County, yeoman, and Rebecca Folke of Chesterfield, Burlington County, spinster.
Feb 19, 1727, John Crague (Cragne), Burlington County, yeoman, and Mary Ellwell of Salem County, spinster.
Apr 1, 1727, William Hollinghead, Burlington County, yeoman, and Hannah Ruderow of same, spinster. [error for 1728].
Apr 3, 1728, John Willcox, Burlington County, blacksmith, and Elizabeth Elkinton of same, widow.
Apr 20, 1728, James Smart, town of Burlington, waterman, and Honour Shallick of same, spinster.
Apr 23, 1728, Josiah Southwick, Burlington County, yeoman, and Elizabeth Parker of same, spinster.
May 14, 1728, Robert Taylor, Burlington County, yeoman, and Sarah Woodard of same, spinster.
May 26, 1728, Joseph Rockhill, Burlington County, mariner, and Sarah Taylor of same, spinster.
Jun 25, 1728, Job Lippincott, Northampton Twp, Burlington,

yeoman, and Anna Ogburn of same, spinster.
Jun 26, 1728, David Lippincott, Burlington County, yeoman, and Mary Chambers of same, spinster.
Jul 1, 1728, Daniel Stockton, Burlington County, yeoman, and Hannah Fisher of same, spinster.
Jul 15, 1728, William Snowden, town of Burlington, hatter, and Hannah White of same.
Jul 19, 1728, Jacob Prickitt, Northampton Twp., Burlington County, yeoman, and Mary Parker of same, spinster.
Jul 26, 1728, George Blackemore, Burlington County, yeoman, and Maria Merritt [Merrit], Mansfield Twp, spinster.
Jul 29, 1728, Obediah Hireton, Jr., Burlington County, and Mary King of same, spinster.
Jul 29, 1728, Thomas Blake, Town of Burlington, mariner, and Anne ---.
Aug 10, 1728, Henry Scott, Burlington County, yeoman, and Jane Hancock of same, spinster.
Aug 14, 1728, Amos Ashead, Burlington County, yeoman, and Cecilla Cheesman of same, spinster.
Sep 16, 1728, Samuel Woodward, Burlington County, yeoman, and Rachel Cowgill of same, spinster.
Sep 12, 1728, Matthew Willson, Burlington County, yeoman, and Anne Guilham of same, widow.
Sep 30, 1728, Benjamin Sharp, Burlington County, yeoman, and Elizabeth Sharp of same, spinster.
Nov 3, 1731, John Fort, Burlington County, and Hannah Marriott of Springfield, Burlington County.
Oct 6, 1732, John Staunton, Little Egg Harbour, Burlington County, yeoman, and Dinah Gale, spinster.
Oct 11, 1732, Henry Oldacres, Evesham, Burlington County, yeoman, and Elinor Borden, spinster.
Nov 24, 1732, John Roberts, New Hanover, Burlington County, husbandman, and Hannah Newberry of same, spinster.
Dec 1, 1732, Richard Eayre, Evesham, Burlington County, yeoman, and Sarah Garwood of same, spinster.
Dec 25, 1732, George White, Burlington, Burlington County, taylor, and Mary Williams of Bristol, Bucks County.
Jun 10, 1732, Thomas Barnes, Jr., Burlington County, yeoman, and Sarah Watson.
Mary 6, 1732, Philippo Tasso, Evesham, Burlington County, sawyer, and Phebe Springer of same, spinster.
Mar 14, 1732, Daniel Sutton, Burlington, Burlington County, blacksmith, and Mary Jackson, spinster.
Apr 12, 1733, Robert Fort, Springfield, Burlington County, husbandman, and Joanna Lebby of same, spinster.
May 7, 1733, Edward Tonkin, Springfield, Burlington County, yeoman, and Mary Cole of Waterford, Gloucester County, spinster.
May 23, 1733, Julius Ewan, Burlington County, yeoman, and Anna Motte, spinster.
May 23, 1733, Samuel Killy, Burlington County, yeoman, and Bathsheba Richards, spinster.
Jul 16, 1733, Samuel Parr, Chester, Burlington County, weaver, and Hannah Burroughs, the younger, of Gloucester County, spinster.
Jul 19, 1733, Jacob Johnson [Richardson in marginal heading],

Northampton, Burlington County, yeoman, and Sarah Fenton of same, widow.
Jul 27, 1733, John Whitehead, Burlington County, cordwainer, and Mary Peachee, spinster.
Sep 1, 1733, Stephen Adams, Springfield, Burlington County, husbandman, and Sarah Rogers of same, spinster.
Sep 17, 1733, Thomas Stevenson, Chesterfield, Burlington County, husbandman, and Experience Cheshire, spinster.
Sep 20, 1733, Jacob Prickett, Northampton, Burlington County, yeoman, and Hannah Bishop, spinster.
Sep 24, 1733, John Springer, Burlington County, husbandman, and Elizabeth Bozworth, spinster.
Sep 28, 1733, Philip Quigley, Nottingham, Burlington County, slavegetter, and Mary Pearson, spinster.
Oct 13, 1733, Robert Saunders, Burlington County, gentleman, and Margaret Cliff of Philadelphia County, widow.
Oct 16, 1733, Henry Tuckney, Burlington County, cordwainer, and Ann Vaughan of same, spinster.
Oct 18, 1733, Joseph Lewis, Evesham, Burlington County, yeoman, and Mary Stratton of same, spinster.
Nov 15, 1733, Jacob Matlack, Evesham, weaver, and Ruth Woodoth.
Jun 5, 1736, Daniel West, Northampton, Burlington County, yeoman, and Rachel Horner, daughter of Isaac Horner of Mansfield.
Jun 21, 1736, Chas. Taylor, Chesterfield, Burlington County, yeoman, and Rachel Evringham of Monmouth County, widow.
Jul 9, 1736, Samuel Hollinshead, Chester, Burlington County, yeoman, and Ann Rosell of same, spinster.
Jul 15, 1736, Abraham Walker, Chester Twp, Burlington County, husbandman, and Rebecca Chambers of same, spinster.
Aug 3, 1736, Edmond Cowgill, Jr., Burlington, weaver, and Marg't Johnson of same, widow.
Aug 9, 1736, John Monroe, Burlington County, sawyer, and Margaret Mitchel, spinster.
Aug 25, 1736, Joseph Aaronson, Chesterfield, Burlington County, yeoman, and Hannah Folwell, spinster.
Sep 18, 1736, Jacob DeCow, Mansfield, Burlington County, husbandman, and Mary Bowker of same, spinster.
Sep 27, 1736, Amos Austin, Evesham, Burlington County, yeoman, and Esther Haines of same, spinster.
Sep 30, 1736, Thomas Earl, New Hanover, Burlington County, husbandman, and Judith Bostedo of Upper Freehold, Monmouth County, spinster.
Oct 30, 1736, Thomas Rogers, Burlington County, yeoman, and Ann Staples of same, spinster.
Nov 1, 1736, Nathan Starkey, New Hanover, Burlington County, yeoman, and Tacey Jones of same, spinster.
Nov 2, 1736, Richard Fenimore, Northampton, Burlington County, husbandman, and Sarah Newell of same, spinster.
Nov 17, 1736, Joseph Chambers, Chesterfield, Burlington County, yeoman, and Sarah Shores of same, spinster.
Nov 18, 1736, Benjamin Butterworth, Burlington County, yeoman, and Ann McCarty of Burlington, widow.
Nov 29, 1736, Dennis Springer, Evesham, Burlington County, husbandman, and Ann Prickett of same, spinster.
Nov 30, 1736, John Huggin, Crosswicks, Burlington County, yeoman,

and Hannah Martin of same, spinster.
Dec 11, 1736, Joseph Spraggs, Mansfield, Burlington County, husbandman, and Elizabeth Wiles of same, widow.
Dec 9, 1736, Reddock Townsend, Great Eggharbour, Burlington County, yeoman, and Mary Covenoven of same, spinster.
Dec 13, 1736, John Gosling, Esq., Burlington, and Sarah Budd of same, widow.
Dec 28, 1736, James Sebet, Chesterfield, Burlington County, cooper, and Hannah James of same, widow.
Dec 29, 1736, Benjamin Fowler, Upper Freehold, Monmouth County, blacksmith, and Miriam Wright of Burlington County, spinster.
Jan 3, 1736, John Pearson, Evesham, Burlington County, husbandman, and Sarah Hamot of Gloucester County, spinster.
Jan 10, 1736, Henry Burr, Northampton, Burlington County, yeoman, and Mary Owen of same, spinster.
Jan 11, 1736, Joseph Scattergood, Burlington, mariner, and Rebecca Watson of Philadelphia, spinster.
Jan 12, 1736, Isaac Atkinson, Northampton, Burlington County, cordwainer, and Elizabeth Reeves, spinster, dau. of William Reeves of same, yeoman.
Feb 9, 1736, John Holder, Burlington, millwright, and Joanna Tindall of Nottingham, Burlington County, widow.
Feb 25, 1736, Job Talman, Mansfield, Burlington County, yeoman, and Sarah Scattergood, spinster, dau of Benjamin Scattergood, yeoman.
Feb 3, 1736, Philip Kenney, Burlington County, husbandman, and Sarah Bryan of Burlington, widow.
Mar 9, 1736, William Price, Chesterfield, Burlington County, blacksmith, and Rebecca Church, spinster dau of --- Church, widow.
Mar 18, 1736, Jonathan Reeves, Northampton, Burlington County, yeoman, and Hannah Budd of same, widow.
May 1, 1736, Charles Netterville, New Hanover, Burlington County, yeoman, and Rachel Wilson of same, spinster.
May 7, 1736, Samuel Wheatcraft, Mansfield, Burlington County, wheelwright, and Sarah Carter of same, spinster.
May 11, 1736, John Davies, Northampton, Burlington County, yeoman, and Hannah Taten of same, widow.
May 12, 1736, Joseph Indicott, Northampton, Burlington County, yeoman, and Ann Gillam of same, spinster.
May 18 1736, Joseph Talman, Mansfield, Burlington County, yeoman, and Mary Woodward, spinster.
May 24, 1736, John Peters, Northampton, Burlington County, carter and Hannah Symonds of same, spinster.
Jul 4, 1737, Samuel Shinn, Northampton Twp., Burlington County, yeoman, and Province Gaskill of same, spinster.
Jul 18, 1737, James Shinn, New Hanover, Burlington County, yeoman, and Hannah Shinn, spinster, daughter of George Shinn, Springfield, Burlington County, yeoman.
Jul 19, 1737, George Clevinger, New Hanover, Burlington County, labourer, and Deliverance Horner, spinster, daughter of Joshua Horner, dec'd.
Jul 25, 1737, Thomas Preston, Burlington, apprentice to Fretwel Wright, tanner, and Martha Moon, spinster, daughter of Susanna Moon, widow.

Aug 1, 1737, Jas. Spencer, Burlington, husbandman, and Sarah Borton of same, widow.

Aug 2, 1737, Amos Shreve, Springfield, Burlington County, yeoman, and Ann Woolston of Northampton, Burlington County, widow.

Aug 10, 1737, Robert Gilham, Springfield, Burlington County, yeoman, and Mary Foster, spinster, daughter of Thos. Foster of same, yeoman.

Aug 15, 1737, John Adams, Springfield Burlington County, yeoman, and Judith Pettitt, spinster, daughter of Moses Pettitt late yeoman, dec'd.

Aug 17, 1737, Bryan Higgins, Burlington County, husbandman, and Sarah Warrick, spinster, daughter of John Warrick late of same yeoman.

Aug 17, 1737, George Bowlby, Springfield, Burlington County, yeoman, and Elizabeth Tonkin, spinster, daughter of John Tonkin late of same, yeoman, dec'd.

Sep 12, 1737, Samuel Danford, Jr., Nottingham, Burlington County, carter, and Mary Groom, spinster, daughter of Peter Groom, dec'd.

Oct 20, 1737, Samuel Lippincott, Northampton Twp, Burlington County, yeoman, and Rebecca Matlack of Chesterfield, Burlington County, spinster.

Oct 22, 1737, John Bishop, Northampton Twp., Burlington County, yeoman, and Rebecca matlack of Chesterfield, Burlington County, spinster.

Nov 1, 1737, John Engle, Evesham, Burlington County, yeoman, and Hannah Middleton, daughter of Sarah Shipton, late Sarah Middleton.

Nov 2, 1737, James Robins, Chesterfield, Burlington County, taylor, and Elizabeth Core, spinster, daughter of Grace Core of same, widow.

Nov 8, 1737, John Price, Evesham, Burlington County, husbandman, and Mary Burne, spinster, daughter of Mary Burne of Gloucester County, widow.

Nov 18, 1737, Thomas Bevis, Chesterfield, Burlington County, yeoman, and Mary Draper, spinster, daughter of Thos. Draper, late of same county, taylor, dec'd.

Nov 23, 1737, John Ewan (?), Northampton Twp., Burlington County, weaver, and Martha Enochs of same, widow.

Nov 23, 1737, George Munrow, Evesham, Burlington County, husbandman, and Sarah Perkins of same, spinster.

Nov 24, 1737, Robert Braddock, Evesham, Burlington County, yeoman, and Elizabeth Bates of same, spinster.

Dec 5. 1838, John Hopper, Deptford, Gloucester County, yeoman, and Ann Garwood, spinster, daughter of Thos. Garwood of Burlington, yeoman.

Dec 8, 1737, Benjamin Allen, Evesham, yeoman, and Patience Borden, spinster, daughter of Jonathan Borden of same, yeoman.

Dec 22, 1737, Joseph Woolston, Northampton Twp., Burlington County, yeoman, and Jane Topping of same, spinster.

Dec 28, 1737, Francis Jervis, Philadelphia, joyner, and Catharine King of Burlington County, widow.

Dec 29, 1737, Joseph Rozell, Evesham, Burlington County, cordwainer, and Ann Alcott of same, spinster, daughter of William Alcott of same, yeoman.

EARLY CHURCH RECORDS OF BURLINGTON COUNTY

Jan 25, 1737, James Browne, Mansfield, Burlington County, yeoman, and Sarah Lindon, spinster, sister of William Lindon of Burlington, smith.

Feb 27, 1737, John Collins, Gloucester, Gloucester County, husbandman, and Elizabeth Moore, spinster, daughter of Benjamin Moore of Burlington County, yeoman.

Mar 7, 1737, James Hughes, Evesham, Burlington County, sawyer, and Rachel Lord, spinster, daughter of Robert Lord, late of same, yeoman, dec'd.

Mar 22, 1737, Francis Surly, Northampton Twp., taylor, and Mary Reeves of same, widow.

Mar 24, 1737, John Harris, Northampton, Burlington County, husbandman, and Sarah Eldridge, daughter of Obadiah Eldridge of same, yeoman.

Mar 25, 1737, Thomas Staples, Springfield, Burlington County, yeoman, and Mary Rogers, spinster, daughter of John Rogers of Burlington, yeoman.

Mar 27, 1737, William Whitton, Evesham, husbandman, and Mary Hammett, spinster, daughter of Sarah Hammett, widow.

Mar 28, 1737, William Budd, Northampton Twp., yeoman, and Susanna Cole, spinster, daughter of Samuel Cole, late of Gloucester County, yeoman, dec'd.

Mar 28, 1737, Joseph Lamb, Northampton, carpenter, and Rebecca Budd, daughter of Elizabeth Budd, widow.

Apr 18, 1737, Robert Elton, son of Revel Elton of Burlington County, Esq., and Sarah Woolman, spinster, dau of Samuel Woolman of same county, yeoman.

Apr 19, 1737, Hugh Copperthwaite, Springfield, Burlington County, carpenter, and Hannah Atkinson, spinster, dau of Jon. Atkinson of Springfield, yeoman.

Apr 29, 1737, William Cunningham, Bordenstown, Burlington County, shipwright, and Elizabeth Ridgeway of same, spinster.

May 18, 1737, Benjamin Gardiner, Evesham, Burlington County, husbandman, and Phebe Borden, spinster, dau of Mary Borden of Hunterdon county, widow.

Jun 1, 1737, William Dennis, New Hanover, Burlington County, yeoman, and Mary Rogers of same, widow.

Jun 1, 1737, Joseph Buckworth, Burlington, sawyer and Esther Ong, spinster, dau of Jacob Ong of New Hanover, Burlington County, yeoman.

Jun 7, 1737, Maham Southwick, Northampton, Burlington County, and Hannah Parker, spinster, dau of William Parker of same, yeoman.

Jun 7, 1737, John Leeds, Egg Harbour, Burlington County, yeoman, and Rebecca Cordry, spinster, dau of William Cordry of same, yeoman.

Apr 17, 1738, Thomas Jones, Springfield, Burlington County, yeoman, and Sarah Page, spinster, daughter of John Page of Chesterfield, yeoman.

Apr 25, 1738, John Munyon, Burlington County, husbandman, and Sarah Cowgill, daughter of Nehemiah Cowgill of same, yeoman.

May 10, 1738, Bryan Donnolly, New Hanover, Burlington County, husbandman, and Susanna Collins, spinster, daughter of Elizabeth Kent.

May 18, 1738, James Cattell, Evesham, carpenter, and Ann Rogers of same, widow.

May 20, 1738, Samuel Swift, Springfield, Burlington County, mason, and Ann Hancock, spinster, daughter of Ann Hancock of same, widow.
May 23, 1738, John Woolston, Northampton Twp., yeoman, and Hannah Tencher, spinster, daughter of Francis Tencher late dec'd.
Jun 12, 1738, Lawrence Surley, Burlington County, husbandman, and Mary Vanhorne of same, spinster.
Aug 2, 1738, Fretwell Wright, Burlington, tanner, and Margaret Ellis, spinster, daughter of Rowland Ellis of Burlington, schoolmaster.
Aug 7, 1738, John Mott, Little Eggharbour, Burlington County, husbandman, and Phebe Cramer, spinster, daughter of Abigail Cramer.
Aug 7, 1738, Thomas Smith, Evesham, yeoman, and Mary White, spinster, daughter of Eliz. White of same.
Aug 1, 1738, Nehemiah Cowgill, Burlington County, yeoman, and Esther Davis of same, widow.
Aug 24, 1738, John Kimball, Burlington, cooper, and Ann Leeds of same, spinster.
Aug 28, 1738, John Bowker New Hanover, Burlington County, yeoman, and Jemima Mills of same, spinster, daughter of Eliza Mills of same, widow.
Sept 4, 1738, John Burr, Jr., Northampton, Burlington County, husbandman and Elizabeth Dawson of same, spinster.
Sep 12, 1738, John Newman, Philadelphia, gentleman, and Hester Heulings of Burlington, spinster, daughter of Abraham Hewlings, Esq. dec'd.
Sep 18, 1738, Cornelius Dorland, Walpeck, Hunterdon County, yeoman, and Mary Walker of Burlington County, widow.
Oct 23, 1738, Nathaniel Thomas, Shrewsbury, Monmouth County, clothier, and Ann Leeds, spinster, daughter of Philo Leeds of Burlington County, yeoman.
Oct 30, 1738, John Rhodes, Burlington, cordwainer, and Mary Caldwell, spinster.
Oct 31, 1738, Content Horner, Upper Freehold, Monmouth County, farmer, and Sarah Hutchin, spinster, daughter of Hugh Hutchin of Burlington, yeoman.
Nov 4, 1738, Jonathan Scott, Burlington, wheelwright and Mary Cassaway of same, widow.
Nov 11, 1738, Thomas Berkinshew, Evesham, Burlington County, husbandman, and Margaret Bliss, spinster, daughter of Elizabeth Bliss, widow.
Jul 1, 1738 , Thomas Esdall, Nottingham, Burlington County, yeoman, and Elizabeth Palmer of same, spinster.
Nov 22, 1738, Thomas Smith, Mansfield, Burlington County, yeoman, and Rebecca Shreeve, spinster, daughter of Joseph Shreeve of same, yeoman.
Dec 2, 1738 , Marmaduke Fort, New Hanover, Burlington County, yeoman, and Mary Cousins, spinster, daughter of John Cousins of Springfield, yeoman.
Jan 16, 1738, Benjamin Gaskill, Northampton, Burlington County, yeoman, and Mary Dennis, spinster, daughter of John Dennis of Freehold, Monmouth County, yeoman.
Feb 13, 1738, Robert Denton, Evesham, Burlington County, yeoman, and Jane Moon of same, spinster.

Feb 23, 1738, John Butcher, Jr., Springfield, Burlington County, yeoman, and Mary Ridgeway, spinster, daughter of Job Ridgeway of same, yeoman.
Feb 26, 1738, David Budd, Northampton, Burlington County, yeoman, and Catharine Allen, spinster, daughter of Henry Allen of Mansfield, same county, yeoman.
Mar 20, 1738, James Dennis, Chesterfield, Burlington County, husbandman, and Sarah Elmore, spinster, daughter of Mathias Elmore of same county, husbandman.
Jan 3, 1739, James Arnell, Burlington, husbandman, and Mary Mott, daughter of Mary Brown, late Mary Mott.
Feb 11, 1739, Peter Cavalier, Jr., Eggharbor, Burlington County, yeoman, and Ann Tearney of Burlington, spinster.
Apr 18, 1739, Gabriel Blond, Burlington County, gentleman, and Susanna Yard of same, widow.
Apr 21, 1739, John Stevenson, Nottingham, Burlington County, yeoman, and Martha Walton, spinster, daughter of Martha Borden, late Martha Walton.
Apr 30, 1739, Ambrose Ewan, husbandman, and Ann Fenton of Northampton, Burlington county, spinster.
May 11, 1739, Samuel Bunting, Chesterfield, Burlington County, yeoman, and Mary Willitts, spinster, daughter of Richard Willitts of Shrewsbury, Monmouth County, yeoman.
May 12, 1739, Benjamin Marriott, Burlington City, cordwainer, and Sarah Crosby of same, spinster.
May 28, 1739, Thomas Dumfe, Burlington County, ropemaker, and Elizabeth White, spinster, daughter of William White, late of Burlington, yeoman, dec'd.
May 29, 1739, Jeremiah Hinds, New Hanover, Burlington County, weaver, and Mary Fitzhuge of Fallowfield, Chester County, widow.
Jun 6, 1739, William Shinn, Springfield, Burlington County, yeoman, and Exercise Corless, spinster, daughter of William Corless of Shrewsbury, Monmouth County, smith.
Jun 16, 1739, James Walsh, New Hanover, Burlington County, labourer, and Margaret Norton of Springfield in same county, spinster.
Jul 16, 1739, William Fenimore, Northampton, Burlington County, husbandman, and Joyce McFaulin of Burlington, widow.
Aug 1, 1739, Cornelius Kelly, Northampton, Burlington County, forgeman, and Penelope McDaniel of same, spinster.
Aug 1, 1739, Thomas Bishop, Northampton, Burlington County, yeoman, and Hannah Lanning of Evesham in same county, widow.
Aug 20, 1739, Daniel Holland, Northampton, Burlington County, labourer, and Mary Smith, spinster, daughter of James Smith of same county.
Sep 11, 1739, Benjamin Inman, Little Eggharbour, Burlington County, blacksmith, and Jemima Brundidge of same, spinster.
Sep 20, 1739, Richard Singleton, City of Burlington, cordwainer, and Elinor Gallagher of same, spinster.
Sep 24, 1739, John Douglass, Burlington County, boatman, and Rachel Pearson, spinster, daughter of Robert Pearson of same, Esq.
Oct 3, 1739, William Baker, Burlington County, husbandman, and Catharine Corkin of same spinster.
Oct 8, 1739, Thos. Gale, Springfield, Burlington County,

labourer, and Elizabeth Kille of same, spinster.
Oct 25, 1739, Peter Homan, Little Eggharbour, Burlington County, husbandman, and Mercy Harding, spinster, daughter of Stephen Harding of same, yeoman.
Nov 1, 1739, Thomas Platt, New Hanover, Burlington County, yeoman, and Sarah Dennis, spinster, daughter of John Dennis of Upper Freehold, yeoman.
Nov 1, 1739, Ezekiel Wright, Great Eggharbour, Burlington County, yeoman, and Mercy Holbard of same, spinster.
Nov 1, 1739, Joshua Milles, New Hanover, Burlington County, sawyer, and Margaret Williams, spinster, daughter of Lydia Ivins, late Lydia Williams.
Nov 24, 1739, John Taylor, Chesterfield, Burlington County, yeoman, and Deliverance Robins, spinster, daughter of Benjamin Robins of same, yeoman.
Nov 27, 1739, George Kimball, Burlington, husbandman, and Mary Elton, spinster, daughter of Revel Elton of Northampton, Burlington County, Esquire.
Dec 31, 1739, William Steward, Burlington, blacksmith, and Elizabeth Robinson, daughter of William Robinson of same city, turner.
Jan 1, 1739, John Handcock, Mansfield, Burlington County, yeoman, and Martha Richardson, daughter of John Richardson of Burlington, yeoman.
Jan 3, 1739, Edward Tagg, Burlington County, carter, and Patience Wainwright, daughter of Nich's Wainwright of Little Eggharbour in same county, yeoman.
Jan 8, 1739, Peter Banyton, Burlington, merchant, and Mary Carpenter of same, widow.
Jan 11, 1739, Zachariah Rozell, Northampton, Burlington County, yeoman, and Mary Morgan of same.
Jan 29, 1739, Joshua Bishop, Northampton, Burlington county, yeoman, and Martha Lanning, spinster, daughter of Hannah Bishop, late Hannah Lanning.
Jan 29, 1739, Thomas Pearson, Nottingham, Burlington County, yeoman, and Sarah Hoff of Trenton, Hunterdon County, spinster, daughter of Wm. Hoff of same, yeoman.
Feb 1, 1739, Daniel Parke, Evesham, Burlington County, husbandman, and Bathsheba Perkins, daughter of Jacob Perkins, late of said county, yeoman, dec'd.
Feb 21, 1739, William Gard, Evesham, Burlington County, husbandman, and Sarah Springer, daughter of Hudson Springer of same, husbandman.
Feb 21, 1739, Isaac Prickett, Evesham, Burlington County, husbandman, and Mary Brookfield, daughter of Levi Brookfield of same, yeoman.
Feb 26, 1739, William Flowers, Burlington, carter, and Martha Norton of same, widow.
Feb 26, 1739, Samuel Rose, Little Eggharbour, Burlington County, yeoman, and Anna Duckworth of Burlington, spinster.
Apr 8, 1740, Thomas Meredyth, City of Burlington, brickmaker, and Jane Norcross, daughter of William Norcross of same, yeoman.
Apr 14, 1740, Benjamin Thorne, Chesterfield, Burlington County, yeoman, and Sarah Bunting, spinster, daughter of William Bunting of same, yeoman.

Apr 19, 1740, William Stevenson, Burlington, gentleman, and Sarah Kimbal, spinster, daughter of Benjamin Kimbal, late of Mansfield, yeoman, dec'd.
Apr 21, 1740, Obadiah Eldridge, Jr., Springfield, Burlington County, gentleman, and Ann Wilson, spinster, daughter of Mathew Wilson of same, yeoman.
May 26, 1740, Zebulon Webb, New Hanover, Burlington County, sawyer, and Edith Lowder of same, spinster.
Jun 5, 1740, John Webb, New Hanover, Burlington County, sawyer, and Rebecca England, spinster, daughter of Daniel England, late of Burlington, yeoman, dec'd.
Jun 9, 1740, Francis Hall, Chesterfield, Burlington County, weaver, and Naomi Middleton, spinster, daughter of John Middleton of Nottingham in said county, yeoman.
Jan 18, 1741, Thomas Herd, Chesterfield, Burlington County, weaver, and Alice Smith, spinster, daughter of Joshua Smith, late of Mansfield, yeoman.
Feb 16, 1741, Patrick Jones, Chester Twp, Burlington County, husbandman, and Martha Chambers, spinster, daughter of John Chambers of same, yeoman.
Feb 19, 1741, Peter Renier ye younger, Mansfield, Burlington County, husbandman, and Jemima Draper of same, spinster.
Feb 20, 1741, Manuel Stratton, Evesham, yeoman, and Mary Joyce, daughter of Martha Joyce of same, widow.
Dec 7, 1741, Micajah Carter, New Hanover Twp, Burlington County, yeoman, and Elizabeth Saint, spinster, daughter of Thomas Saint.
Jan 17, 1742, Mathew Wright, Burlington County, yeoman, and Penelope Jones of same, spinster.
Jan 9, 1743/4, Thomas Gill, Evesham, Burlington County, yeoman, and Hannah Hollinshead of same, spinster.
Jan 27, 1743, John Stapleford, Philadelphia, merchant, and Elizabeth Derkindirrin of city of Burlington, spinster.
Jan 1, 1743, David Stout, city of Burlington, gentleman, and Margaret Vollow of Bergen County, spinster.
Jun 18, 1744, James Moon, Burlington, waggoner, and Alice Barry of same.
Jan 30, 1748, Stephen Gaskill, Northampton, Burlington County, and Lavinah Gaskell, spinster. (Bond reads Levinah, 1747-48:84.)
Feb 18, 1748, George Elkington, Northampton, Burlington County, and Sarah Pimm, spinster.
Mar 13, 1748, James Sherwin, Burlington County, yeoman, and Edith Kimble of same, spinster.
Mar 15, 1748, Thomas Cunningham, Hanover, Burlington County, husbandman, and Sarah Bowler, spinster.
Mar 29, 1749, Samuel Murrell, Northampton, Burlington County, and Rachel Hooper of same, spinster.
Apr 3, 1749, Valentine Arps, New Hanover, Burlington County, labourer, and Elizabeth Parker of same, spinster.
Apr 8, 1749, John Gibson, Springfield, Burlington County, and Sarah Marriott of same, spinster.
May 13, 1749, John Driver, Little Egg Harbour, Burlington County, and Mary Sparks of Evesham, spinster. (The bond shows her name as Parks, and Paul Parks of Evesham was bondsman. A-W:121.)
May 15, 1749, Joseph Burr, Jr., Northampton, yeoman, and Mary

Mullen of same, spinster.
May 19, 1749, Abell Gale, Little Eggharbour, Burlington County, yeoman, and Mary Gale of same, widow. (But the bond shows that Abel obtained the license for John Stanton of Little Egg Harbour, labourer, and Mary Gale. A-W:362.)
May 24, 1749, John Guinnop, Nottingham, Burlington County, waterman, and Anne Brittain of Monmouth County, spinster.
Jun 12, 1749, Thomas Bowlby, Morris County, yeoman, and Mary Turley of Burlington County, widow.
Jul 3, 1749, John Berryman, Springfield Twp, weaver, and Margaret Marriott of same, spinster.
Jul 10, 1749, Thomas Addis, Mansfield, Burlington County, and Anne English of same, spinster.
Jul 26, 1749, Abraham Brown, Chesterfield, Burlington County, and Susanna Richardson of same, spinster. (The bond is signed Ara: Brown Jr. and her residence is stated as "the County aforesaid." A-W:36.)
Aug 7, 1749, Henry Scott, City of Burlington, yeoman, and Priscilla Turner of same, spinster.
Aug 8, 1749, Solomon Rockhill, Burlington County, yeoman, and Susannah Taylor of Chesterfield, spinster.
Aug 10, 1749, John Murfey, Burlington County, yeoman, and Sarah Jones of Springfield. (In one of three places on the bond, the name appears as Murfin. He signed with his mark. A-W:272.)
Aug 10, 1749, William Jones, New Hanover, Burlington County, and Mary Birdsell of same, spinster. (Bond is dated Aug 24, 1749. A-W:231.)
Aug 25, 1749, Adam Forker, Northampton, Burlington County, blacksmith, and Hannah Gaskill of same, spinster. (Bond is signed "Adam Farquhar". A-W:151.)
Aug 29, 1949, John Norton, Springfield, labourer, and Grace Gillum of same, widdow.
Sep 9, 1749, William Hill, Chesterfield, Burlington County, labourer, and Elizabeth Ashton of same, spinster.
Sep 14, 1749, Gabriel Puneo and Mary Hort "of the same place," spinster. (Bond states his residence as Evesham, Burlington County. A-W:37.)
Sep 21, 1749, Ebenezer Dotey, Northampton, Burlington County, blacksmith, and Margaret Woolston of same, spinster.
Sep 30, 1749, James Butler and Elizabeth Stull "of the same place," spinster. (Bond describes him as of Bridgetown, Burlington County, hammer-man. A-W:37.)
Oct 5, 1749, Thomas Baker, Mansfield, Burlington County, and Sarah Hazleton of same, spinster.
Jan 1, 1750, Abraham Potts, City of Burlington, cordwainer, and Mary Lee of same.
Jan 23, 1750, Nicholas Stiles, Chester, Burlington County, yeoman, and Elizabeth Sherwin, spinster.
Sep 25, 1750, Joseph Nutt, Mansfield, Burlington County, and Venah Broadhome of Springfield, Burlington County.
Sep 26, 1750, Richard Bowker, Hanover, Burlington County, labourer, and Esther Gwin of Evesham, widow.
Oct 23, 1750, Leonard Vandegrief, and Charity Haines of Burlington County, spinster. (Bond is signed by Leonard Vandegrift, of Bensalem, Bucks County, yeoman. W:96.)

Oct 23, 1750, James Willis, Philadelphia, shipwright and Rachel Lovell of Burlington, spinster (Bond signed by James Wells, W:95).
Nov 2, 1750, George Beck and Mary Griffiths, both of Bridgetown, Burlington County.
Nov 7, 1750, Phillip Dingwell, Borden Town, Burlington County, skinner, and Mary Daily of same, widdow. (Entered again on page 151 1/2, with date Nov 17, 1751, but bond [E:28] is dated Nov 7, 1750).
Jan 23, 1751, John Lord, Gloucester County, yeoman, and Mary Borton, of Burlington, spinster.
May 8, 1751, Joseph Raneir, Mansfield, Burlington County, and Sarah Wood of same, spinster.
May 9, 1751, Robert Webb, Jr., Stratton Island, New York, and Barthia Crammue (?) of Burlington County, spinster. (The bond was executed by Hezekiah Wright, of Stratton Island, New York, to obtain license for Robert Webb, Jr., of Burlington County, and Barthia Crammer of same, spinster. W:100.)
May 20, 1751, George Miers, Evesham, yeoman, and Mary Prickett of Northampton, spinster. (The bond gives his occupation as labourer, and is signed "George Mirs." M:88.)
June 26, 1751, George Bliss, Borden Town, Burlington County, and Susannah Preston of Mansfield, widdow.
Jul 8, 1751, Edward Browning, Waterford, Gloucester County, blacksmith and Grace Oldale, Burlington County, spinster.

ST. ANDREWS PE CHURCH - TRINITY PE CHURCH
MT. HOLLY, NEW JERSY

Marriages all Solemnized by Rev. Spragg

21, Nov, 1785 - Elias Stealman and Ann Little, Mount Holly.
26, Oct, 1786 - Simon Simonson and Mary Ferguson of the New York City, m. at Mount Holly.
16, Nov, 1786 - Thomas Potts and Sarah Vansciver, m. at Mount Holly
21, Jan, 1787 - Clement Kinsey and Mary Plum, Mt. Holly
19, Feb, 1787 - John Smith and Rachel Evans
12, Mar, 1787 - Jonathan Gaskill and Elizabeth Southwick
19, Mar, 1787 - Jesse Ellison and Lydia Hayne
16, Apr, 1787 - Thomas White and Isabelle Friend
29, Jul, 1787 - Continue Chew and Martha Ewen
31, Jul, 1787 - Daniel Gorden and Izilah Reddrick
29, Oct, 1787 - Joseph Mason and Hepziba Eves
29, Nov, 1787 - George Woolston and Abigail Ellis
5, Dec, 1787 - Prince Solomon and Belinda Rash
11, Dec, 1787 - William Dimpsey and Amey Whitaker
7, Jan, 1788 - Abraham Harris and Rebeckah Hollingshead
9, Jan, 1788 - William Price and Katharine Holland
24, Jan, 1788 - Aaron Pickett and Ann Oliphant
31, Jan, 1788 - Joseph Collins and Elizabeth Mullen
2, Feb, 1788 - William Ridgway and Betsey Test
14, Apr, 1788 - John Plum and Sarah Kinsey
14, May, 1788 - Alexander Peacock and Hanah Sharp
14, May, 1788 - Hollingshead Hilliard and Ann Mullen
14, May, 1788 - Thomas Green and Lydia Hilliard
1, Jun, 1788 - William Davis and Lydia Connaroe
31, Jul, 1788 - Josiah Wilkins and Hester Sharp
12, Aug, 1788 - William Steward and Mary Major
2, Sep, 1788 - Joseph Kimble and Barbara Adams
11, Sep, 1788 - John Peters and Mary Scever
11, Sep, 1788 - John Barry and Jane Bond
24, Sep, 1788 - John Walker and Mary Lees
6, Oct, 1788 - Job Lippincot and Anna Warren
23, Oct, 1788 - Thomas Porter and Mary Wiley
30, Oct, 1788 - Thomas Clark and Rebeckah Pierson
20, Nov, 1788 - John McElroy and Sarah Goodman, m. in Borough of Bristol, PA.
21, Nov, 1788 - David Briggs and Mary Stapleton
31, Dec, 1788 - Joseph Denight and Martha Brown
7, Jan, 1789 - Thomas Jones and Elizabeth Cox
8, Jan, 1789 - George Bachelor and Hannah Munyan
10, Jan, 1789 - George Haines and Ruth Gaskill
20, Jan, 1789 - Thomas Taylor and Elizabeth Bud
25, Jan, 1789 - John Carman and Mary Jones
10, Feb, 1789 - Daniel Brown and Katharine Lynch
23, Feb, 1789 - Joseph Truax and Hannah Burr
24, Feb, 1789 - James Maguire and Hannah Hughes
5, Mar, 1789 - Isaiah Bowler and Martha Allcot
8, Apr, 1789 - Thomas Buckley and Martha Chubb

EARLY CHURCH RECORDS OF BURLINGTON COUNTY

3, May, 1789 - John Jones and Elizabeth Field
28, May, 1789 - Israel Mills and Ruth Parker
25, Jun, 1789 - Joshua Porter and Hope Smith
27, Jul, 1789 - John Bowden and Margaret Shepherd
30, Jul, 1789 - Samuel Lewis and Rachel Dobbins
6, Aug, 1789 - Benjamin Haines and Mary Smallwood
2, Sep, 1789 - Thomas Joyce and Mary Woodrow
17, Sep, 1789 - Jesse King and Sheba Smith
22, Sep, 1789 - William Taylor and Marriette Mooney

Marriages all solemnized by Rev. Andrew Fowler and recorded in the County Clerk's office, July 12, 1979.

1, Dec, 1796 - Samuel Hunt and Deborah Bennet in Chester at house of Henry Bennet.
18, Jan, 1797 - William Richards and Marget Wood, Mt. Holly
9, Feb, 1797 - Thomas Stokes and Mary Chambers at home of John Wilkins in Chester twp.
12, Feb, 1797 - Daniel Marss and Amy Clutch
26, Mar, 1797 - Curtis Dicks and Elizabeth Bennet, Mt. Holly
9, Apr, 1797 - Volkert VanHurzan and Elizabeth Bennet, Mt. Holly
20, Apr, 1797 - Jacob Gaskill and Esther Rudderow, Mt. Holly
25, Jun, 1797 - Benjamin Fish and Elizabeth Lee at Gloucester County.
5, Jul, 1797 - John Shears and Martha Pearse.
21, Jul, 1797 - Gamalion Shin and Bulah Eastwood, Mt. Holly.
1, Aug, 1797 - John L. Clark and Sophia M. Ross, Mt. Holly.
31, Oct, 1797 - William Crompton and Elizabeth Neale, Mt. Holly.
30, Dec, 1797 - William Small and Hannah Wheeler, home of George Woolston
27, Dec, 1797 - William Rudderow and Rachel Rowing of Waterford Twp at home of Joseph Coles.
27, Dec, 1797 - Samuel Albertson and Sarah Barret at home of John Cathcart.
18, Jan, 1797 - Peter Shin (Slim?} and Rebeccah Lippincott, Mt. Holly.
11, Feb, 1797 - Thomas Wilkins and Elizabeth Miller at home of Mrs. Ellis, Mt. Holly.
28, Feb, 1798 - Jacob Williams and Rebeccah Curtis at Lumberton.

BAPTISMS AT ST. ANDREW'S P.E. CHURCH, MT. HOLLY

Elizabeth Bennet, dau. of Joseph and Martha Bennet, b. 24th da, 11th mo, 1768, baptized 2nd da, Oct, 1785.
Children of Joseph and Mary Cooper: Samuel Cooper, b. 3rd da, Sep, 1771; Joseph Cooper, b. 18th da, Mar, 1780; William Cooper, b. 13th Feb, 1783; John Cooper, b. 20th Sep, 1784, all baptized 2nd da, Oct, 1785.
Children of Mathias and Katharine Lane: Henry Lane, b. 8th da, May, 1775; Elizabeth Lane, b. 3rd da, Oct, 1777; James Lane, b. 25th da, May, 1783, all baptized 20th da, Nov, 1785.
George Bartram Shiras, son of Alexander and Martha Shiras, b. 15th da, Dec, 1785, baptized 9th da, Mar, 1786.
Children of Nathan and Rebecah Haines: Elizabeth Haines, b. 9th da, Feb, 1757; Nathan Haines, b. 20th da, Aug, 1759, baptized 9th da, Mar, 1786.
Children of Nathan and Dorcas Haines: Henry Pendergrass Haines, b. 18th da, Sep,1763; Sarah Haines, b. 7th da, Dec, 1764; Joseph Haines, b. 26th da, Jul, 1765; Catharine Haines, b. 15th da, Jul, 1766; Marrion Hannah Haines, b. 24th da, Feb, 1767; Keziah Haines, b. 10th da, Jan, 1773, all baptized 9th da, Mar, 1786.
Child of George and Margaret Painter: Martha Painter, b. 18th da, Jul, 1786, baptized 26th da, Oct, 1786.
Child of William Lees, Jr and Hannah: William Spraggs Lees, b. 5th da, Apr, 1788, baptized 26th da, Oct 1786.
Children of Alexander and Martha Shiras: Alexander Shiras, b. 12th da, Jun, 1790, baptized 30th da, Sep, 1792.
Children of Joseph and Mary Cooper: Joseph Cooper, b. 1st da, Sep, 1786; Collin Cooper, b. 12th da, Nov, 1788; Thomas Cooper and Mary Cooper, b. 20th da, Oct, 1790, baptized 30th da, Sep, 1792.
Children of John and Esther Perry: Charles Perry, b. 13th da, Jan, 1782; Elias Perry, b. 18th da, Aug, 1784; Samuel Perry, b. 28th da, Dec, 1786; Elizabeth Perry b. 24th da, Oct, 178?, baptized 30th da, Sep, 1792.
Child of John and Ann Phillips: Joseph Rossell Phillips, b. 29th Mar, 1786, baptized 30th da, Sep, 1792.
Child of Peter and Elizabeth Van Pelt: Alexander Shiras Van Pelt, b. 6th da, Jan, 1797, baptized 12th da, Feb, 1797.
Child of Samuel and Elizabeth Baxter: Margaret Baxter, b. no date, baptized 19th da, Mar, 1797.
Children of Robert and Ann Davidson: Mary Davidson, b. 1791; Peggy Davidson, b. 1793; Benjamin John Davidson, b. 1795; Robert Davidson, b. 1797, baptized 27th da, Aug, 1797.
Children of Richard and Jane Cox: Rebeccah Cox, b. 16th da, Sep 1787; Elizabeth Cox, b. 6th da, Feb, 1790; Maryann Hannah Cox, b. 28th Aug, 1791, baptized 27th da, Aug, 1797.
Child of Andrew and Rene Low: Joseph Read Low, b. 3rd da, May, 1798, baptized 25th da, Nov, 1798.
Children of Thomas and Abigail Curtis: Margaret Curtis, b. 31st da, Oct, 1778; Thomas Curtis, b. 12th da, Jun, 1784; Isaac Antrim Curtis, b. 24th da, Aug, 1798, baptized 9th da, Dec, 1798.
Peter Van Pelt, b. 29th da, Sep, 1798, baptized 15th da, Nov, 1799.

EARLY CHURCH RECORDS OF BURLINGTON COUNTY

NEW JERSEY CATHOLIC BAPTISMS RECORDS FROM 1759-1781
extracted Janet Drumm Dirnberger

Baptisms performed by the Catholic missionaries of Old St. Joseph's Church, Philadelphia and originally published in *The Catholic Churches in New Jersey*, by Rev. Joseph M. Flynn, M.R., V. F.

At Burlington.
Elizabeth of John and Hannah Bradshaw, b. Oct, 1755; bapt. Aug 26, 1773. sub. condit.; John and Catherine Hoyle.
William of William and Eleanor Egan, b. May 29, 1773; bapt. Aug 26, 1773. Spon: John Davelin and Anna Kearns.
John of William and Eleanor Egan, b. Aug 19, 1775; bapt. Jun 18, 1776. Spon: Patrick Kearns and Margaret Scott.
John of John and Catherine Hoy, b. Jan, 1763, bapt. Aug 26, 1763. Spon: Patrick and Rosa Kearns, sub. condit.
Margaret of John and Catherine Hoy, b. May, 1767; bapt. Aug 26, 1773. Spon: Patrick and Rosa Kearns, sub. condit.
Asa Joseph of John and Catharine Hoy, b. Mar 25, 1774; bapt. Jun 15, 1774. Spon: William and Eleanor Egan.
George of John and Catharine Hoy, b. Jul 26, 1776; bapt. Jun 24, 1779. Spon: John Scott and Catharine Hogan.
John of John and Ann Mary Klemmer, b. Dec 23, 1776; bapt. Jun 22, 1779. Spon: Joseph Hoay.
Mary (Meridith) of John and Margarety Muny, b. Apr 8, 1768; bapt. Nov 12, 1772. Spon: Nicholas and Ann Workman.
John of John and Margaret Muny, b. Oct 31, 1769; bapt. Nov 12, 1771. Spon: Nicholas and Ann Workman.
Mary of James and Sarah Ryan, b. Jun 8, 1765; bapt. Aug 26, 1773. Spon: John and Catherine Hoy, sub. condit.
Mary of John and Margaret Scott, b. May 29, 1779; bapt. Jun 23, 1779. Spon: Patrick Kearns and Catharine Hogan.
Samuel of John and Elizabeth Sculley, b. Feb 22, 1870; bapt. Nov 21, 1781. Spon: John and Margaret Scott.

THE REGISTER of the CHURCH of ST. ANN'S, BURLINGTON COUNTY

Memorandum. This Church was called St. Ann's (in the first Charter granted Oct 4, 1704 by Lord Cornbury) after the name of the Queen; but when a more ample charter was granted in 1709, Jan 25 by Lieut. Governor Ingoldsby, Church was called St. Mary's and so continued to be denominated, on account of its first foundation, none having been laid on the 25th of March which was in 1703, but this it seems was not adverted to till afterwards - Apr 7, 1768. Jonathan Odell.

R. C. Well Feb 28 Anno Domini Jesu Christi

John of Roger Parke, bapt. 1702/3 by Mt. John Talbot.
Ann of Roger Parke, bapt. by Mr. John Talbot 1702/3.
Thomas of Andrew Smith, bapt. Feb 20, 1702/3.
Andrew of Andrew Smith, bapt. Feb 20, 1702/3.
Elizabeth of Andrew Smith, bapt. Feb 20, 1702/3.
Mary of Andrew Smith, bapt. Feb 20, 1702/3.
Hannah of Andrew Smith, bapt. Feb 20, 1702/3.
William Schooley, son to Robert Schooley bapt. Feb 20, 1702/3.
John of Roger Park, bapt. Feb 20, 1702/3.
Ann of Roger Park, bapt. Feb 20, 1702/3.
Mary of Thomas Tyndal, bapt. Feb 7, 1704.
Eliz of Thomas Tyndal, bapt. Feb 7, 1704.
Thomas of Thomas Tyndal, bapt. Feb 7, 1704.
Ann of Thomas Tyndal, bapt. Feb 7, 1704.
William of Thomas Tyndal, bapt. Feb 7, 1704.
John of Thomas Tyndal, bapt. Feb 7, 1704.
Sarah of Thomas Tyndal, bapt. Feb 7, 1704.
Robert of Thomas Tyndal, bapt. Feb 7, 1704.
Roger the son of Roger Park, bapt. Feb 7, 1704.
Mary of John Chambers, bapt. Feb 7, 1704.
Ann of James Lacy, bapt. Feb 7, 1704.
William of John Choroneth (?), bapt. Aug 27, 1704.
Martha of John Tomkin, bapt. Feb 10, ---.
Phebe of Thos. Pocho, bapt. Feb 10, ---.
John Stockton, bapt. Feb 24, ---.
Philo Leeds, bapt. Feb 24, ---.
Mary, wife of Philo Leeds, bapt. Feb 24, ---.
Japos of Mary and Philo Leeds, b. Oct 24, 1863, bapt. Feb, 1704/5.
Mary of Mary and Philo Leeds, b. Apr 19, 1685, bapt. Feb 9, 1704.
Holise of Mary and Philo Leeds, b. Jul 27, 1687, bapt. Feb 1704.
Roshannah of Mary and Philo Leeds, b. Mar 24, 1692/3, bapt. Apr 9, 1705.
Ann of Mary and Philo Leeds, b. Feb 17, 1694/5, bapt. Apr 9, 1705.
Daniel of Mary and Philo Leeds, b. Jun 5, 1697, bapt. Apr 9, 1705.
Filan of Mary and Philo Leeds, b. Aug 25, 1699, bapt. Apr 9, 1705.
Rebekah Wheeler, bapt. by Mr. G. Keith on Sun, Feb 22, 1702/3. and her children,

John of Rebekah Wheeler, bapt. by Mr. G. Keith on Sun, Feb 22, 1702/3.
Rebekah of Rebekah Wheeler, bapt. by Mr. G. Keith on Sun, Feb 22, 1702/3.
Robert of Rebekah Wheeler, bapt. by Mr. G. Keith on Sun, Feb 22, 1702/3.
Mary of Rebekah Wheeler, bapt. by Mr. G. Keith on Sun, Feb 22, 1702/3.

Burlington County
Sarah Cook, the first baptized in the church here, Mar 10, 1703.
Moses Longhoff, bapt. Mar 10, 1703.
Deborah Longhoff, bapt. Mar 10, 1703.
James Longhoff, bapt. Mar 10, 1703.
Elizabeth Longhoff, bapt. Mar 10, 1703.
Laban Longhoff, bapt. Mar 10, 1703.
Isaac Perkins, bapt. Nov 20, 170-.
Benjamine Perkins, bapt. Nov 20, 170-.
Isaac Perkins, bapt. Nov 20, 170-.
Jacob Perkins, bapt. Nov 20, 170-.
Mary Perkins, bapt. Nov 20, 170-.
Thomas Peachy, bapt. Nov 20, 170-.
Ann Peachy, bapt. Nov 20, 170-.
Elizabeth Fenton, bapt. Nov 21, 170-.
Jeremiah Fenton, bapt. Nov 21, 170-.
Enoch Fenton, bapt. Nov 21, 170-.
Eliezer Fenton, bapt. Nov 21, 170-.
Judeth Fenton, bapt. Nov 21, 170-.
Elizabeth Knott, bapt. Nov 21, 170-.
John Tonkin bapt. Feb 1, 1703/4.
Susanna Tonkin, wife of John, bapt. Feb 1, 1703/4.
Mary of John and Susanna Tonkin, bapt. Feb 1, 1703/4.
John of John and Susanna Tonkin, bapt. Feb 1, 1703/4.
Charles of John and Susanna Tonkin, bapt. Feb 1, 1703/4.
Bathsheba of John and Susanna Tonkin, , bapt. Feb 1, 1703/4.

New Castle
Richard Reynolds, bapt. Feb 23, 170-.
Robert Wotten, bapt. Feb 23, 170-.
Sarah Carter, bapt. Feb 23, 170-.

Burlington
Mary Stewart, bapt. Feb 8, 17--.
Thomas Lasey, bapt. Feb 8, 17--.
--- Smith, bapt. Feb 8, 17--.
Christian Silver, bapt. Feb 8, 17--.
James Silver, bapt. Feb 8, 17--.
Ann Scott, bapt. Feb 8, 17--.
Thomas Scott, bapt. Feb 8, 17--.
Henry Scott, bapt. Feb 8, 17--.
The son of Margaret and Hugh Huddy, bapt. May 17--.
Mary Andrews, bapt. Apr 10, bapt. May, 17--.

William Fasset and Ann Downey married Dec 25, ---.

Amboy
Catherine Barclay buried Jan 6, 1703.

Burlington
John Newman and Margaret Hienloke married Feb 8, 1703.
Philip Edington and Abigail Pain married Feb 18, 1704.

Long Island, Oyster Bay. Francis Britton, bapt. Sep 12, 1702.

Freehold
Mary Napper and her daughters, Margaret, Rebecca, and Eliza.
bapt. Oct 18, 1702.
Hanah and Helen Reid, bapt. Oct 25, 1702.
William and Mary Leeds, bapt. Oct 25, 1702.

Amboy
Margaret Nicholson, bapt. Feb 10, ---.
John Brown, bapt. Feb 10, ---.
Catherine Barclay, bapt. Jan 6, 1703.

Raway
William Whitehead, bapt. Jun 19, 1704.
John Johnson, bapt. Jun 19, 1704.
Grace Baremore, bapt. Jun 19, 1704.
Mary Hall, bapt. Jun 19, 1704.
John Ervers, Jr. (Ewers), bapt. Jun 19, 1704.
Henry Baremore, bapt. Jun 19, 1704.
Hanah Baremore, bapt. Jun 19, 1704.
Mary Baremore, bapt. Jun 19, 1704.
Phebe Baremore, bapt. Jun 19, 1704.
Elizabeth Johnson, bapt. Jun 19, 1704.
John Johnson, bapt. Jun 19, 1704.
Ann of John and Elizabeth Johnson, bapt. Jun 19, 1704.
Sarah of John and Elizabeth Johnson, bapt. Jun 19, 1704.
Mary Dennis, bapt. Jun 19, 1704.
Abigail Dennis, bapt. Jun 19, 1704.
William Hall, bapt. Jun 19, 1704.
Rebecca Parker, bapt. ---.
Philip Parker, bapt. ---.
Sarah Parker, bapt. ---.
Elizabeth Rodoro, bapt. ---.
Bridgit Rodoro, bapt. ---.
Mary Rodoro, bapt. ---.
John Rodoro, bapt. ---.
Sarah Rodoro, bapt. ---.
Ann Rodoro, bapt. ---.
Rebecca Rodoro, bapt. ---.
Mary Budd, bapt. Sep 9, 1704.
Susanna Budd, bapt. Sep 6, 1704.
Thomas Budd, bapt. Dec 3, 1708.
William Budd, bapt. Jan 2, 1711.
David Budd, bapt. Jul 14, 1712.
Rebecca Budd, bapt. Nov 4, 1714.
Abigail Budd, bapt. May 15, 1716.

Sarah Budd, bapt. Mar 11, 1718.

Chesqueack near Raritan River At the house of Francis Loots bapt. 1709.
Elizabeth of Thomas Smyth, bapt. 1709.
Jean of Thomas Smyth, bapt. 1709.
William of Thomas Smyth, bapt. 1709.
Margaret of Thomas Smyth, bapt. 1709.
Ann of Thomas Smyth, bapt. 1709. Mary of Thomas Smyth, bapt. 1709.

Joseph of Benjamin Hall, bapt. 1709.
Daniel of Benjamin Hall, bapt. 1709.
David of Benjamin Hall, bapt. 1709.
Sarah of Benjamin Hall, bapt. 1709.
Samuel of Thomas and Mary Warn(?), bapt. 1709.
Janet of Charles Jolly, bapt. 1709.
John of Francis Loots, bapt. 1709.
Elizabeth of Francis Loots, bapt. 1709.
John of John Melvil, bapt. 1709.
Frederick of John Melvil, bapt. 1709.
Will of John Melvil, bapt. 1709.
Marget of (Bowe) Buraleau, bapt. 1709.
Mary of (Bowe) Buraleau, bapt. 1709.
Lydia of (Bowe) Buraleau, bapt. 1709.
Solomon of Benjamin Hall, bapt. 1709.
Mary wife of Walter Newman, bapt. Aug 9, 1709.
John of Walter and Mary Newman, bapt. Aug 9, 1709.
Mary of Walter and Mary Newman, bapt. Aug 9, 1709.
Rachael of Walter and Mary Newman, bapt. Aug 9, 1709.
Martha of Walter and Mary Newman, bapt. Aug 9, 1709.
Walter of Walter and Mary Newman, bapt. Aug 9, 1709.
Sarah of Walter and Mary Newman, bapt. Aug 9, 1709.
Rebecca of Walter and Mary Newman, bapt. Aug 9, 1709.
William of Walter and Mary Newman, bapt. Aug 9, 1709.
Richard of Walter and Mary Newman, bapt. Aug 9, 1709.
Thomas of William (Therborn), bapt. Aug 9, 1709.
Mary of Jacob Hall, bapt. Aug 9, 1709.
William of William Leek, bapt. Aug 9, 1709.
Sarah of William Leek, bapt. Aug 9, 1709.

Notaun: That Theophilus Tolly, son of Lewis Tolly by Margaret, his wife was bapt. on the 20 Nov 1710 at Burlington, in West Jersey by the Rev'd. Mr. John Talbot, Minister of St. Ann's Church there.

Copewell Church
Marma Duke, bapt. Feb 27, 1705.
Isaac and Eliz. Hutchinson, bapt. Feb 27, 1705.
John Heath, bapt. Feb 27, 1705.
Andrew Heath, bapt. Feb 27, 1705.
Eliz. Sarah Heath, bapt. Feb 27, 1705.

John Butler, bapt. Oct 18, ---.
Mary Butler, bapt. Oct 18, ---.

RECORDS OF ST. ANN'S CHURCH (ST. MARY'S)

Elizabeth Hancock bapt. May 10, 1710.
Mary Normanday, bapt. Jun 10, 1710.
Mary Thomson, bapt. Jun 1, 1710.
Margt. and Hanah John Allen, bapt. Ju- 22, 1710. (?) Burlington
John of Samuel and Susanna Woolston, bapt. May 6, 1712.
Ann (Adcock), bapt. Jun 1, 1712.
Martha of Dorothy and Robert Naylor, bapt. Jun 10, 1712.
Margaret of William Merrail, bapt. Jun 11, 1712.
Elizabeth of (Ralfe Coare), bapt. Jun 11, 1712.
George of John Park, bapt. Jun 11, 1712.
Elizabeth of Jane and Tho. Platt, bapt. Jun 29, 1712.
Martha of Mary and Richard Franey(?), bapt. Jun 30, 1712.
Richard Allison, bapt. Mary, 1714.
Thomas Earle, adult, bapt. Jun 29, 171-.
Hestor (?) and Solomon Nathaniel Curtis, bapt. Jul 27, 171-.
Richard of Row Ellis, bapt. Aug 26, 171-.
Hanah of Jacob and Sarah Perkins, bapt. Sep --, 171-.
Catharine of Eliz and John (Hamel, Jr.?), bapt. 8, 171-.
Thomas of Hanah and Thomas Clark, bapt. Oct 6, 171-.
Susannah of Eliz. and David Kendal, bapt. Nov 2, 171-.
George of Mary and George Willis, bapt. Nov 2, 171-.
Richard of Mary and Richard Medley, bapt. Dec 2, 171-.

Nathaniel Curtis and Eliz. Hewlings, married Jun 10, 1712.
Roger Hawkins and Eliz. Holman, married Jun 11, 1712.
Andrew and Rebekah Nicholas married Sep 9, 1715.
Rowland Ellis and Sarah Allison married Apr 17, 1715.

"Philadelphia, November 30, 1727. Yesterday, died at Burlington, the Reverend Mr. John Talbot, formerly Minister of that Place, who was a pious good Man, and much lamented." (Note. The above is a true copy of an extract from the American Weekly Mercury for Nov 23-30, 1727, published in Philadelphia, and is placed upon this register, to record the decease of the first Rector of St. Mary's Church, which seems to have been omitted, this tenth Day of December 1868, by me. Wm. Allen Johnson, Rector.)

Catherine of Mary and Peter Rose, bapt. Feb 27, 1719.
Samuel of Sarah and Jonathan Lovott, bapt. Mar 15, 1719.
William of Dorothy and Robert Naylor, bapt. Mar 24, 1719.
Esther of Mary and Abram ---, bapt. Mar 20, 1719.
Mary Martha of Dinah and Peter Bard, bapt. Mar 20, 1719.
Samuel Woolston of Samuel and Eliz, bapt. Jul 26, 1719.
Jacob Perkins of Bathsheba, bapt. Jul 26, 1719.
Thomas of Hanah and John Allen, bapt. Aug 23, 1719.
Andrew of Lewis and Margt Jolly, bapt. Aug 23, 1719.
Elizabeth of William and Susanna Robinson, bapt. Sep 6, 1719.
Richard of Wm. and Mary Booker, bapt. Sep 13, 1719.
John of Thomas and Mary Platt, bapt. Sep 13, 1719.
John of Tho. and Mary Foster, bapt. Sep 13, 1719.
Mary of Ann and R. Elton, bapt. Nov --, 1719.
William of William and Mary Callum, bapt. Nov 9, 1719.

Mary of Abigail and Philo Leeds, bapt. Jan 1, --
Margaret Budd, bapt. Feb 25, ---.
Susanna and Mary Huntley, bapt. Feb 25, ---.
Sarah Griffith, bapt. Feb 25, ---.
James of Mary and Hugh McClutchy, bapt. ---.
Martha Dawson, bapt. May 11, ---.

Lawrence Surley to Mary Vanhorn married Jun 14, 1738.
Thos. Evary and Diana Cassol married Jul 9, 1738.

Andrew Bishop and Margaret Sutton, both of Burlington married Aug 20, 1738 at Allenton.
John Kimble and Anna Leeds married Aug 27, 1738 at Burlington.
Charles Shepherd and Margaret Powel both of Burlington married Jun 5, 1739 at Burlington.
George Hatfield and Mary Moses married Jul 6, 1739 at Burlington.

Jas Johnston and Lucy Saltan married Jul 6, 1739 at Burlington.

Elizabeth of John and Jennet Neale, b. Dec 3, 1733, bapt. by Parson Wamon Misher at Burlington.
Martha of John and Jennet Neale, b. Feb 9, 1735, bapt. by Parson Wamon Misher at Burlington.
John of John and Jennett Neale, b. Dec 29, 1737, bapt. by Parson Wamon Misher at Burlington.
Thomson of John and Jennett Neale, b. Jun 22, 1744, bapt. by Parson Campbell.
Jennet of John and Jennet Neale, b. Feb 16, 1750, bapt. by Mr. Campbell.
Catherin of John and Jennet Neale, bapt. by Mr. Campbell, 1753.

Jennet Neale, Sr. buried in the church burying ground in Burlington by Rev. Collin Campbell.
John Neale, Sr. buried in Feb, 1765 in the church burying ground in Burlington by the Rev. Colin Campbell.

Margret of Rowland Ellis and his wife, Sarah, b. Sep 17, 1716, bapt. 1st of November.
Richard of Rowland Ellis and his wife, Sarah, b. Jul 6, bapt. Aug 26, 1716.
Johannes, Filius, Rowland, Ellis and Sarah Uoris (Eyres), bapt. 19 Jun, 1720.
William of Rowland Ellis and Sarah, his wife b. Sep 25, 1722, bapt. the latter end of Oct, 1722.
Joseph of Rowland Ellis and Sarah his wife, b. Sep 23, 1722, bapt. Dec 2, 1724.
Samuel of Thos Clarke and Hannah his wife, bapt. Oct 20, 1724.
(All baptized by Colin Campbell, AM)

Burlington
Martha Golchorn, bapt. Jun 30, 1738.
Bathsheba Tomkins, bapt. Jun 11, 1738.

Allentown
A female child named Charity bapt. Jun 18, 1738.

RECORDS OF ST. ANN'S CHURCH (ST. MARY'S)

Robert Elton of Anthony Elton, bapt. Jul 9, 1738 at (Burlingtone).
John Rogers, bapt. at Allenstowne Aug 13, 1738.
Grace of Samuel Bustill bapt. Aug 27, 1738.
Mary of Mr. Granden bapt. Sep 19, 1378.
Charles of John Wulson, barber, Bristoll, PA, bapt. Oct 25, 1738.
Daniel of Roger Smith bapt. at Mt. Holly. [no date].
Gasper of Roger Smith bapt. at Mt. Holly. [no date].
Leonard of Frederick Heiland at Mt. Holly. [no date].
John of Charles Tomkins of Burlingtone, bapt. Dec 30, 1738.
John of Jeremy Stillwell, bapt. Feb, 1738/9 at Allentown.
Sarah of Mr. Jones, bapt. Feb 1738/9 at Allentown.
Thomas of Rowland Ellis, bapt. Mar 7, 1738/9.
Baptisms by Mr. Colin Campbell, Missionary at Burlington, 1739

James to Mr. Noble, bapt. Jul 22, 1739 at Burlington.
John of John Rowth, bapt. Jul 28, 1739 at Burlington.
John Abraham of Peter Bard, bapt. Aug 3, 1739 at Bristol
Elizabeth of John Kimble, bapt. Aug 17, 1739 at Burlington.
Two female children to Mr. Henry Brown, Oct 9, 1739 at Burlington.
John of Mr. Tomkins, bapt. Oct 21, 1739 at Burlington.
Anthony, bapt. Dec 15, 1739 at Burlington.
Mary of Wm. and Susanna Stebs, bapt. Dec 15, 1739. at Burlington. [hand written into records.]
A male child for George Page, bapt. Jan 9, 1739 at Burlington.
Samuel of James Bud, bapt. Apr 6, 1739.
George of Mr. Foster, bapt. May 26, 1739 at Burlington.
Jeremiah of Jeremiah Stillwell, bapt. June, 1739.
John to John Neil, bapt. at Burlington. Mary to John Neil, bapt. at Burlington. [handwritten]

The Rev'd Mr. Collin Campbell, Missionary at Burlington was married to Miss Mary Martha Bard of the same place by the Rev'd. Mr. Currie, June, 1742.

Mary Ann Campbell of Colin and Mary Campbell, b. Jul 2, 1743, bapt. Jul 10, 1743 by the Rev'd Mr. Jenney, Rector of Christ Church Philadelphia and Commissary Pensilvania.
Mary, the second daughter of Colin and Mary Campbell, b. Aug 13, 1745, bapt. Jan 18, 1747 by the Rev'd Commissary Jenney.
Hugh of Colin and Mary Campbell, bapt. Jan 18, 1747.
Rebecca of Colin and Mary Campbell, bapt. Mar, 1750.
Colin, second son of Colin and Mary, b. Dec 15, 1751, bapt. Dec, 1751.
Charlott of Peter and Mary Bard, bapt. Nov 28, 1753.
John Campbell, b. Feb 24, 1754, bapt. Mar 24, 1754 in St. Mary's Church, Burlington by the Rev'd Mr. Sturgeon.
Elizabeth of John and Ann Lawrence, bapt. Aug 28, 1754.
Sarah Bard of Peter and Mary Bard, bapt. Dec 28, 1754.
James of Anthony DeNormandie and his wife, Mary, bapt. Dec 28, 1754.
Jane of Colin and Mary Campbell, b. Nov 6, 1755, bapt. Dec, 1755 at St. Mary's Church, Burlington.

Archibald of Colin and Mary Campbell, b. Oct 25, 1758, bapt. Nov, 1758 at St. Mary's Church, Burlington.
Mary of Thomas Robinson, a strymaker, and Ann, his wife, bapt. Nov, 1758.
John of Thomas Robinson, a strymaker, and Ann, bapt. Dec 26, 1761.
The 5 adults in the Family of Felix Leeds, from above Mt. Holly, bapt. Jul 27, 1740.
A female of Jehu Claypool, bapt. Jun, 1741.
Mary of Jo's Johnson, bapt. Aug 10, 1740 at Allenton.
William son of Malachi Walton [Waltonarn] and Mary, bapt. Jul 15, 1741 at Bristol.
Benjamin of Peter Baynton, Esq. bapt. Dec 21, 1741.
Elizabeth Darkinder, cousin of Peter Baynton, (?) bapt. Dec 21, 1741.
James Bryant bapt. Aug, 1741 at Mt. Holly.
James of Bennet Bard, bapt. Oct, 1741 at Burlington.
Jeremiah of Jeremiah Stilwell, bapt. Nov, 1741.
James of Jeremiah Stilwell, bapt. Nov, 1741.
Jasper, a Dutch child bapt. Dec, 1741 at Mt. Holly.
Peter of Fretwell Wright, bapt. Jan, 1741.
Barnard of Bartholemie Rowley, bapt. Mar, 1741.
Charles of Charles Read, bapt. Apr, 1742.
James of Jeremiah Stilwell, bapt. May 18, 1742.
Helena of Andrew Gordon, bapt. May 18, 1742.
Ursilla of Stephen Warren, bapt. May 18, 1742.

St. Ann's Church at Burlington Register.

Daniel of Rowland Ellis and Sarah, his wife, b. Feb 5, 1727, bapt. Mar, 1727 by Mr. Nath. Harwood, missionary.
Rowland of Rowland Ellis and Sarah, his wife, b. Aug 16, 1734, bapt. May, 1735 by Mr. Robert Weyman.
George of Rowland Ellis and Sarah, his wife, b. Sep 18, 1736, bapt. Dec 26, 1736 by the Rev'd Mr. Peters.
Thomas of Rowland Ellis and Sarah, his wife, b. Jan 13, 1738, bapt. Feb, 1738 by the Rev'd Mr. Colin Campbell, missionary.
Ann of Nathaniel Thomas and Ann, his wife, bapt. Apr 28, 1746 at Mt. Holly.
Patience, adult child of Joseph and Mary Shinn; bapt. May 30, 1746 at Mt. Holly.
Rebecca, adult child of Joseph and Mary Shinn; bapt. May 30, 1746 at Mt. Holly.
William, adult child of Joseph and Mary Shinn; bapt. May 30, 1746 at Mt. Holly.
Vestai of Joseph and Mary Shinn; bapt. May 30, 1746 at Mt. Holly.
Joseph of Joseph and Mary Shinn; bapt. May 30, 1746 at Mt. Holly.
Benjamin of Joseph and Mary Shinn; bapt. May 30, 1746 at Mt. Holly.
John of Joseph and Mary Shinn; bapt. May 30, 1746 at Mt. Holly.
Francis of Joseph and Mary Shinn; bapt. May 30, 1746 at Mt. Holly.
Abigail of Joseph and Mary Shinn; bapt. May 30, 1746 at Mt. Holly.
Amariah, adult child of Thomas and Mary Foster; bapt. May 30,

1746 at Mt. Holly.
Josiali, adult child of Thomas and Mary Foster; bapt. May 30, 1746 at Mt. Holly.
Abner of Thomas and Mary Foster; bapt. May 30, 1746 at Mt. Holly.
Content of Thomas and Mary Foster; bapt. May 30, 1746 at Mt. Holly.
Elizabeth of Thomas and Mary Foster; bapt. May 30, 1746 at Mt. Holly.
Barzillai, an adult child of Michael Woolston and Sarah, his wife; bapt. May 30, 1746 at Mt. Holly.
Ann of Michael Woolston and Sarah, his wife; bapt. May 30, 1746 at Mt. Holly.
John of John and Ann Fort; bapt. May 30, 1746 at Mt. Holly.
Abraham of John and Ann Fort; bapt. May 30, 1746 at Mt. Holly.
Ann of John and Ann Fort; bapt. May 30, 1746 at Mt. Holly.
Hannah of John and Ann Fort; bapt. May 30, 1746 at Mt. Holly.
Daniel of Richard Bowker and Joanna, his wife; bapt. May 30, 1746 at Mt. Holly.
Barzillai of Richard Bowker and Joanna, his wife; bapt. May 30, 1746 at Mt. Holly.
Margaret of John Tackbachtoll and Rachel, his wife; bapt. May 30, 1746 at Mt. Holly.
David of Thomas Jones, bapt. May 30, 1746 by Mr. Colin Campbell, missionary at Burlington.

Memorandum: This day likewise came to hear one preach at the house of Henry Cooper in Northampton Twp, the widow Bell; born in New England, a poor woman maintained by said Twp, aged as she told me before my whole congregation there, one hundred and two years, had her eye sight and hearing versedly well, walked upright and had the entire use of all her other faculties; Witness Colin Campbell, missionary Burlington.

Jonathan of Jonathan Lovet, bapt. Jun 8, 1746.
Elizabeth of Jonathan Lovet, bapt. Jun 8, 1746.
Samuel of Samuel Lovet, bapt. Jun 8, 1746.
John of Philip Streaker, bapt. Jun 8, 1746.
Arant of Arant and Janet Scuyler, bapt. Apr 1749.
John of Arant and Janet Scuyler, bapt. Jul 1, 1751.
Anna of Arant and Janet Scuyler, bapt. Jan 11, 1754.
Peter of Arant and Janet Scuyler, bapt. Feb, 1755.
Mary of Arant and Janet Scuyler, bapt. Feb, 1755.
Abraham of Arant and Janet Scuyler, bapt. Feb, 1755.

Joseph Bryant of Mt. Holly and Mary White of Burlington married Aug 14, 1746 by Parson Colin Campbell by publication.
Isaac Heuling and Ruth Snowden married in the Church of Burlington, Dec 15, 1752 by publication.
Joseph Boardman and Catherine Departeene married by publication Jan 6, 1753.
Thomas Wallin and Hope Dawson married by publication Jan 6, 1753.
Joseph Adams and Mary Elmer married Oct 6, 1755.

William of William and Hannah DeNormandie, bapt. Nov, 1747.
Edward of Bernard Grandon and Sarah, his wife, b. Jun 12, 1744;

bapt. Jul 15, the following.
John of Richard Allen and Sarah, his wife, b. Aug 27, 1749; bapt. Oct 10, the following, at Bristol, Pennsylvania.
Sarah of Richard Allen and Sarah, his wife, b. Jan 6, 1754; bapt. Mar 29, 1761 in the church at Burlington by Colin Campbell, missionary.
Elizabeth of Richard Allen and Sarah, his wife, b. May 27, 1757; bapt. Mar 29, 1761 in the church at Burlington by Colin Campbell, missionary.
Mary of Richard Allen and Sarah, his wife, b. Jul 19, 1759; bapt. Mar 29, 1761 in the church at Burlington by Colin Campbell, missionary
John David Limbeck, bapt. Nov 12, 1752.
John Jacob Limbeck, bapt. Nov 12, 1752.
John of Alexander Ross, bapt. Apr, 1753 at Burlington.
Fretwell Wright bapt. Sep 11, 1754 in St. Mary's Church, Burlington.
Jonathan of Fretwell Wright; bapt. Sep 11, 1754 in St. Mary's Church, Burlington.
Ellis of Fretwell Wright; bapt. Sep 11, 1754 in St. Mary's Church, Burlington.
William of Fretwell Wright; bapt. Sep 11, 1754 in St. Mary's Church, Burlington.
Issack of Fretwell Wright; bapt. Sep 11, 1754 in St. Mary's Church, Burlington.
Marion Hannah of Alexander Ross, bapt. Sep 15, 1754.
Joseph of Daniel Ellis, bapt. May, 1755.
William of John Pool and Sarah, his wife, bapt. Oct 8, 1755.

Sir John St. Clair, Barronet and Elizabeth Morelan, gentlewoman married Mar 17, 1752 by Colin Campbell according to the rites and ceremony of the Church of England, licensed by His Excellency, Josiah Hardy.

Charles Campbell bapt. Mar 17, 1765 at Burlington by the Rev'd. Mr. Sturgeon.
Ann of Walter and Hannah Vanskiver, bapt. Nov 14, 1760 at Burlington.
Martha, wife of John Lawrence, bapt. Apr 20, 1764 at Burlington.
Sarah of John Lawrence and wife, Martha, bapt. Apr 20, 1765 at Burlington.
Catherine of John Lawrence and wife, Martha, bapt. Apr 20, 1765 at Burlington.
Abraham of Godfrey Hancock, bapt. Apr 23, 1764 at Burlington.
Isaack of Godfrey Hancock, bapt. Apr 23, 1764 at Burlington.
Mary of Godfrey Hancock, bapt. Apr 23, 1764 at Burlington.
Rebeckah of Godfrey Hancock, bapt. Apr 23, 1764 at Burlington.
Thomas of Jonathan Tuly and Martha, his wife; bapt. Apr 23, 1764 at Burlington.
John of Jonathan Tuly and Martha, his wife; bapt. Apr 23, 1764 at Burlington.
Joseph of Jonathan Tuly and Martha, his wife; bapt. Apr 23, 1764 at Burlington.
Mary of Jonathan Tuly and Martha, his wife; bapt. Apr 23, 1764 at Burlington.

RECORDS OF ST. ANN'S CHURCH (ST. MARY'S)

Elizabeth of Robert Elton and Margaret, his wife, bapt. Sep, 1764 at Burlington.
Letice, wife of James Dobbins, bapt. Oct 30, 1764 at Burlington.
Sarah, adult child of James and Letice Dobbins, bapt. Oct 30, 1764 at Burlington.
Zebedee, adult child of James and Letice Dobbins, bapt. Oct 30, 1764 at Burlington.
Joab, adult child of James and Letice Dobbins, bapt. Oct 30, 1764 at Burlington.
James, adult child of James and Letice Dobbins, bapt. Oct 30, 1764 at Burlington.
Michael, an infant of James and Letice Dobbins, bapt. Oct 30, 1764 at Burlington.
Sarah, wife of Philo Leeds, bapt. Oct 30, 1764 at Burlington.
Samuel, adult child of Philo Leeds and his wife, Sarah, bapt. Oct 30, 1764 at Burlington.
Theodosia Lee, an adult bapt. Oct 30, 1764 at Burlington.
Ann of Noah and Rebeckah Ridgway, bapt. Oct 30, 1764 at Burlington.

The Rev'd Colin Campbell departed this life on the 9th of Aug, 1766.

Jonathan Odell, M.A. was appointed, by the Society for Propagating the Gospel in foreign parts, to succeed Mr. Campbell, as missionary at Burlington, Dec 25, 1766, and he arrived at Burlington on the 25 of Jul, 1767, and was the next day regularly inducted in St. Ann's (now St. Mary's) Church, in the said city of Burlington, by his Excellency Wm. Franklin, Esq., Governor of the province of New Jersey.

Anno Domini 1767. Parish Register of St. Mary's Church in Burlington (with occasional entries relating to neighboring places) continued by J. Odell, Missionary.

John the seventh child of John and Edy Carty, b. Jan 19, 1766 at Burlington, bapt. Jul 26, 1767.

George Bass of Springfield in the County of Burlington and Ann Appleton, of the city of Burlington, were married at Burlington Aug 3, 1767.
Garret Vandergrift, of the county of Philadelphia and Agnes Harris of the twp of Bristol in the province of Pennsylvania were married at Burlington Aug 14, 1767.
Thomas Lippincott, of Chester Twp in Burlington County, and Elizabeth Haines of Northampton in said county, were married at Burlington Aug 15, 1767.
Joseph Bruton [Burton] of Bristol, Pennsylvania and Bridget Kelly of the same place were married at Burlington Aug 30, 1767.

Robert Jenney the first born of Samuel and Mary Bard, b. Aug 9, 1767 at Bridge Town (alias Mt. Holly), bapt. Aug 23, 1767.
Mary the second child of Samuel and Theodosia Allen, b. Dec 27, 1764, bapt. Sep 4, 1767 at New Mills, the place of their nativity, Hanover Twp, West New Jersey.

EARLY CHURCH RECORDS OF BURLINGTON COUNTY

George the third child of Samuel and Theodosia Allen, b. Oct 26, 1766, bapt. Sep 4, 1767 at New Mills, the place of their nativity, Hanover Twp, West New Jersey.
Jennet the third child of John Neal and Eleanor, his wife, b. Aug 11, 1767, bapt. Sep 13, 1767 at Burlington.
Abraham the sixth child of Abraham Vanskiver and Mary, his wife, b. Jun 21, 1767, bapt. Sep 13, 1767 at Burlington.

Barbara, wife of Thomas Barnsley, Esq. of the twp of Bensalem, Bucks County, Pennsylvania d. Aug 18, 1767, bur. Aug 21, 1767 at Bristol, Bucks County, Pennsylvania.
Lawrence Hand was buried at Burlington Aug 30, 1767.
Sarah the first born of Samuel and Cyllania Woolston of Mt. Holly, buried at Mt. Holly, Sep 14, 1767.

Note: The authenticity of the above attested at a meeting of the vestry Apr 4, 1768. John Odell, Minister of St. Mary's Church. William Lyndon and Abrm Hewlings, church wardens.

1767
Ann Cocker, of the city of Liverpoole and county of Lancaster in the kingdom of Great Britain, was buried in Burlington, Sep 10, 1767.
Ann of John and Mary Harris, b. Jan, 1764, buried Sep 15, 1767 at Burlington.

Mary the fourth child of Reuben Baxnell, late a soldier in his Majesty's 48th Regt. of Foot, and Sarah, his wife, bapt. Sep 27, 1767.

Abraham the fifth child of Arent Schuyler and Jennet, his wife, buried at Burlington, Sep 29, 1767.
Samuel Rutherford, Esq., late a Captain in his Majesty's 15th Reg. of Foot, was buried at Trenton, Oct 21, 1767.

Elnathan Stevenson and Bathsheba Norcross, both of Burlington County, married at Mt. Holly, Oct 25, 1767.

Ann the fifth child of Thomas Cooper and Elizabeth, his wife, b. Aug 30, 1767; bapt. Nov 8, 1767 at Mt. Holly.

Jacob Brian, of Springfield in the county of Burlington, buried Nov 17, 1767.

Gabriel Vanhorne, of Middletown in the county of Bucks and province of Pennsylvania, yeoman, and Susannah Ashton, of the same place, married at Burlington, Nov 18, 1767.

Mary the third child of Robert and Mary Bill, b. Nov 21, 1767, bapt. Nov 29, 1767 at Mt. Holly.
Mary of Joseph Bruton and Bridget, his wife, b. Nov, 1767 at Bristol, bapt. Dec 6, 1767 at Burlington.

Jonathan Atkinson, of Northampton, Burlington County, and Mary Hillyer of the same place, married at Burlington, Dec 7, 1767.

RECORDS OF ST. ANN'S CHURCH (ST. MARY'S) 131

Rebecca, wife of George Deacon, bapt. Dec 9, 1767 at Burlington.
James the fourth child of James Dobbins and Ruth, his wife, b.
Nov 1, 1767, bapt. Dec 15, 1767 at Mt. Holly.
David of David Crowne (or Crahan) and Catherine Hendric, b. In
the Spring of 1764, bapt. Dec 26, 1767 at Burlington.

Daniel Toy, one of the vestrymen of St. Andrew's Church at Mt.
Holly buried near said church, Dec 28, 1767.

April 4, 1768 Above attested by John Odell, Minister and William
Lyndon and Abrm Hewlings, church wardens.

1767
Barnet Vanhorne, of Northampton, Burlington county and Levina
Bogart, of the same place, married at Burlington Dec 30, 1767.

James the eighth child of John and Edy Carty, b. Dec 23, 1767,
bapt. Dec 20, 1767 at Burlington.

1768
John Esdall of Burlington and Sarah Ellis, of the same place,
married at Burlington Jan 3, 1768.

James the eighth child of John and Edy Carty buried at Burlington
Jan 6, 1768.

Richard Long and Mary Whitace, both of the parish of Burlington,
married at Burlington Jan 20, 1768.

Rebecca, wife of George Deacon was buried at Burlington, Jan 20,
1768.
William Skeeles, one of the vestrymen at St. Mary's Church,
Burlington buried near said church, Jan 24, 1768.

Joseph Betts and Elizabeth Fort, both of the County of Burlington
married at Burlington Jan 24, 1768.
David Vaughan of Springfield and Mary Renier of Mansfield, both
of the county of Burlington, married at Burlington Jan 31, 1768.
George West and Mary Clark, both of the county of Burlington were
married at Burlington Feb 2, 1768.

Anne of Thomas and Edy Price, of Mt. Holly, bapt. Feb 14, 1768
age 18 in St. Andrew's church at Mt. Holly.
Francis of Francis Gibbons and Elizabeth North, b. Nov 18, 1767,
bapt. Mar 23, 1768 in St. Mary's church, Burlington.
Anne, the reputed daughter of Francis Gibbons and Elizabeth
North, b. Nov 18, 1767, bapt. Mar 23, 1768 in St. Mary's church,
Burlington.
Mary the third child of Garret and Joanna Keating, b. Oct 26,
1767, bapt. Mar 30, 1768 at Burlington.
Rachael, a black female child belonging to Rebecca Allen of
Burlington, bapt. Apr 3, 1768 at Burlington.

April 4, 1768 attested by John Odell, Minister, William Lyndon and Abrm Hewlings, church wardens.

1768
John Dawson and Grace Searle, both of the province of Pennsylvania married Apr 5, 1768 at Burlington.

Edward Tonkins, one of the vestrymen of St. Mary's Church was buried Apr 7, 1768 in the said churchyard, at Burlington.

Zebulon Bozarth, of Wellenborough in the county of Burlington and Margaret Regions of the same place married Apr 11, 1768, at Burlington.
Joseph Kelly, of the County of Bucks in Pennsylvania and Phobe Buckman, of the same place, married Apr 13, 1768, at Burlington.

Mary Neale was buried Apr 25, 1768, at Burlington.

Richard Stockton, of the county of Burlington and Hannah Crispin, of the same place, were married May 2, 1768, at Burlington.

Judith Weaver, sister-in-law to Lambert Barnes, buried May 5, 1768 at Burlington.

Robert Adeir and Rebecca Huddleston, both of the province of Pennsylvania married May 21, 1768 at Burlington.
Edward Kemble and Levina Atkinson, both of Springfield in the county of Burlington married May 22, 1768 at Mt. Holly.
David Larrew and Sarah Larzelere, both of Bucks County in the province of Pennsylvania married Jun 2, 1768 at the house of Nicholas Larzelere in said county.

Sarah the first born of Thomas and Anne Butcher, b. Dec 7, 1766, bapt. Jun 2, 1768 in Maxfield Twp, Bucks County and province of Pennsylvania.

William Putten, formerly a soldier of the 48th Regt. was buried Jun 3, 1768 at Burlington.

Mary the eighth child of Samuel and Syllania Woolston, b. Jan 13, 1766, bapt. May 8, 1768 at Mt. Holly.

Attested by John Odell, Minister and William Lyndon and Abrm Hewlings, Church wardens.

1768
William Harcourt first born of Thomas and Hannah Freeman, b. Dec 27, 1767 at Jamaica on Long Island, bapt.
Joseph of Joseph Morgan and Mary White of Waterford in Gloucester County, bapt. Jun 9, 1768 at Burlington.

John Larzelere and Margaret Vanhorne, both of Bucks County of the province of Pennsylvania married at Middletown in said county, Jun 16, 1768.
The Rev'd William Frazer, of Amwell and Rebecca Campbell of Burlington married Jul 13, 1768.

Reuben Boxendale, of Lancashire in England, late a soldier in his Majesty's 48th Regt. of Foot, was buried at Burlington Jul 14, 1768.
Jemima, wife of Thomas Bud, Sr. was buried at Mt. Holly, Jul 18, 1768.

George Smith and Hannah Stockton, both of Wellenburgh in the county of Burlington, married at Burlington, Aug 9, 1768.

Jemima of William and Susannah Norton of Mt. Holly, bapt. Aug 14, 1768 at Mt. Holly.

Jacob Bennet and Hannah Hogeland, both of Bucks County, in Pennsylvania married at Burlington, Aug 14, 1768.

Joseph of John and Christine Wistor, bapt. at Mt. Holly, Aug 28, 1768.

Hope Walling was buried at Burlington, Aug 24, 1768.
Joseph of Charles and Sarah Pettit of Burlington, was bapt. and buried Aug 31, 1768 at Burlington.

April 4, 1768 attested by John Odell, Minister, William Lyndon and Abrm Hewlings, church wardens.

Anno Domini 1768. Charlotte the second born of Samuel and Mary Bard of Mt. Holly, b. Aug 27, 1768, bapt. Sep 11, 1768.

William Taylor and Abigail Carter, both of Springfield in the county of Burlington, married at Burlington Sep 18, 1768.
Thomas Browne and Mary Nutt, both of Mansfield, in the county of Burlington, married at Burlington Sep 19, 1768.
James Bruce and Winefee Franklin married at Burlington, Sep 20, 1768.

Sarah, wife of David Larrew, of Bucks County, Pennsylvania, buried in Bristol in said county, Sep 21, 1768.

James the fourth child of John and Rozanna Hogan of Evesham, from Limerick in Ireland, b. Dec 17, 1767, bapt. Sep 25, 1768.
Benjamin the eighth child of John and Elizabeth Clark, b. Aug 13, 1768, bapt. Nov 7, 1768 at Mt. Holly.

Elizabeth, the widow of James Thomson of Burlington was buried at Burlington, Nov 7, 1768 in the 84th year of her age.

Mary of Arent Schuyler and Jane, his second wife, b. Oct 3, 1768, bapt. Nov 16, 1768, buried Nov 29, 1769 at Burlington.

John the third child of John and Elizabeth Poole, b. May 1, 1768, bapt. Nov 21, 1768 at Burlington.

Anne, the wife of Revel Elton of Northampton, bapt. at the said Revel's house, Dec 19, 1768.

Revel of Revel and Anne Elton, bapt. Dec 19, 1768.

Anne, the wife of Revel Elton, of Northampton, was buried at Burlington, Dec 24, 1768.

Attested by John Odell, Minister, William Lyndon and Abrm Hewlings, church wardens.

Anno Domini 1769

Lewis the third child of Lewis and Bridget Taylor, b. Dec 4, 1768 at Mt. Holly, bapt. Jan 1, 1769.

Thomas Reynolds, Esq. and Mary, the widow of Jacob Bryan, both of Burlington county, married Jan 4, 1769 at Mt. Holly.

Susannah the third child of Adam and Margaret Shepherd, b. Apr 19, 1768, bapt. Jan 8, 1769 at Burlington.

Samuel Davis, Jr. of Chester Twp in the county of Burlington, was buried at the church in Waterford (alias Colestown), Jan 14, 1769.

Lucy the fourth child of John and Lucy Murrell, b. Dec 20, 1768, bapt. Jan 15, 1769 at Mt. Holly.

Sarah, the widow of Daniel Toy, of Mt. Holly, bapt. in St. Andrew's church, Jan 29, 1769.

Joshua Renier and Rosanna Foster, both of Mansfield Twp in the county of Burlington, married Feb 7, 1769 at Burlington.

Samuel the ninth child of Samuel and Cyllania Woolston of Northampton Twp, b. Aug 22, 1768, bapt. Feb 12, 1769 at Mt. Holly.

Richard, the son of Richard Milligan, dec'd and Rachel (now the wife of Thomas Esdall) was buried in Burlington, Feb 14, 1769.

Elizabeth of Daniel Toy (late of Mt. Holly) and Sarah, his widow, b. Jul 5, 1758, bapt. Feb 26, 1769 in St. Andrew's church.

Frederick of Daniel Toy (late of Mt. Holly) and Sarah, his widow, b. Nov 16, 1759, bapt. Feb 26, 1769 in St. Andrew's church.

Mary of Daniel Toy (late of Mt. Holly) and Sarah, his widow, b. Feb 9, 1762, bapt. Feb 26, 1769 in St. Andrew's church.

John of Daniel Toy (late of Mt. Holly) and Sarah, his widow, b. Jan 25, 1764, bapt. Feb 26, 1769 in St. Andrew's church.

RECORDS OF ST. ANN'S CHURCH (ST. MARY'S)

Daniel of Daniel Toy (late of Mt. Holly) and Sarah, his widow, b. Feb 15, 1766, bapt. Feb 26, 1769 in St. Andrew's church.
Jemima, the wife of Peter Renier was baptized at Burlington Mar 20, 1769.
Mary the fourth child of Frederick and Catherine Lowden, b. Sep 19, 1768, bapt. Mar 26, 1769 in St. Mary's church, Burlington.
Rachel the eighth child of Ralph and Grace Boon, b. Feb 4, 1769, bapt. Mar 26, 1769 in St. Mary's church, Burlington.

Attested by John Odell, Minister, William Lyndon and Abrm Hewlings, church wardens.

Anno Domini 1769. Elizabeth of Thomas and Rachel Esdall, b. Feb 23, 1769, bapt. Apr 9, 1769 at Burlington.

John Vanskiver and Mary Crouss both of Burlington married Apr 9, 1769.

Jane Cole, of Burlington, d. Apr 16, 1769 in the 48th year of her age; buried Apr 19, 1769 at Burlington.

Eber Taylor and Sarah Ferguson, both of Burlington married Apr 21, 1769 at Burlington.

Joseph Richardson of Burlington, bapt. Apr 23, 1769 in the 41st year of age.
Anne of Joseph Richardson and Esther, his wife, b. Oct 20, 1756, bapt. Apr 23, 1769.
John of Joseph Richardson and Esther, his wife, b. Nov 13, 1758, bapt. Apr 23, 1769.
Joseph of Joseph Richardson and Esther, his wife, b. Oct 17, 1761, bapt. Apr 23, 1769.
Benjamin of Joseph Richardson and Esther, his wife, b. May 1, 1763, bapt. Apr 23, 1769.
Mary of Joseph Richardson and Esther, his wife, b. Nov 13, 1764, bapt. Apr 23, 1769.
Jane of John Richardson and wife, Rebecca, b. Nov 24, 1748, bapt. Apr 23, 1769.
John of John Richardson and wife, Rebecca, b. Apr 17, 1753, bapt. Apr 23, 1769.
Joseph of John Richardson and wife, Rebecca, b. Dec 12, 1755, bapt. Apr 23, 1769.
William of John Richardson and wife, Rebecca, b. Jun 18, 1758, bapt. Apr 23, 1769.
Rebecca of John Richardson and wife, Rebecca, b. Jan 27, 1761, bapt. Apr 23, 1769.

Henry Mitchell and Martha Vanhorne, both of Bucks County in the province of Pennsylvania, married Apr 25, 1769.

Francis Griffin of Burlington buried Apr 30, 1769.

Asher Mott of Amwell Twp, county of Hunterdon and province of New Jersey, and Ann Biles of Falls Twp, County of Bucks and province of Pennsylvania, married May 10, 1769.

Thomas of George and Elizabeth Stockham, of Bristol Twp, in the county of Bucks, Pennsylvania, b. Apr 14, 1769, bapt. May 15, 1769.

Abel Person was buried at Burlington May 29, 1769.

Peter the first born of Frederick and Elizabeth Light of Bucks County, Pennsylvania, aged 3 months, bapt. Jun 4, 1769 by Rev'd Wm. Frazer, at Burlington.

Attested by John Odell, Minister, William Lyndon and Abrm Hewlings, church wardens.

Anno Domini 1769
Leonard Murray (otherwise called Smith) was buried at Burlington, Jun 8, 1769.
Peter Bard, Jr. of New York was buried at Burlington Jun 14, 1769.

Tyrringham Palmer and Anne Kemble both of Burlington, married Jun 15, 1769.
Thomas Murphin and Anne Brooks, both of Burlington county married at Bristol in Pennsylvania Jun 24, 1769.

Mary the fifth child of James and Anne Holland of Evesham, b. Apr 19, 1769, bapt. Jun 25, 1769 at Mt. Holly.
Colin the first born of the Rev'd Wm. Frazer of Amwell and Rebecca, his wife, b. May 24, 1769, bapt. Jun 21, 1769 at Burlington.
Martha the eighth child of Daniel and Bathsheba Ellis, b. May 27, 1769, bapt. Jul 2, 1769 at Burlington.

Anne, the widow of Revel Elton, Esq. of Burlington was buried at Burlington, Jul 4, 1769.
Sarah, widow of Rowland Ellis, deceased of Burlington, buried Jul 18, 1769 at Burlington.
Charlotte the second child of Samuel and Mary Bard of Mt. Holly, was buried at Mt. Holly, Jul 19, 1769.

Margaret the first child of Hugh and Sarah McKlean of Burlington, b. Nov 14, 1768, bapt. Jul 30, 1769.
Joseph Murrill, b. Feb 29, 1731, bapt. Aug 6, 1769 at Mt. Holly.
Anne, wife of Joseph Murrill, b. Sep 5, 1733, bapt. Aug 6, 1769 at Mt. Holly.
William of Joseph Murrill and Anne, his wife, b. Sep 13, 1759, bapt. Aug 6, 1769 at Mt. Holly.
Mary of Joseph Murrill and Anne, his wife, b. Jul 26, 1761, bapt. Aug 6, 1769 at Mt. Holly.
Margaret of Joseph Murrill and Anne, his wife, b. Dec 25, 1766, bapt. Aug 6, 1769 at Mt. Holly.
John a fifth child of John Lawrence, Esq. and Martha, his wife, b. Sep 27, 1768, bapt. Aug 7, 1769 at Burlington.
Jacob the second child of Jacob and Catherine Moser, b. Jul 23,

1769, bapt. Aug 11, 1769.

Attested by John Odell, Minister, William Lyndon and Abrm Hewlings, church wardens.

Anno Domini 1769
Isaac the fourth child of John and Eleanor Neale of Burlington, b. Jul 16, 1769, bapt. Aug 13, 1769 at St. Mary's church, Burlington.
Peter Aris of John and Mary Hodgkinson, b. Jun 2, 1769, bapt. Aug 13, 1769 in St. Mary's church, Burlington.

Joseph Vandergrift of Burlington and Lydia Brelsford of Bristol married at Burlington, Aug 18, 1769.

Mary the sixth child of Thomas and Elizabeth Cooper of Mt. Holly, b. Jul 22, 1769, bapt. Aug 20, 1769 at Mt. Holly.
Alexander Robertson the third child of William and Mary Burn, b. Nov 17, 1768, bapt. Sep 3, 1769 at Mt. Holly.

James Longstaff, of Springfield, aged 80 years, died Sep 9, 1769; was buried at Mt. Holly, Sep 10, 1769.

Thomas of Henry and Mary Dalton, b. Sep 23, 1769, bapt. Oct 2, 1769 at Burlington.
Joseph of Henry and Mary Dalton, b. Sep 23, 1769, bapt. Oct 2, 1769 at Burlington.

Joseph Archer and Martha Tuly, both of the County of Burlington, were married at Burlington, Oct 3, 1769.

Sarah, the wife of John Esdall, died Oct 2, 1769; buried Oct 3, 1769 at Burlington.
Thomas the first born of John and Mehitable Tribet, b. Oct 11, 1767, bapt. Oct 29, 1769 and buried Oct 30, 1769.

Ellis of John Esdall and Sarah, his late wife, b. Oct 4, 1769, bapt. Nov 10, 1769 at Burlington.
Samuel the eleventh child of David and Deborah Force, b. Sep 18, 1769, bapt. Nov 14, 1769 at Burlington.

Alice, the wife of Charles Read, Esq. of Burlington, died Nov 13, 1769; buried Nov 15, 1769.
Peter Bard of Mt. Holly died Nov 30, 1769 at the age of 56 years; buried Dec 2, 1769 at Burlington.

Attested by John Odell, Minister and William Lyndon and Abrm Hewlings, Church wardens.

Anno Domini 1769. Jacob the fourth born of Abraham and Mary Collin, b. Oct 1, 1769, bapt. Dec 3, 1769 at Burlington.

Samuel Bard, Esq. of Mt. Holly died at Bristol, Dec 14, 1769 in the 29th year of his age; buried Dec 17, 1769 at Burlington.

1770

John Powell and Sarah Bateman, both of Chester Twp in the county of Burlington married Jan 1, 1770 at Burlington.

Henry Nordyke, of Willenborough, died Jan 2, 1770; buried Jan 4, 1770 at Burlington.

Anne the third child of Michael and Mary Parker, b. Nov 1, 1769, bapt. Jan 7, 1770 at Mt. Holly.

William Mitchell and Mary Hutchin, both of Mansfield married at Burlington, Jan 14, 1770.

John the first child of Richard and Mary Long, b. Feb 5, 1769, bapt. Jan 20, 1770.

Joseph Weaver and Rachel Robinson, both of Mt. Holly married at Mt. Holly, Jan 21, 1770.
Isaac Wood and Mary Rossell, both of Mt. Holly married at Mt. Holly, Jan 25, 1770.

William of Nicholas and Lydia Dicker, b. Apr 26, 1768, bapt. Feb 18, 1770 at Mt. Holly.

Jane Campbell second daughter of the late Mr. Campbell, Minister of this church, b. Nov 6, 1755; died Feb 19, 1770; buried Feb 21, 1770.
John Rowe died Feb 20, 1770 in the 47th year of his age; buried Feb 22, 1770.

William Austin and Hannah Claypoole, both of Willenburgh in the County of Burlington married at Willenburgh Mar 1, 1770.

Anne of John and Francess Crook, b. Feb 28, 1770, bapt. Mar 25, 1770 at Burlington.
Margaret, a negro woman belonging to Mrs. Treadwell of Bristol in Pennsylvania, bapt. Apr 8, 1770 at Burlington.

John Wollard, in a very advanced age, died Apr 12, 1770; buried Apr 13, 1770 at Burlington.

Asa, a black male infant belonging to Rebecca Allen, bapt. Apr 15, 1770 at Burlington.
Richard the fourth child of William and Elizabeth Blair, b. Dec 5, 1769, bapt. Apr 16, 1770 at Burlington.
Elizabeth the fourth child of George and Deborah Haywood, b. Dec 18, 1760, bapt. Apr 22, 1770 at Mt. Holly.

Joshua Wright and Sarah Mitchell, both of Bucks County in Pennsylvania, married Apr 26, 1770 at Burlington.

William Lyndon, one of the wardens of this church, died May 3, 1770; buried May 5, 1770 at Burlington.

RECORDS OF ST. ANN'S CHURCH (ST. MARY'S)

Samuel Tintard, Esq., Captain in his Majesty's 25th Regt. of Foot and Abigail Stockton of Princeton married at Princeton, May 23, 1770.

Elizabeth, the widow of Nicholas Powell, buried Jun 7, 1770 at Burlington.

Cornelius Vandyke and Elizabeth Yerkus, both of Bucks County in Pennsylvania, married at Bristol in the said county, Jun 7, 1770.
Fanny Luke, black female infant belonging to John Ayers, bapt. Jun 24, 1770 at Burlington.
Charles the eighth child of Arent Schuyler, b. May 19, 1770, bapt. Jun 27, 1770 at Burlington.
Susannah the tenth child of Jacob and Catherine Sydenham, b. Apr 7, 1770, bapt. Jun 27, 1770 at Burlington.
Anne the sixth child of Barnaby and Rachael VanSkyver, b. Aug, 1768, bapt. Jun 27, 1770 at Burlington.
Isaac the fourth child of John and Elizabeth Poole, b. May 18, 1770, bapt. Jul 8, 1770 at Burlington.
Anne the seventh child of Abraham and Mary VanSkyver, b. Apr 15, 1770, bapt. Jul 8, 1770 at Burlington.
Charles, a black male infant belonging to Mrs. Wright of Bristol, bapt. Jul 8, 1770 at Burlington.

Sarah Peachy buried Jul 10, 1770 at Burlington.

John Fox and Alice Hutchin, both of Mansfield, married Jul 15, 1770 at Burlington.

Elizabeth, the wife of John Shaw, died Jul 22, 1770; buried Jul 23, 1770 at Burlington.

Anne the sixth child of Chichester and Margaret Reynolds, b. Jan 12, 1768, bapt. Jul 29, 1770 at Mt. Holly.

Rachel, daughter of Ralph and Grace Boon, b. Feb 4, 1769; buried Aug 3, 1770.

Isaac Vanhorne and Sarah Fury, both of Northampton, married Aug 5, 1770 in St. Mary's Church, Burlington.

Elizabeth the second child of George and Elizabeth Stockham of Bristol in Pennsylvania, b. Jun 21, 1770, bapt. Aug 5, 1770.
John and Mary, second and third children of John and Mehitabel Tribet, b. Oct 7, 1769, bapt. Aug 5, 1770 at Burlington.

John Mackie of Philadelphia and Hannah Butterworth of Burlington married Aug 7, 1770 at Burlington.

Joseph the youngest son of Henry and Mary Dalton buried in Burlington, Aug 9, 1770.

Simon Tribet and Elizabeth Hawkins, both of Burlington married

Aug 12, 1770 at Burlington.

Rowland the fifth child of Daniel and Bathsheba Ellis, buried at Burlington Aug 15, 1770.
Elizabeth of William and Elizabeth Blair buried in Burlington Aug 18, 1770.
Jacob the youngest child of Abraham and Mary Collin buried at Burlington Aug 23, 1770.
Anne of Abraham and Hannah Tooley of Philadelphia buried at Burlington, Aug 24, 1770.
Hannah, widow of John Deacon buried at Burlington Aug 26, 1770.
William Budd, Sr., one of the vestryman of St. Andrew's church, Mt. Holly buried Aug 29, 1770 at Mt. Holly.

Jacob Nordyke and Anne Betts, both of Mansfield, were married in Burlington, Sep 3, 1770.

Elizabeth, the wife of William Shadaker, buried in Burlington, Sep 4, 1770.

James the fourth child of William and Mary Murphy, b. Sep 15, bapt. Sep 7, 1770.
Hans George the fourth child of John and Catherine Hälle, b. Jun 19, 1763, bapt. Sep 8, 1770 in Burlington.
Rebecka the seventh child of Chichester and Margaret Reynolds, b. Feb 27, 1770, bapt. Sep 9, 1770 in Mt. Holly.
Isaac of James and Suzanna Bourchier, b. May 2, 1769, bapt. Sep 9, 1770 at Mt. Holly.

Hans George the fourth child of John and Catherine Halle buried in Burlington, Dec 14, 1770.

Grace, the widow of Edward Browning, bapt. Sep 16, 1770 in Burlington.
Cornelia the first born of John and Mary Vanskyver, b. Aug 20, 1769, bapt. Sep 16, 1770.

Martha, wife of James Flanigan died Sep 18, 1770, buried Sep 19, 1770 in Burlington.
Hannah, the wife of Micajah Reeve, died Oct 14, 1770, buried Oct 16, 1770 at Mt. Holly.
Henry Delatush of Mansfield, buried Oct 18, 1770.

Rachel the eleventh child of William and Susannah Norton of Mt. Holly, b. Oct 7, 1770, bapt. Nov 4, 1770.
Sarah first born of Richard and Sarah Jackson of Northampton, b. Nov 3, 1770, bapt. Nov 5, 1770.

Peter Shiras and Rebecca Thomas both of Mt. Holly married November 11, 1770.

Reuben Harding the ninth child of Henry and Elizabeth Knight, b. Jul 25, 1770, bapt. Nov 18, 1770 at Mt. Holly.

Patrick Cowan buried Dec 3, 1770 at Burlington.

Joseph Bullock and Esther Baynton both of Philadelphia married at Philadelphia Dec 6, 1770.
Thomas Neale and Mary Moon, both of Burlington, married in St. Mary's Church, Burlington, Dec 12, 1770.
Dennis Gunnin and Eleanor Connor both of Evesham married at Mt. Holly, Dec 16, 1770.

John the tenth child of Samuel and Cyllania Woolston of Mt. Holly, b. Oct 27, 1770, bapt. Dec 16, 1770 at Mt. Holly.
Hugh the first born of Henry and Anne Cowan of Evesham, b. Mar 4, 1770, bapt. Dec 16, 1770 at Mt. Holly.

David Thomas buried at Burlington, Dec 19, 1770.

Sebastian, a negro man belonging to Mr. Wright of Trenton, and Rosetta, his infant daughter, belonging to Mrs. Treadwell of Bristol, both bapt. Jan 6, 1771 at Burlington.
Daniel the thirteenth child of William and Mary Coxe, b. Sep 25, 1769 at Philadelphia, bapt. Jan 9, 1771 at Sunbury, Bucks County.
Mary Patterson, a widow, late of Pennsylvania, bapt. Jan 13, 1771 at Mt. Holly.
Jane the first child of Mathew and Hannah Currey, b. Mar 19, 1769, bapt. Jan 14, 1771.
Mary the fourth child of Dougal and Sarah Cameron, b. May 5, 1770, bapt. Jan 14, 1771.

Mary, the wife of John Irick, buried at Mt. Holly, Jan 16, 1771.

Thomas Craven and Elizabeth Sydenham both of Burlington married at Burlington, Feb 7, 1771.
Joseph Read, Esq., Attorney at Law, and Martha Rossell both of Mt. Holly married at Mt. Holly Feb 7, 1771.
William Colwell of Evesham and Lucretia Mary Marling of Chesterfield married at Burlington, Feb 11, 1771.

Latitia, wife of Andrew Cole, buried at Mt. Holly, Mar 6, 1771.

William Biddle and Elizabeth Berry married at Burlington Apr 3, 1771.

Rebecca, the wife of John Richardson, of Springfield buried Apr 3, 1771.

Thomas Hunloke and Mary Bard both of Mt. Holly married in St. Andrew's Church Apr 11, 1771.

Hepzibah of John and Barbara Acey, b. Apr 13, 1770, bapt. Apr 21, 1771 at Mt. Holly.
Samuel of Frederic and Catherine Lowdon, b. Dec 28, 1770, bapt. Apr 28, 1771 at Burlington.
Elizabeth of Nicolas and Lydia Dicker, b. Nov 16, 1770, bapt. May 5, 1771 at Mt. Holly.

Joseph Porter of Evesham and Hannah Knight of Mt. Holly married May 19, 1771.

Anna Maria Powell of Elizabeth Martine, b. Nov 12, 1770, bapt. May 22, 1771 at Burlington.

James Lidden and Anne Lane, both of Bucks County, Pennsylvania married May 30, 1771.

Mary the fifth child of David and Rebecca Walton, of Bucks County, in Pennsylvania b. Feb 28, 1771, bapt. May 30, 1771 at Bristol.

Rebecca, widow of Benjamin Towne, late of Bucks County, buried May 30, 1771.

Samuel Stiles and Jane Dobson, both of Burlington, married Jun 26, 1771.

Alicia, widow of James Moon of Burlington buried Jul 16, 1771.

Mary of Isaac and Mary Wood, b. Jan 7, 1771, bapt. Jul 28, 1771 at Mt. Holly.

Deborah of Benjamin and Rebecca Towne, late of Bucks County, Pennsylvania, buried Aug 2, 1771 at Bristol.

Joseph of John and Lucy Murrell, b. Jun 23, 1771, bapt. Aug 10, 1771 at Mt. Holly.
Elizabeth, wife of James Harrison, a free negro, and her two infant daughters, bapt. Aug 18, 1771 at Burlington.
Rowland of Daniel and Bathsheba Ellis, b. Jul 8, 1771, bapt. Aug 28, 1771 at Burlington.
Anne of Simon and Elizabeth Tribet, b. Jun 22, 1770, bapt. Aug 21, 1771 at Burlington.
William of James and Anne Holland, b. Feb 18, 1771, bapt. Aug 21, 1771.

Peter Van Horne and Sarah Mode both of Bucks County, Pennsylvania married Sep 4, 1771.
Michael Dicker and Catherine Sutphine both of Northampton married Sep 9, 1771.

John first child of Jacob and Rachel Shafer, b. Jan 13, 1755, bapt. Sep 15, 1771 at Burlington.
Tamar, a free negro woman, bapt. Sep 29, 1771 at Burlington.

Rev'd Mr. Jonathan Downes, late a fellow of St. John's College and Rector of St. Peter's in Barbados, buried Oct 14, 1771 at Burlington.
William Blair buried Oct 15, 1771 at Burlington.
Daniel Jones, one of the vestrymen at Mt. Holly buried Oct 16, 1771.

James Justice and Martha Norton, both of Mt. Holly married Oct

31, 1771.
James Page and Hannah Evringham married Nov 18, 1771.

Thomas Barnsley of Bensalem buried in Bristol, Nov 13, 1771.

Ephraim Green and Susannah Renier married Nov, 1771.
James Carr and Mary Calvert, both of Bristol in Pennsylvania, married Nov 23, 1771.
Lucy of John and Martha Lawrence, bapt. Nov 24, 1771 at Burlington.
Charles of John and Eleanor Neale, b. Oct 8, 1771, bapt. Nov 24, 1771 at Burlington.
William Bullos, b. Nov 24, 1771, bapt. Nov 24, 1771 at Burlington.

Allan McCollin and Rebecca Jolly, both of Burlington married Nov 25, 1771.
Hugh Ross and Anne Clay married Dec 20, 1771.
John Weitzel and Sabitha Morris, both of Philadelphia married Dec 25, 1771.
John Rainier and Suzanna English, both of Mansfield, married Dec 26, 1771.

Sarah, widow of Michael Woolston, late of Northampton, buried Dec 26, 1771 at Mt. Holly.

William Mannington and Sarah Coxe married at Burlington Feb 14, 1772.
Henry Reeves and Hannah Furnace married at Mt. Holly Feb 23, 1772.

Hannah, wife of Jonathan Reeves, buried at Mt. Holly Mar 29, 1772.

Elizabeth of Devalt and Elizabeth Fish, b. Jan 14, 1772, bapt. Apr 19, 1772 at Burlington.

Joseph of Ephraim and Elizabeth Philips buried Apr 24, 1772 at Burlington.

Anna of Thomson and Mary Neale, b. Nov 16, 1771, bapt. Apr 24, 1772 at Burlington.
Sarah of William Blair, dec'd and Elizabeth, his wife, b. Feb 17, 1772, bapt. May 3, 1772 at Burlington.
Sarah of Symon and Elizabeth Tribbet, bapt. May 5, 1772 at Burlington.

Rev'd Jonathan Odell and Anne De'Cou married at Burlington May 6, 1772 by Wm. Thomson, missionary at Trenton.

Hannah, daughter of a negro woman belonging to Mrs. Allen of Bristol in Pennsylvania bapt. May 24, 1772.
Maria, daughter of a negro woman belonging to Mrs. Wright of Bristol, bapt. May 24, 1772.

George of Joseph Taylor and Dorothy Moulton, bapt. Jun 6, 1772 at Burlington.
Mary, widow of Thomas Gill bapt. Jun 6, 1772 at Colestown.
Marion Hannah the fifth child of George and Deborah Haywood, b. Mar 24, 1772, bapt. Jun 7, 1772.
Abraham of John and Elizabeth Poole, b. Feb 24, 1772, bapt. Jun 24, 1772 at Burlington.

Benjamin Dunham and Jane Ogden both of Burlington County married Jun 27, 1772 at Burlington.
Charles Bevan of Philadelphia and Mary Kemble of Burlington married Jul 9, 1772 at Burlington.
Joseph Barber of Pennsylvania and Elizabeth Morford, New Jersey married Jul 24, 1772 at Burlington.

William of James and Ruth Dobbins, b. Oct 4, 1771, bapt. Aug 2, 1772.
Joseph first born of John and Mary Rogers, b. Jul 5, 1769, bapt. Aug 12, 1772, buried Aug 16, 1772.
Catherine of Barnaby and Sarah Higarty, b. May 14, 1772, bapt. Sep 13, 1772 at Mt. Holly.

Elizabeth of John Henry, buried Sep 20, 1772 at Burlington.

Catherine, wife of Jacob Mowzer, bapt. Sep 21, 1772 at Burlington.
William son of Jacob and Catherine Mowzer, b. Jun 7, 1771, bapt. Sept 21, 1772 at Burlington.
Lydia of James and Elizabeth Isdale, b. Dec 28, 1768, bapt. Sep 21, 1772.
Mary of James and Elizabeth Isdale, b. Feb 16, 1769, bapt. Sep 21, 1772.
Richard of James and Elizabeth Isdale, b. Jan 13, 1772, bapt. Sep 21, 1772.

John Singleton and Elizabeth Shadaker, both of Burlington married Oct 21, 1772 at Burlington.

Anne of Henry and Elizabeth Knight, b. Apr 22, 1772, bapt. Oct 25, 1772.
Isaac of Jacob and Elizabeth Perkins, b. Mar 22, 1765, bapt. Oct 26, 1772.
Jacob of Jacob and Elizabeth Perkins, b. Jan 3, 1767, bapt. Oct 26, 1772.
William of Jacob and Elizabeth Perkins, b. Feb 10, 1769, bapt. Oct 26, 1772.
Sarah of Jacob and Elizabeth Perkins, b. Mar 5, 1771, bapt. Oct 26, 1772.

James Dick and Lucia Richardson, both of Mansfield, married Oct 29, 1772.
Robert Boothe and Agness Braithwaite, both of Trenton, married Nov 5, 1772.

Martha of Daniel and Bathsheba Ellis, buried Nov 13, 1772.

RECORDS OF ST. ANN'S CHURCH (ST. MARY'S) 145

Mary of Edward and Isabella Murphy, b. Oct 22, 1772, bapt. Nov 22, 1772.
Elizabeth of Edward and Esther Diggins, b. Oct 29, 1772, bapt. Nov 22, 1772.

Grace of William and Suzanna Norton buried Nov 28, 1772 at Mt. Holly.

Empson Wright and Amy Wood, both of Mansfield, married Nov 29, 1772.

Esther of William and Suzanna Norton buried Dec 1, 1772 at Mt. Holly.

Sarah of Thomas and Mary Hunlock, b. Oct 16, 1772, bapt. Dec 6, 1772 at Mt. Holly.
Godfrey Hancock, Jr. bapt. Dec 23, 1772.
Thomas of Godfrey Hancock and Anne, his wife, b. Jun 30, 1766, bapt. Dec 23, 1772.
Godfrey of Godfrey Hancock and Anne, his wife, b. Apr 28, 1768, bapt. Dec 23, 1772.
Anne of Godfrey Hancock and Anne, his wife, b. Aug 15, 1769, bapt. Dec 23, 1772.
Sarah of Godfrey Hancock and Anne, his wife, b. Feb 15, 1772, bapt. Dec 23, 1772.
John of Margaret Brandeburgh, b. Oct 15, 1770, bapt. Dec 27, 1772.

Cyllania, wife of Samuel Woolston of Mt. Holly buried Jan 1, 1773.

Alice of Henry and Mary Bolton, bapt. Jan 3, 1773 at Mt. Holly.

John Connor and Mary Roberts, both of Burlington Island, married Jan 11, 1773.

Mary, wife of John Byrns, late of Mt. Holly bapt. Jan 31, 1773 at Mt. Holly.

Thomas Wilkinson and Elizabeth Early married Jan 31, 1773.

Seth Lucas, aged 42 years bapt. Feb 4, 1773 at Burlington.
Mary the fourth child of Elton and Sarah Kemble, b. the 3rd instant, bapt. Feb 22, 1773, buried Feb 24, 1773.

David Antram and Rebecca Bryan married Feb 8, 1773 at Mt. Holly.
Michael Newton and Mary Buckhill, both of Burlington married Feb 23, 1773.

Grace the twelfth child of William and Suzanna Norton, b. Jan 21, 1773, bapt. Feb 28, 1773.

Mary wife of Philip Streaker buried Mar 23, 1773.
John of Anthony and Mary Armsrister buried Apr 10, 1773 at

Burlington.

Rose, a negro woman bapt. Apr 12, 1773 at Burlington.

Seth Lucas buried Apr 15, 1773 at Burlington.

Mary the first born of Jonathan Odell and Anne, his wife, b. Mar 19, 1773, bapt. Apr 21, 1773.
Martha of John and Martha Lawrence, b. Feb 24, 1773, bapt. Apr 21, 1773.

Joseph Taylor and Dorothy Mouton both of Burlington married Apr 29, 1773.

James of Jacob Spencer and Anne Patterson, b. Apr 27, 1773, bapt. May 18, 1773.

Thomas Wall buried Jun 3, 1773 at Burlington.

Robert of Seth and Esther Lucas of Burlington, b. Oct 17, 1761, bapt. Jun 11, 1773.
William of Seth and Esther Lucas of Burlington, b. Sep 26, 1763, bapt. Jun 11, 1773.
John of Seth and Esther Lucas of Burlington, b. Aug 8, 1765, bapt. Jun 11, 1773.
Seth of Seth and Esther Lucas of Burlington, b. Sep 20, 1767, bapt. Jun 11, 1773.
Esther of Seth and Esther Lucas of Burlington, b. Jan 22, 1770, bapt. Jun 11, 1773.
Edward of Seth and Esther Lucas of Burlington, b. Feb 2, 1772, bapt. Jun 11, 1773.

William Jackson and Anne Kennedy both of Mt. Holly married Jun 13, 1773.

Henry Sollar, of Germany, buried Jun 14, 1773 at Burlington.

Jeremiah Bloomfield and Elizabeth Cowen, both of Burlington, married Jun 28, 1773.

Martha of James Justice, buried at Mt. Holly Jul 2, 1773.
Isaac of John Pool buried at Burlington Jul 11, 1773.
Elizabeth of Anthony Elton buried at Burlington Jul 15, 1773.

Gertrude of Abraham and Mary VanSkiver, b. Apr 13, 1773, bapt. Jul 18, 1773.

James Cullum buried at Burlington Jul 28, 1773.

Mary of Thomas and Ellen Potter, b. Oct 28, 1770, bapt. Aug 3, 1773.
Jane of Thomas and Ellen Potter, b. Apr 11, 1773, bapt. Aug 3, 1773.

Samuel Woolston buried at Mt. Holly Aug 6, 1773.

The wife of Alexander Patterson buried at Burlington Aug 7, 1773.
Thomas of Jonathan and Peggy Johnson, b. Dec 2, 1772 in Maryland, bapt. Aug 8, 1773.
Abraham of Aarent and Jane Schuyler, b. Dec 25, 1772, bapt. Aug 12, 1773.
Thomas of Samuel and Sarah Allen, b. Sep 9, 1772, bapt. Aug 12, 1773.
John of John and Anna Hayes, b. Nov 19, 1771, bapt. Aug 12, 1773.
William of William and Rachel Hayes, b. Sep 18, 1770, bapt. Aug 12, 1773.
Sarah of John and Mary Campbell, b. Mar 14, 1772, bapt. Aug 15, 1773.
Joseph of Joseph and Rebecca Hait, b. Sep 16, 1767, bapt. Aug 16, 1773.
Charles of Joseph and Rebecca Hait, b. Jul 31, 1768, bapt. Aug 16, 1773.
Benjamin of Joseph and Rebecca Hait, b. Oct 5, 1770, bapt. Aug 16, 1773, buried Aug 20, 1773.
Cornelius of Joseph and Rebecca Hait, b. Dec 23, 1772, bapt. Aug 16, 1773.
Richard and Sarah, twin children of Daniel and Bathsheba Ellis, b. Aug 13, 1773, bapt. Aug 22, 1773. Sarah Ellis, buried Aug 25, 1773.

George of Joseph and Dorothy Taylor buried Aug 31, 1773 at Burlington.

Jasper Moon and Martha Cripps, both of Burlington married Sep 1, 1773.

Martha of John and Martha Lawrence buried Sep 14, 1773 at Burlington.
Anne Heathcoate buried Sep 25, 1773 at Burlington.

Thomasine of George and Elizabeth Stockham, b. Jan 31, 1773, bapt. Sep 26, 1773 at Burlington.

Jacob Hibbs buried Oct 5, 1773 at Bristol.
Marrion of Alex and Elizabeth Ross buried Oct 15, 1773 at Mt. Holly.

Doctor William McIllvaine and Margaret Rodman, both of Burlington married Nov 6, 1773.
Richard Huff and Alice Herd, both of Chesterfield married Dec 29, 1773.

Mary, widow of Casparus Schuyler buried Dec 30, 1773.
John Williamson buried at Bucks County, no date.
A child of James Esdall buried, no date.
Elizabeth of Rev'd Mr. Frazer buried Aug 22.

Thimothy Thomas and Bathsheba Gardiner married, no date.

John of John and Sarah Muschentyne, b. Jun 1, ---, bapt. Sep 4.

Anthony Harley, a child of Knowlton, a negro man of Governor Franklin, bapt. no date.

John Smith and Rebecca Borden married, no date.
John of Benjamin and Jane McIllhany, b. Jul 1770 at Bristol, bapt. no date.

Joseph Barristatler and Suzanne Sullyvan married, no date.

Sarah of Joseph and Dorothy Taylor, b. Aug 3, 1773, bapt. Oct 2, ---.
Elizabeth of Simon and Elizabeth Tribbet, b. Jul 15, 1773, bapt. no date.
William of Simon and Elizabeth Tribbet, b. Jul 15, 1773, bapt. no date.

Wife of Samuel Bullas buried no date.

Jacob Winner and Elizabeth Hellings married, no date.

Barbara, wife of Adam Ingar, Mount Holly, buried Jan 26, 1774.

Jane the fourth child of Alexander and Mary McMullen, b. Jan 4, 1774, bapt. Feb 15, 1774.
Ann first child of John and Elizabeth Wood, b. Nov 7, 1774, bapt. Feb 20, 1774.
Thomas, son of Alexander and Christian Chrisolm, b. 4th Instant, bapt. Feb 20, 1774.

John North, buried 1774.
Catherine, Widow of Edward Pearce, buried Mar 30, 1774.

Anne, of John and Eleanor Neale, b. Feb 16, 1774, bapt. Apr 1, 1774.

John Fox and Rebecca Borden, married Apr 7, 1774.
Thomas Carpenter and Mary Tonkin, married ---, 13, 1774.
Mathew Maquire and Anne Manington, married ---, 17, 1774.

John Kempton, buried 1774.

Henry of Thomas and Elizabeth Cooper, b. Jan 12, 1774 at Mt. Holly, bapt. --- 24, 1774.
Mary of William Wilson and Elizabeth Martin, b. April 10, 1774, bapt. May 1, 1774.
Sarah of Jeremiah and Elizabeth Bloomfield, b. March 30, 1774, bapt. --- 29, 1774.

Alexander Browne and Anne Bickham, married Jun 9, 1774.

Rachel of James and Elizabeth Esdall, b. May 8th, 1774, bapt. --- 12, 1774.

Michael Kearney and Elizabeth Lawrence married --- 30, 1774.

RECORDS OF ST. ANN'S CHURCH (ST. MARY'S)

Elizabeth of William and Elizabeth Grinding, b. Sept 7, 1770, bapt. Jul 3, 1774.
William of William and Elizabeth Grinding, b. Dec 28, 1771, bapt. Jul 3, 1774.
Samuel of William and Elizabeth Grinding, b. Feb 24, 1774, bapt. Jul 3, 1774 at Mount Holly.

--- Millington at Bristol, buried Jul 5, 1774.
James Carr buried --- 12, 1774.
Anthony Elton buried --- 15, 1774.
Widow of --- Raworth, buried Oct 5, 1774.

William Franklin the second child of Jonathan and Anne Odell, b. Oct 19, 1774, bapt. Nov 13, 1774.
Elizabeth the sixth child of Elton and Sarah Kemble, b. Oct 22, 1774, bapt. Dec 4, 1774.

John Smith and Mary Lyphers married Oct 23, 1774.
Christopher Basser and Anne Mason married --- 30, 1774.
Thomas Clark and Sarah Wright married ---, 22, 1774.
Baldwin Wake, Esq. and Anna Schuyler married 1774.

Mary of Thomson and Mary Neale b. June 29, bapt. 1774, bapt. Dec 26, 1774.
Hester, wife of David Wright, bapt. Dec 30, 1774.
Daniel Hancock and Phoebe his wife, bapt. Dec 30, 1774, adult.
George, an adult child of Sarah and Thomas Hancock, bapt. Dec 30, 1774, Adult.
Levi of Daniel and Phoebe Hancock, b. Jul 10th, bapt. Dec 30, 1774.
Sarah seventh child of Joseph and Rebecca Haight, b. Dec 17th, 1774, bapt. Jan 22, 1775.
Collin of Edward and Levina Kemble, b. Oct 7th, 1768, bapt. Feb 19, 1775.
Anne of Edward and Levina Kemble, b. Jan 22, 1771, bapt. Feb 19, 1775.
Elizabeth Leeds of Edward and Levina Kemble, b. Jan 27, 1773, bapt. Feb 19, 1775.
William of William and Susanna Norton, bapt. --- 26, 1775 at Mt. Holly.

Elizabeth Leeds, child of Edward and Levina Kemble, buried --- 26, 1775.

John Miller and Catherine Rowe, married --- 28, 1775.

William Vanskiver, buried Mar 1, 1775.
Henry Barber and Rachel Morford(?), married --- 2, 1775.
Joseph Worrell Esq., buried at Trenton --- 7, 1775.
Joseph Sandys, buried --- 22, 1775.

Jacob Stooksbury and Charity Reeves, married --- 30, 1775.

Hannah, wife of Jabez Eldridge, Mt. Holly buried Apr 2, 1775.

Wife of John Hank b, Mt. Holly, bapt. Apr 21, 1775.
Elizabeth, of John Poole, b. Nov 21, 1774, bapt. Apr 23, 1775.
Nancy of Frederic and Catherine London, b. Oct 30, 1774, bapt. --- 23, 1775.

Jacob Shedaker and Rachel Isdall, married --- 24, 1775.

Baldwin of Drury and Frances Wake, b. Aug 3, 1774, bapt. May 5, 1775.
John of William and Charity Atkinson, b. Nov 5, 1772, bapt. May 5, 1775.
William of William and Charity Atkinson, b. April 12, 1775, bapt. May 5, 1775.
Jane of Barnaby and Rachel VanSkiver, b. April 17, 1772, bapt. 1775.
Charles of Barnaby and Rachel VanSkiver, b. Aug 13, 1774, bapt. 1775.
Sarah of Samuel and Sarah Allen, b. Feb 2, 1775, bapt. 1775.
John of Joseph and Mercy Force, b. Dec 14, 1774, bapt. 1775.
Reuben, of Edward and Sarah Lewis, b. Mar 4, 1774 Mt. Holly, bapt. May 8, 1775.

Timothy Merrick and Sarah Keys married --- 13, 1775.
William Moore and Margaret Kerr married --- 18, 1775.
William Shute and Sarah Jones Mt. Holly, married --- 21, 1775.

Mary, Widow of --- Wollard, buried 1775.

John Broom and Sarah Esdall, married Jun 20, 1775.

Elisha Talman, of John and Martha Lawrence, b. Feb 23, 1775, bapt. --- 21, 1775.
Rebecca, of John and Catherine Jacobs, Mt. Holly, b. Dec 25, 1776, bapt. Jul 16, 1775 [as records read].

William Bell and Elizabeth Philips, married Aug 6, 1775.
David Johnson and Sarah Creaton, married --- 9, 1775.
Samuel Bullas and Mary Toy, married --- 13, 1775.

Tirringham Palmer of Philip and Margaret North, b. Jul 4, 1775, bapt. 1775.

Rachel, Widow of Nathaniel Wilkinson, buried --- 15, 1775.

Margaret, of Thoms and Elizabeth Carvin, b. --- 1773, bapt. Sep 3, 1775.

Samuel Frost, buried --- 7, 1775.
John Austin, buried --- 9, 1775.

Jeremiah of Edward and Izabella Murphy, Mt. Holly, b. Jul 31, 1775, bapt. --- 10, 1775.

Nathaniel Leader and Barbara Coxe, married --- 12, 1775.

RECORDS OF ST. ANN'S CHURCH (ST. MARY'S)

A child of Joseph Taylor buried, 1775.

John of Retonnock and Suzanna Dixon, b. Oct 27, 1775, bapt. Oct 9, 1775.

Elizabeth, of Thomas and Elizabeth Murphy, b. ye 2d Inst., bapt. --- 21, 1775.
Samuel, of Jonathan and Margaret Johnson, Mt. Holly, b. Oct 27, 1775, bapt. Nov 5, 1775.

Sarah, child of Joseph Taylor, buried --- 6, 1775.

Henry Murphy and Suzanna Foster, married --- 7, 1775.

Thomas, child of John Leigh, buried ---, 1775.

Sarah of Joseph and Dorothy Taylor, b. Sept 14, 1775, bapt. ---, 12, 1775.
Mary of Joseph and Dorothy Taylor, b. Sept 15, 1775, bapt. --- 12, 1775.
Samuel of John and Mary Hodjkinson, b. Sep 22, 1775, bapt. 1775.

James Hunter and Rachel Murphy, married --- 12, 1775.

Maria, of Bowes and Margaret Reed, b. Nov 11, 1775, bapt. Dec 5, 1775.

Thomas Budd Sr. Mt. Holly, buried --- 7, 1775.

David Collins and Ann Harding Mt. Holly married 1775.
William Pitman and Mary Noble married --- 12, 1775.

Deborah of Abraham and Mary Vansciver, b. Nov 9, 1775, bapt. Good Friday, 1776.
Bowman How of Thomas and Mary Hunlock, b. Mar 30, 1776, bapt. Apr 28, 1776.
John of Catherine Rowe, age 9 months old, bapt. Aug 6, 1776.
Mary of Alexander and Mary McMullen, b. Jul 29, 1776, bapt. 1776.
Mary of Henry and Suzannah Murphy, b. Aug 31, 1775, bapt. 1776.
Levina, wife of Edward Kemble, bapt. Sep 3, 1776.
John of Samuel and Mary Bullas, b. Aug 11, 1776, bapt. Sept 8, 1776.
Rowland of Rowland and Hannah Ellis, b. Nov 5, 1774, bapt. --- 26, 1776.
Anne of Job and Mary Field, b. Jul 17, 1778, bapt. Oct 6, 1776.
James of Job and Mary Field, b. Mar 5, 1775, bapt. Oct 6, 1776.
Margaret of Patrick and Suzannah Viergang, bapt. Nov 17, 1776.
Elizabeth of Thomson and Mary Neale, b. Jun 25, 1776, bapt. --- 24, 1776.
Lucy Anne of Jonathan and Anne Odell, b. Nov 14, 1776, bapt. Feb 24, 1779 by the Rev'd Mr. Montgomery.
Charles Pettit of Bowes and Margaret Reed, b. April 6, 1778, bapt. 1779.

William Smith of Thomson and Mary Neale, b. Jul 16, 1778, bapt. 1779.
Joseph of Joseph and Dorothy Taylor, bapt. Nov 14, 1781 by the Rev'd Mr. Frazer.
Ann Burnet of Bowes and Margaret Reed, bapt. Nov 14, 1781.
James of John and Martha Lawrence, bapt. Nov 14, 1781 at Elizthown by the Rev'd Mr. Odell.
Sarah Anne, of Jonathan and Anne Odell, b. Aug 11, 1781, bapt. Apr 14, 1782.

Samuel Roe was Licenced to officiate as a Reader in the Episcopal Church by the Rev'd Clergy of New York, October 7 and was rec'd by the Wardens, Vestry and congregation of the Church of St. Mary's in the city of Burlington, Oct 18th to be their Reader - He was ordained Deacon Sept 16 and Priest the 18th, 1785 in the City of New Haven, in the State of Connecticut, by the Right Rev'd Dr. Samuel Seabury.

Parish Register of St. Mary's Church in Burlington (with occasional entries relating to Neighboring places) 1785 continued by Saml Roe, Minister of Sd. Church

Arney Heulings wife of Isaac Heulings, buried Jan 16, 1785.
Susanna Holinshead, wife of Joseph Holingshead, buried Jan 16, 1785.
Price of Burlington, who died the Jan 24, 1785, buried Jan 25, 1785.
Martha Furguson, Widow of Gnd Furguson of Burlington, buried Jan 30, 1785.
William Hewlings, a Vestryman of St. Mary's Church, buried Mar 28, 1785.
John Gollohan, at Burlington, buried Apr 17, 1785.
Mary Sterling, Wife of James Sterling, merchant in Burlington, buried Aor 20, 1785.
Ann Skiler, daughter of Aaron Skiler, buried May 8, 1785 at Burlington.
Mrs. Fort, Wife of John Fort, Vestryman of the Church of St. Mary's, buried May 11, 1785.

Martha of Thompson and Mary Neal b. Sept 24,1785, bapt. Oct 1, 1785.
Elizabeth of Cornelius and Julia Elderton, b. April 9th 1785, bapt. Oct 2, 1785.
Levina of Edward and Hannah Kemble, b. Jul 12th, 1778, bapt. Oct 3, 1785.
Charles of Edward and Hannah Kemble, b. Nov 10, 1780, bapt. Oct 3, 1785.
John of Edward and Hannah Kemble, b. Feb 17 1784, bapt. Oct 3, 1785.

George Painter and Margaret Ferguson both of Burlington, married Oct 5, 1785.

Ann of Bowes and Margaret Reed, b. Oct 31, 1784, bapt. 1785.

Joseph Ellis of Daniel Ellis of Burlington who departed this life after a very short illness, on the night of the 7th, buried --- 9, 1785.

William of Robert and Elizabeth Graves, b. ------, bapt. --- 9, 1785.

William Lowden and Ann Peacock, both of Burlington, married --- 13, 1785.

Catharine, Wife of Betha. Hodjinson of Burlington, buried Oct 30, 1785.

Susanna of Samuel and Mary Bullus b. Sept 15, 1780, bapt. Nov 17, 1785.
Charles son of Charles Bussinett of Bristol in Pennsylvania, b. the Sep 20, preceeding, bapt. Nov 19, 1785.
Polly Collin, an adult, bapt. Dec 26, 1785.
Isaac of John and Polly Collin, b. Aug 20, the preceding, bapt. 1785, buried Dec 29, 1785.

John George of Mrs. Priestly in Bristol in Pennsylvania, b. 31st Jul 1785, bapt. Jan 1, 1786.
Alexander Henry of Richard and Frances Durden of Pensylvania b. Dec 22, 1785, bapt. Jan 15, 1786.
Randolph of John Jacob and Mary Sluyter of Burlington, b. Dec 21, 1785 and bapt. Jan 26, 1786.

Asa Schooly and Mary Kimble both of Burlington County married Jan 26th, 1786.

Nancy Murphy of Pennsylvania, b. Jan, 1786 and bapt. at Burlington Feb 19, 1986.
Mercy Alexander, a slave of Joseph Bloomfield, b. Jan 6, 1785, bapt. Feb 19, 1786.

Isaac of Blath Jones of Burlington, bapt. Feb 13, 1786. [This entry in error in its proper places].

Edward Kimble buried Mar 13, 1786 at Burlington.

Donald of John Malcomb Pennsylvania, b. Jan 1784, bapt. 1786.
Neal of Doctor Malcomb, b. Nov 24th 1785, bapt. 1786.

John Kennedy at Bristol in Pennsylvania, buried Mar 13, 1786.

Abraham Kelly and Deborah Hammell both of Burlington married Mar 23, 1786.
Jacob Gosling and Margaret Gale of Bristol in Pennsylvania married Apr 24, 1786.
Thomas Green and Mary Stockton at Burlington, married Apr 27, 1786.

Widow Anderson at Coles Church, buried May 6, 1786.

John of John and Nancy Stephenson, b. Oct 18th, 1785, bapt. May 19, 1786.
Maria of the Rev'd Sam Roe and Isabella his wife, b. Mar 27, 1785, May 20, 1786.

John of John and Nancy Stephenson, buried May 22, 1786.

Samuel Branson and Susanna Farley both of Burlington married Jun 9th, 1786.

Jane of John Denny of Burlington, bapt. Jul 27, 1786, buried Jul 28, 1786.

Aaron Anderson and Elizabeth Williamson both of Burlington County, married Jul 27, 1786.

Benjamin the son of John and Elizabeth Smick, b. May 12th 1781, bapt. Dec 8, 1782 by the Revd Mr. Frazer.
Mary of John and Elizabeth Smick, b. Jul 20th, 1783, bapt. Apr 26, by Rev'd Mr. Beach [or Bach], buried Oct 13, Oct 1784.
Peter the Son of John and Elizabeth Smick, b. June 10th, bapt. Jul 17th 1785 by the Rev Mr. Blackwell.
Mary the Daughter of John and Elizabeth Smick, b. June 10th Bapt. Jul 17th 1785 by the Revd Mr. Blackwell.

David Kinkead and Mary Land? both of Chester township in the State of New Jersey on the fifth day of May 1787.

John of Abraham Vansciver and Mary, his wife, bapt. Mar 19, 1788 per John Wade.

Corrected and Certified a True copy, 19 Feb 1970, by the Rev Aurthur Egaus M.A. St. Pauls, Rutger University.

Elizabeth Lindsey, buried Sep 7, 1776.

John M. Vanharlingen and Mary Stiles married by Dr. Wharton Apr 16, 1797.
Florimond Joseph Dussar and Elizabeth Mortimer, married by Dr. Wharton May 25, 1797.
John Sims and Mary Neale in St. Mary's Church, married by Dr. Wharton Jul 18, 1797.
William Crompton and Elizabeth Neale married by Rev'd Andrew Fowler Oct 31st 1797 at Mt. Holly.

1798 March 15th. Dr. Charles H. Wharton arrived at Burlington with his family having been regularly elected to the Rectoship of St. Mary's Church in this City in consequence of his acceding to an unanimous and unsollicited call from the Vestry of said Church communicated to him a few months before.

William Mott and Jane Jeffries married Apr 19, 1798.

Jun 2d Died Mary C. Wharton the most beloved wife of Dr. Wharton,

RECORDS OF ST. ANN'S CHURCH (ST. MARY'S)

died at Phila, Jun 2, 1798, buried Jun 3, 1798 near the S.W. Corner of St. Peter's burial ground in said city, 1798.
Buried my poor negro man Frederick drowned the day before in Delaware, buried Jun 25, 1798.

Margaret Smick a child daughter of Jo and Elizabeth Smick, bapt. Aug 13, 1798.

Levi Hancock a young man, buried Aug 19, 1798.
Jennett Painter wife of George Painter, buried Aug 26, 1798.

William Neale Sims, an infant son of John and Mary Sims, bapt. Sep 2, 1798.

Mr. James Walker of Philadelphia at Bristol, buried Sep 15, 1798.
Sept 16th Buried Martha Griffin 1798.
Buried Benjamin Kimble buried Nov 28, 1798.

John Meyers and Ann Bisham married Dec 31, 1798.
Mary McIlvanine of Wm and Mary McIlvaine, bapt. Jan 1, 1799.

buried William Peacock, buried Feb 10, 1799.
Cesar Murray a black man, buried Mar 5, 1799.
Thomas Elton, buried Mar 8, 1799.
Thomas Oakly, buried Mar 30, 1799.

Richard Haycock Durdin bapt. May 14, 1799.
Robert Shippen Lee bapt. May 14, 1799.
Ann Burton an infant, Jul 31, 1799.
Mary Bates an Infant daughter of Elizabeth and Wm. Bates, Aug 8, 1799.

Lewis Lemaud and Mary Wall married Aug 29, 1799.

John Schyler buried Sep 1, 1799.

Joseph Jackson and Clara Taylor, black people, married Sep 5, 1799.

Samuel Lowden, an infant, bapt. Sept 24, 1799.
George Lowden, an infant, bapt. Sep 24, 1799.
William Lowden, an infant, bapt. Sep 24, 1799.

George Painter and Margaret Neale married Oct 3, 1799.
Joseph Bispham and Rebecca Elton married Oct 24, 1799.

Richard Footman of Philadelphia buried Oct 27, 1799.

C. H. Wharton, DD to Anne Kinsey married Nov 28, 1799 by Rev. James Albercrombie.

Mrs. Gordon buried by Dr. C. H. Wharton, Rector, Feb 8, 1800.

John Fennymore and Mary Meyers married Mar 20, 1800.

Anne Martyr, an adult, bapt. Jun 8, 1800.
Elizabeth Neale, an infant of John and Mary Neale, bapt. Jul 20, 1800.
William Hartshorne and Infant, bapt. Aug 3, 1800.
Mary Coxe wife of Wm. Coxe, Senr., buried Aug 27, 1800.

John M'Dermot and Hannah Vandergrift married Sep 14, 1800.
William Sytle and Ann Lowden married Sep 20, 1800.
Dennis Villette and Ann Pene, French persons married Oct 9, 1800.

Thomas, an infant of William and Elizabeth Crampton Thomson, bapt. Oct 20, 1801.
Neale Simms, an Infant son of John and Mary Sims, bapt. 1800.
Jane Lee, buried by Dr. C. H. Wharton, Rector Feb 6, 1801.
Patrick Higgins buried Mar 2, 1801.

Elizabeth of Edward and Elizabeth Shippen, bapt. May 2, 1801.
Mary of Edward and Elizabeth Shippen, bapt. May 2, 1801.
Ann of Edward and Elizabeth Shippen, bapt. May 2, 1801.
Richard of Edward and Elizabeth Shippen, bapt. May 2, 1801.
Frances of Edward and Elizabeth Shippen, bapt. May 2, 1801.
Sarah of Edward and Elizabeth Shippen, bapt. May 2, 1801.

Rebecca Farrel buried May 16, 1801.

Anne Wharton, wife to Dr. C. H. Wharton., bapt. May 22, 1801 by Bishop White in Philadelphia.
Margaret Coxe, infant daughter of William and Rachel Coxe, bapt. Aug 29, 1801.

Margaret Coxe and Nancy Price buried Aug 30, 1801.
William Coxe, Senr. buried Oct 12, 1801.
Sarah Kimble buried Oct 13, 1801.
Mary Hetfield buried Dec 24, 1801.

Sarah Burton, an Infant, bapt. Dec 26, 1801 by Dr. Charles H. Wharton, Rector.
Maria of William and Rachel Coxe, bapt. Jan 3, 1802.
Emily of Wm. and Rachel Coxe, bapt. Jan 3, 1802.
Elizabeth Haye, an adult, bapt. Jan 13, 1802 at Mt. Holly.

George West and Amy English married Jan 21, 1802.

James Hodgson buried Jan 30, 1802 at Mt. Holly.
An Infant son of Mr. and Mrs. M'Kinzie from Jamaica, buried Mar 27, 1802.

Thomas Craven and Elizabeth Sydenham, both of Burlington married Feb 3, 1771.
William Colwell of Evesham and Lueretia married Feb 10, 1771.
Mary Marling of Chesterfield, Burlington Co. married 1771.
Samuel Stiles and Jane Dobson both of Burlington married Jun 9, 1771.
Michael Dicker and Catherine Sutphine, both of Northampton,

married Sep 8, 1771.
James Justice and Martha Norton both of Mount Holly, married Oct 27, 1771.
Ephraim Green and Susannah Renier, Mansfield, married Nov 3, 1771.
James Page and Hannah Evringham of Springfield, married Nov 10, 1771.
John Rainier and Suzannah English of Mansfield married Dec 25, 1771.
Henry Reeves and Hannah Furnace, both of Northampton, married Feb 23, 1771.
John Singleton and Elizabeth Shadaker, both of Burlington, married Oct 18, 1771.
James Dick and Lucia Richardson, both of Mansfield, married Oct 18, 1771.
Empson Wright and Amey Wood, both of Mansfield, married Nov 29, 1771.
John Connor and Mary Roberts of Burlington Island, married Dec 20, 1771.
Thomas Wilkinson and Elizabeth Earley, of Burlington, married Jan 31, 1773.

Register of the publication of the banns of marriage, by the Revd Sam Roe.

Jacob Gosling and Margaret Gale of Bristol, maried Apr 23, 1786.
David Vaughan of Springfield and Mary Renier of Mansfield, County of Burlington married Jan 24, 1768.
George Smith and Hannah Stockton both of the Township of Willenborough and County of Burlington, married Aug 7, 1768.
William Taylor and Abigail Carter, both of Springfield, married Aug 21, 1768.
Thomas Browne and Mary Nutt, both of Mansfield, married Sep 18, 1768.
Joshua Renier and Rosanna Foster, both of Mansfield, married Feb 5, 1769.
John Vanskiver and Mary Crouss, both of Burlington, married Mar 28, 1769.
Eber Taylor and Sarah Ferguson both of Burlington, married Apr 16, 1769.
John Powell and Sarah Bateman, both of Chester married Dec 27, 1769.
William Mitchel and Mary Hutchin, both of Mansfield, married Dec 27, 1769.
William Austun and Hannah Claypole, both of Willenborough and County of Burlington, married Feb 25, 1770.
John Fox and Alice Hutchin, both of Mansfield, married Jun 3, 1770.
Isaac Vanhorne and Sarah Fury, both of Northampton, married Jul 22, 1770.
Simon Tribet and Elizabeth Hawkings, both of Burlington, married Jul 12, 1770.
Jacob Nordyke and Anne Betts, both of Mansfield, married Sep 3, 1770.
Dennis Gunning and Elinor Connar, both of Northampton, married

Dec 2, 1770.
Thomson Neale and Mary Moon, both of Burlington, married Dec 9, 1770.

John Williamson, Bucks County, buried 1774.
A child of James Esdall, buried 1774.
Elizabeth of Rev'd Mr. Frazier, buried Aug 22, 1774.
William Hancock, buried Aug 23, 1774.

Thimothy Thomas and Bathsheba Gardiner, married 1774.

John of John and Sarah Muschentyne, b. June 1, bapt. Sep 4, 1774.
Anthony Harley, child of Knowlton, a negro man of Govenour Franklin, bapt. 1774.

John Smith and Rebecca Borden, married 1774.

John of Benjamin and Jane McIlhany b. Jul 1770 at Bristol, bapt. 1774.

Joseph Barrickstatler and Suzanne Sullyvan, married 1774.

Wife of Samuel Bullas, buried 1774.

Jacob Winner and Elizabeth Hellins, married 1774.

Sarah of Joseph and Dorothy Taylor, b. Aug 3d, 1773, bapt. Oct 2, 1774.
Elizabeth of Joseph and Dorothy Taylor, b. Aug 29th, 1774, bapt. Oct 2, 1774.
William of Simon and Elizabeth Tribbet, b. Jul 15, 1774, bapt. Oct 2, 1774.

INDEX

INDEX

-A-

AARONS, Elizabeth, 58
AARONSON, Abigail F., 30
  Ann, 30
  Benjamin, 19
  Caleb, 33
  Elizabeth, 30
  Ephraim C., 30
  Frances R., 31
  Hope, 19
  John, 30, 33
  Joseph, 105
  Lydia, 33
  Mary Ann, 30
  Nathan R., 31
  Rebecca, 30
  Samuel, 30
  Sarah, 30
ABBOTT, Ann, 25, 65
  Samuel, 25
  Timothy, 35, 49
ACEY, Barbara, 141
  Hepzibah, 141
  John, 141
ADAMS, Barbara, 115
  John, 12, 100, 107
  Joseph, 127
  Stephen, 105
ADCOCK, Ann, 123
ADDIS, Thomas, 113
ADDOMS, Mary, 102
ADEIR, Robert, 132
ALBERCROMBIE, James, 155
ALBERTSON, Samuel, 116
ALCOTT, Ann, 107
ALLCOT, Martha, 115
ALLEN, Benjamin, 107
  Catharine, 110
  David, 100
  Elizabeth, 128
  George, 130
  Hanah, 123
  Hannah John, 123
  Henry, 110
  James, 72, 102
  John, 102, 123, 128
  Joseph, 5, 60
  Margt., 123
  Mary, 56, 128, 129
  Meriam, 5
  Mrs., 143
  Nathan, 92
  Peter, 102
  Ralf, 5
  Rebecca, 131, 138
  Richard, 128
  Samuel, 129, 130, 147, 150
  Sarah, 92, 128, 147, 150
  Theodosia, 129, 130
  Thomas, 123, 147
ALLIN, Miriam, 42
  Ralph, 42
ALLINSON, David, 96
  Elizabeth, 95
  James, 90
  John, 95
  Margaret, 95
  Martha, 94, 95
  Mary, 95
  Samuel, 94
  Sybil, 95
ALLISON, Richard, 123
  Sarah, 123
ANDERSON, Aaron, 154
  Elizabeth, 102
  Widow, 153
ANDREW, Elizabeth, 79
  Esther, 79
  Hannah, 79
  Isaac, 79
  Lydia, 79
  Mary, 79
  Rebecca, 79
  William, 79
ANDREWS, Hannah, 5
  Isaac, 71, 88
  Jacob, 5
  John, 5
  Mary, 120
  Rebecca, 88
  William, 96, 97
ANTRAM, Abigail, 52
  Ann, 52
  Caleb, 52
  Charity, 52
  David, 101, 145
  Isaac, 52
  John, 52
  Thomas, 52
ANTRIM, Abigail, 22, 41
  Ann, 22
  Bathsheba, 26
  Caleb, 22
  Charity, 22
  Isaac, 22, 26, 28
  Jane, 22
  John, 22, 41, 53
  Joseph, 36
  Martha, 38
  Sarah, 58
  Susanna, 36, 64
  Thomas, 36, 56
ANTRUM, Abigail, 13
  Ann, 2
  Benjamin, 2, 33
  Charity, 66
  Ebenezer, 25
  Hannah, 2
  John, 2
  Joseph, 2, 13
  Martha, 2
  Sarah, 2, 17, 33
  Susannah, 2
  Thomas, 17
APPLETON, Ann, 129
ARCHER, Joseph, 137
ARMSRISTER, Anthony, 145
  John, 145
  Mary, 145
ARMSTRONG, Elizabth, 87
ARNELL, James, 110
ARNOLD, Rebecca, 103

ASHEAD, Abel, 78, 96
  Amos, 78, 88, 91, 104
  Anna, 97
  Eleanor, 78
  Ellenor, 91
  John, 78
  Lydia, 78
  Mary, 78
  Moses, 78, 91
  Sarah, 88
ASHTON, Elizabeth, 35, 49, 53, 113
  Susannah, 130
ATKINSON, Alice, 11
  Amos, 17
  Ann, 2, 14, 17, 18, 32, 33
  Benjamin, 2, 14, 17, 32, 33
  Beulah, 86, 97
  Chalkey, 18, 32
  Charity, 150
  Christian, 103
  Clayton G., 17
  Elizabeth, 14, 95
  Francis, 11
  Hannah, 32, 108
  Hope, 2, 14
  Isaac, 2, 106
  Jane, 2, 14, 15
  Job, 2
  Joel, 17, 42
  John, 2, 14, 15, 17, 90, 92, 95, 108, 150
  Jonathan, 102, 130
  Joseph, 2, 14
  Levina, 132
  Lydia, 33
  Lydia Ann, 17
  Mahlon Stacy, 70, 86
  Mary, 32, 86
  Nathan, 17, 33
  Sarah, 14, 15, 17
  Sara, 2
  William, 2, 15, 150
AUSTIN, Amos, 105
  Elizabeth, 74, 85
  Hope, 102
  John, 150

  Jonathan, 85
  Josiah, 71
  Prudence, 96
  Rebecca, 75
  Rek, 85
  Sarah, 75
  William, 81, 138, 157
AYERS, John, 139

-B-

BACH, Revd., 154
BACHELOR, George, 115
BAK, Asa, 1
BAKER, Peter, 11
  Phebe, 11
  Thomas, 113
  William, 110
BALLENGER, Esther, 98
  Isaac, 97
  Jacob, 91
  Mary, 103
  Sybilla, 97
  Thomas, 93, 97
BALLINGER,
  Elizabeth, 69
  Isaac, 71
  Joshua, 69, 82
  Martha, 74, 84, 85
  Naomi, 69
  Rachel, 71
  Rebecca, 89
  Susan, 84
  Thomas, 84
BANYTON, Peter, 111
BARBER, Elizabeth, 21
  Henry, 149
  Joseph, 144
BARCLAY, Catherine, 121
BARD, Bennet, 126
  Charlott, 125
  Charlotte, 133, 136
  Dinah, 123
  James, 126
  John Abraham, 125
  Mary, 125, 129, 133, 136, 141
  Mary Martha, 123, 125
  Peter, 123, 125, 136, 137
  Robert Jenney, 129
  Samuel, 129, 133, 136, 137
  Sarah, 125
BAREMORE, Grace, 121
  Hanah, 121
  Henry, 121
  Mary, 121
  Phebe, 121
BARNES, Lambert, 132
  Thomas, 104
BARNSLEY, Barbara, 130
  Thomas, 130, 143
BARRET, Sarah, 116
BARRICKSTATLER, Joseph, 158
BARRISTATLER, Joseph, 148
BARRY, Alice, 112
  John, 115
BARTON, Aaron, 12, 44, 45, 50, 63
  Barzailla, 60
  Barzillai, 3, 29
  Bathsheba, 12, 44, 45
  David, 3, 29
  Hannah, 12
  Isaac, 12, 44, 51
  Jane, 45, 50
  John, 3, 29, 63
  Jonathan, 3, 29
  Mary, 81
  Sarah, 3, 29, 50
  Sempta, 12
BASS, George, 129
BASSER,
  Christopher, 149
BATE, Elizabeth, 2
BATEMAN, Sarah, 138, 157
BATES, Abigail, 92, 99
  Amy, 99
  Ann, 86
  Elizabeth, 99, 107, 155
  John, 75, 99

INDEX

99
 Amy, 99
 Ann, 86
 Elizabeth, 99, 107, 155
 John, 75, 99
 Mary, 155
 William, 155
BAXNELL, Mary, 130
 Reuben, 130
 Sarah, 130
BAXTER, Elizabeth, 117
 Margaret, 117
 Samuel, 117
BAYNTON, Benjamin, 126
 Esther, 141
 Peter, 126
BEACH, Revd., 154
BEAKES, Edmond, 101
BEAKS, Edmond, 24
 Mary, 24
BEATY, Elizabeth, 35
BECK, Alice, 28
 Anna, 29
 George, 114
 Godfrey, 29
 John, 23, 28
 Mary, 23, 65, 66
 Sarah, 100
BELL, Elizabeth, 80
 James, 80
 Priscilla, 80
 Widow, 127
 William, 150
BENNET, Deborah, 116
 Elizabeth, 116, 117
 Henry, 116
 Jacob, 133
 Joseph, 117
 Martha, 117
 Mary, 3
 Titus, 40, 54
BENNETT, Titus, 63
BERKINSHEW, Thomas, 109
BERRY, Elizabeth, 141
BERRYMAN, John, 113
BETTS, Anne, 140, 157

Joseph, 131
BETZLER, George, 102
BEVAN, Charles, 144
BEVIS, Thomas, 107
BIBBLE, Joseph, 1
 Sarah, 1
BICKEY, Anne, 12
BICKHAM, Anne, 148
BICKNEY, Rachel, 23
BIDDLE, Beulah, 45, 51
 Charlotte, 60
 Joseph, 45
 Sarah, 18, 45
 William, 141
BILES, Ann, 135
BILL, Mary, 130
 Robert, 130
BIRDSELL, Mary, 113
BIRDSILL, Ann, 85
 Elijah, 79
 Mary, 79
 Sarah, 79
BISHAM, Ann, 155
BISHOP, Andrew, 124
 Ann, 32
 Eliza, 33
 Hannah, 105, 111
 John, 32, 33, 102
 Joshua, 111
 Mary, 32, 33
 Robert, 103
 Thomas, 110
BISPHAM, Abigail, 71, 81
 Hannah, 81
 Joseph, 155
 Thomas, 81
BLACK, ---, 12
 Achsah, 3, 21, 25, 29, 39
 Amey, 44
 Amy, 3, 16, 18, 29
 Ann, 2, 18, 32, 74
 Charles, 2, 18
 Christian, 40, 68
 Edward, 45
 Elizabeth, 25, 40
 Ezra, 3, 16, 18, 29, 44
 George, 18
 Hope, 2, 18

Jobe, 40
 John, 3, 6, 11, 40, 49, 55, 57
 Joseph, 40
 Lydia, 49
 Mary, 18, 25, 40, 57, 74
 Nathan W., 18
 Rebecca, 18
 Samuel, 18, 25
 Sarah, 3, 6, 29, 40
 William, 2, 3, 12, 18, 21, 25, 29, 32, 39, 45, 49, 51, 74
BLACKEMORE, George, 104
BLACKWELL, Revd., 154
BLAIR, Elizabeth, 138, 140, 143
 Richard, 138
 Sarah, 143
 William, 138, 140, 142, 143
BLAKE, Thomas, 104
BLISS, Elizabeth, 109
 George, 114
 Margaret, 109
BLOND, Gabriel, 110
BLOOMFIELD,
 Elizabeth, 148
 Jeremiah, 146, 148
 Jospeh, 153
 Sarah, 148
BOARDMAN, Joseph, 127
BOGART, Levina, 131
BOKINS, Edward, 3
 Joice, 3
 Nathan, 3
BOLTON, Alice, 145
 Henry, 145
 Mary, 145
 Sarah, 103
BOND, Jane, 115
 Sarah, 44, 57
 Thomas, 93
BOOKER, Mary, 123
 Richard, 123
 William, 123
BOON, Grace, 135,

139
  Rachel, 135, 139
  Ralph, 135, 139
BOOTHE, Robert, 144
BORDEN, Charles, 38
  Elinor, 104
  Jonathan, 107
  Joseph, 101
  Martha, 110
  Mary, 108
  Patience, 107
  Phebe, 108
  Rebecca, 148, 158
  Sarah, 38, 55
  Tacy, 38, 55
  Thomas, 38
  William, 38, 55, 59
BOROUGH, Lydia, 99
BORTON, Aaron, 26, 27
  Abraham, 77
  Ann, 77
  Bathsheba, 26, 27
  Deborah, 80
  Edward, 26, 76
  Elizabeth, 77, 79
  Esther, 80, 87
  Hannah, 27, 79, 87
  Hope, 77
  Isaac, 27, 69, 76
  Jacob, 69, 76, 77
  Jane, 27
  Jemima, 69, 76
  John, 76, 77
  Jonathan, 87
  Josiah, 88
  Mary, 26, 69, 76, 114
  Rachel, 77
  Rek, 88
  Sarah, 27, 77, 88, 101, 107
  Serepta, 27
  Uriah, 69
  William, 79, 80
BOSTEDO, Judith, 105
BOULTON, Alce, 95
  Alice, 82
  Azuba, 90
  Azubah, 95
  Edward, 76, 82, 95, 98
  Hannah, 82, 86
  Joseph, 90, 95
  Lydia, 82
  Margaret, 95
  Phebe, 82
  Reuben, 82
  William, 82, 95
BOURCHIER, Isaac, 140
  James, 140
  Suzanna, 140
BOURTON, Abraham, 96
  Caleb, 95, 97, 99
  Hope, 91
  Jacob, 98
  Jemima, 98
  John, 98
  Mary, 96
  Richard, 99
  Sarah, 99
  Uriah, 96
BOWDEN, John, 116
BOWE, Lydia, 122
  Marget, 122
  Mary, 122
BOWKER, Barzillai, 127
  Daniel, 127
  Joanna, 127
  John, 109
  Mary, 105
  Richard, 113, 127
BOWLBY, George, 107
  Thomas, 113
BOWLER, Isaiah, 115
  Sarah, 112
BOWNE, Edith, 7
  James, 7
  Sarah, 58
  William, 11
BOXENDALE, Reuben, 133
BOYD, Keturah, 51
BOZARTH, Zebulon, 132
BOZWORTH,
  Elizabeth, 105
BRADDOCK, Abigail, 80
  Barzillai, 78, 93
  Bathsheba, 76
  Charlotte, 96
  Daniel, 78, 97
  Darnel, 76, 87
  Elizabeth, 76, 78, 80, 94
  Frances, 79, 86
  Francis, 78, 79
  Hannah, 76, 78, 96
  Hubert, 86
  Jemima, 76, 98
  Jerusha, 78
  Job, 76, 96
  John, 78
  Lydia, 80
  Mariah, 96
  Mary, 78
  Nev, 95
  Phebe, 76
  Rachel, 76, 99
  Rehoboam, 98
  Rehobram, 76
  Reuben, 80, 94, 99
  Robert, 76, 78, 79, 86, 107
  Samuel, 80
  Sarah, 79, 80, 86, 87, 98
  Selany, 95
  Thomas, 80
  William, 76
BRADSHAW,
  Elizabeth, 118
  Hannah, 118
  John, 118
BRADY, Marggrett, 100
BRAITHWAITE,
  Agness, 144
BRANDEBURGH, John, 145
  Margaret, 145
BRANIN, Abigail, 87, 88
  Abijah, 88
  Abner, 88
  Burzilla, 102
  Elizabeth, 73, 87, 88
  Ezra, 88
  Hope, 88
  Michael, 73, 87
  Nathaniel, 88
  Rachel, 88
  Thomas, 87
  William, 87, 88
BRANNEN, Michael,

INDEX

96
  William, 90
BRANNIN, Isabel, 91
  William, 98
BRANSON, Achsah,
  11, 62
  Alice, 1, 11
  Asa, 1, 11, 51,
  61
  D., 22
  David, 25, 62
  Elizabeth, 11
  Esther, 20
  Jonathan, 1, 11
  Lydia, 11
  Mary, 11, 22
  Mercy, 11
  Meribah, 59
  Moses, 25
  Samuel, 11, 25,
  62, 154
  Sarah, 1, 11, 25,
  33, 51, 53, 62
  Stacy, 25, 62
  Susannah, 5, 33
BRAZENTON, Samuel,
  79
BRELSFORD, Lydia,
  137
BRIAN, Jacob, 130
BRIDGIT, Ann, 121
  Elizabeth, 121
  John, 121
  Mary, 121
  Rebecca, 121
  Sarah, 121
BRIGGS, David, 115
BRITTAIN, Anne, 113
BRITTON, Francis,
  121
BROADHOME, Venah,
  113
BROCK, Talman, 3
BROOKFIELD, Mary,
  111
BROOKS, Anne, 136
  Elizabeth, 87,
  102
  John, 88
  Susanna, 88
BROOM, John, 150
BROWN, Abigail, 30
  Abraham, 30, 31,
  46, 113
  Alice, 79

Allen, 30
Ann, 6, 44, 79
Ara:, 113
Asher, 6, 30, 57
Beulah, 79
Clayton, 37, 44,
  79, 98
Daniel, 115
Elijah, 41, 64,
  67
Elizabeth, 6, 37,
  88
Ezra, 30
Hannah, 30, 31,
  41, 103
Henry, 125
Ira, 30
Isaac, 89
Israel, 30
James, 41, 46, 64
Jane, 30
John, 6, 32, 79,
  88, 98, 121
Joseph, 6, 30,
  31, 57, 79
Mahlon, 79
Margaret, 6
Martha, 115
Mary, 1, 6, 79,
  102, 110
Phebe, 32
Rebecca, 6, 60
Rebeckah, 46
Ruben, 30
Ruth, 88
Samuel, 30, 44,
  79
Sarah, 88, 89
Susanna, 32, 63
Virgin, 79, 88
Virginia, 79
William, 79
BROWNE, Alexander,
  148
  James, 108
  Thomas, 133, 157
BROWNING, Edward,
  114, 140
  Grace, 140
BRUCE, James, 133
BRUNDIDGE, Jemima,
  110
BRUTON, Bridget,
  130
  Joseph, 129, 130

Mary, 130
BRYAN, Jacob, 134
  James, 126
  Mary, 134
  Rebecca, 145
  Sarah, 106
BRYANT, Joseph, 127
BUCKHILL, Mary, 145
BUCKLEY, Thomas,
  115
BUCKMAN, Phobe, 132
BUCKWORTH, Joseph,
  108
BUD, Elizabeth, 115
  James, 125
  Jemima, 133
  Samuel, 125
  Thomas, 133
BUDD, Abigail, 121
  David, 110, 121
  Elizabeth, 108
  Hananh, 106
  Margaret, 124
  Mary, 121
  Rebecca, 7, 108,
  121
  Sarah, 106, 122
  Susanna, 121
  Thomas, 121, 151
  William, 7, 108,
  121, 140
BUDDEN, James, 102
BUDEY, Peter, 102
BUFFIN, Abigail, 2,
  15
  Ann, 15
  Clayton, 15
  Elizabeth, 2
  Hannah, 2, 15
  Levina, 15
  Michael, 2, 15
  Penelope, 2, 15
  Richard, 2, 15,
  100
  Sarah, 2, 15
BULLAS, John, 151
  Mary, 151
  Samuel, 148, 150,
  151, 158
BULLEN, Mary, 102
BULLOCK, Amos, 21,
  35
  Amy, 5, 20, 21
  Anthony, 4, 24,
  66

Caleb, 21
David Barton, 21
Deborah, 32
Edith, 5, 24, 33
Edward, 5, 20, 38, 63
Elizabeth, 4, 5, 20, 21, 32
George, 5, 24, 33
Hannah, 5, 24, 33
Isaac, 5, 20, 32, 65, 68
Jemina, 4
John, 4, 20
Joseph, 4, 5, 21, 24, 33, 36, 51, 55, 141
Joshua, 21, 32
Lydia, 36, 51, 56
Margaret, 5, 20, 21, 24, 33
Mary, 21, 36, 51, 56
Nathan, 21
Rebecca, 4
Sarah, 4, 20, 21
Susanna, 36, 51
Susannah, 56
Thomas, 21
William, 5, 24, 33
BULLOS, William, 143
BULLUS, Mary, 153
Samuel, 153
Susanna, 153
BUNET, Mary, 3
BUNTING, Benjamin, 30
Ebeneazer, 4
Ebenezer, 30
Elizabeth, 4, 30, 41, 64, 68
Isaac, 4, 30, 56
James, 100
Joshua, 101
Lydia, 38, 49
Mary, 20
Samuel, 3, 30, 55, 110
Sarah, 111
Sophia, 100
William, 111
BURALEAU, Lydia, 122

Marget, 122
Mary, 122
BURDSALL, Anna, 86
Charles, 86
Elijah, 85, 86, 93
Elizabeth, 37
Heturah, 86
Heziah, 85
John, 86
Lydia, 85
Mary, 85, 86
Richard, 37, 44, 57
Sarah, 85, 86
Stephen, 44
William, 86
Wills, 86, 94
BURLING, Benjamin, 32
Mercy, 32
BURN, Alexander Robertson, 137
Mary, 137
William, 137
BURNE, Mary, 107
BURNET, Deborah, 29, 51
Elizabeth, 29
Mary, 29, 39
BURNS, Sarepty, 26
BURNSIDE, James, 103
BURR, Hannah, 115
Henry, 72, 106
John, 109
Joseph, 32, 113
Leah, 37, 56
Marge, 72
Mary S., 32
Rachel, 72
BURROUGH, Abel, 73
Ann, 73
Eber, 73
Lydia, 74
Samuel, 73, 74, 89
Sarah, 73, 74, 89
Thomas, 73
BURROUGHS, Hannah, 104
BURTIS, Mariam, 62
Meriam, 40
Miriam, 65
William, 40

BURTON, Ann, 155
Joseph, 129
Sarah, 156
BUSBY, Nicolaus, 39
BUSSINETT, Charles, 153
BUSSOM, Joseph, 100
BUSTILL, Grace, 125
Samuel, 125
BUTCHER, Anne, 132
Elizabeth, 74, 88, 90
John, 110
Joseph, 74, 88
Margaret, 21
Mary, 88
Prudence, 74
Samuel, 74, 88, 98
Sarah, 74, 132
Thomas, 21, 132
BUTLER, Benjamin, 93, 94
Hannah, 94
Israel, 28
James, 113
John, 93, 122
Mary, 28, 122
BUTTER, Benjamin, 85
BUTTERWORTH, Benjamin, 105
Hannah, 139
BUZBY, Jabez, 71
Jeboz, 89
Nicholas, 55
Sarah, 89
BYRNE, Patrick, 103
BYRNS, John, 145
Mary, 145

-C-

CALDWELL, Mary, 109
CALLUM, Mary, 123
William, 123
CALVERT, Mary, 143
CAMERON, Dougal, 141
Mary, 141
Sarah, 141
CAMPBELL,
Archibald, 126
Charles, 128
Colin, 124, 125,

INDEX

126, 127, 128, 129
Collin, 125
Hugh, 125
Jane, 125, 138
John, 125, 147
Mary, 126, 147
Mary Ann, 125
Mr., 124, 138
Rebecca, 125, 133
Sarah, 147
CARMAN, John, 115
CARPENTER, Mary, 111
Thomas, 148
CARR, James, 143, 149
CARSLAKE, Abigail, 16, 33
Abigial, 32
Ann, 16
Anna, 32
Clayton, 16
Edward, 16
Joel, 16, 32
Joseph, 16, 33
Mary, 16
Sarah, 16
William, 16, 32, 33, 48
CARTER, Abigail, 133, 157
Anne, 62
Micajah, 112
Sara, 106
Sarah, 120
CARTY, Edy, 129, 131
James, 131
John, 129, 131
CARVIN, Elizabeth, 150
Margaret, 150
Thomas, 150
CASSADAY, Thomas, 100
CASSAWAY, Mary, 109
CASSOL, Diana, 124
CATHCART, John, 116
CATHERAL, Benjamin, 48
Sarah, 48
CATHERALL, Benjamin, 33
Sarah, 33
CATHRALL, Benjamin,

5, 6
Sarah, 5, 6
CATTELL, James, 108
CATTLE, Abigail, 102
Ann, 91
Deborah, 91
Hope, 91, 92
James, 91
Jane, 91, 92
Rachel, 91, 92
CAVALIER, Peter, 110
CHAMBERS, John, 112, 119
Joseph, 105
Martha, 112
Mary, 104, 116, 119
Rebecca, 105
CHAPMAN, Abraham, 101
Huldah, 40, 56, 60
Joseph, 100
Rebecca, 44
Sarah, 37
William, 44, 56
CHEESMAN, Cecilla, 104
CHESHIRE, Experience, 105
CHEW, Continue, 115
CHORONETH, John, 119
William, 119
CHRISOLM, Alexander, 148
Christian, 148
Thomas, 148
CHUBB, Martha, 115
CHURCH, Rebecca, 106
CIVIL, Abigail, 65
CLARK, Benjamin, 133
Elizabeth, 133
Hanah, 123
John, 133
John L., 116
Mary, 131
Thomas, 115, 123, 149
CLARKE, Hannah, 124
Samuel, 124

Thomas, 124
CLAY, Anne, 143
CLAYPOLE, Hannah, 157
CLAYPOOL, Jehu, 126
CLAYPOOLE, Hannah, 138
CLAYTON, Susanna, 39
Susannah, 61
CLEAR, Sarah, 102
CLEMENT, Samuel, 102
CLEMENTS, Samuel, 72
CLEVENGER, Huldah, 66
Jerusa, 101
John, 66
Rebecca, 66
Rhoda, 66
Samuel, 66
Sarah, 9, 57, 66
Thomas, 66
Urcilla, 66
Zachariah, 66
CLEVINGER, George, 106
CLIFF, Margaret, 105
CLINE, Ephraim, 102
CLOTHIER, Caleb, 70, 98
Elizabeth, 98
James, 98
CLUTCH, Amy, 116
COARE, Elizabeth, 123
Ralfe, 123
COCKER, Ann, 130
COGILL, Jospeh, 100
COHEAN, Rebecca, 102
COLE, Andrew, 141
Jane, 135
Latitia, 141
Mary, 14, 104
Samuel, 14, 108
Susanna, 108
COLEMAN, Hannah, 12
COLES, Joseph, 116
COLLEY, Amy, 56
Samuel, 56
COLLIN, Abraham, 137, 140

Isaac, 153
Jacob, 137, 140
John, 153
Mary, 137, 140
Polly, 153
COLLINS, Ann, 69
David, 151
Elizabeth, 69, 87, 95, 97
Esther, 87
Ezra, 69
Frances, 69
Hope, 69
Isaac, 69
Jacob, 69
Job, 69, 75, 87, 93, 96
John, 69, 70, 78, 87, 108
Joseph, 115
Josiah, 69
Lydia, 69, 87
Mary, 69, 96
Mercy, 71
Naomi, 69
Ruth, 78
Sabillah, 88
Sarah, 69, 87, 90
Susanna, 108
Susannah, 78
COLLY, Amy, 40
COLWELL, Lueretia, 156
William, 141, 156
CONAROE, Antrim, 58
CONARROE, Antrim, 51
CONEROW, Andrew, 103
CONNAR, Elinor, 157
CONNAROE, Lydia, 115
CONNOR, Eleanor, 141
John, 145, 157
COOK, Charity, 66
Elizabeth, 32
Hannah, 44
Lydia, 42, 44
Phebe, 42
Richard, 31
Sarah, 120
Thomas, 31
William, 19, 34, 42, 44, 49

COOKE, Hannah, 4
Phebe, 4
William, 101
COOPER, Achsah, 74
Ann, 74, 82, 95, 130
Benjamin, 74, 82, 95
Benjamin C., 74
COOPER, Collin, 117
COOPER, Deborah, 74, 95
Elizabeth, 82, 130, 137, 148
Hannah, 96
Henry, 127, 148
James, 25, 66, 74, 82
John, 117
Joseph, 117
Mary, 74, 117, 137
Matilda, 74
Rebecca, 74, 95
Samuel, 74, 95, 117
Sarah, 25
Thomas, 117, 130, 137, 148
William, 74, 96, 117
COPE, Elizabeth, 38
COPELAND, Ann, 35
Copperthwaite, 35
David, 35
Lydia, 35
William, 35
COPERTHWAIT, Martha, 94
COPPERTHWAITE, Hugh, 108
COPPWERTHWAITE, Thomas, 5
COPWERTHWAITE, John, 6
CORDRY, Rebecca, 108
CORE, Elizabeth, 107
Enoch, 27
Grace, 107
Sarah, 27
CORKIN, Catharine, 110
CORLASS, John, 64

CORLESS, Deborah, 32
Exercise, 110
Joseph, 32
William, 110
CORLIS, John, 56
COSTLOW, Josiah, 74
COUSINS, John, 109
Mary, 109
COVENOVEN, Mary, 106
COWAN, Anne, 141
Henry, 141
Hugh, 141
Patrick, 140
COWEN, Elizabeth, 146
COWGILL, Edmond, 105
Nehemiah, 108, 109
Rachel, 104
Sarah, 108
COWPERTHWAITE, Hugh, 81
John, 21, 55
Rebecca, 71, 81
William, 86
COX, Elizabeth, 115, 117
Hannah, 32
Jane, 117
Joseph, 32
Lydia, 85
Maryann Hannah, 117
Rachel, 102
Rebeccah, 117
Richard, 117
COXE, Barbara, 150
Daniel, 141
Emily, 156
Margaret, 156
Maria, 156
Mary, 141, 156
Rachel, 156
Sarah, 143
William, 141, 156
COZENS, Anne, 103
CRAFT, Ann, 16, 40
Deborah, 16
Elizabeth, 16, 67
George, 16, 40, 45, 59
Hannah, 45

INDEX

Hester, 67
Jesse, 67
Job, 67
John, 67
Joseph, 67
Ridgway, 67
Samuel, 45
Thomas, 67
CRAGUE, John, 103
CRAHAN, David, 131
CRAMER, Abigail, 109
Phebe, 109
Sarah, 7
Stephen, 7
CRAMMER, Barthia, 114
Stephen, 29
CRAMMUE, Barthia, 114
CRAVEN, Thomas, 141, 156
CREATON, Sarah, 150
CRIPPS, Martha, 147
CRISPIN, Hannah, 132
Selany, 91
Seth, 102
CRISPS, John, 13
Mary, 13
CROMPTON, William, 116, 154
CROOK, Anne, 138
Francess, 138
John, 138
CROSBY, Sarah, 110
CROSHAW, Elizabeth, 1, 9
George, 1, 31
Hannah, 1, 31
John, 1, 2, 9
Mary, 31
Samuel, 1, 9, 31
Sarah, 9
CROUSS, Mary, 135, 157
CROWNE, David, 131
CROWSHAW, George, 9
Hannah, 9
CRUSHER, Rachel, 84
Thomas, 84
CULLUM, James, 146
CUNNINGHAM, Thomas, 112
William, 108

CURREY, Hannah, 141
Jane, 141
Mathew, 141
CURRIE, Revd, 125
CURTES, Rachel, 95
CURTICE, Alice, 51
Ann, 51
Asa, 51
Mary, 51
Sarah, 51
Thomas, 51
CURTIS, Abigail, 117
Achsah, 16, 40, 59, 65
Alice, 3, 28, 46, 51
Ann, 28, 51, 61
Asa, 28, 51
Benjamin, 28
Elizabeth, 28, 36
Hestor, 123
Isaac Antrim, 117
Jane, 55
John, 16, 28, 43
Jonathan, 31, 43, 54, 93, 97
Margaret, 117
Mary, 28, 31, 51
Mercy, 43
Nataniel, 123
Rachel, 93
Rebeccah, 116
Sarah, 16, 28, 40, 46, 51, 59, 65
Solomon Nathiel, 123
Susannah, 28
Thomas, 3, 28, 46, 51, 117
Tilton, 16, 40, 59, 65
CURTISS, Peter, 100

-D-

DAILY, Mary, 114
DALTON, Henry, 137, 139
Joseph, 137, 139
Mary, 137, 139
Thomas, 137
DANFORD, Samuel, 107
DARKINDER,

Elizabeth, 126
DARNEL, Hannah, 76
Jemima, 76
John, 76
DAVELIN, John, 118
DAVENPORT, Emanuel, 5
Mary, 34
Mercy, 5
DAVIDSON, Ann, 117
Benjamin John, 117
Elizabeth, 93
Mary, 93, 117
Peggy, 117
Robert, 117
William, 93
DAVIES, John, 106
DAVIS, Abigail, 28
Ann, 28, 85
David, 77, 96
Esther, 109
Hannah, 28
Isaac, 28, 55
Ivins, 28
Job, 28
Jonathan, 28, 66
Martha, 77
Mary, 28, 58, 77, 97
Meribah, 28, 59
Samuel, 134
Samuel C., 85
Samuel Cole, 85
William, 28, 115
DAWSON, Elizabeth, 109
Hannah, 56
Hope, 127
John, 132
Martha, 124
Rachel, 35, 48
Rhoda, 40, 61
DEACON, George, 131
Hannah, 140
John, 140
Rebecca, 131
DEATS, H. E., 100
DE'COU, Anne, 143
DECOW, Abigail, 17
Achsah, 14, 19, 36, 45, 46, 54, 59
Ann, 17
Anna T., 17
Clayton, 19, 36,

54, 59
Daniel, 14, 17
Eben, 60
Eber, 17
Edward, 3
Elizabeth, 17
Esther, 30
George, 17
Isaac, 3, 14, 17, 40
Jacob, 30
DECOW, Jacob, 105
DECOW, James, 17
Joel, 3, 14
John, 17, 38
Joseph, 19, 36, 46, 59
Lydia, 17
Margaret, 17
Mary, 3, 14, 17, 19, 25, 36, 46, 59
Nathan, 14
Prudence, 17
Robert, 17
Samuel, 3, 14, 40
Sarah, 14, 17, 61
Stacy, 3, 14, 41, 68
Thomas, 25, 67
William, 61
DELATUSH, Henry, 140
DENIGHT, Joseph, 115
DENNIS, Abigail, 121
James, 110
John, 109, 111
Mary, 109, 121
Phebe, 62
Philip, 101
Sarah, 111
William, 108
DENNY, Jane, 154
John, 154
DENORMANDIE,
Anthony, 125
Hannah, 127
James, 125
Mary, 125
William, 127
DENTON, Robert, 109
DEPARTEENE,
Catherine, 127
DERKINDIRRIN,
Elizabeth, 112
DEVIT, Elizabeth, 102
DICK, James, 144, 157
DICKER, Elizabeth, 141
Lydia, 138
Michael, 142, 156
Nicholas, 138
Nicolas, 141
William, 138
DICKS, Curtis, 116
DIGGINS, Edward, 145
Elizabeth, 145
Esther, 145
DIMPSEY, William, 115
DINGWELL, Phillip, 114
DIRNBERGER, Janet Drumm, 118
DIXON, John, 151
Retonnock, 151
Suzanna, 151
DOBBINS, James, 129, 131, 144
Joab, 129
Letice, 129
Michael, 129
Rachel, 116
Ruth, 131, 144
Sarah, 129
William, 144
Zebedee, 129
DOBSON, Jane, 142, 156
DONALDSON, Arthur, 37, 42
Elizabeth, 37, 53
Margaret, 37, 55, 62
DONNOLLY, Bryan, 108
DORLAND, Cornelius, 109
DOTEY, Ebenezer, 113
DOUGHTY, Daniel, 34
DOUGLASS, John, 110
William, 26
DOWNES, Jonathan, 142
DOWNEY, Ann, 120
DRAPER, Jemima, 112
Mary, 107
Thomas, 107
DRIVER, John, 112
DUCKWORTH, Anna, 111
DUDLEY, Francis, 73
John, 76
Rachel, 73
DUGLESS, Joseph, 101
DUKE, Marma, 122
DUMFE, Thomas, 110
DUNHAM, Benjamin, 144
DURDEN,
Alexander Henry, 153
Frances, 153
Richard, 153
DURDIN,
Richard Haycock, 155
DUREL, Lydia, 97
Sybilla, 94
DURELL, Lydia, 92
DUSSAR, Florimond Joseph, 154

-E-

EARL, Ann C., 31
Anthony, 2, 10
Caleb, 6, 10, 36
Clayton, 7, 67, 68
Daniel, 1, 6, 66
Edith, 2, 10, 31
Elizabeth, 1, 6, 43
Elizabeth S., 25
Esther, 36
John, 1, 6, 7, 31, 35, 66
Joseph, 1, 6, 36, 42
Leah, 7, 10
Leticia, 6, 10
Lydia, 25
Martha, 7, 25
Mary, 1, 6, 8, 10, 13, 25, 42, 43, 44, 45, 49
Mercy, 1, 6, 7, 9, 32

INDEX

Michael, 7, 25, 46
Rebecca, 7, 25, 32, 46
Sarah, 4, 25, 39
Susannah, 7
Tantom, 6, 13, 42, 43
Tanton, 1, 6, 10
Tantum, 10
Taunton, 45
Theodosia, 36
Thomas, 2, 6, 7, 10, 25, 31, 32, 46, 105
Tucker, 42
Tucker William, 7
William, 9, 49
EARLE, Clayton, 1
John, 1
Martha, 1
Michael, 1
Rebecca, 1
Susannah, 1
Thomas, 1, 123
Tucker, 1
EARLY, Elizabeth, 145, 157
EASTWOOD, Bulah, 116
EAYRE, Elizabeth, 86
John, 86
Rebecca, 86
Richard, 104
EDINGTON, Philip, 121
EGAN, Eleanor, 118
John, 118
William, 118
EGAUS, Aurthur, 154
ELDERTON,
Cornelius, 152
Elizabeth, 152
Julia, 152
ELDRIDGE, Hannah, 149
Jabez, 149
James, 71
Obadiah, 108, 112
Sarah, 108
ELHATON, Frances, 94
ELIS, Leah, 63
William, 59, 111

ELKATON, Frances, 94
ELKINGTON, George, 112
ELKINTON, Amy, 75
Elizabeth, 103
Joseph, 75
ELLIS, Abigail, 17, 115
Amos, 3, 14, 17, 32, 45, 56
Ann, 17
Barzillai, 4, 24, 31
Bathsheba, 136, 140, 142, 144, 147
Benjamin C., 17
Charles, 17
Daniel, 126, 128, 136, 140, 142, 144, 147, 153
David, 4, 24
Elizabeth, 3, 4, 14, 17, 24, 31, 32
Elizabeth Howard, 24
George, 126
Hannah, 14, 102, 151
John, 4, 23, 24, 31, 32, 45
Joseph, 4, 23, 50, 124, 128, 153
Joshua, 24
Josiah, 17
Leah, 3, 14
Lucy, 23, 24, 45
Margaret, 109, 124
Mariam, 3
Martha, 136, 144
Martha R., 24
Mary, 3, 14, 17, 31, 32
Meribah, 4, 24
Miriam, 14, 17, 45
Mrs., 116
Nathan W., 24
Peter, 3, 14, 17, 24, 45
Peter H., 14
Phebe, 3, 4, 14, 23, 24, 32, 43
Rebecca, 24

Rebecca N., 24
Richard, 123, 124, 147
Row, 123
Rowland, 109, 123, 124, 125, 126, 136, 140, 142, 151
Samuel, 4, 14, 23, 24, 32, 45
Sarah, 3, 14, 17, 124, 126, 131, 136, 147
Susannah, 24
Thomas, 125, 126
Thomas Biddle, 17
William, 4, 14, 67, 124
William Hunt, 23
William M., 17
William N., 24
ELLISON, Jesse, 115
ELLWELL, Mary, 103
ELMER, Mary, 127
ELMORE, Mathias, 110
Sarah, 110
ELTON, Ann, 123
Anne, 134, 136
Anthony, 125, 146, 149
Elizabeth, 129, 146
Margaret, 129
Mary, 111, 123
R., 123
Rebecca, 155
Revel, 108, 111, 134, 136
Robert, 108, 125, 129
ELY, Ann, 36
John, 55
ELYS, Ann, 54
EMELY, Elizabeth, 1
John, 1
Mary, 1
Robert, 1
Susannah, 1
EMLEY, Abigail, 17
Catherine, 6
Elizabeth, 9, 17
Hannah, 17
John, 9, 17
Joseph, 17

Mary, 9, 17
Robert, 9, 17, 34
Samuel, 6
Susanna, 9
Susannah, 34
William, 17
EMLY, Elizabeth, 34
Hannah, 63
John, 34, 63
Mary, 34
Robert, 34, 48
ENGLAND, Daniel, 112
Rebecca, 112
ENGLE, Aaron, 80, 83, 88
Ann, 80
Deborah, 83
Deborah E., 88
Elizabeth, 83
Esther, 83, 88
Esther T., 83
Job, 88
John, 88, 107
Joseph, 80, 83
Marg, 83
Mary, 80
Maryann, 83
Patience, 88
Paul, 83
Sarah, 88
ENGLISH, Amy, 3, 28, 38, 156
Anne, 113
Arthur, 28
Elisha, 28, 38
Elizabeth, 18, 61
Israel, 18, 28, 38
J., 18
John, 3, 28, 39, 60
Joseph, 3, 14, 18, 28, 33, 62
Leah, 63
Mary, 28
Mary E., 18
Mercy, 3, 38
Rebecca, 18
Sarah, 3, 14, 18, 28, 38
Sarah Ann, 18
Suzanna, 143
Suzannah, 157
Tryphena, 33

ENOCHS, Martha, 107
ERVERS, John, 121
ESDALL, Elizabeth, 135, 148
Ellis, 137
James, 147, 148, 158
John, 131, 137
Rachel, 134, 135, 148
Sarah, 137, 150
Thomas, 109, 134, 135
EVANS, Abigail, 81
Abraham, 77
Amos, 77, 89
Ann, 81, 89
Barsheba, 102
Caleb, 69
Carlton, 77
Deborah, 70
Eli, 93
Elizabeth, 69, 89
Enoch, 70, 71, 77, 81, 93
Esther, 69, 70, 71, 81
Hannah, 70, 71, 77
Isaac, 69
Jacob, 69, 77, 80, 81, 89, 90, 91
Jamima, 69
Joel, 71
John, 70, 71, 81, 92, 93, 96
Jonathan, 90
Joseph, 71, 81
Joseph B., 77
Joshua, 69
Jospeh, 89
Lydia, 71, 77
Martha, 69, 81
Mary, 70, 71, 77, 81, 89
Nathan, 69
Rachel, 77, 89, 91, 115
Rachel B., 77
Rebecca, 69, 70, 71, 79, 81, 89, 97
S., 102
Sarah, 70, 71, 79, 81, 89
Susanna, 81

Syllania, 77, 89
Thomas, 69, 70, 71, 81, 89
Uriah, 77
William, 69, 70, 71, 79, 81
EVARY, Thomas, 124
EVENS, Thomas, 74
EVERHAM, Unity, 39, 62
EVES, Hepziba, 115
Samuel, 93
EVILMAN, John, 20
Mary, 20
EVRINGHAM, Hannah, 143, 157
Rachel, 105
EWAN, Ambrose, 110
John, 107
Julius, 104
EWEN, Martha, 115
EWERS, John, 121
EYERS, Elizabeth
Ann, 42, 66
EYRE, Elizabeth
Ann, 66
Habakkuk, 71
Martha, 71
Mary, 71
EYRES, Ellis, 124
Filius, 124
Johannes, 124
Rowland, 124
Sarah, 124

-F-

FAOLKE, Eneker, 38
Jane, 38
FARLEY, Susanna, 154
FARQUHAR, Adam, 113
FARREL, Rebecca, 156
FASSET, William, 120
FELLOW, John, 65
FENIMORE, Richard, 105
William, 110
FENNYMORE, John, 155
FENTON, Ann, 110
Eliezer, 120
Elizabeth, 120

INDEX

Enoch, 120
Jeremiah, 120
Judeth, 120
Sarah, 105
FERGUSON, Margaret, 152
Mary, 115
Sarah, 135, 157
FIELD, Abigail, 16
Anne, 151
Benjamin, 3, 16, 31
Caleb, 3, 16, 31
Catherine, 31
Eli, 96
Elizabeth, 116
Hannah, 96
Isaac, 16
James, 151
Job, 16, 151
John, 66
Joseph, 3, 16, 31
Martha, 31, 96
Mary, 151
Mercy, 66
Rebecca, 3, 16, 31
Thomas, 3, 16, 42
William, 16, 38, 66
FISH, Devalt, 143
Elizabeth, 143
FISHER, Benjamin, 116
Elizabeth, 32
Hannah, 104
Thomas, 32
FITZHUGE, Mary, 110
FLANIGAN, James, 140
Martha, 140
FLOWERS, William, 111
FLYNN, Joseph M., 118
FOLKE, Rebecca, 103
FOLLWELL, William, 103
FOLWELL, Hannah, 105
Hope, 50
John, 41
Nathan, 41
Sarah, 41, 56, 67
FOOTMAN, Richard, 155
FORCE, David, 137
Deborah, 137
John, 150
Joseph, 150
Mercy, 150
Samuel, 137
FORKER, Adam, 113
FORMAN, Ann, 35
Barzillai, 28
Elizabeth, 28, 53
George, 35
Hannah, 28
Isaac, 34, 64
John, 36, 52, 55, 61
Josiah, 35
Matilda, 28
Rebecca, 51
Richard Way, 35
Ruth, 61
Susannah, 35
Thomas, 34, 52, 58
William, 64
FORSYTH, Ann, 28
Joseph, 28, 45, 59
FORSYTHE, Ann, 38, 63
Joseph, 38
Mathew, 68
FORT, Abraham, 127
Ann, 127
Elizabeth, 131
Hannah, 127
Johanna, 103
John, 104, 127, 152
Marmaduke, 109
Mrs., 152
Robert, 104
FORTENBURG, Penelope, 58
FOSTER, Abner, 127
Agness, 85
Amariah, 9, 126
Charles, 85
Content, 127
Elizabeth, 85, 127
George, 125
Grace, 18
Hannah, 72
John, 123
Joshua, 18
Josiah, 72, 85, 93, 94, 95, 102
Josiali, 127
Lettice, 9
Lydia, 72, 95
Mary, 8, 72, 85, 102, 107, 123, 126, 127
Rachel, 72
Rebecca, 72, 94
Rosanna, 134, 157
Suzanna, 151
Thomas, 107, 123, 126, 127
Uriah, 102
William, 8, 72, 85, 92
FOULKE, Cadawalder, 36
Cadwalader, 43, 51
Isacher, 45, 58
Phebe, 36
Priscilla, 45
William, 45
FOWLER, Andrew, 116, 154
Benjamin, 106
Elizabeth, 24
Joseph, 4, 24, 43
Mary, 4, 43
Meribah, 4, 43, 49, 68
FOX, John, 139, 148, 157
Lemuel, 5
Samuel, 55
Sarah, 2, 34, 53
Sary, 53
William, 2, 52
FRANEY, Martha, 123
Mary, 123
Richard, 123
FRANKLIN, 148, 158
Thomas, 42
William, 129
Winefee, 133
FRASHER, Robert, 101
FRAZER, Colin, 136
Elizabeth, 147
Rebecca, 136
Revd., 154
William, 133, 136

FRAZIER, Elizabeth, 158
  Revd., 158
FREEMAN, Hannah, 133
  Thomas, 133
  William Harcourt, 133
FRENCH, Ames, 23
  Amos, 39, 61
  Amy, 31, 46, 63
  Charles, 18
  Elizabeth, 46
  Hannah, 23
  Hope, 18
  Jacob, 31, 46
  John, 6, 23, 39, 61
  Lydia, 23
  Mahlon, 39, 61
  Rachael, 6
  Rachel, 23, 39, 61
  William, 6, 23, 39, 61
FRIEDLAND, Jonas, 37
FRIEND, Isabelle, 115
FROST, Samuel, 150
FURGUSON, Gnd, 152
  Martha, 152
FURMAN, Ann, 48
  Barzillai, 3, 16
  Elizabeth, 3, 5, 16
  George Middleton, 48
  Hannah, 3, 16
  Isaac, 5, 40
  James, 5
  John, 5, 43, 57
  Josiah, 43, 48
  Mahlon, 16
  Matilda, 3
  Rebecca, 5
  Richard, 32
  Richard Way, 48, 50
  Ruth, 48
  Sarah, 5
  Susannah, 32
  Theodosia, 5
  Thomas, 5, 32
  William, 5, 40
FURNACE, Hananh, 157
  Hannah, 143
FURY, Sarah, 139, 157

-G-

GALE, Abell, 113
  Dinah, 104
  Margaret, 153, 157
  Mary, 113
  Thomas, 111
GALLAGHER, Elinor, 110
GALLIFER, Thomas, 102
GANT, John, 80
  Phebe, 80
GARD, William, 111
GARDINER,
  Bathsheba, 147, 158
  Benjamin, 108
  Catherine, 10
  Hannah, 89
  John, 10, 89
  Joseph, 89
  Mary, 89
GARRISON, Sarah, 53
GARWOOD, Alice, 88
  Ann, 107
  Charity, 1, 10, 27
  Daniel, 78
  Elizabeth, 78
  Hannah, 78
  Hope, 78
  Isaac, 88
  Isaiah, 88
  Jacob, 2
  Japhit, 98
  Jophet, 75
  Jopheth, 78
  Joseph, 102
  Margaret, 78
  Mary, 88
  Priscilla, 10
  Rachel, 78
  Sarah, 78, 104
  Susannah, 78
  Thomas, 78, 107
  William, 102
GASKILL, Aaron, 6, 39, 48, 49
  Abigail, 31
  Abraham, 49
  Barzillai, 65
  Benjamin, 109
  Caleb, 1, 7, 41
  Charles, 1, 7, 31
  Charles E., 25
  Clayton, 1, 7, 36
  Cornelia C., 25
  Ebenezer, 27, 37, 39, 52, 58
  Edith, 1, 7, 25, 31, 55
  Elizabeth, 6, 27, 37, 39, 42,, 48, 50, 58
  Esther, 9, 37, 39, 50, 58
  Grace, 79, 83
  Hannah, 25, 113
  Hudson, 9, 65
  Isaac, 9, 59
  Jacob, 116
  Jane, 71
  Job, 9, 10
  John, 6, 39, 48
  Jonathan, 71, 115
  Joseph, 39, 79, 83
  Lavinah, 112
  Levi, 10
  Louis, 9
  Lydia, 27, 37, 39, 50, 58
  Mary, 6, 10, 44, 48
  Moses, 49
  Nathaniel, 6
  Province, 106
  Rachel, 39, 48, 71
  Rachell, 6
  Robert, 25
  Ruth, 48, 61, 115
  Samuel, 6, 39, 44, 48
  Sarah, 1, 6, 7, 25, 39, 48, 62
  Sibilla, 39
  Stephen, 112
  Sybella, 48
  Sybilla, 6, 44
  Thomas, 1, 7, 25, 31, 34, 50

Virgin, 79
William, 7, 9, 25, 59
GASKIN, Barzilla, 101
GAUNT, Ann, 28, 29, 45, 53, 64
Arthur, 53
Asher, 7
Daniel, 29
Elizabeth, 7, 29
Hannah, 6, 29, 44, 62
Jane, 29, 45
John, 28, 29, 45
Judah, 6
Larsta, 7
Mary, 29, 54
Peter, 7, 36
Phebe, 29
Reuben, 7
Samuel, 6, 29, 44, 45
Sarah, 6
Uz, 6, 44, 63
GAUNTT, Ann, 14, 59
Asher, 1
Benjamin, 12
Daniel, 65
Elihu, 1
Elisha, 12
Hannah, 1, 9, 12, 44
Hannaniah, 14
Israel, 12
Jane, 59
Jefferson, 12
John, 19, 59
Lewis, 12
Mary, 59
Peter, 1
Phebe, 59
Reuben, 58
Reubine, 1
Samuel, 1, 9, 11, 12, 19, 27, 44, 59
Sarah, 11, 44
Sarspeta, 1
Sempta, 12
Serepta, 27
Uz, 1, 11
GIBBONS, Anne, 131
Francis, 131
GIBBS, Abel, 3
Able, 33

Amos, 2, 25
Ann, 17, 22
Anna, 25
Asa, 2, 46
Benjamin, 25, 32, 35, 50
Caleb, 9
Elizabeth, 9, 32, 64
Hannah, 4, 25, 38, 40, 44, 54, 61
Isaac, 4, 22, 39
Jane, 25
Joel, 2, 56
John, 2, 9, 25, 66
Joseph, 32
Joshua, 4, 38, 40, 44, 52, 61
Martin, 2, 14, 17, 25, 46
Mary, 2, 25, 38, 40, 61
Mercy, 9
Miles, 34, 50, 53
Miles H., 38
Phebe, 2, 14, 46
Rebecah, 35
Rebecca, 2, 4, 14, 17, 22, 40, 61, 66
Rebekah, 35, 50
Reuben, 4, 52, 55
Rheuben, 40
Samuel, 2, 9
Sarah, 4, 35, 36, 52, 57
Sophua, 101
Tanton, 9, 22
Taunt, 57
Taunton, 59
Theodocia, 97
William Earl, 2
GIBSON, Jacob, 100
John, 112
Simon, 24
GIFFORD, William, 76
GILHAM, Robert, 107
GILL, Mary, 144
Thomas, 112, 144
GILLAM, Ann, 106
Anna, 33
Isaac, 33
Margaret, 33

Mary, 33
Simon, 33
GILLIAM, Anna, 30
Isaac, 30
Mary, 30
Simon, 30
William, 30
GILLUM, Grace, 113
GODFREY, Mary, 103
GOFORTH, Samuel, 102
GOLCHORN, Martha, 124
GOLLOHAN, John, 152
GOODMAN, Sarah, 115
GORDON, Andrew, 126
Daniel, 115
Helena, 126
Mrs., 155
GOSLIN, Phoebe, 102
GOSLING, Jacob, 153, 157
John, 106
GRANDEN, Mary, 125
GRANDON, Bernard, 127
Edward, 127
Sarah, 127
GRAVES, Robert, 153
William, 153
GREEN, Ephraim, 143, 157
Joseph, 29, 36, 54, 56, 59
Sarah, 67
Thomas, 115, 153
GRIFFIN, Francis, 135
Hannah, 72, 73
Jonathan, 73
Martha, 155
GRIFFITH, Isaac, 90
James, 90
Sarah, 124
GRIFFITHS, Mary, 114
GRINDING,
Elizabeth, 149
Samuel, 149
William, 149
GROOM, Mary, 107
Peter, 107
GUILHAM, Anne, 104
GUINNOP, John, 113
GUNNIN, Dennis, 141

GUNNING, Dennis, 157
GWIN, Esther, 113

-H-

HAIGHT, Joseph, 149
  Rebecca, 149
  Sarah, 149
HAINE, Habakkuk, 71
  Martha, 71
HAINES, Abigail, 31, 45, 75, 88, 89
  Abigial, 64
  Abraham, 83, 88
  Ann, 12, 69, 82
  Anna, 84
  Anne, 12
  Anner, 76
  Benjamin, 70, 83, 116
  Bethuel, 70
  Beulah, 84
  C., 6
  Caleb, 31, 70, 102
  Carlisle, 71
  Catharine, 117
  Chalkley, 70
  Charity, 114
  Charles, 75, 84, 89
  Clayton, 75, 83
  Core, 71, 82, 91
  David, 75
  Deborah E., 88
  Dorcas, 117
  Elisha, 84
  Elizabeth, 12, 70, 71, 74, 83, 84, 85, 117, 129
  Empson, 83
  Ephraim, 74
  Esther, 69, 71, 74, 84, 105
  George, 75, 89, 115
  Grace, 82
  Hannah, 69, 74, 75, 84
  Henry Pendergrass, 117
  Hephzibah, 74
  Ira, 84
  Isaac, 13, 74, 75, 84, 85
  Isaac B., 84
  Isaiah, 82, 91
  Jacob, 75, 84
  Jane, 71
  Jesse, 71
  Job, 74, 84, 85, 87
  John, 55, 69, 70, 76, 81, 82, 87, 92
  John M., 70
  Jonathan, 69, 74, 75, 84, 85
  Joseph, 76, 88, 117
  Joshua, 84, 87
  Josiah, 17, 18, 45, 74, 75
  Keturah, 70
  Keziah, 117
  Levi, 71
  Lydia, 75
  Mahlon, 13
  Mark, 82
  Marrion Hannah, 117
  Martha, 72, 82, 84, 85
  Mary, 6, 17, 45, 60, 70, 74, 75, 76, 82, 83, 84, 85, 87, 89, 91
  Mercy, 71
  Nathan, 83, 84, 117
  Nehemiah, 75, 88, 89, 90
  Noah, 75
  Phebe, 71
  Rachel, 25, 70, 71, 75, 83
  Rebecah, 117
  Rebecca, 33, 70, 71, 83, 102
  Reuben, 70
  Ruth, 71, 82
  Samuel, 11, 12, 83, 84
  Sarah, 11, 18, 56, 60, 71, 82, 83, 87, 88, 117
  Sarah W., 89
  Solomon, 71
  Theodocia, 88
  Thomas, 84, 85
  William, 71, 83, 85
HAINS, Ann, 93
  Anna, 97
  Charlotte, 96
  Core, 93
  Deborah, 96
  Edmond, 96
  Edward, 99
  Elizabeth, 92, 95, 96, 99
  Esther, 97
  Hannah, 95
  Isaac, 90
  Job, 90, 91
  John, 96, 97
  Joshua, 91
  Josiah, 97
  Leeds, 96
  Martha, 91
  Mary, 93, 96
  Nehemiah, 90
  Reuben, 96
  Samuel, 91, 95
  Solomon, 92, 95
  William, 92
HAIT, Benjamin, 147
  Charles, 147
  Cornelius, 147
  Joseph, 147
  Rebecca, 147
HALBERT, Beulah, 90
HALL, Benjamin, 122
  Daniel, 122
  David, 122
  Francis, 112
  Jacob, 122
  Joseph, 122
  Mary, 103, 121, 122
  Naomi, 37
  Rebecca, 62
  Sarah, 122
  Solomon, 122
  William, 121
HALLE, Hans George, 140
  John, 140
HAMEL, Catharine, 123
  Eliz, 123
  John, 123
HAMMELL, Deborah, 153
HAMMETT, Mary, 108

INDEX

Sarah, 108
HAMMIT, Elizabeth, 75
  Sabillah, 75
  Samuel, 75
HAMOT, Sarah, 106
HANCE, Ann, 26
  David, 26
  Edward, 26
  Eliza, 26
  Hannah, 26
  Isaac, 26
  Jediah, 26
  Sarepty, 26
  Timothy, 49
HANCOCK, Abraham, 128
  Ann, 109
  Anne, 145
  Daniel, 149
  Elizabeth, 123
  George, 149
  Godfrey, 14, 29, 128, 145
  Isaack, 128
  Jane, 104
  Levi, 149, 155
  Mary, 14, 29, 128
  Phoebe, 149
  Rebeckah, 128
  Sarah, 145, 149
  Thomas, 145, 149
  William, 158
HAND, Lawrence, 130
HANDCOCK, John, 111
HANK, John, 150
HARBER, Sarah, 102
HARDING, Ann, 151
  Mercy, 111
  Reuben, 140
  Stephen, 111
HARDY, Josiah, 128
HARKER, Sarah, 53
HARLEY, Anthony, 148, 158
HARRIS, Abraham, 115
  Agnes, 129
  Alice, 9
  Ann, 130
  Christian, 67
  Edith, 9
  Frances, 9
  James, 9
  Jane, 9

John, 108, 130
Joseph, 9, 64
Mary, 130
Phebe, 9
Ruth, 9
Samuel, 9
Thomas, 9, 67
William, 9, 49
HARRISON, Benjamin, 35, 42
  Deborah, 56
  Diadamia, 4, 34, 42
  Elizabeth, 142
  Isaac, 4
  James, 142
  Latham, 35
  Meriam, 35
  Rebecca, 5, 62, 63
  Rebekah, 34
  Tacy, 51
  Thomas, 42
  Tracy, 35
  William, 35
HARTSHORNE, William, 156
HARVEY, Ann, 3, 29
  Charlotte, 17
  Elizabeth, 17, 32
  Job, 2, 14, 17, 29, 54
  John, 2, 3, 14, 29, 53
  Lawrence, 17
  Mary, 2, 4, 14, 17, 29, 54
  Minor, 17
  Peter, 2, 14, 17, 29, 32, 51, 54
  Rebecca, 17
  Sarah, 17, 32, 54
HARWOOD, Nathaniel, 126
HATFIELD, George, 124
HAVENS, Thomas, 65
HAWKINGS, Elizabeth, 157
HAWKINS, Elizabeth, 139
  Roger, 123
HAY, Hannah, 69
  Isaac, 69
  Jemima, 69

William, 101
HAYE, Elizabeth, 156
HAYES, Anna, 147
  John, 147
  Rachel, 147
  William, 147
HAYNE, Lydia, 115
HAYWOOD, Deborah, 138, 144
  Elizabeth, 138
  George, 138, 144
  Marion Hannah, 144
HAZLETON, Sarah, 113
HEARTLY, Roger, 103
HEATH, Andrew, 122
  Eliz. Sarah, 122
  John, 122
HEATHCOATE, Anne, 147
HEATTON, Hannah, 63
HEILAND, Frederick, 125
  Leonard, 125
HELLINGS, Elizabeth, 148
HELLINS, Elizabeth, 158
HENDRIC, Catherine, 131
HENDRICKS, Mary, 103
HENRY, Elizabeth, 24, 45, 59, 144
  John, 24, 45, 144
  Susanna, 45
  William, 38, 53, 58, 66
HERD, Alice, 147
  John, 100
  Thomas, 112
HERITAGE, Joseph, 48
HERLIN, Elizabeth, 2
  Mathias, 2
HETFIELD, Mary, 156
HEULING, Isaac, 127
HEULINGS, Arney, 152
  Hester, 109
  Isaac, 152
HEWLINGS, Abraham,

109
Abrm, 130, 131, 133-137
Eliz., 123
Elizabeth, 81
Jonathan, 81
Mary, 81
William, 152
HIBBS, Jacob, 147
HIENLOKE, Margaret, 121
HIGARTY, Barnaby, 144
  Catherine, 144
  Sarah, 144
HIGGINS, Bryan, 107
  Patrick, 156
HILES, Joseph, 96
  Margaret, 95
  Nicholas, 96
HILL, William, 113
HILLIARD,
  Hollingshead, 115
  Lydia, 115
HILLYER, Mary, 130
HINCHAM, John, 87
HINDS, Jeremiah, 110
HIRETON, Obediah, 104
HOAY, Joseph, 118
HODGKINSON, John, 137
  Mary, 137
  Peter Aris, 137
HODGSON, James, 156
HODJINSON, Betha., 153
  Catharine, 153
HODJKINSON, John, 151
  Mary, 151
  Samuel, 151
HODSON, Anne, 103
HOFF, Sarah, 111
  William, 111
HOGAN, Catharine, 118
  James, 133
  John, 133
  Rozanna, 133
HOGELAND, Hannah, 133
HOILE, Andrew, 80
  Elizabeth, 80, 82

Enoch, 80
Hannah, 80
James, 80
Joseph, 80
Joshua, 80
Levi, 80
Margaret, 80
Martha, 80
Nicholas, 80, 82
Priscilla, 80, 82
HOLBARD, Mercy, 111
HOLBERT, Joshua, 102
HOLDER, John, 106
HOLINSHEAD, Joseph, 152
  Susanna, 152
HOLLAND, Anne, 136, 142
  Daniel, 110
  James, 136, 142
  Katharine, 115
  Mary, 136
  William, 142
HOLLINGHEAD,
  William, 103
HOLLINGSHEAD,
  Edmund, 72
  Rebeckah, 115
HOLLINGSWORTH,
  Agness, 84
  Elanor, 84
  Hugh, 84
HOLLINSHEAD,
  Hannah, 112
  Samuel, 105
HOLLOWAY,
  Elizabeth, 5, 36, 53
  George, 5, 36, 53, 54
  Mary, 5, 36, 53
  Sarah, 5, 36, 53
  Thomas, 36, 53
  William, 5, 36, 53
HOLMAN, Eliz., 123
HOLMES, Rachel, 86
HOMAN, Peter, 111
HOOPER, Rachel, 112
HOOTON, Bathsheba, 77
  Deborah, 77
  Thomas, 77
HOPPER, John, 107

HORNER, Achsah, 10, 13
  Anna, 13
  Chalkley, 13
  Content, 109
  Deborah, 13
  Deliverance, 106
  Hannah, 13
  Isaac, 13, 54, 105
  John, 10
  Jonathan, 13
  Joseph, 23, 54
  Joshua, 106
  Mary, 13, 53
  Mercy, 58
  Rachel, 105
  Rebecca, 13
  Sarah, 13
  Susannah, 13
  Thomas, 13
HORSEMAN, Samuel, 103
HORT, Mary, 113
HOSKINS, John, 16
  Mary, 16
HOUGH, Mary, 11
HOWARD, Alexander, 4, 24
  Edith, 35, 53
  Elizabeth, 4, 24
  Martha, 4, 24
  Mary, 24
  Rebecca, 4, 24
  Thomas, 4, 11
  Thomas M., 24
HOY, Catherine, 118
  George, 118
  John, 118
HOYLE, Catherine, 118
  John, 118
HUDDLESTON,
  Rebecca, 132
HUDDY, Hugh, 120
  Margaret, 120
HUFF, Ann, 72
  Richard, 147
HUGG, Joseph, 102
HUGGIN, John, 105
HUGHES, Hannah, 115
  James, 108
HULSE, James, 100
HUNLOCK, Bowman How, 151

INDEX

Mary, 151
Sarah, 145
Thomas, 145, 151
HUNLOKE, Thomas, 141
HUNT, Isaiah, 75
Samuel, 116
HUNTER, James, 151
HUNTLEY, Mary, 124
Susanna, 124
HURLEY, Benjamin, 83
Elizabeth, 83
Rachel, 83
HUTCHIN, Alice, 139, 157
Ann, 5
Hugh, 5, 109
Isaac, 22, 58
Jane, 22
Mary, 23, 138, 157
Rebecca, 23
Sarah, 23, 109
William, 23
HUTCHINS, Isaac, 45
John, 45
Sarah, 45
HUTCHINSON, Eliz., 122
Isac, 122
HUTTEN, Mary, 76
HYETT, Samuel, 12

-I-

INDICOTT, Joseph, 106
INGAR, Adam, 148
Barbara, 148
INGOLDSBY, Governor, 119
INMAN, Benjamin, 110
IRICK, John, 141
Mary, 141
IRVINS, Aaron, 53
Ann, 53
Berkley, 53
Isaac, 53
Mary, 53
Samuel, 53
IRWIN, Ann, 102
ISDALE, Elizabeth, 144

James, 144
Lydia, 144
Mary, 144
Richard, 144
ISDALL, Rachel, 150
IVINS, Aaron, 38, 39, 45, 58
Ann, 4, 27, 36, 38, 45, 55, 58
Barclay, 38
Barzillai, 46
Berkly, 58
Elizabeth, 27
George, 39
Hannah, 46
Isaac, 4, 27, 28, 38
Israel, 27
Joseph, 27
Lydia, 111
Mahlon, 27
Margaret, 41, 46
Mary, 22, 27, 28, 38, 43, 58
Meriam, 39
Rebecca, 66
Samuel, 22, 27, 38, 43, 44, 54, 55, 58
Sarah, 5, 44

-J-

JACKSON, Catennor, 102
Joseph, 155
Mary, 104
Sarah, 140
William, 146
JACOBS, Catherine, 150
John, 150
Rebecca, 150
JAMES, Hannah, 106
JEFFRIES, Jane, 154
JENKINSON, Hannah, 90, 96
JENNEY, Revd, 125
JERVIS, Francis, 107
JEVINS, Sollomon, 101
Susannah, 101
JOHNSON, Ann, 121
Asa, 65

David, 150
Elizabeth, 121
Heziah, 65
Jacob, 104
Jervas, 95
Jo's., 126
John, 121
Jonathan, 147, 151
Margaret, 105, 151
Mary, 126
Peggy, 147
Samuel, 151
Sarah, 121
Thomas, 147
William Allen, 123
JOHNSTON, James, 124
JOLLY, Andrew, 123
Charles, 122
Janet, 122
Lewis, 123
Margt, 123
Rebecca, 143
JONES, Benjamin, 11, 22, 27, 44, 79
Blath, 153
Charity, 42
Charity C., 22
Charles, 22, 35, 42, 43, 51, 52, 55
Daniel, 142
David, 72, 94, 127
Elizabeth, 22, 27, 42, 44, 48, 70, 79, 98
Elizabeth Sophia, 22
Esther, 27
Hannah, 70
Hester, 48
Isaac, 153
Israel, 27, 48, 61
Jeremiah, 43
Jesse, 70, 90
John, 116
Jonathan, 70, 90, 94, 98
Joseph, 27, 48
Mary, 22, 27, 35, 42, 48, 55, 70,

115
Owen, 70
Patrick, 112
Penelope, 112
Phebe, 53
Samuel, 22, 102
Sarah, 11, 22, 27, 42, 44, 48, 70, 79, 113, 125, 150
Tacey, 105
Thomas, 108, 115, 127
William, 70, 85, 94, 96, 98, 113
JORDAN, Sarah, 53
JOYCE, Allen, 72
  Martha, 112
  Mary, 112
  Thomas, 116
JUSTICE, James, 142, 146, 157
  Martha, 146

-K-

KAY, Hannah, 76
  Isaac, 76
  Jemima, 76, 77
KEARNEY, Michael, 148
KEARNS, Anna, 118
  Patrick, 118
  Rosa, 118
KEATING, Garret, 131
  Joanna, 131
  Mary, 131
KEITH, G., 119, 120
KELLY, Abraham, 153
  Bridget, 129
  Cornelius, 110
  Joseph, 132
  Sarah, 26
KEMBLE, Anne, 136, 149
  Collin, 149
  Edward, 132, 149, 151, 152
  Elizabeth Leeds, 149
  Elton, 145
  Hannah, 152
  John, 152
  Levina, 149, 151, 152
  Mary, 144, 145
  Sarah, 145
KEMINGS, James, 103
KEMPTON, John, 148
KENDAL, David, 123
  Eliz., 123
  Susannah, 123
KENNEDY, Anne, 146
  John, 153
KENNEY, Philip, 106
KENT, Elizabeth, 108
KERBY, Rachel, 64
KERLIN, Elizabeth, 18, 53
  Grace, 2, 18
  Margaret, 18
  Mathias, 18
  Sarah, 18
  Thomas, 2
KERR, Margaret, 150
KETTLE, Ann, 90
  Deborah, 90
  Hope, 92
  James, 90
  Jane, 92
  Rachel, 92
KEYS, Sarah, 150
KILLE, Elizabeth, 111
KILLY, Samuel, 104
KIMBAL, Benjamin, 112
  Sarah, 112
KIMBALL, George, 111
  John, 109
KIMBLE, Benjamin, 155
  Edith, 112
  Edward, 153
  Elizabeth, 125
  John, 124
  Joseph, 115
  Mary, 153
  Ruth, 90
  Sarah, 156
KING, Catharine, 107
  Jesse, 116
  John, 102
  Mary, 104
KINKEAD, David, 154
KINSEY, Anne, 155
Clement, 115
Sarah, 115
KIRBY, Aaron, 23
  Abel, 40
  Abraham, 4
  Achsah, 4, 61
  Amy, 21, 23, 24, 43
  Ann, 4, 5, 56, 61, 90
  Benjamin, 4, 5, 35
  Charlotte, 23
  Edmond B., 24
  Elizabeth, 4, 5, 24, 36
  Emphson, 51
  Empson, 5, 61
  Israel, 4, 23, 43
  James I., 24
  Job, 4, 57
  John, 24, 32
  Joseph, 100
  Maria, 32
  Martha, 24
  Mary, 24, 32
  Phebe, 4
  Rachel, 4, 23, 35, 41
  Rebecca, 63
  Robert, 4, 21, 24, 32, 40, 43
  Sarah, 23
  William N., 24
KLEMMER, Ann Mary, 118
  John, 118
KNIGHT, Anne, 144
  Elizabeth, 140, 144
  Hannah, 142
  Henry, 140, 144
KNOTT, Elizabeth, 120
KOBSON, James, 100

-L-

LACY, Ann, 119
  James, 119
LAMB, Charlotte, 9
  Charttee, 2
  Ejaias, 9
  Elizabeth, 29, 64
  Esaias, 2

Esasias, 63
Jacob, 73
Joseph, 1, 2, 7, 8, 11, 29, 58, 108
Lettice, 9
Lottice, 2
Lydia, 73
Mary, 2, 8, 9
Mercy, 2, 8
Nehemiah, 2, 9
Rebecca, 1, 2, 7, 9
Samuel, 2, 9, 68
Sarah, 73
Susanna, 64
LAND, Mary, 154
LANE, Anne, 142
Elizabeth, 117
James, 117
Katharine, 117
Mathias, 117
LANNING, Hannah, 110, 111
Martha, 111
LARREW, David, 132, 133
Sarah, 133
LARZELERE, John, 133
Nicholas, 132
Sarah, 132
LASEY, Thomas, 120
LAURIE, James, 31
Mary, 31
LAVORY, William, 35, 36
LAWRANCE, Thomas, 34
LAWREN, Edith, 56
LAWRENCE, Ann, 125
Catherine, 128
Elizabeth, 125, 148
Jacob, 101
James, 152
John, 125, 128, 136, 143, 146, 147, 150, 152
John B., 11
Lucy, 143
Margaret, 59, 62
Martha, 128, 136, 143, 146, 147, 150, 152
Sarah, 11, 128

Thomas, 48
LAWRIE, Achsah, 5, 21, 46
Ann, 5, 21, 37, 44
Beulah, 32
Deborah, 30
Edith, 36
Elizabeth, 5, 21, 46
James, 43
John, 5, 21, 46, 65, 66
Joseph H., 32
Joseph Murfin, 44
Mary, 43
Thomas, 5, 30, 37, 43, 44, 54, 55
William, 5, 21, 57
LEADER, Nathaniel, 150
LEBBY, Joanna, 104
LEE, Elizabeth, 116
Jane, 156
John, 103
Mary, 113
Robert Shippen, 155
Theodosia, 129
LEEDS, Abigail, 124
Ann, 109, 119
Anna, 124
Daniel, 119
Elizabeth, 86, 91
Felix, 126
Filan, 119
Hannah, 7
Holise, 119
Japhet, 7
Japos, 119
John, 108
Mary, 119, 121, 124
Philo, 109, 119, 124, 129
Roshannah, 119
Samuel, 129
Sarah, 129
William, 121
LEEK, Sarah, 122
William, 122
LEES, Hannah, 117
Mary, 115
William, 117

William Spraggs, 117
LEIGH, John, 151
Thomas, 151
LEMAUD, Lewis, 155
LEONARD, Catharine, 54
Frances, 36
Francis, 1
John, 100
LEROY, Catharine, 11
LESTER, Thomas, 102
LETCHWORTH, Hannah, 32
Sarah, 31
Thomas, 31
William, 32
LEVIN, Heziah, 5
Moses, 5
LEVINS, Barzillai, 4
Hannah, 4
Margaret, 4
LEVIS, Sarah, 5
LEWIS, Edward, 150
Joseph, 105
Reuben, 150
Samuel, 116
Sarah, 150
LEYLAND, Thomas, 100
LIDDEN, James, 142
LIGHT, Elizabeth, 136
Frederick, 136
Peter, 136
LIMBECK, John David, 128
John Jacob, 128
LINDON, Sarah, 108
William, 108
LINDSEY, Elizabeth, 154
LINTON, Benjamin, 14, 24
Hannah, 24
Jane, 14
Martha, 3, 23
Sarah, 3, 33
LIPINCOTT, Elizabeth, 52
Joseph, 52
Rebecca, 52
Samuel, 52

Stacy, 60
LIPPINCOT, Sarah, 98
LIPPINCOTT, Aaron, 74, 81, 95, 98
  Aaron Tomlinson, 90
  Agneys, 76
  Ahab, 70
  Amaziel, 88
  Anner, 76
  Benjamin, 81, 91
  Beulah, 70, 86, 87
  Caleb, 70
  Charles, 76
  Clayton, 76
  David, 104
  Dorothy, 81, 89, 91
  Eliza. S., 82
  Elizabeth, 5, 22, 35, 73, 74, 81, 91, 97
  Esther, 70
  Freedom, 73
  Hannah, 70, 73, 87
  Hope, 70, 76
  J., 22
  Jacob, 95
  Job, 89, 102, 103, 115
  John, 82
  John H., 76
  Joseph, 5, 35, 81
  Joshua, 70, 73, 89, 90, 93
  Josiah, 102
  Lydia, 76
  Mark, 76
  Mary, 4, 34, 70, 73, 81, 82, 89, 98
  Moses, 81, 86, 91, 94
  Nathan, 73, 76, 89
  Rachel, 70, 73, 86, 87
  Rebecca, 5, 23, 73
  Rebeccah, 116
  Rebekah, 35
  Samuel, 5, 23, 35, 76, 107
  Sarah, 30, 81, 82, 87, 88, 89, 91, 92, 93, 94
  Stacy, 39
  Theodosia, 76
  Thomas, 70, 86, 87, 93, 129
  William Cooper, 76
LISHMAEL, Susannah, 58
LITTLE, Ann, 115
LLOYD, Hannah, 34, 48
  Levi, 48
LONDON, Catherine, 150
  Frederic, 150
  Nancy, 150
LONG, Heziah, 95
  John, 138
  Keziah, 97
  Mary, 138
  Richard, 131, 138
LONGHOFF, Deborah, 120
  Elizabeth, 120
  James, 120
  Laban, 120
  Moses, 120
LONGSTAFF, James, 137
LOOTS, Elizabeth, 122
  Francis, 122
  John, 122
LORD, John, 114
  Joshua, 102
  Rachel, 108
  Robert, 108
LOUNES, Esther, 12
LOVELL, Rachel, 114
LOVET, Elizabeth, 127
  Jonathan, 127
  Samuel, 127
LOVOTT, Jonathan, 123
  Samuel, 123
  Sarah, 123
LOW, Andrew, 117
  Joseph Read, 117
  Rene, 117
LOWDEN, Ann, 156
  Catherine, 135
  Frederick, 135
  George, 155
  Mary, 135
  Samuel, 155
  William, 153, 155
LOWDER, Edith, 112
LOWDON, Catherine, 141
  Frederic, 141
  Samuel, 141
LUCAS, Benjamin, 27
  Eben, 3
  Edward, 146
  Elizabeth, 3
  Esther, 146
  John, 3, 146
  Mary, 27
  Robert, 146
  Sarah, 3
  Seth, 145, 146
  Thomas, 3
  William, 3, 146
LUKE, Fanny, 139
LUND, Rachel, 59
LYNCH, Catharine, 86
  Katharine, 115
LYNDON, William, 130, 131, 132, 133, 134, 135, 136, 137, 138
LYPHERS, Mary, 149

—M—

MCCARTY, Ann, 105
MCCLUTCHY, Hugh, 124
  James, 124
  Mary, 124
MCCOLLIN, Allan, 143
MCDANIEL, Penelope, 110
M'DERMOT, John, 156
MCELROY, John, 115
MCFAULIN, Joyce, 110
MCILLHANY,
  Benjamin, 148, 158
  Jane, 148, 158
  John, 148, 158
MCILLVAINE,
  William, 147
MCILLVANINE, Mary,

155
William, 155
MACKIE, John, 139
M'KINZIE, M., 156
MCKLEAN, Hugh, 136
Margaret, 136
Sarah, 136
MCMULLEN,
Alexander, 148, 151
Jane, 148
Mary, 148, 151
MAGUIRE, James, 115
MAJOR, Mary, 115
MALCOMB, Doctor, 153
Donald, 153
John, 153
Neal, 153
MANINGTON, Anne, 148
MANNINGTON,
William, 143
MAQUIRE, Mathew, 148
MARLIN, Mary, 156
MARLING, Mary, 141
MARRIOTT, Benjamin, 110
Hananh, 104
Margaret, 113
Sarah, 112
MARSHALL, Isaac, 101
MARSS, Daniel, 116
MARTIN, Andrew, 100
Elizabeth, 100, 148
Hannah, 106
John, 100
Mary, 33, 101
Mary G., 24
Thomas, 33
MARTINE, Elizabeth, 142
MARTYR, Anne, 156
MASE, Asa, 3
MASON, Anne, 149
Joseph, 115
William, 102
MATLACK, Abraham, 77
Dorothy, 89
Eliza, 77
Jacob, 105

Joseph, 89
Rebecca, 77, 107
Sarah, 89
MATLOCK, Abram, 102
Deborah, 102
Joseph, 81
William, 81
MEDLEY, Mary, 123
Richard, 123
MEIRS, Unity, 61
MELVIL, Frederick, 122
John, 122
Will, 122
MEREDYTH, Thomas, 111
MERRAIL, Margaret, 123
William, 123
MERRICK, Timothy, 150
MERRIT, Maria, 104
Thomas, 100
MERRITT, Maria, 104
MEYERS, John, 155
MIDDLETON, Amos, 14
Ann, 82
Charity, 93
David, 34, 42, 48
Dinah, 45, 50
Elizabeth, 16, 28, 34
Esther, 90
George, 16, 28, 45
Hannah, 107
John, 93, 102, 112
Jonathan, 101
Josiah, 32
Maria, 32
Miriam, 14, 45, 50
Naomi, 112
Patience, 50
Phebe, 82
Rhoda, 50
Rhode, 3
Samuel, 82
Sarah, 63, 107
Thomas, 65
MIERS, George, 114
MILLER, Amy, 102
Elizabeth, 116
John, 149

Josiah, 87
Leatitia, 87
MILLES, Joshua, 111
MILLIGAN, Rachel, 134
Richard, 134
MILLINGTON, ---, 149
MILLS, Eliza, 109
Israel, 116
Jemima, 109
Priscilla, 88
Rachel, 88
Zebidee M., 88
MIM, John, 101
MINGIN, Margaret, 102
MINION, Margaret, 75
Stephen, 75
MINOR, Catharine, 43, 54
Cathrine, 28
Charlotte, 28, 44, 54
Elizabeth, 28, 43, 44, 46, 54
Lawrence, 17, 28, 43, 44, 46, 54
Rebecca, 28, 46, 54
Sarah, 17, 28
Thomas, 28
MIRS, George, 114
MISHER, Wamon, 124
MITCHEL, Margaret, 33, 105
Samuel, 33
William, 157
MITCHELL, Henry, 135
Sarah, 138
William, 138
MODE, Sarah, 142
MONROE, John, 105
MONROW, George, 102
MONTGOMERY, Revd, 151
MOODY, Martin, 91, 93, 97
MOON, Alicia, 142
James, 112, 142
Jane, 109
Jasper, 147
Martha, 106

Mary, 141, 158
Rebecca, 60
Susanna, 106
MOONEY, Marriette, 116
MOORE, Benjamin, 70, 108
  Bethuel, 78
  Elizabeth, 70, 108
  Martha, 78
  Mary, 70
  Priscilla, 74
  Sarah, 102
  William, 150
MORELAN, Elizabeth, 128
MORFORD, Elizabeth, 144
  Rachel, 149
MORGAN, Joseph, 71, 133
  Mary, 111
MORRE, Ruth, 88
MORRIS, A., 15
  Abraham Z., 26
  Alice, 2, 7
  Anthony, 2, 7, 26, 34, 50
  Bathsheba, 88
  Caleb, 26
  Eliza, 50
  Elizabeth, 2, 7, 34
  Esther, 2, 7, 26, 36
  George, 7
  Hannah, 7
  John, 7, 26
  Joseph, 2, 25, 26, 36, 53, 55
  Josepy, 7
  Mary, 7, 88
  Rachel, 25, 26
  Rebecca, 26
  Sabitha, 143
  Sarah, 2, 7, 26, 34, 50
  Stephen, 7, 88
  Susannah, 15
  Thomason, 26
MORRISON, Rachel, 9
  Sarah, 22
  Thomas, 9
MORSE, Jonathan, 102
MORTIMER, Elizabeth, 154
MORTON, Aaron, 8
  Joseph, 103
  Sarah, 8
MOSER, Catherine, 136
  Jacob, 136
MOSES, Mary, 124
MOTT, Asher, 135
  John, 109
  Mary, 110
  William, 154
MOTTE, Anna, 104
MOULTON, Dorothy, 144
MOUNT, Theodosia, 52
MOUTON, Dorothy, 146
MOWZER, Catherine, 144
  Jacob, 144
  William, 144
MULLEN, Ann, 115
  Elizabeth, 99, 115
  Mary, 113
MULLIN, John, 86
MUNROW, George, 107
MUNY, John, 118
  Margarety, 118
  Mary, 118
  Meridith, 118
MUNYAN, Hannah, 115
MUNYON, John, 108
MURFEY, John, 113
MURFIN, John, 113
  Joseph, 55
MURPHIN, Thomas, 136
MURPHY, Edward, 145, 150
  Elizabeth, 151
  Henry, 151
  Isabella, 145
  Izabella, 150
  James, 140
  Jeremiah, 150
  Mary, 140, 145, 151
  Nancy, 153
  Rachel, 151
  Suzannah, 151
  Thomas, 151
  William, 140
MURRAY, Leonard, 136
MURRELL, John, 134, 142
  Joseph, 142
  Lucy, 134, 142
  Rachel, 102
  Samuel, 112
MURRILL, Anne, 136
  Jospeh, 136
  Margaret, 136
  Mary, 136
  William, 136
MUSCHENTYNE, John, 147, 158
  Sarah, 147, 158
MUSGRAVE, Mary, 102
MUSKOTT, Frederick, 101
MYERS, Mary, 155
MYOVERIA, Elizabeth, 102

-N-

NAPPER, Eliza, 121
  Margaret, 121
  Mary, 121
  Rebecca, 121
NAYLOR, Dorothy, 123
  Martha, 123
  Robert, 123
  William, 123
NEAL, Eleanor, 130
  Jennet, 130
  John, 130
  Martha, 152
NEALE, Anna, 143
  Anne, 148
  Catherin, 124
  Charles, 143
  Eleanor, 137, 148
  Elizabeth, 116, 124, 151, 154, 156
  Isaac, 137
  Jennet, 124
  John, 124, 137, 143, 148, 156
  Margaret, 155
  Martha, 124
  Mary, 132, 143, 149, 151, 152,

INDEX

154, 156
Thomas, 141, 158
Thomson, 124,
143, 149, 151, 152
  William Smith,
152
NEGRO, Asa, 138
  Charles, 139
  Dinah, 100
  Frederick, 155
  Hannah, 143
  Jack, 100
  Knowlton, 148,
158
  Margaret, 138
  Maria, 143
  Mercy Alexander,
153
  Pleasant, 100
  Rachel, 131
  Rose, 146
  Rosetta, 141
  Sabeack, 100
  Sebastian, 141
  Tamar, 101, 142
  Tom, 100
NEIL, John, 125
  Mary, 125
NETTERVILLE,
  Charles, 106
NEVELL, Jane, 101
NEWBERRY, Hannah,
104
NEWBOLD, Achsah, 11
  Ann, 1, 3, 11,
12, 44
  Anthony, 12
  B., 29
  Barzella, 56
  Barzillai, 1, 7,
27
  Barzillia, 11
  Beulah, 1, 32
  Caleb, 1, 11, 33,
59, 62, 67, 68
  Charles, 27
  Charlotte, 8
  Clayton, 1, 8,
12, 32, 33, 42, 46
  Cleayton, 1
  Daniel, 1, 11
  Deborah, 1, 35,
52
  Edith, 1, 11, 12,
27, 44

  Elizabeth, 1, 8,
39, 62
  Enoch, 11, 27
  George, 1, 8, 12,
42
  Hannah, 1, 8, 11,
12, 27, 33, 35,
51, 57
  Henry, 1
  John, 1, 3, 8,
14, 27, 37, 43,
44, 46, 62, 82
  Joseph, 8, 58
  Joseph W., 12
  Joshua, 27
  Lydia, 1, 11
  Margaret, 1, 11,
27
  Martha, 3, 14,
16, 40, 43
  Mary, 1, 3, 6, 8,
11, 12, 14, 16,
27, 32, 40, 43,
44, 46, 50, 51,
55, 56, 58, 68, 82
  Michael, 1, 7, 8,
9, 11, 12, 27, 37,
57
  Molly, 11
  Rachel, 1, 11,
12, 14, 27, 46
  Rebecca, 1, 7, 8,
46
  Samuel, 1, 3, 11,
12, 14, 16, 57,
58, 67, 68
  Sarah, 1, 7, 11,
12, 27, 29, 33,
37, 41, 68
  Susan, 1
  Susan C., 12
  Susanna, 46
  Susannah, 1, 8,
27, 33, 44
  Thomas, 1, 6, 11,
12, 27, 37, 50,
54, 55, 100
  Thomas J., 12
  Watson, 12
  William, 1, 8,
12, 27, 33, 44,
46, 64, 65, 67,
68, 100
  William F., 12
NEWELL, John, 101

  Sarah, 105
NEWMAN, John, 109,
121
  Martha, 122
  May, 122
  Rachel, 122
  Rebecca, 122
  Richard, 122
  Sarah, 122
  Walter, 122
  William, 122
NEWTON, Mary, 86
  Michael, 145
  Samuel, 31
  Sarah, 31
NICHOLAS, Andrew,
123
  Rebekah, 123
NICHOLSON,
  Margaret, 121
NIXON, William, 102
NOBLE, James, 125
  Mary, 151
NORCROSS,
  Bathsheba, 130
  Jane, 111
  William, 111
NORDYKE, Henry, 138
  Jacob, 140, 157
NORMANDAY, Mary,
123
NORTH, Elizabeth,
131
  John, 148
  Margaret, 150
  Philip, 150
  Tirringham
  Palmer, 150
NORTON, Esther, 145
  Grace, 145
  Jemima, 133
  John, 113
  Margaret, 110
  Martha, 111, 142,
157
  Rachel, 140
  Susanna, 149
  Susannah, 133,
140
  Suzanna, 145
  William, 133,
140, 145, 149
NUTT, Abigail, 37
  Ann, 39, 56
  Charlotte, 37

Edward, 56
Elizabeth, 37,
38, 44, 49, 56, 57
Hannah, 37
Joseph, 113
Levy, 44
Mary, 133, 157
Moses, 37, 38

-O-

ODELL, Anne, 146,
151, 152
John, 130, 131,
132, 133, 134,
135, 136, 137
Jonathan, 119,
129, 143, 146,
151, 152
Lucy Anne, 151
Mary, 146
Revd., 152
Sarah Anne, 152
OFFLEY, Ann, 36
Daniel, 36, 43,
44, 55
Rachel, 44
OGBORN, Ann, 37, 54
Caleb, 37, 54
Daniel, 37
Elizabeth, 88
Esther, 88
Joseph, 4, 37,
40, 60
Joseph F., 88
Samuel, 37, 88
William, 37
OGBURN, Anna, 104
John, 101
Joseph, 38
OGDEN, Jane, 144
OLDACRES, Henry,
104
OLDALE, Grace, 114
OLIPHANT, Ann, 115
OLIPHEN, Hope, 95
ONEAL, George, 25
O'NEAL, George, 44,
54
ONEAL, Sarah, 25
O'NEIL, George, 9
Sarah, 9
ONG, Esther, 108
Jacob, 108
ORSEN, Leland, 86

Margaret, 86
Prudence, 86
OWEN, Benjamin, 91
David, 91
Elizabeth, 91
Jesse, 91
Joseph, 91
Joshua, 90, 91
Mary, 70, 106
Prudence, 70, 91
Rachel, 91
Roland, 91
Rowland, 70
Sarah, 91
Sidney, 91

-P-

PAGE, Abigail, 84
Agnes, 89
Agness, 84
Alice, 84
Clayton H., 84
Edward, 101
Elizabeth, 84, 89
George, 125
James, 143, 157
John, 108
Sarah, 84, 108
Thomas, 84, 89
William, 84, 89
PAIN, Abigail, 121
PAINTER, George,
117, 152, 155
Jennett, 155
Margaret, 117
Martha, 117
PALMER, Ann, 76
Elizabeth, 109
Hannah, 76
Jonathan, 76
Tyrringham, 136
PANCOAST, Abbe Ann,
25
Abigail, 8
Ann, 25, 66
Asa, 3, 39
Benjamin, 3, 34,
49
Daniel A., 12
Elizabeth, 3, 8,
12, 25
George L., 25
Grace, 10
Hannah, 8, 12,
25, 39, 47

James, 42, 65
John, 8, 25, 65,
66, 68
Joseph, 3, 8, 25,
39, 47, 68, 100,
101
Lucy A., 25
Mary, 3, 36
Rebecca, 51
Samuel, 3, 66
Samuel A., 25
Sarah, 3, 8, 25,
38, 47, 101
Solomon, 3, 34
Thomas, 10
Thomasin, 3
Thomson, 39
Unity, 3, 34, 39,
50, 101
William, 25
PANCOST, Abigial, 1
Hannah, 1
John, 1
Joseph, 1
Sarah, 1
PARENT, Thomas, 101
PARK, Ann, 119
John, 119
Roger, 119
PARKE, Ann, 119
Daniel, 111
John, 119
Roger, 119
PARKER, Anne, 138
Edward, 5, 55
Elizabeth, 5,
103, 112
Hannah, 108
John, 101
Joseph, 6, 55
Mary, 104, 138
Michael, 138
Philip, 121
Rebecca, 103, 121
Ruth, 116
Sarah, 121
Solomon, 102
Thomas, 39, 59
William, 108
PARKS, Mary, 112
Paul, 112
PARR, Samuel, 104
PATTERSON,
Alexander, 147
Anne, 146

INDEX

Mary, 141
PATTISON, Rebecca, 103
PATTIT, Keziah, 49
PAXSON, Anna, 30
  Benjamin, 40, 46, 65, 66
  Jane, 46
  Rachel, 40, 65
  Thomas, 46
  William, 30
PEACHEE, Mary, 105
PEACHY, Ann, 120
  Sarah, 139
  Thomas, 120
PEACOCK, Alexander, 115
  Ann, 72, 73, 153
  Anna, 73
  Elizabeth, 73, 92
  Hannah, 73
  John, 72
  Joseph, 72
  Joshua, 72, 73
  Rachel, 90
  Susannah, 72, 73
  William, 73
PEARCE, Catherine, 148
  Edward, 148
PEARSE, Martha, 116
PEARSON, John, 106
  Mary, 105
  Rachel, 110
  Robert, 110
  Thomas, 111
PEDDLE, Edith, 102
PENE, Ann, 156
PENQUITE, Gersham, 94
PERKINS, Bathsheba, 111, 123
  Benjamine, 120
  Elizabeth, 144
  Hanah, 123
  Isaac, 120, 144
  Jacob, 111, 120, 123, 144
  Mary, 120
  Rebekah, 56
  Sarah, 107, 123, 144
  William, 144
PERRY, Charles, 117
  Elias, 117

Elizabeth, 117
Esther, 117
John, 117
Samuel, 117
PERSON, Abel, 136
PETERS, John, 106, 115
  Mr., 126
PETTIT, Adam, 30
  Charles, 133
  Jospeh, 133
  Keziah, 30
  Sarah, 133
PETTITT, Judith, 107
  Moses, 107
PHILIPPS, Mary, 102
PHILIPS, Elizabeth, 75, 150
  Ephraim, 143
  Joseph, 143
  Peter, 75
  Sarah, 75, 102
PHILLIPS, Ann, 117
  Catharine, 66
  John, 117
  Joseph Rossell, 117
  Margaret, 86
PIERCE, Hannah, 96
  Joseph, 96
  Mary, 96, 99
  Rachel, 96
  Susanna, 96
PIERSON, Rebeckah, 115
PIMM, Sarah, 112
PIMMOCK, Tallman, 58
PINE, Benjamin, 102
  John, 87
  Mary, 87
  Rachel, 87
PITMAN, Aaron, 31
  Frances, 59
  John, 13
  Mary, 13, 40
  Matida, 31
  Sarah, 41
  William, 151
PITTMAN, Abel, 30
  Elizabeth, 30
  Ephraim, 30, 37, 56
  Frances, 30

Mary, 30, 35
Robert, 30
Sarah, 30, 33, 50
PLATT, Alice, 22, 42
  Elizabeth, 22, 42, 123
  George, 22, 42
  Jane, 123
  John, 22, 42, 48, 123
  Martha, 22
  Mary, 22, 42, 123
  Thomas, 42, 111, 123
  William, 22, 42
PLUM, John, 115
  Mary, 115
POCHO, Phebe, 119
  Thomas, 119
POINTSEH, Asa, 28
  Peter, 28
POINTSET, Asa, 42
POINTSIT, Asa, 64
POOL, Isaac, 146
  John, 146
  Sarah, 128
  William, 128
POOLE, Abraham, 144
  Elizabeth, 134, 139, 144, 150
  Isaac, 139
  John, 134, 139, 144, 150
POPE, Amy, 31
  Ann, 2, 29, 37
  Clayton, 2, 29, 38
  Elizabeth, 2, 18, 29, 49, 89
  John, 2, 15, 29, 31, 38, 46, 89
  Joseph, 2, 18, 29, 63
  Mary, 15
  Nathaniel, 2, 15, 29, 31, 39, 46, 101
  Rebecak, 37
  Rebecca, 2
  Rebekah, 29
  Richard, 15
  Samuel, 15
  Sara, 65
  Sarah, 2, 15, 31,

39, 46
 Thomas, 2, 15, 39
 Unity, 15
 William, 2, 15
PORTER, Joseph, 142
 Joshua, 116
 Thomas, 115
POTTER, Constant, 51
 Ellen, 146
 Jane, 146
 Mary, 146
 Thomas, 146
POTTS, Abraham, 113
 Anne, 103
 Richard, 5, 100
 Thomas, 115
POULTNEY, Benjamin, 34, 42
 Eleanor, 42
 Phebe, 34
 Thomas, 42
POWELL, Anna Maria, 142
 Elizabeth, 139
 John, 138, 157
 Margaret, 124
 Nicholas, 139
PRESTON, Susannah, 114
 Thomas, 106
PRICE, ---, 152
 Ann, 13
 Anne, 131
 Edy, 131
 John, 107
 Nancy, 156
 Thomas, 13, 131
 William, 106, 115
PRICKET, Hepziba, 99
 Job, 97, 98
 John, 99
 Sabylla, 99
PRICKETT, Aaron, 115
 Ann, 72, 105
 Barzillai, 72
 Elizabeth, 72
 Isaac, 9, 111
 Jacob, 105
 Job, 72
 Josiah, 72
 Louis, 9
 Mary, 114

Rachel, 72, 102
 Sabillah, 72
 Stacy, 72
PRICKITT, Aaron, 75
 Elizabeth, 75
 Hannah, 75
 Hepehziah, 75
 Jacob, 75, 104
 John, 75
 Samuel, 75
PRIESTLY, John George, 153
 Mars., 153
PUNEO, Gabriel, 113
PUTTEN, William, 132

-Q-

QUICKFALL, Samuel, 100
QUICKSALL, Amy, 16
 Samuel, 16
QUIGLEY, Philip, 105

-R-

RAINIER, John, 143, 157
RAKELTRAN, Abraham, 101
RANDOLPH, Daniel, 101
RANEIR, Joseph, 114
RASH, Belinda, 115
RAWORTH, ---, 149
READ, Alice, 137
 Charles, 126, 137
 Hannah, 85
 Joseph, 141
RECKLESS, Joseph, 100
REDDRICK, Izilah, 115
REED, Ann, 152
 Ann Burnet, 152
 Bowes, 151, 152
 Charles Pettit, 151
 Margaret, 151, 152
 Maria, 151
REEVE, Ann, 87
 Casper, 83, 98
 Clayton, 83
 Elizabeth, 82, 87, 98

Emmor, 87
 Franklin, 83
 Hannah, 43, 82, 83, 87, 98, 140
 Hannah Ann, 83
 Job, 83
 Job Whitall, 83
 John N., 82
 John W., 89
 Josiah, 35, 43, 53, 82, 89
 Josiah Miller, 87
 Leatitia, 87
 Mark, 43, 82, 87, 98
 Martha, 35, 82, 89
 Micajah, 140
 Priscilla, 87, 89
 Rebecca, 83
 Richard Miller, 87
 Robert, 83, 98
 Samuel, 98
 Sarah Whitall, 83
 William, 87
 William F., 87
REEVES, Amriah Ann, 84
 Ann, 84, 93
 Charity, 149
 Elizabeth, 84, 106
 Hannah, 84, 143
 Henry, 143, 157
 Jonathan, 106, 143
 Josiah, 93
 Leatitia, 93
 Mahlon, 84
 Martha, 84
 Mary, 108
 Samuel, 73, 84
 Sarah, 55
 Susanna, 36, 51, 92
 Susannah, 90
 Thomas, 84
 William, 93, 106
REGIONS, Margaret, 132
REID, Hanah, 121
 Helen, 121
RENIER, Jemima, 135

INDEX

Joshua, 134, 157
Mary, 131, 157
Peter, 112, 135
Susannah, 143, 157
RENIOR, Lettice, 54
REYNOLDS, Anne, 139
  Chichester, 139, 140
  Margaret, 139, 140
  Rebecka, 140
  Richard, 120
  Thomas, 134
RHODES, John, 109
RICHARDS,
  Bathsheba, 104
  William, 116
RICHARDSON, Anne, 135
  Benjamin, 135
  Elizabeth, 46
  Esther, 135
  Jane, 9, 135
  John, 9, 111, 135, 141
  Joseph, 41, 46, 67, 135
  Lucia, 144, 157
  Martha, 111
  Mary, 135
  Rebecca, 41, 135, 141
  Susanna, 113
  William, 46, 135
RIDGEWAY, Ann, 10
  Elizabeth, 10, 108
  Hannah, 11
  Henry, 10, 11
  Mary, 10, 11
  Rebecca, 11
  Samuel W., 10
  Sarah, 11
  Solomon, 10
  William, 11
RIDGWAY, Aaron, 98
  Andrew C., 22, 32
  Ann, 2, 3, 26, 37, 129
  Barzilla, 102
  Caleb, 21, 49
  Catherine, 16
  Daniel, 57, 64
  David, 21, 40

David W., 22
Eli, 34, 48, 98
Eliza, 33
Elizabeth, 2, 4, 16, 21, 26, 32, 37, 45, 46, 49, 60, 98
Ellis, 34, 48
H., 32
Hannah, 26, 57, 60
Hannaniah, 14
Henrietta, 32
Henry, 2, 26, 37, 60, 62
Isabell, 4
Jacob, 4, 14, 16, 20, 21, 34, 5, 48, 94, 98
Job, 3, 7, 25, 46, 55
John, 21, 32, 46, 49, 103
Jonathan, 7
Joseph, 8, 16, 32
Lucy, 23
Lydia, 98
Mary, 2, 4, 7, 25, 26, 32, 35, 37, 38, 43, 46, 52, 60, 110
Noah, 129
Phebe, 20
Rebecca, 7, 25, 26, 37, 46, 60
Rebeckah, 129
Richard, 23
Samuel, 2, 37, 60, 65
Samuel W., 26
Sarah, 2, 8, 21, 26, 37, 46, 49, 60, 98
Solomon, 2, 26, 37, 43, 60
Susanna, 48
Susannah, 34, 98
Thomas, 22, 40, 60
William, 26, 35, 43, 51, 115
RIGERS, John, 4
  Ruth, 4
  Theodosia, 4
ROBBINS, Amy, 18

Anna, 18, 29
Edward, 18, 44, 57
Elizabeth, 18
Joice, 29, 39
Mariah, 18
Nathan, 18, 29, 39, 44
Rebecca, 18
Sarah, 18
William, 18
ROBERTS, Clayton, 89
  Elizabeth, 89
  Esther, 81, 89, 95
  Isaac, 69
  Izy, 78
  Jacob, 81, 89
  John, 81, 89, 95, 104
  John e., 81
  Joseph, 81
  Joshua, 89
  Mary, 81, 145, 157
  Phebe, 81
  Rebecca, 81
  Reuben, 70, 81
  Sarah, 69
  Susan, 81
  Syllania, 89
  Thomas E., 81
ROBERTSON, James, 33
ROBINS, Ann, 12
  Benjamin, 111
  Deliverance, 111
  James, 107
  Joice, 51
  Nathaniel, 12
ROBINSON, Ann, 126
  Elizabeth, 95, 111, 123
  James, 5
  John, 126
  Mary, 126
  Rachel, 138
  Sarah, 102
  Susanna, 123
  Thomas, 126
  William, 123
ROCKHILL, Aaron, 2, 15, 40
  Abigail, 26

Amos, 2, 15, 16
Amy, 3, 16, 43
Caleb, 3, 58
E., 20
Edward, 3, 14, 15, 16, 18, 19, 39, 40, 42, 43, 44, 61, 64
Elizabeth, 3, 14, 16, 20, 42, 43, 44
George, 3
Grace, 18, 39, 61, 64
Hannah, 2, 15, 19, 40
Hannah Cook, 41
Hope, 68
Jerusha, 2, 16, 15, 40
John, 2, 3, 15, 26, 40, 52
Joseph, 103
Joshua, 2
Martha, 3, 19
Mary, 3, 16, 42, 58
Mercy, 2, 11
Meribah, 15
Nathan, 3, 16, 19, 41, 44, 64
Samuel, 2, 15, 40
Sarah, 3, 15, 40
Solomon, 100, 113
Susannah, 15
Tabitha, 16
Thomas, 2, 11
William, 15, 40
RODMAN, Isaac Person, 97
Margaret, 147
RODORO, Elizabeth, 121
ROE, Isabella, 154
Maria, 154
Sam, 154, 157
Samuel, 152
ROGERS, Abigail, 87
Abner, 87
Allen, 78
Amey, 36
Ann, 6, 20, 76, 78, 108
Beulah, 93
Catharine, 57
David, 78
Elizabeth, 27, 43
Grace, 77, 78
Hope, 87
John, 57, 108, 125, 144
Joseph, 78, 144
Josiah, 78
Martha, 78
Mary, 5, 6, 23, 53, 77, 78, 88, 108, 144
Michael, 6, 20, 50
Phebe, 50
Rachel, 78
Ruth, 52
Samuel, 6, 36, 43, 101
Sarah, 76, 78, 105
Thomas, 105
William, 27, 77, 78, 87, 90, 93
William D., 78
ROSE, Catherine, 123
Mary, 123
Peter, 123
Samuel, 111
ROSELL, Ann, 105
ROSS, Alex, 147
Alexander, 128
Elizabeth, 147
Hugh, 143
John, 128
Marion Hannah, 128
Marrion, 147
Sophia M., 116
ROSSELL, Martha, 141
Mary, 138
ROWE, Catherine, 149, 151
John, 138, 151
ROWING, Rachel, 116
ROWLAND, John, 12
ROWLEY, Barnard, 126
Batholemie, 126
ROWTH, John, 125
ROY, Rebecca, 102
ROZELL, Joseph, 107
Zachariah, 111
RUDDEROW, Esther, 116
William, 116
RUDEROW, Hannah, 103
RUNDALL, Elijah, 93
RUTHERFORD, Samuel, 130
RYAN, James, 118
Mary, 118
Sarah, 118

-S-

SAINT, Elizabeth, 112
Thomas, 112
ST. CLAIR, John, 128
SALTAN, Lucy, 124
SALTER, Joseph, 102
Mary, 98
Rachel, 102
Sarah, 96, 98
William, 96, 98, 102
SANDYS, Joseph, 149
SANSOM, Beulah, 38
Hannah, 45
Jospeh, 38, 45
Samuel, 45
SATERTHWAITE, Elizabeth, 65
Joseph, 65
William, 67
SATTERGOOD, Benjamin, 4
Caleb, 4, 57
Joshua, 4
Martha, 4
Mary, 4
Sarah, 4
SATTERTHWAITE, Abigail, 3, 13, 18
Ann, 3, 13, 43
Benjamin, 3, 13, 18, 41, 60
Caleb, 18, 41
Daniel, 19
Deborah, 19
Elizabeth, 3, 13, 19, 32, 44, 55
George, 103
Hannah, 3, 13, 24, 32
Jane, 3, 13, 22,

29, 43, 45, 46
Joel, 18, 41
John, 3, 13
Joseph, 3, 13,
19, 32, 55
Martha, 3, 13, 46
Mary, 3, 13, 14,
18, 19, 44
Reuben, 13, 19
Reubine, 3
Samuel, 3, 13,
14, 19, 24, 29,
32, 44, 46, 56
Sarah, 18, 41
William, 3, 13,
14, 22, 43, 45, 46
SAUNDERS,
Elizabeth, 74
John, 74, 99
Robert, 105
Solomon, 74, 99
Solomon L., 74
SAVAGE, John, 102
SAVORY, William,
35, 36
SAXTON, Elizabeth,
64
James, 101
SCATTERGOOD, Ann,
24
Benjamin, 29, 30,
41, 67, 106
Caleb, 24, 25,
29, 46, 67
Elizabeth, 29, 30
Hannah, 25
John A., 25
Jonathan, 24
Joseph, 24
Joshua, 29, 60
Martha, 25, 29,
65
Mary, 24, 25, 29,
46
Nathan, 25
Sarah, 24, 25,
29, 58, 61, 67,
106
Thomas, 2, 34,
36, 37
William, 25
SCEVER, Mary, 115
SCHOLEY, James, 103
SCHOOLEY, Abigail,
10

J., 7
John, 10, 26
Mary, 7
Rebecca, 26
Robert, 119
William, 119
SCHOOLY, Asa, 153
SCHUYLER, Aarent,
147
Abraham, 130, 147
Anna, 149
Arent, 130, 134,
139
Casparus, 147
Charles, 139
Jane, 134, 147
Jennet, 130
Mary, 134, 147
SCHYLER, John, 155
SCOTT, Ann, 120
Henry, 104, 113,
120
Jonathan, 109
Margaret, 118
Martha, 65
Mary, 32, 118
Thomas, 32, 120
SCULLEY, Elizabeth,
118
John, 118
Samuel, 118
SCUYLER, Abraham,
127
Anna, 127
Arant, 127
Janet, 127
John, 127
Mary, 127
Peter, 127
SEABURY, Samuel,
152
SEARLE, Grace, 132
SEBET, James, 106
SEVER, Benjamin,
102
SHADAKER,
Elizabeth, 140,
144, 157
William, 140
SHAFER, Jacob, 142
John, 142
Rachel, 142
SHALLICK, Honour,
103
SHARKEY, Alice, 9

James, 9
SHARP, Aaron, 102
Amos, 72
Ann, 72
Benjamin, 104
Deborah, 72, 102
Elizabeth, 104
Enoch, 102
George, 94
Hanah, 115
Hannah, 75, 85
Hester, 115
Hugh, 85, 93
Job, 85
John, 102
Joshua, 71
Mary, 102
Rebecca, 71
Sibillah, 85
Thomas, 75, 85
Timothy, 102
William, 71, 75,
85, 92
SHARPE, Ann, 72
SHARPLESS, Joseph,
41, 59, 68
SHAW, Elizabeth,
139
John, 139
SHEARS, John, 116
SHEDAKER, Jacob,
150
SHEELER, Hannah,
116
SHEPHERD, Adam, 134
Charles, 124
Margaret, 116,
134
Susannah, 134
SHEPPARD, John, 89,
95
Lydia, 95
Mary, 89
Priscilla, 89
Richard, 72, 95
SHEROD, Ann, 61
SHERWIN, Elizabeth,
113
James, 112
SHIN, David, 58
Gamalion, 116
Grace, 58
Hannah, 58
John, 58
Peter, 58, 116

Rachel, 58
SHINN, Abigail, 5, 23, 31, 126
Abraham, 83
Alice, 88
Anna, 19
Asa, 100
Benjamin, 79, 96, 126
Caleb, 27, 52, 59, 60, 79
Clement, 83
David, 39, 83, 86, 94
Elizabeth, 5, 19, 64, 83, 87
Francis, 74, 126
George, 23, 106
Grace, 39, 83, 86, 88, 94
Hannah, 39, 83, 86, 87, 88, 98, 106
James, 5, 23, 53, 106
Jane, 94
John, 39, 76, 79, 83, 86, 88, 93, 94, 96, 126
Jonas, 87
Joseph, 83, 126
Kedar, 28, 40, 52
Laber?, 88
Levi, 87, 88
Levina, 5, 23
Mahlon, 39, 83
Margaret, 5, 23, 62
Mariam, 23
Mary, 5, 20, 27, 52, 54, 57, 59, 60, 126
Maylon, 94
Mehatable, 79
Meribah, 20
Meuin, 5
Patience, 126
Peter, 39, 83, 86, 94
Rachel, 5, 19, 23, 39, 43, 76, 83, 88, 94
Rebecca, 126
Ruth, 87
Sabillah, 88

Samuel, 93, 106
Sarah, 5, 15, 19, 20, 23, 28, 31, 43, 52, 59, 63, 79, 96
Solomon, 5, 15, 19, 66, 67
Susannah, 103
Thomas, 5, 19, 20, 23, 28, 31, 41, 43, 52, 66, 94
Unity, 5, 19, 61
Vestai, 126
Vincent, 5
Vinecomb, 19
William, 110, 126
Zilpah, 20
SHIPPEN, Ann, 156
Edward, 156
Elizabeth, 156
Frances, 156
Mary, 156
Richard, 156
Sarah, 156
SHIPTON, Sarah, 107
SHIRAS, Alexander, 117
George Bartram, 117
Martha, 117
Peter, 140
SHIVERS, Rachel, 102
SHORES, Sarah, 105
SHREEVE, Abigail, 3
Alexander, 2
Charles, 2
Gresham, 2
Isaiah, 2
James, 2
Joseph, 3, 109
Joshua, 2, 75
Leah, 2
Rebecca, 2, 3, 109
Sarah, 3
Stacy, 93
Theodocia, 2
SHREVE, Abigail, 13, 15, 19, 28, 35, 36, 44, 53, 54, 62
Alexander, 8, 13, 44
Amos, 107

Amy, 15
Ann, 10, 15, 20
Benjamin, 10, 34, 42, 50
C., 22
Caleb, 1, 10, 13, 15, 16, 18, 19, 20, 28, 39, 44, 46, 54, 58, 60, 62
Charles, 8
Charlotte, 15, 18
Elizabeth, 15, 19, 31, 35, 49, 62, 95
Gersham, 8, 57
Grace, 1, 10, 46
Hannah, 19, 35
Isaac, 28
James, 8, 31
Jane, 22, 28
Job, 19, 28, 35, 49, 62
John, 36, 54
Joseph, 15, 28, 36, 54
Joshua, 8, 13, 31, 42, 44, 75
Keziah, 53, 55
Leah, 8
Margaret, 38, 49
Mary, 10, 13, 28, 39
Mary Ann, 13
Mercy, 19
Penelope, 28
Phebe, 10
Rebecah, 10, 28
Rebecca, 8, 12, 13, 15, 16, 19, 31, 42, 44
Rebekah, 42
Reuben, 1, 39, 46
Richard, 38
Ruben, 10
Samuel, 15, 19
Samuell, 101
Sarah, 8, 13, 15, 28, 38
Susannah, 34, 51
Tanton E., 13
Theodosia, 8, 42
Thomas, 1, 10, 15, 19, 40, 62
SHRIEVE, Abigail, 43

INDEX

Caleb, 43, 90
SHRIVE, Penelope, 43
SHUFF, Grace, 37, 50
SHUTE, William, 150
SIDDEL, James, 103
SIDDENS, Jane, 95
SILVER, Christian, 120
  James, 120
  Rebecca, 31
  S., 31
SIMMS, Neale, 156
SIMONSON, Simon, 115
SIMS, John, 154, 155
  Mary, 155
  William Neale, 155
SINGLETON, John, 144, 157
  Richard, 110
SKEELES, William, 131
SKILER, Aaron, 152
  Ann, 152
SLEEPER, Jane, 88
  John, 76, 88
  Jonathan, 102
  Lydia, 88
  Mary, 102
SLEEPERS, Benjamin, 96
  Jane, 96
  John, 96
  Sarah, 96
SLUYTER, John
  Jacob, 153
  Mary, 153
  Randolph, 153
SMALL, William, 116
SMALLWOOD, Mary, 116
SMART, James, 103
SMICHK, Benjamin, 154
  Elizabeth, 154
  John, 154
SMICK, Elizabeth, 155
  Jo, 155
  Margaret, 155
  Mary, 154

Peter, 154
SMITH, Abigail, 10, 102
  Alice, 112
  Amos, 15
  Ann, 33, 44, 50, 72
  Charles, 10
  Cowperthaite, 50
  Daniel, 31, 39, 125
  David, 50
  Deborah, 35, 49
  Elizabeth, 31, 72, 119
  Esther, 83, 88
  Gasper, 125
  George, 133, 157
  Hannah, 41, 119
  Hope, 116
  James, 37, 41, 47, 110
  Job, 2, 15
  John, 10, 115, 148, 149, 158
  Joshua, 15, 112
  Leonard, 136
  Lydia, 50
  Margaret, 15
  Mary, 2, 15, 32, 33, 35, 110, 119
  Meribah, 2, 15, 32, 88
  Rachel, 47
  Ralph, 9, 44
  Rebecca, 2, 15
  Rebekah, 88
  Samuel, 10, 15, 42, 49
  Samuel R., 88
  Samuel S., 10
  Sarah, 2, 9, 15, 36, 44
  Sheba, 116
  Thomas, 2, 15, 32, 34, 35, 37, 42, 49, 72, 88, 109, 119
  Timothy, 36
  Tryphena, 42
  William, 10, 50, 83
SMYTH, Ann, 122
  Elizabeth, 122
  Jean, 122

Margaret, 122
Mary, 122
Thomas, 122
William, 122
SNOWDEN, Hannah, 76
  Ruth, 127
  William, 104
SNUFFIN, Rachel, 102
SOLLAR, Henry, 146
SOLOMON, Prince, 115
SOUTHWICH, Joseph, 59
  Maham, 108
  Mary, 59
  Peter, 59
  Phebe, 59
  Samuel, 59
SOUTHWICK,
  Elizabeth, 115
  Hannah, 11
  Joseph, 11
  Josiah, 103
  Mary, 11
  Peter, 11
  Phebe, 11
  Rebecca, 11
  Samuel, 11
SPARKS, Mary, 112
SPENCER, Jacob, 146
  James, 107, 146
SPRAGG, Revd., 115
SPRAGGS, Joseph, 106
SPRINGER, Amos, 102
  Dennis, 105
  Hudson, 111
  John, 105
  Phebe, 104
  Sarah, 111
STANTON, John, 113
STAPLEFORD, John, 112
STAPLES, Ann, 105
  Thomas, 108
STAPLETON, Mary, 115
STARKEY, Abel, 100
  Ann, 66
  Nathan, 105
STAUNTON, John, 104
STEALMAN, Elias, 115
STEBS, Mary, 125

Susanna, 125
William, 125
STEEPENS, Jane, 96
STEPHENSON, John, 154
Nancy, 154
STERLING, James, 152
Mary, 152
STEVANSON, Alice, 22
Cornell, 19
Mary, 20
William, 20, 22
STEVENS, John, 6
Lucretia, 6
STEVENSON, Achsah, 62
Alice, 4, 42
Catharine, 37, 67
Elnathan, 130
James, 4, 42, 59
John, 4, 35, 51, 110
Margaret, 4, 42
Mary, 4, 37, 43, 54
Rebecca M., 67
Samuel, 4, 37, 43, 67
Susanna, 63
Susannah, 4
Thomas, 105
Thomas M., 67
William, 4, 34, 42, 43, 112
STEWARD, Abner, 4, 18
Alice, 52
Ann, 12, 34
Anne, 1
Bridget, 1, 4, 12, 20, 34, 43
Elizabeth, 1, 12, 34
John, 12, 100
Jonathan, 5, 61, 62
Joseph, 1, 4, 12, 34, 43
Mary, 4, 49
Nathan, 12
Sarah, 35
Susanna, 43, 52
Susannah, 4

Thomas, 4, 48, 49
William, 111, 115
STEWART, Ann, 64
Elizabeth, 64
Mary, 120
STILES, Mary, 154
Nicholas, 113
Samuel, 142, 156
STILLWELL,
Jeremiah, 125
Jeremy, 125
STILWELL, Jeremiah, 126
STOCKHAM,
Elizabeth, 136, 139, 147
George, 136, 139, 147
Thomas, 136
Thomasine, 147
STOCKTON, Abigail, 139
Ann, 1, 30
Anna, 8
Daid, 8
Daniel, 104
David, 2
Doughty, 8
Elizabeth, 1, 2, 8, 9
George, 1
George W., 8
Hannah, 9, 133, 157
Israel, 1, 39
Israel F., 8
Job, 2, 8, 16, 58
John, 119
Joseph, 1, 8, 9, 57
Mary, 1, 2, 8, 9, 54, 153
Mercy, 2
Obediah, 2, 9, 40, 65
Richard, 1, 8, 132
Ruth, 8, 26, 48
Samuel, 2, 23, 30, 49, 63, 64
Sarah, 1, 8
STOKES, Amy, 84
Ann, 88
Atlanick, 84
Atlantick, 77

Beulah, 84, 87, 88, 89
Caleb, 84, 87
Deborah, 77
Elizabeth, 80
Frances, 86
Hannah, 17, 86, 92
Hezikah, 86
Hope, 86
Isaac, 69, 84, 87
Jacob, 84
John, 84, 87, 88, 89
Joseph, 17, 77,
Joshua, 71, 77, 90, 97
Josiah, 77, 91, 92
Lydia, 77, 87
Mary, 84, 86
Rachel, 84
Rebecca, 77, 97
Ruth, 87
Samuel, 84, 86
Sarah, 80
Thomas, 80, 91, 116
William, 65, 82, 84, 88
STOUT, David, 112
STRATTEN, Alce, 95
Elizabeth, 3
Ephraim, 95
Martha, 94
STRATTON, Aaren, 72
Aaron, 73
Abi, 73
Abigail, 75
Achsah, 73
Alice, 75, 76, 82
Amy, 75
Ann, 73, 75
Anner, 75
Asa, 73
Beulah, 86, 90, 102
Caleb, 72
Daniel, 72, 73
David, 81, 86
Dorothy, 73
Eber, 72
Eli, 72, 94
Elisabeth, 34
Elizabeth, 73,

INDEX

75, 93
Enoch, 73, 75, 89
Ephraim, 75, 76, 82
Grace, 102
Hannah, 89
Hephzibah, 86
Hepsiba, 93
Hope, 75
Isaac, 102
Isaiah, 75
Job, 72
John, 73, 75, 76, 86, 98 Jonathan, 72
Joseph, 86, 94
Joshua, 73
Josiah, 75
Levi, 75
Lydia, 73, 76
Manuel, 112
Margaret, 75
Mark, 75, 92
Martha, 86
Mary, 72, 73, 82, 105
Michael, 73
Naomi, 72
Noah, 72, 92
Phebe, 73
Phoebe, 102
Prudence, 72
Rachel, 76
Rebecca, 81, 86
Reuben, 76
Ruth, 75
Samuel, 86
Sarah, 72, 86
Stacy, 73, 92
Susannah, 102
William, 72, 73
STREAKER, John, 127
Mary, 145
Philip, 127, 145
STULL, Elizabeth, 113
STURGEON, Revd, 125, 128
SULLYVAN, Suzanne, 148, 158
SURLEY, Lawrence, 109, 124
SURLY, Francis, 108
SUTPHINE,
Catherine, 142, 156
SUTTON, Daniel, 104
Margaret, 124
SWIFT, Samuel, 109
SYDENHAM,
Catherine, 139
Elizabeth, 141, 156
Jacob, 139
Susannah, 139
SYKES, Ann, 7, 42
Anthony, 1, 6, 10, 31, 33, 58
Benjamin, 1, 6, 7, 42
Charles, 1
Edith, 1, 6, 10
Elizabeth, 7, 42
Hannah, 1, 7, 42
John, 1, 6, 35, 39
Katherine, 1, 6
Mary, 1, 6, 10, 31
Rabbecah, 42
Rebecca, 1, 7
Samuel, 1, 6
Thomas, 1, 6, 31, 40, 51, 63, 64
William, 1
SYMONDS, Hannah, 106
SYTLE, William, 156

-T-

TACKBACHTOLL, John, 127
Margaret, 127
Rachel, 127
TAGG, Edward, 111
TALBERT, Rachel, 2
William, 2
TALBOT, John, 119, 122, 123
TALLMAN, Deborah, 29
Joseph, 29, 45
Martha, 29
Mary, 29
Sarah, 28, 45
Thomas, 28
TALMAN, Augustin, 19
Deborah, 3
Deborah Ann, 19
Elisha, 150
J., 31
Job, 106
Joseph, 3, 18, 51, 106
Martha, 3, 31
Mary, 3
Sarah, 3, 18, 19
Valeriah, 19
TALOR, Eber, 102
TANTUM, David, 31
David K., 26
Joseph, 26
Sarah, 26
Susannah, 31
Warren, 31
TASSO, Philippo, 104
TATEN, Hannah, 106
TAYLOR, Abigail, 46
Abner, 22
Achsah, 19, 45
Amos, 22, 39
Amy, 16, 29
Andrew, 100
Anthony, 12, 100
Bridget, 134
Caleb, 22
Charles, 22, 56, 105
Clara, 155
Daniel, 22, 56
David, 31
Dorothy, 147, 148, 152, 158
Eber, 135, 157
Elizabeth, 14, 22, 31, 56, 92, 158
George, 144, 147
Hannah, 22
James, 46
John, 14, 16, 19, 22, 45, 56, 111
John Henry, 11
Joseph, 97, 144, 146, 147, 148, 151, 152, 158
Lewis, 134
Margaret, 17
Martha, 41
Mary, 12, 14, 22, 151
Robert, 22, 56,

103
  Samuel, 14, 15, 16, 17, 29, 66
  Sarah, 15, 16, 103, 148, 151, 158
  Susannah, 113
  Thomas, 42, 46, 102, 115
  William, 116, 133, 157
TEARNEY, Ann, 110
TENCHER, Francis, 109
  Hannah, 109
TEST, Betsey, 115
THERBORN, Thomas, 122
  William, 122
THOMAS, Ann, 126
  Anna, 90
  Catherine, 31
  David, 101, 141
  Elizabeth, 18
  Hope, 102
  Nathaniel, 109, 126
  Rebecca, 140
  S., 31
  Thimothy, 147, 158
  Timothy, 18
  Webster, 92
THOMSON, Elizabeth, 134
  Elizabeth Crampton, 156
  James, 134
  Mary, 123
  Thomas, 156
  William, 156
THORN, Abraham, 38, 54
  Amos, 101
  Diadamia, 38, 54
  Elizabeth, 38
  John, 38, 54
  Joseph, 90, 93, 97
  Mary, 38
  Samuel, 69, 90
  Sarah, 90
  Tacy, 38, 54
  Thomas, 90
THORNE, Abraham, 38
  Benjamin, 111
  Diadamia, 38
  Elizabeth, 38
  John, 38
  Mary, 38
  Tacy, 38
TILTON, Abraham, 31, 59
  Ann, 14
  Daniel, 14, 27
  Elizabeth, 31
  Samuel, 8
  Sarah, 8, 27
TINDALL, Joanna, 106
TINTARD, Samuel, 139
TINTON, Elizabeth, 8
  O., 8
TOLHAMOUS, Achsah, 61
TOLLY, Lewis, 122
  Margaret, 122
  Theophilus, 122
TOMKIN, John, 119
  Martha, 119
TOMKINS, Bathsheba, 124
  Charles, 125
  John, 125
TOMLIN, Tamson, 102
TONKIN, Bathsheba, 120
  Charles, 120
  Edward, 104
  Elizabeth, 107
  John, 107, 120
  Mary, 120, 148
  Susanna, 120
TONKINS, Edward, 132
TOOLEY, Abraham, 140
  Anne, 140
  Hannah, 140
TOPPING, Jane, 107
TORR, Elizabeth, 94
  Jaboel, 92
  John, 92
  Josiah, 92
TOWNE, Benjamin, 142
  Deborah, 142
  Rebecca, 142
TOWNSEND, Reddock, 106
TOY, Daniel, 131, 134, 135
  Elizabeth, 134
  Frederick, 134
  John, 134
  Mary, 134, 150
  Sarah, 134, 135
TREADWELL, Mrs., 138, 141
TRIBBET, Elizabeth, 143, 148, 158
  Sary, 143
  Simon, 148, 158
  Symon, 143
  William, 148, 158
TRIBET, Anne, 142
  Elizabeth, 142
  John, 137, 139
  Mary, 139
  Mehitabel, 137, 139
  Simon, 139, 142, 157
  Thomas, 137
TROTH, Ann, 80, 89, 94
  Charles, 80
  Deborah, 80
  Elizabeth, 91
  Esther, 80, 94
  Huldah, 80
  Isaac, 80
  Jacob, 80, 91
  James, 91
  John, 80, 89, 94
  Lucy Ann, 80
  Mary, 89, 94
  Paul, 80, 91, 97
  Susannah, 80
  William, 80, 91, 94
TROTTEN, Susan H., 12
TROTTER, Joseph, 33
  Susannah, 33
TRUAX, Joseph, 115
TUCKER, John, 7
  Leah, 7
TUCKNEY, Henry, 105
TULY, John, 128
  Jonathan, 128
  Joseph, 128
  Martha, 128, 137
  Mary, 128

INDEX

Thomas, 128
TURLEY, Mary, 113
TURNER, Priscilla, 113
TYLOR, Mary, 56
  Samuel, 56
TYNDAL, Ann, 119
  Eliz, 119
  John, 119
  Mary, 119
  Robert, 119
  sarah, 119
  Thomas, 119
  William, 119

-U-

UORIS, Ellis, 124
  Filius, 124
  Johannes, 124
  Rowland, 124
  Sarah, 124

-V-

VAN, Hannah, 60
VAN HORNE, Peter, 142
VAN PELT,
  Alexander Shiras, 117
  Elizabeth, 117
  Peter, 117
VANDEGRIF, Leonard, 114
VANDEGRIFT, Leonard, 114
VANDERGRIFT,
  Garret, 129
  Hannah, 156
  Joseph, 137
VANDYKE, Cornelius, 139
VANHARLINGEN, John M., 154
VANHORN, Mary, 124
VANHORNE, Barnet, 131
  Gabriel, 130
  Isaac, 139, 157
  Margaret, 133
  Martha, 135
  Mary, 109
VANHURZAN, Volkert, 116
VANLAW, Joseph, 6, 34
VANSCIVER, Abraham, 151, 154
  Deborah, 151
  John, 154
  Mary, 151, 154
  Sarah, 115
VANSKIVER, Abraham, 130, 146
  Ann, 128
  Barnaby, 150
  Charles, 150
  Gertrude, 146
  Hannah, 128
  Jane, 150
  John, 135, 157
  Mary, 130, 146
  Rachel, 150
  Walter, 128
  William, 149
VANSKYVER, Abraham, 139
  Anne, 139
  Barnaby, 139
  Cornelia, 140
  John, 140
  Mary, 139, 140
  Rachael, 139
VAUGHAN, Ann, 105
  David, 131, 157
VENNABLE, Arthur, 84
  Charles, 84
  Esther, 84
  John, 84
  Joseph, 84
  Martha, 84
  Mary Ann, 84
  Rachel, 84
  Thomas, 84
  William, 84
VIERGANG, Margaret, 151
  Patrick, 151
  Suzannah, 151
VILLETTE, Dennis, 156
VINNACOMB, William, 91
VOLLOW, Margaret, 112

-W-

WADE, John, 154
WAINWRIGHT,
  Nicholas, 111
  Patience, 111
WAKE, Baldwin, 149, 150
  Drury, 150
  Frances, 150
WALKER, Abraham, 105
  James, 155
  John, 115
  Mary, 109
WALL, Mary, 155
  Thomas, 146
WALLIN, Thomas, 127
WALLING, Hope, 133
WALLINS, Drucilla, 102
WALN, Elizabeth, 4, 20, 42, 46, 65
  Hannah, 4, 65
  Jacob, 4
  Jacob Shoebaker, 39
  Joseph, 4, 36
  Mary, 4, 42
  Nicholas, 4, 31, 46
  Rebecca, 4
  Richard, 4, 20, 31, 36, 42, 46, 63
  Sarah, 31
WALSH, James, 110
WALTON, David, 142
  Malachi, 126
  Martha, 110
  Mary, 126, 142
  Rebecca, 142
  William, 126
WALTONARN, Malachi, 126
  Mary, 126
  William, 126
WARDALL, Antony, 54
  Elizabeth, 41, 54
  Sarah, 40, 54
  Thomas, 40, 54
WARDEL, Mary, 5
  Samuel, 5
  Sarah, 5
WARE, Andrew, 29, 52
  Asa, 51
  Edith, 29

Miriam, 29
WARN, Mary, 122
  Samuel, 122
  Thomas, 122
WARNER, Hannah, 103
WARREN, Achsah, 1, 30, 35, 55
  Achsash, 52
  Anna, 30, 115
  Benjamin, 9
  Beulah, 9
  Caleb, 9
  Gamaliel, 30
  John, 1, 9, 30
  Mary, 49
  Meribah, 30
  Nathan, 30
  Rachel, 1, 9
  Robert, 30
  Samuel, 37, 57
  Sarah, 1, 9
  Stephen, 9, 126
  Susanna, 64
  Susannah, 1, 9, 30
  Thomas, 30
  Ursilla, 126
WARRICK, Elizabeth, 53
  John, 107
  Sarah, 107
WATERMAN, Samuel, 103
WATKINS, Deborah, 59
WATSON, Abner, 79, 95
  Ann, 79
  Deborah, 79
  Elizabeth, 95
  Hannah, 12
  John, 12
  Mark, 79
  Mary, 79, 95
  Phebe, 79
  Rebecca, 106
  Sarah, 104
  William, 79
WEAVER, Joseph, 138
  Judith, 132
WEBB, John, 112
  Robert, 114
  Zebulon, 112
WEBSTER, Ann, 91
  Hannah, 85, 93

Laurance, 85, 86
Laurence, 93
Lawrence, 90
Levi, 85, 91
  Samuel, 85, 92
  Sarah, 85
  Thomas, 85
  William, 85
WEITZEL, John, 143
WELL, R. C., 119
WELLS, James, 114
WEST, Batho., 103
  Daniel, 105
  George, 131, 156
WESTAR, Richard, 42
  Sarah, 42
  Thomas, 42
WEYMAN, Robert, 126
WHARTON, Anne, 156
  C. H., 155, 156
  Charles H., 154, 155
  Dr., 154
  Mary C., 154
WHEATCRAFT, Edward, 101
  Samuel, 106
WHEATLEY, William, 101
WHEELER, John, 120
  Mary, 120
  Rebekah, 119, 120
  Robert, 120
WHITACE, Mary, 131
WHITAKER, Amey, 115
WHITALL, Hannah, 83
  Job, 83
  Sarah, 83
WHITE, Bishop, 156
  Eliz., 109
  Elizabeth, 3, 30, 110
  Esther, 30
  George, 104
  Hannah, 38, 87, 104
  Joseph, 38
  Lydia, 38
  Mary, 3, 30, 38, 109, 127, 133
  Peter, 3, 30
  Sabilla, 87
  Samuel, 87
  Thomas, 87, 93, 115

William, 3, 30, 34, 50, 51, 110
WHITEHEAD, John, 105
  William, 121
WHITTON, William, 108
WIGGUS, Elizabeth, 6
  John, 6
WILCOX, Joseph, 71
  Mary, 71
  Sarah, 71
WILES, Elizabeth, 106
  Joseph, 5
WILETS, Ann, 64
  David, 64
  Eliakim, 64
  Elizabeth, 64
  Mary, 64
  Phebe, 64
  Sarah, 64
WILEY, Mary, 115
WILKAMS, Elizabeth, 35
WILKINS, Ann, 85
  Anna, 85
  Elizabeth, 81, 85
  Esther, 85
  Jacob, 76
  James, 85
  John, 116
  Josiah, 115
  Mary, 74, 75, 85
  Theodocia, 97
  Thomas, 71, 74, 116
WILKINSON, Nathaniel, 150
  Rachel, 150
  Thomas, 145, 157
WILLARD, Rebeckah, 100
WILLCOX, John, 103
WILLETS, Ann, 20
  David, 20, 37, 56
  Eliakim, 20, 37, 56
  Elizabeth, 20, 37, 56
  Jacob, 20
  Joseph, 50, 51, 60
  Mary, 20, 37, 56

INDEX

Phebe, 20, 37, 56
Rebecca, 20
Samuel, 20
Sarah, 20, 37
WILLIAM, Lydia, 56
WILLIAMS,
  Elizabeth, 5, 51
  Ester, 5
  George, 51
  Jacob, 116
  Joel, 5, 52
  John, 5, 102
  Joseph, 5, 50, 51, 68
  Josiah, 5
  Lydia, 38, 51, 98, 111
  Margaret, 51, 111
  Mary, 104
  Phebe, 51
  Sarah, 5, 35, 51
WILLIAMSON,
  Elizabeth, 154
  John, 147, 158
WILLIS, George, 123
  James, 114
  Joseph, 5
  Mary, 123
WILLITS, Benjamin, 97
  Hipseba, 93
  Joseph, 60
WILLITTS, Mary, 110
  Richard, 110
WILLS, Ann C., 31
  Beulah, 87, 88
  Daniel, 85, 87
  Hannah, 85, 89, 91
  Mary, 70, 85
  Priscilla, 83, 89
  Rebecca, 83
  Sarah, 87
  W., 31
  Zebedoe, 83
WILLSON, Ezekiah, 103
  Mary, 103
  Matthew, 104
WILSEY, Simeon, 97
WILSHEAR, Abigail, 102
WILSON, Abigail, 26, 56, 66, 82
  Abraham, 26, 60

Ann, 13, 38, 41, 51, 57, 68, 93, 112
Anna, 82
Benjamin, 66
Benjamin L., 26
Charles, 125
Christian, 56
Christianna, 26
Elizabeth, 13, 41, 57, 86
Hannah, 13, 41, 57, 86
Ira, 82
Isaac, 82, 93
John, 13, 26, 41, 82, 125
Joseph, 13, 41
Lydia, 13, 57
Mary, 13, 26, 82, 93, 148
Mathew, 112
Mordecai, 82
Nathan W., 82
Phebe, 82, 93
Rachel, 13, 38, 57, 106
Rebecca, 82
Samuel, 82
Sarah, 13, 26, 41, 57
Thomas, 13, 41, 42, 57, 68, 86
Triphena, 3
Tryphena, 26
Tryphosia, 26
William, 13, 26, 41, 59, 66, 82, 148
WILTSE, Elizabeth, 86
  Henry, 86
  John C., 86
  Martin, 86
  Simeon, 86
  William, 86
WINNER, Jacob, 148, 158
WISTAR, Mary, 35
  Richard, 42
  Sarah, 42
  Thomas, 35, 42, 50
WISTOR, Christine, 133

John, 133
Joseph, 133
WITCRAFT, Abraham, 102
WOLLARD, John, 138
  Mary, 150
WOLSTON, Lydia, 93
WOOD, Amey, 157
  Amy, 145
  Ann, 1, 30, 33, 148
  Anna, 27
  Deborah, 42
  Edith, 27
  Elisabeth, 33
  Elizabeth, 1, 27, 148
  Hannah, 24, 27, 33
  Isaac, 4, 138, 142
  Jesse, 4
  John, 1, 42, 101, 148
  John E., 62
  Margaret, 1, 27
  Marget, 116
  Mary, 1, 4, 27, 34, 142
  Samuel, 27
  Sarah, 114
  Susan, 1, 4, 27
  Susanna, 33, 37, 42, 48, 50
  Thomas, 1, 54
  William, 1, 24, 27, 30
WOODARD, Sarah, 103
WOODMAN, Hannah, 6
  Samuel, 6
WOODMANCY, Anne, 61
  Miriam, 61
  Sille, 61
  William, 61
WOODOTH, Ruth, 105
WOODROW, Mary, 116
WOODWARD, Abner, 5, 20, 43, 52, 67
  Achsah, 20
  Alice, 20
  Ann, 20, 21
  Anthony, 5, 19, 20, 21, 42, 43, 45, 48, 100
  Apollo, 20

Benjamin, 5, 52
Beulah, 23
Caleb A., 23
Charlotte, 20
Clemence, 20, 21, 43
Constant, 5
Cressy, 100
Deborah, 5, 38, 42, 45, 52, 58
Eliza, 20
Elizabeth, 5, 20, 21, 38, 52, 58
Forman, 5, 20, 65
George, 5
Hannah, 21
Hannorah, 100
Henrietta, 32
Horace, 20
Increase, 21, 38, 43, 52, 58
Isaac, 5, 48
Israel, 20, 23, 32
James, 20
Jethro, 21, 62
Job, 23
John, 5, 62, 100
John E., 20, 23
Jonathan, 21
Joseph, 20, 100, 103
Joshua, 61
Josiah, 21, 57
Keturah, 5
Mary, 5, 20, 21, 32, 38, 106
Mary Annah, 23
Nimrod, 5, 48
Phebe, 21, 62
Rebecah, 38
Rebecca, 5, 23, 63
Rebeckah, 100
Robert, 5, 20
Samuel, 5, 20, 32, 104
Samuel L., 23
Sarah, 20, 21, 53
Susanna, 43
Susannah, 5, 20
Thomas, 5, 20, 43
Valeriah, 19, 45
Velariah, 5
William, 21, 100

WOOLSTON, Ann, 107, 127
Barzillai, 127
Cyllania, 130, 134, 141, 145
Eliz., 123
George, 115
John, 109, 123, 141
Joseph, 107
Margaret, 113
Mary, 132
Michael, 127, 143
Samuel, 123, 130, 132, 134, 141, 145, 146
Sarah, 127, 130, 143
Susanna, 123
Syllania, 132
WORKMAN, Ann, 118
Nicholas, 118
WORRELL, Joseph, 149
WORSTER, Tacy, 92
WOTTEN, Robert, 120
WRIGHT, Abednego, 96
Abigail, 26
Abner, 5, 22
Achsah, 5, 10, 25, 45, 57
Achsash, 22
Ann, 4, 5, 22, 32, 34, 36
Anna, 32
Benjamin, 10, 46
Caleb, 1, 10
Catherine, 1, 4, 10, 16
David, 4, 5, 6, 21, 22, 32, 40, 63, 149
Deborah, 10
Ebenezer, 5, 31, 34
Elihu, 21, 41
Elisha, 10, 57
Elizabeth, 1, 2, 5, 6, 10, 21, 22, 26, 32, 34, 39, 41, 50, 51, 63, 84
Ellis, 128
Empson, 145, 157
Esther, 10

Ezekiel, 111
Frances, 1, 26, 36, 61
Fretwell, 106, 109, 126, 128
George, 41, 46, 67
Hannah, 21, 40, 50
Henry, 10
Hester, 149
Hezekiah, 114
Isaac, 5, 6, 21, 39, 60, 61
Isaack, 128
Jane, 4, 36
Job, 2
John, 2, 5, 7, 10, 21, 22, 32, 41, 50, 57, 59, 84
Jonathan, 2, 21, 50, 63, 66, 128
Joseph, 1, 4, 5, 10, 26, 34, 36
Joshua, 4, 49, 138
Mahlon, 4, 64
Martha, 84
Mary, 1, 2, 4, 5, 6, 7, 10, 21, 22, 26, 31, 34, 35, 36, 40, 41, 50, 57, 58, 63
Mathew, 112
Miriam, 106
Moses, 4
Mr., 141
Mrs., 139, 143
Nathan, 4, 21, 22, 36, 41
Peter, 126
Priscilla, 10, 34, 50
Rebecca, 1, 2, 4, 10, 21, 22, 26, 31, 32, 34, 36, 62, 97
Rebekah, 50
Rebekuh, 48
Richard, 10
Ruth, 46
Samuel, 1, 2, 4, 6, 10, 22, 26, 36, 41, 49, 66
Samuel G., 10

Sarah, 1, 4, 5, 21, 22, 26, 41, 50, 149
Scholey, 33
Schooley, 1, 26
Stacy, 5
Stephen, 34, 50
Thomas, 4, 5, 22, 25, 45
Thompson, 62
William, 4, 10, 16, 26, 31, 32, 67, 128
William C., 32

-Y-

YARD, Susanna, 110
YERKUS, Elizabeth, 139

-Z-

ZELLEY, George, 19
ZELLY, Daniel, 43, 73
  John, 43
  Rachel, 43
ZILLA, Daniel, 35
  Penelope, 35
ZILLAH, Daniel, 89
  Dorothy, 89
ZILLAI, George, 19
ZILLY, Bathsheba, 91, 93
  Daniel, 41, 52, 93
  David, 91
  George, 41, 67
  Jemima, 93
  Job, 91, 93
  John, 26
  Rachel, 25
  Silvanus, 58
  Silvenus, 63
  Sylvanus, 40
  William Braddock, 92, 93

Other Heritage Books by Charlotte Meldrum:

Abstracts of Bucks County, Pennsylvania Land Records, 1684-1723

Early Church Records of Burlington County, New Jersey Volumes 1-3

Early Church Records of Chester County, Pennsylvania, Volume 2
Charlotte Meldrum and Martha Reamy

Early Church Records of Gloucester County, New Jersey

Early Church Records of Salem County, New Jersey

Early Records of Cumberland County, New Jersey

Johnston County, North Carolina Marriages, 1764-1867

Marriages and Deaths of Montgomery County, Pennsylvania, 1685-1800

www.ingramcontent.com/pod-product-compliance
Lightning Source LLC
Chambersburg PA
CBHW070741160426
43192CB00009B/1526